W9-BRX-810

937.05   Langguth, A. J.
Lan   1933-
c.1   A noise of war

MY   '99

MOUNT LAUREL LIBRARY
100 Walt Whitman Avenue
Mount Laurel, NJ 08054
609/234-7319

DEMCO

WITHDRAWN

WITHDRAWN

ALSO BY A. J. LANGGUTH

Patriots (1988)
Saki (1981)
Hidden Terrors (1978)
Macumba (1975)
Marksman (1974)
Wedlock (1972)
Jesus Christs (1968)

A.J.Langguth

Caesar,
Pompey,
Octavian
and
the Struggle
for Rome

SIMON & SCHUSTER
NEW YORK   LONDON   TORONTO
SYDNEY   TOKYO   SINGAPORE

A

NOISE

OF

WAR

Mount Laurel Library
100 Walt Whitman Avenue
Mt. Laurel, N.J. 08054-9539
(609) 234-7319

In Memory of
Ethel Narvid

SIMON & SCHUSTER
Simon & Schuster Building
Rockefeller Center
1230 Avenue of the Americas
New York, New York 10020

Copyright © 1994 by A. J. Langguth
All rights reserved
including the right of reproduction
in whole or in part in any form.
SIMON & SCHUSTER and colophon are
registered trademarks of Simon & Schuster Inc.
Design and picture research by Edith Fowler
Additional picture research by Natalie Goldstein
Map by Jeanyee Wong
Manufactured in the United States of America

10   9   8   7   6   5   4   3   2   1

Library of Congress Cataloging-in-Publication Data

Langguth, A. J., date.
  A noise of war : Caesar, Pompey, Octavian and
the struggle for Rome / A. J. Langguth.
    p.   cm.
  Includes bibliographical references and index.
  1. Rome—History—Republic, 265–30 B.C.
I. Title.
DG254.L36   1994
937'.05—dc20   93-39196   CIP
ISBN: 0-671-70829-5

Some display elements are based on material in
Arthur Baker's Historic Calligraphic Alphabets,
Dover Publications, Inc.

CONTENTS

THE CAST IN ROME

Vipsanius Marcus AGRIPPA   Skilled naval tactician; defeated Antony at Actium.

Marcus ANTONIUS Creticus   Mark Antony's father; died soon after an inept campaign against pirates.

Mark ANTONY   (83 or 82–30 B.C.): Caesar's tribune in 49 B.C.; triumvir with Octavian and Lepidus; wives included Octavia and Cleopatra.

AURELIA   Caesar's mother. Died 54 B.C.

Marcus Junius BRUTUS   (85–42 B.C.): Son of Servilia and the Marcus Brutus executed by Pompey in 77 B.C.; led the conspiracy to assassinate Caesar.

Gaius Julius CAESAR   (July 13, 100–March 15, 44 B.C.)

CALPURNIA   Daughter of Lucius Calpurnius Piso; married Caesar (59 B.C.)

Lucius Sergius CATILINE   Accused by Cicero of conspiring to overthrow the state. Driven into exile in 63 B.C. and killed in battle the next year.

Marcus Porcius CATO   (95–46 B.C.): Great-grandson of Cato the Censor; forced by Clodius to oversee annexation of Cyprus (58 B.C.); supported Pompey in the Civil War.

Gaius Valerius CATULLUS   (c. 84–54 B.C.): Poet born in Verona; courted Clodia with poems in which he called her "Lesbia."

Quintus Lutatius CATULUS   Leader of the patrician faction; defeated by Caesar for Pontifex Maximus.

Marcus Tullius CICERO   (January 3, 106–December 7, 43 B.C.): Consul in 63 B.C.; his son, also Marcus Tullius Cicero (born 65 B.C.), survived his father to become consul under Octavian in 30 B.C.

Quintus Tullius CICERO   (102–43 B.C.): Cicero's younger brother; both he and the son (66–43 B.C.) named for him were killed in the proscriptions of Antony, Octavian and Lepidus.

CLODIA   (born c. 95 B.C.): Known for her affairs, particularly with the poet Catullus.

Publius CLODIUS Pulcher   (92–52 B.C.): Clodia's brother; tried for profaning the Bona Dea ceremony (62 B.C.); led the movement to exile Cicero; killed by Milo.

CORNELIA   Caesar's first wife; died 69 B.C.

Marcus Licinius CRASSUS   Rich merchant who led the war against Spartacus (72–71 B.C.); served as consul with Pompey (70 B.C., 55 B.C.); joined with Caesar and Pompey in pact to control Rome; was defeated and killed in the East (53 B.C.).

Gaius Scribonius CURIO   Mark Antony's youthful friend, Cicero's protégé; as tribune (50 B.C.), he defected to Caesar.

Lucius DOMITIUS Ahenobarbus   Selected by the senate in 49 B.C. to replace Caesar in Gaul.

Aulus GABINIUS   As tribune, led the movement to give command against the pirates to Pompey (67 B.C.); accepted a bribe to restore Ptolemy Auletes to the Egyptian throne.

JULIA   Caesar's father's sister; married to Marius. Another Julia, Caesar's daughter (83–54 B.C.), married Pompey.

Titus LABIENUS   (c. 100–45 B.C.): Caesar's legate in Gaul; defected to Pompey; died at Munda.

Marcus Aemilius LEPIDUS   Consul in 78 B.C.; opposed Sulla's changes, and led an army against Rome but was defeated and died in exile. His son, also Marcus Aemilius Lepidus, backed Caesar against Pompey, then became a triumvir with Antony and Octavian.

Lucius Licinius LUCULLUS   Supported Sulla in the march on Rome; fought Mithridates until the senate transferred command to Pompey.

Gaius MARIUS   (c. 157–86 B.C.): Married Caesar's aunt; consul seven times.

Titus Annius MILO   Tribune (57 B.C.); raised gangs to oppose Clodius, whom he killed; defended by Cicero (52 B.C.).

OCTAVIA   Daughter of Caesar's niece; Octavian's sister; Antony's fourth wife (40 B.C.).

Caius OCTAVIAN (Augustus)   (63 B.C.–A.D. 14): His mother, Atia, was Caesar's niece; triumvir with Antony and Lepidus from 43 B.C.

POMPEIA   Sulla's granddaughter; Caesar's second wife but divorced after the Bona Dea scandal (62 B.C.).

Gnaeus POMPEY Magnus   (106–48 B.C.): Pompey the Great. His father was the general Pompeius Strabo. His elder son, Gnaeus Pompeius, was executed after defeat by Caesar at Munda (45 B.C.). His younger son Sextus was put to death by Octavian's allies (36 B.C.).

PORTIA   Cato's daughter; wife of Marcus Brutus.

Quintus SERTORIUS   Marius' ally; fought Sulla's generals to hold Spain; defeated by Pompey and Metellus; murdered by one of his officers.

SERVILIA   Influential Roman matron; Caesar's mistress; Marcus Brutus' mother.

SPARTACUS   Thracian slave who led revolt of 73–71 B.C.

Lucius Cornelius SULLA Felix   (c. 138–78 B.C.): Dictator of Rome; enemy of Marius; sponsor of laws to strengthen the patrician senate.

THE CAST ABROAD

ANTIPATER   Governor of Idumaea, father of Herod. Helped restore Ptolemy Auletes (55 B.C.); supported Pompey, then came to Caesar's aid at Alexandria (48 B.C.).

CLEOPATRA VII   (69–30 B.C.): Queen of Egypt.

MITHRIDATES VI   King of Pontus; led battles against Rome from 88 B.C. until his death in 68 B.C.

NICOMEDES IV   King of Bithynia. Rumors about sexual relations with Caesar (80 B.C.) plagued Caesar throughout his life.

PHRAATES IV   King of Parthia; defeated Antony in Media Atropatene in 36 B.C.

PTOLEMY XII AULETES   Father of Cleopatra; restored to throne by Gabinius and Antony. His two sons served at different times as king with Cleopatra until their deaths in 47 and 44 B.C.

VERCINGETORIX   Arverni chieftain in Gaul; defeated by Caesar at Alesia in 52 B.C.

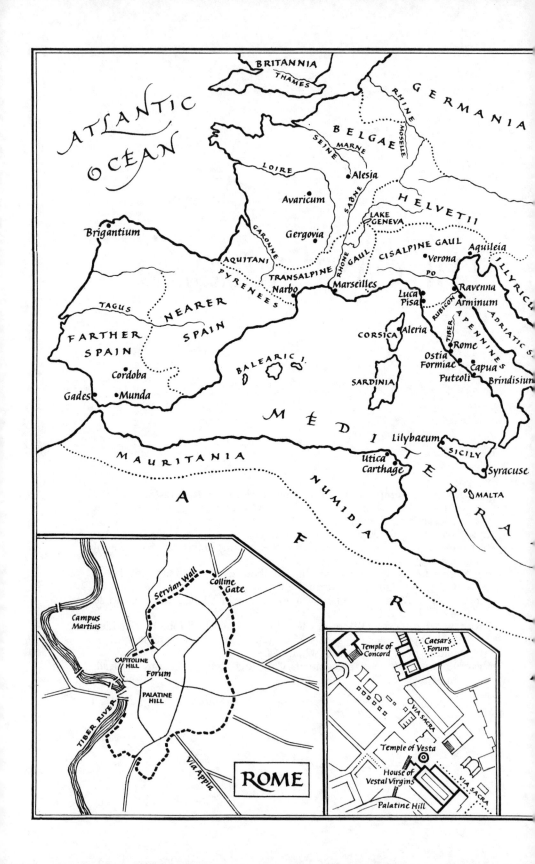

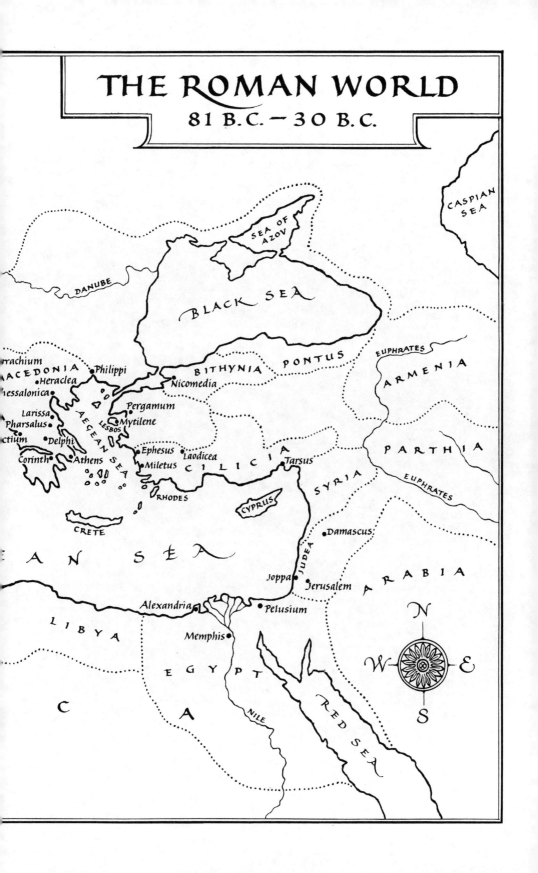

THE ROMAN WORLD
81 B.C. – 30 B.C.

CASPIAN SEA

SEA OF AZOV

DANUBE

BLACK SEA

BITHYNIA

PONTUS

EUPHRATES

ARMENIA

rachium

MACEDONIA

Heraclea

hessalonica

Philippi

Nicomedia

PARTHIA

Larissa

Pergamum

Pharsalus

Mytilene

LESBOS

ctium

Delphi

AEGEAN SEA

Ephesus

Corinth

Athens

Miletus

Laodicea

CILICIA

Tarsus

SYRIA

EUPHRATES

RHODES

CYPRUS

CRETE

AN SEA

Damascus

JUDEA

Joppa

Jerusalem

ARABIA

Alexandria

Pelusium

N

LIBYA

Memphis

W

E

EGYPT

C

A

NILE

RED SEA

S

Marius was once rebuked for granting Roman citizenship illegally to 1,000 men of Camerinum who had fought for him in a recent battle. Marius answered that the law spoke too softly to be heard in such a noise of war.

—Plutarch's Life of Gaius Marius

I

CAESAR AND CICERO

81 B.C.

Gaius Julius Caesar stood before Sulla, the dictator of Rome, and weighed a decision that could cost him his life. Sulla had seized the city by force and was bending the political opposition to his will. To ensure the loyalty of Rome's young aristocrats, he had ordered several of them to leave their wives and marry women he had selected. Most had obeyed, and now he was demanding that the 19-year-old Caesar sue for divorce and take a more politically acceptable bride.

Sulla was not pleased with Caesar's appearance. He didn't care for the modish fringe on the sleeve of his toga or the way he let his belt hang loose at the waist. The young man looked as though he fussed too much over his appearance. Roman men had been clean-shaven for many years, but Caesar went further and had the barber pluck out his stray facial hairs.

The result of all that attention was a stylish, handsome

Bust of Julius Caesar in his prime. Art Resource.

young man—tall for a Roman at five feet, eight inches—with pale skin, prominent cheekbones, wide-set dark eyes and a long, straight nose.

Sulla's lineage was equally patrician, but he had been poverty-stricken in his youth. After he had conquered Rome, he heard of a slave who was gossiping that he had once lived in the same boardinghouse as the new dictator. Sulla had him executed. At 57, Sulla's white skin was scarred by raging acne. Behind his back, people compared his face to a mulberry with oatmeal scattered across it. Sulla's eyes, however, were blue and sharp.

The young man standing before him should have reminded Sulla of himself in his youth. He may even have expected Caesar to look back knowingly at him. Conservative Romans prized the virtue of *gravitas*, their earnest sense of duty. But Sulla had always shown a tolerance for *levitas*, the flippancy with which lighter-minded men responded to the world. From his adolescence, Sulla had surrounded himself with dancers and comedians, and he had inherited his first bit of money from an easy older woman. His longest liaison had been with Metrobius, a female impersonator.

But Caesar was staring at him with black, cold eyes. His stubbornness was an affront and a puzzle to Sulla. Caesar's family had demonstrated once before that when self-interest required a change of brides, Caesar would do as he was told. He had been hardly more than a child when his parents betrothed him to a girl from a family richer than his but from a lower class, the *equites*. They were the knights who had once supplied Rome with cavalry but now were businessmen who lent money and collected taxes. They ranked higher than the plebeians but well below Caesar's patrician circle, the men who took membership in the senate as their birthright.

When Caesar's first engagement had been broken for political reasons, he had married Cornelia, a young aristocrat whose father had been named four times as consul, Rome's highest political honor. Since he knew all about that change of brides, Sulla could reasonably expect Caesar to rewrite his marriage vows again.

But Caesar answered no, he would not divorce Cornelia. Apparently he loved her, and in a day of widespread divorce his marriage ceremony had been traditional and binding, the same one that had united his own parents. By defying Sulla, Caesar was honoring not only his mother and father but also his aunt Julia and Gaius Marius, her late husband. Marius was the renowned general who had restored great prestige and power to Caesar's family. He was also Sulla's most hated enemy.

To punish Caesar, Sulla confiscated his inheritance and Cornelia's dowry. Fearing for his life, Caesar fled south to the mountains of Samnium. For many days he stayed hidden, bribing men for a different place to sleep each night. The strain began to tell on Caesar's health, which was unreliable. He was sometimes filled with energy, at other times weak and fatigued. He began to shake from an ailment the Romans called quartan fever since it brought on violent paroxysms every fourth day.

Malaria was not Caesar's only enemy. When Sulla's soldiers discovered him hiding in a peasant's hut, he had to bribe their leader with two talents—50 times a soldier's annual pay—to persuade the men to let him escape.

As Caesar moved from house to house, his family was mounting an appeal to the dictator. Allegiances between the followers of Sulla and Marius were constantly shifting, and Caesar's mother, Aurelia, called on her conservative relatives to protect her son. She also had friends among the Vestal Virgins. Even a dictator had to listen to their pleas.

Sulla agreed to spare the young man. With absolute power, he had become dissipated and drunken but remained a shrewd judge of men. He had paid more attention to Caesar's hard eyes than to his foppish clothes. When his advisers congratulated him on the decision, Sulla replied, "You are stupid if you don't see that in this boy there are many Mariuses."

Julius Caesar didn't believe that he could stop running. He arranged for a post that would take him far from Rome, although it meant a long absence from his wife and Julia, his two-year-old daughter. But it put an ocean between him and the dictator.

While Julius Caesar was defying Sulla, another young man was deciding if he too could stand up to the dictator. Family pride had moved Caesar to take the risk; Marcus Tullius Cicero had the opposite motive. He was a "new man," Rome's slighting term for someone who entered politics from a family that had never produced a consul. In a society based on heritage, a new man's position was unenviable. Two aristocratic families, the Valerians and the Fabians, had each held the consulship 45 times since the day the Republic was founded, Cicero's ancestors not once. But as it happened, Cicero had been born in Arpinum, 70 miles southwest of Rome, the same hill town that had produced Marius.

Arpinum had enjoyed Roman citizenship for more than a century, and its residents had adopted the city's speech and manners. Yet getting to Rome took two or three days, and when natives of Arpinum arrived, many Romans considered them underbred, however distinguished they might be at home. With no Roman ancestors to make his ambition legitimate, Cicero needed to find a bold action that would win the city's respect.

In Arpinum, Cicero's grandfather was remembered for leading the successful campaign against secret ballots in town elections. Older families had feared the practice would reduce their influence on the vote. The Ciceros had won a solid local standing despite their name—a *cicer* was a chickpea—which may have described an ancestor with a wart on the end of his nose. The family was proudly defensive about their name, and Marcus Cicero had vowed at an early age that he would become so famous no one would ever laugh at it again.

Cicero's father, plagued by a lifetime of minor ailments, found refuge in reading. His mother was not the confident Roman matron Julius Caesar's mother, Aurelia, was. She was fearful and suspicious and would set traps for her servants to see if they were stealing from her. The father's ill health kept the family in Arpinum, but as Marcus and his younger brother Quintus grew older, he sent them to live in a modest house in Rome, where they could absorb the city's culture and refine their accents. Cicero's father had cultivated Roman connections—lawyers, political leaders, the city's most renowned orators—to look after the boys. They found Cicero precocious. His classmates were soon carrying home stories of his quick intelligence, and some fathers went to the school to see the prodigy for themselves. Other Romans, less impressed by bookishness, were annoyed to find their sons deferring to a boy from the provinces.

Cicero spent many hours during his teenage years at a patron's house in the elegant district of Palatine Hill. While most Romans lived in single rooms in four-story tenements, houses in the hills could be spacious and airy with chambers built around an atrium. Rich men furnished their homes in marble, ivory and fine wood. Because Rome had no police force, they built heavy doors—but seldom windows—into the walls that faced the street. Behind those bolted doors, Cicero listened as scholarly Romans whiled away their days. He first memorized poetry from books—the papyrus scrolls copied by slaves—then tried writing his own poems. He learned Greek, and loved Homer and the tragedies of Euripides. He wrote a poem about a fisherman who became a sea god, and it was published, further enhancing his youthful reputation.

When the time came at 16 for him put on his man's toga, Cicero was at least as well educated as any boy born in Rome. Since there was no set course of study for a lawyer, he began an informal apprenticeship with a famous jurist. His teacher, a former consul, was writing the first analysis of Roman civil law.

The Romans' firm ideas about duty dated from an age of high civic principles. A patrician did not accept money for serving as consul or in other offices, at least not while he was within the city's walls. But abroad, as military governor or proconsul—an assignment considered payment for services rendered to Rome—he was free to make his fortune. Men who couldn't win fame as a soldier had the second, lesser option of gaining prominence through their oratory, by pleading cases in court. Although lawyers could not take a fee, they were handsomely repaid in gratitude and political support. In the Forum, several lawsuits would be heard at the same time, each with a jury of 75 or 80 men, and spectators wandered from one hearing to the next, looking for the best show.

Cicero memorized stanzas of famous poetry in order to incorporate their phrases in his orations. But he realized that reciting other men's words would only win him a reputation for a good memory. So he wrote more of his own uninspired poetry, and during the years that Marius ruled Rome, young Cicero's verses praised his fellow native of Arpinum.

Cicero was in his late teens when he enlisted in a war against other Italian towns by joining the staff of Pompeius Strabo. A young man who aspired to public office had once been expected to serve in several military campaigns, but that requirement was no longer stringently observed. If Cicero had ever considered the army as his road to fame, his first experience taught him better. Tall but weedy, Cicero might hope to train his voice for oratory but never for barking orders.

During his service, Cicero came to know Strabo's son Pompey, who was the same age but already marked for military greatness. Cicero had to envy Pompey's vigor, his direct soldier's mind, his skill in commanding troops. Those were not Cicero's talents. He completed his service by fighting in Campania and then returned to Rome, his uncongenial duty done.

At 21, Cicero began to study with Apollonius Molon, a celebrated teacher of oratory from the island of Rhodes. He also listened regularly to Hortensius, considered Rome's best younger speaker. Performing for a crowd, Hortensius became a dervish of broad gestures and bombast. Cicero had found the soldier Pompey daunting, but Hortensius aroused his competitive instincts.

In front of friends, Cicero practiced a style of declaiming that concentrated more on argument than histrionics. The Greek philosopher Zeno had once described eloquence as a closed fist, logic as an open palm. Cicero chose the palm. He began an ambitious book on rhetoric, listing 15 topics that roused men to indignation and another 16 that moved them to pity. Reading it over, Cicero found the book immature and put it aside.

By the time Sulla swept to power, Cicero supported him. He might mount a safe challenge to the dictator if it advanced his career, but otherwise Cicero endorsed Sulla's program for restoring the authority of the patricians in the senate.

A young man born to high rank like Julius Caesar could be grateful for his privileges and yet sympathetic to the average man's resentments. But Marcus Cicero, who had come to Rome to make his name, didn't want the rules changed while he was still trying to master them. As a new man, Cicero would ally himself with the aristocrats.

II

POMPEY

81 B.C.

Romans knew that their city had been built on rape and murder, but the kind of menace that Julius Caesar was facing from Sulla dated back only about 50 years. During Rome's first six centuries, friction had often developed among the city's social classes, but Romans had been proud of the civilized way they resolved political disputes. They had fought the strangers outside their walls, not each other.

The origin of Rome's name had been lost over the centuries. A popular myth held that the city had been founded by Romulus, a cast-off infant suckled by a wolf; *ruma* was the Latin word for teat. In the same story, Romulus had killed his twin brother Remus. Then he drew circles with a plow to mark the Comitium, where the people were to assemble, and the Pomoerium, a sacred space within Rome's walls. Romans thought that Romulus had begun building his new city on April 21, and they were still celebrating that date when Caesar was born six and a half centuries later.

Romulus was supposed to have organized his soldiers into

units he called legions. Those men who could identify their fathers became *patres*—patricians—to distinguish them from the orphans and runaways who were flocking to his settlement. The patricians became Romulus' advisers, his senate. Because many of the Roman males were unmarried, Romulus devised public games to attract a party of women from the nearby Sabine tribe. When the women arrived, the Romans seized them as wives. In the battle that followed, Romulus defeated the Sabine king and offered his suit of armor to the god Jupiter. That began the tradition called a triumph, a conquering general leading a parade through the city. But later military victories swelled Romulus' arrogance until, in his thirty-eighth year as king, he vanished. Romans suspected the senators of killing him, but his body was never found.

Those were the myths. Less fanciful versions of Rome's beginnings were almost as unreliable. All that was known was that tribes of Etruscans, Umbrians, Samnites and Latins had once roamed the nearby hills. Latins who wanted a river outpost may have come down from their ancient city of Alba Longa to set up a fort on the left bank of the Tiber River, 15 miles from the Mediterranean. Possibly it was that nest of earthworks and huts on Palatine Hill that became Rome.

Rome's early leaders ruled as kings, and when the Etruscans conquered the city they continued the monarchy. They brought the Greek alphabet to Rome, along with their own Etruscan architecture. Romans seemed to absorb alien cultures effortlessly. "Better to copy," they said, "than to envy."

For a century and a half, those Tarquin kings built walls and sewers and began to construct Rome's Capitol. But the patricians increasingly resented the king's power. When the son of Tarquinius the Proud raped a virtuous matron named Lucretia, Romans used that excuse to lock the seventh Etruscan king outside their city walls and establish a republic.

The Romans were protective of their new independence. Parceling out the king's duties to a variety of religious and civil officials, they devised ingenious ways to keep the supreme power—which they called the imperium, the right of command—fragmented and temporary. Sovereignty would now rest with the senate and with the Roman people. Every year, an assembly elected two praetors, or leaders, who would hold absolute power, except that one leader could overrule the other. In time, the name of that high office was changed to "consul."

When threats from an enemy tribe jeopardized their careful legal safeguards, Romans allowed the assembly to elect a dictator with full imperium. But only for six months. After that, the crisis should be over, and the dictator was expected to step aside and return power to the elected officials. In the Republic's 400 years before Caesar's birth, Rome had seldom required a dictator and never for more than six months.

Over the centuries, Romans defeated formidable enemies, each victory expanding their power. They were not forced to confront Philip II, king of Macedonia, or his son Alexander the Great, since the Macedonians drove their kingdom far into the East—to Persia, Syria, Egypt—instead of attacking Rome. But the Romans did triumph over Hannibal, the Phoenician king of Carthage, when he tried to conquer Italy. During that war, the Romans acquired from the Phoenicians a new form of punishment called crucifixion.

Roving tribes from the north, Gauls and Goths, also menaced the city, and one Gallic rampage destroyed Rome's archives. Romans lost every record of their first four and a half centuries that hadn't been engraved on stone. Yet through the battles and raids, Rome prevailed and prospered. Two generations before Caesar's birth, all direct taxes in Italy had been dropped because Rome's generals had lately brought back 31,000 pounds of gold and 670,000 pounds of silver. The conquered provinces remained heavily taxed, however, and supplied a growing number of slaves. Romans considered the tribute from subject peoples as only proper. Complacently, they regarded the entire Mediterranean as Mare Nostrum, "Our Sea."

The number of plebeians had been expanding with Rome's territories. They were the citizens who couldn't boast a noble heritage and included a class called the *proletarii*, men and women who had no property but their children, their *proles*. For many years, the plebeians had resented the law that allowed only noblemen to perform sacrifices, a restriction that barred a plebeian from holding the highest civic offices. They also wanted protection against the arbitrary death sentences being handed down by patrician judges. They proposed a guarantee that any citizen condemned to die could appeal the judgment to a meeting of the people. Some of those complaints had been heard and resolved. But when patricians in the senate blocked other basic reforms, rebellious plebians marched to a hill outside Rome and created their own city.

The threat of economic chaos brought quick concessions. Plebeians were allowed to share in Rome's government, and the office of tribune was created to look after the people's interests. The tribunes, whose number expanded gradually from two to 10, could not hold the imperium, could not direct the state, as the consuls did, but they could overrule the decree of any official, no matter how high-ranking.

Reforms alone could not end the ill feeling between Rome's classes. Patricians still used their senate membership to hoard power. The city's businessmen had become international bankers, traders and tax collectors in the provinces. Plebeians were expected to till the land or run the city's small shops. When times turned bad, plebeians left their farms to find work in Rome, where they had to compete with the slaves who flooded the city after each military victory.

One plebeian revolt had forced the patricians to commit Rome's laws to writing. The Twelve Tables were memorized by every Roman schoolboy. They formed a constitution that was meant to protect Roman freedom, but over time they had become rigidly interpreted and difficult to change. Some regulations were mundane: citizens were responsible for maintaining the roads at the edge of their property. To avoid fires and health hazards, cremation and burial were not allowed within the city limits. But other provisions went to the core of Roman life. The code gave each *pater*, or father, the right to decide life and death for his wife, children and slaves. Table IV, for example, began, "Quickly kill a dreadfully deformed child." By Caesar's time, very few Roman fathers killed a member of their household, although female infants were sometimes left outside to perish if they weren't adopted by a passerby.

As Roman life sprawled far beyond its narrow constitution, the Roman matron took on an influence not foreseen by the authors of the Twelve Tables. Women cherished a story that dated from Hannibal's assault on Rome, when the senate had passed an emergency defense measure to raise money. Called the Oppian Law, it limited the amount that a Roman woman could spend on luxuries and made it illegal for her to own more than half an ounce of gold. Twenty years later, Hannibal's threat was gone but the

austerity remained. Roman women asked to have their rights restored, and when mildness failed, they took to the streets. Cato
the Censor, the sternest conservative voice of his age, was appalled to see women accosting senators to plead their cause. He
lectured his fellow patricians that they must start controlling their
wives. But other men took a different lesson from the demonstra-
tion, and the Oppian Law was repealed.

That was Rome's idea of political uproar—until the generation before Caesar's birth. Then an aristocrat named Tiberius
Gracchus was elected tribune and challenged the structure of his
society, and Romans learned how entrenched the patricians'
power had become. Tribunes in the past had been content to
correct specific injustices and leave broader policy to the senate.
Tiberius was proposing a massive land reform. After a military
victory, Rome routinely took territory away from conquered tribes
and declared it the property of the Roman people. Senators decided whether to sell the land or keep it as state property. Tiberius
argued that farmland seized in recent wars should be divided
among the men who had fought for it.

The roots of the debate went back to the Republic's early
days when plebeians accused patricians of keeping most of the
conquered land for themselves. For three and a half centuries
before Tiberius, the people's leaders had been arguing for a fairer
distribution of property. But progress had been slow, and now
large estates in Sicily and Africa were driving the smaller farmers
off their land by shipping cheap grain to Rome. While the estates
were expanding into raising cattle and growing olives for oil and
grapes for wine, their absentee owners lived and voted in Rome to
protect their rights. It was those privileges that Tiberius was threatening.

Patrician senators immediately protested against resettling
veterans on the conquered land. They argued that the farms made
up most of the public wealth that allowed Romans to pay no taxes.
But everyone knew that those same senators made vast profits by
leasing the public land back to themselves at low fees. A more
legitimate objection arose among Italians around the peninsula
who were already living on the disputed land. Tiberius intended
to compensate them with full Roman citizenship, but the patricians resisted: extending the vote would dilute their influence.

The people's assembly passed Tiberius' program, but his

reforms were barely under way when his term ended. Tiberius campaigned immediately for reelection, defying the tradition of letting at least a year elapse between terms. When Tiberius won again, his opponents turned to force. They smashed the senate's wooden benches into clubs; a former consul hiked up his toga to lead a gang into the streets. The patricians pushed their way through the people who were protecting their tribune. Seeing the danger, Tiberius began to run. A senator grabbed his toga. Tiberius let it fall and tried to escape in his tunic. He had almost reached the Temple of Jupiter, when an enemy caught up with him and shattered his skull with the heavy foot of a senate chair.

For centuries, Romans had depended on their Pomoerium, Romulus' safety zone within the city's walls. Soldiers were forbidden to bring their weapons into it, and Romans thought they didn't need police because they had the Pomoerium. Now, the mêlée ended with Tiberius and 300 other men dead, not from swords or daggers but from clubs and rocks, and the sanctuary ground was drenched in blood. For the first time in the Republic's history, Romans had resolved a political debate with murder.

A decade later, Tiberius' brother, Gaius, was elected tribune and took up his crusade. Gaius was a better speaker and more politically adroit, but the issue of land reform still divided the senate from most Romans. And even if his plan succeeded, unemployed and desperate Romans couldn't all be shipped abroad to work the land. For them, he recommended setting a price on grain less than half the market price, low enough to guarantee that no one went hungry. Gaius also renewed the call for extending Roman citizenship throughout the peninsula.

The senators balked, and in the brawl that followed Gaius too was killed. His enemies cut off his head and then fought for the honor of carrying it to the patrician consul. They wanted to claim the reward—the weight of Gaius' head in gold. On a scale, however, the head was suspiciously heavy. Closer inspection showed that Gaius' skull had been hollowed out and the brain chamber filled with lead.

Several leaders spoke for the popular movement that the Gracchus brothers had aroused, but none had the impact of Julius Caesar's uncle, Marius. He was no patrician. His parents had been day laborers, which meant that he was simply Gaius Marius, with no third name, and he had become an adult before he ever saw a city. But arriving from Arpinum, Marius had attached himself to the noble house of Metellus, and the family had promoted his fortunes.

The other patricians did not like the rugged soldier with an appetite for glory, although they had to admit that Marius was an exceptional military organizer. He rose quickly through the ranks, and as his reputation spread, he stood for tribune, a harmless honor for a man of the people—although the year was significant: it was the first election after the murder of Gaius Gracchus. Marius kept presuming above his station and slipped through an election to win a praetorship. That should have been the upper limit for a new man. But Marius went on to gather enough popular support to be elected consul. His aristocratic wife, Caesar's aunt Julia, was not surprised. A Syrian clairvoyant had assured her that Marius was destined to hold the consulship seven times, more than any man in Roman history.

At first, the prophecy unrolled smoothly. Marius shouldn't have been eligible for a second consecutive year as consul, but the tradition had already been flouted. Marius was fighting in Africa and couldn't reach Rome in time for the election, but that also proved no impediment. He became the first man in Roman history to be elected consul in absentia.

Marius' true strength was not simply his popularity with the civilians, it was the loyalty of his troops. Over his career, Marius had set about making Rome's army more professional. In the days of the kings, serving as a soldier had been a privilege granted only to nobles. But when hill tribes menaced the city and the number of patricians wasn't large enough to repel them, the army was opened to wealthy traders and then even to plebeians. It had taken 350 years until soldiers were paid; before that, honor and self-defense had been motive enough.

Marius eliminated the last property requirements for service and made every citizen eligible. To replace the unpopular practice of drafting farmers, he began calling for volunteers among the city's poor and quickly drew as many troops as he needed. Men now signed up for a specific term, not simply until a campaign ended. Under Marius, volunteers took their oath of allegiance to a general, not to that year's consuls. Patricians still furnished the officers, but a young aristocrat usually served his apprenticeship far from the gritty legions, and few of them stayed in the army long enough to become veterans. By the time an aristocrat's political skills in Rome had won him a generalship, he was likely to be middle-aged, with scant military knowledge. At best, he might draw up a sound tactical plan. But its success would depend on the centurions who had spent their lives waging war.

Soldiering was a rough, disciplined life, and the men who chose it became Rome's sinew. Peasants from Italy or Crete or the Balearic Islands, they were men with no standing in Rome who had discovered a powerful trade to ply. Their loyalty to a commander outweighed anything they felt for an abstraction like the Roman republic.

Julius Caesar was born during his uncle's sixth term as consul. That same year, Marius botched a political crisis when two former allies threatened to seize Rome. Marius hesitated to enforce the senate's "ultimate decree," a suspension of rights that ordered the consul to put down any threat to Rome, using whatever force necessary. As a result of his bungling, when his sixth consulship ended Marius was forced into exile in Asia. It seemed the sooth-sayer had been wrong.

And the year had been marked by another galling failure. For years Marius had pursued Jugurtha, Rome's enemy in Africa, but when the king was finally captured, a patrician officer, Cornelius Sulla, took the credit. Twenty years younger than Marius, driven by ambition and allied with the patricians, Sulla became Marius' implacable enemy.

Without support from Marius' popular movement, Italians outside Rome realized that the nobility would never willingly grant them citizenship. Forces combined around the peninsula, and their three-year assault was called the Social War—Romans were fighting against their *socii*, their former allies. Demoralized senators seemed ready to capitulate and vote citizenship to every Italian when Sulla persuaded his troops in southern Italy to march on their own capital.

Taking over Rome, Sulla installed conservative politicians to look after the nation's business and then set off again to enrich his soldiers by fighting in Asia. A patrician named Lucius Cinna deserted the senate's cause and joined the huge band of Italians eager for their voting rights. It was Marius' chance for revenge, and leading remnants of his army he and Cinna took Rome back from Sulla's supporters. The result was Marius' seventh consulship.

Romans speculated afterward that six terms as consul had eroded Marius' humanity and left him unfit for power. Hoary with age, frenzied from the indignities of exile, Marius seemed determined to wash Rome's streets with blood. In recent times, men of both factions had been silenced by murder, but what followed was butchery. After repaying his own grudges, Cinna tried to restrain his co-consul. But Marius roamed the streets with slaves who were killing men at a nod of his head. When a former praetor greeted him, Marius was distracted and didn't respond. The slaves took that apparent snub as their cue and ran the man through with their swords. As the story spread, even Marius' allies became afraid to approach him.

Thirteen days into his seventh consulship, Marius, 70 years old, wracked by alcohol and insomnia, died in bed from pneumonia, fighting old enemies in his delirium. Cinna continued to rule, illegally prolonging his terms as consul but acting with moderation until a band of rebellious troops killed him.

Sulla stormed back to take the city and guarantee that his faction wouldn't be dislodged again. After a decisive victory north of Rome at the Colline Gate, he waited anxiously for news of Pompey, who was leading a private army to Rome to support him. Pompey was already considered a brilliant soldier, though he was only in his early twenties.

As his legions drew within sight of the city, Pompey ordered his officers to march in strict formation, fully armed. Sulla was impressed by their discipline, as he was meant to be. When Pompey saluted Sulla as "Imperator," Sulla repeated that exalted title back to him—a 23-year-old who had never held elected office.

Sulla sent Pompey to Sicily and Libya to quell the lingering resistance there, and his successes were equally notable. But so were the complaints that he was ruthless, even sadistic. In Africa, Pompey slaughtered lions and elephants, to make sure, he said, that even the beasts of Libya feared the Roman army.

When it was time for Pompey to return to Rome, Sulla instructed him to send his troops back first. Sensing a trick, Pompey's men threatened to mutiny until Pompey urged them to follow orders. Weeping, he assured them that he would kill himself before he would violate instructions from Rome.

His reaction was melodramatic but not insincere. Tears

came easily to Pompey; his courage guaranteed that no one would mock him for them. His weeping also testified to a young man unusually sensitive to Rome's opinion. His family had been influential in Picenum, northeast of Rome, but the Pompeii couldn't compare in prestige to the Metelli or to Caesar's Julii. Pompey wanted to be accepted by the senate's ruling class, and that need made him vulnerable and touchy.

Like other ambitious Roman soldiers, he took Alexander the Great as his model. In the two and a half centuries since Alexander died of fever at 33, no one had conquered the world as he did. On their march back to Rome, Pompey's devoted troops flattered him by adding "Magnus" to his name, making him Pompey the Great. The title not only had majestic echoes, it solved an annoyance: he would never again be called by his father's name, Pompeius Strabo, "Pompey the Squinter."

This time, Sulla went outside the city walls to welcome Pompey home. But when Pompey asked for a triumph to celebrate his victories, the dictator felt compelled to deny it. A triumph was bound by specific rules and traditions.

Long in the past, when Rome's army had been made up of farmers called from their fields, their commander had led them in rituals to cleanse them of the impurity of killing. By Pompey's day, professional soldiers had become less squeamish. Now a triumph offered spectacles and games even more extravagant than those of the feast days. At the front of the procession, military guards led the battle's most distinguished prisoners of war. As the march neared the Capitol, they were usually pulled out of line and strangled in the public prison. After them came chariots of plunder— gold, silver, jewels, statuary. Next rode the man who was being honored, the triumphator, a son of Jupiter, with his cheeks painted blood red. Romans worried that looking down on so much gold and adulation might arouse the true gods to jealousy, so while the civilians were shouting praise, the general's legions followed behind and cursed him with vile insults.

Only the senate could declare a triumph, and only for a consul or praetor. Generals whose victories far outshone any by Pompey had respected that tradition and hadn't asked for the honor. Sulla argued that he couldn't allow Pompey, who had never been elected to any office, to ride down the Sacra Via. The people would be incensed at the boy for demanding a triumph, Sulla said, and at him for permitting it.

Pompey's answer came so low that Sulla missed it. But when the dictator saw his courtiers looking shocked, he asked, Pompey to repeat what he had said. Pompey said again that more people worshiped the sun when it rose than when it set. The image annoyed Sulla, but he said, "Let him have his triumph! Let him have his triumph!"

Pompey's great day proved less than glorious. He had intended to enter Rome in a chariot drawn by four elephants brought as booty from Libya, but the city gate was too narrow for them. Pompey had to settle for horses. The morning of the triumph, his troops learned for the first time how little of the spoils he was allotting to them. Angry and disappointed, they threatened to disrupt his procession, but Pompey held firm and won the grudging admiration of the senate's patricians. Despite Sulla's fears, most Romans were taking the entire spectacle in good humor, enjoying the fact that a man who didn't qualify for a triumph had wrested one from the reluctant senators.

Now that Pompey was home, it was hard to credit the stories about his viciousness abroad. Seen close up, the young man was handsome but in a soft and rounded way. His cheeks were full, his chin retreating into early jowls. With his wavy hair and eyes that seemed to promise compassion, Pompey's boyish face could look reassuring, even sweet.

Flora, an aging and celebrated courtesan, told a somewhat different story. Pompey's wife had died young, and Pompey, who needed a woman in his life, was finding consolation where he could. A well-born Roman woman might have expected tenderness and respect. Not Flora. After the nights she and Pompey made love, she boasted to friends about the bites all over her body.

Sulla's atrocities were becoming plain for all to see. He not only sentenced 80 opposition senators to death but also let his followers confiscate their property. To his first list of 80 names, he began adding—3,600 businessmen, more than 2,000 other Romans. The heads of victims were stuck up on poles in the Forum as a warning that the populist age had ended and Rome was back in patrician hands.

Under Marius, Rome's poor had risen up in envy; under Sulla, the patricians were surpassing them in greed. First came his soldiers, who regarded pillaging as their veterans' bonus. Sulla confiscated the land of the communities that had opposed him and turned it over to his soldiers as they left the army. But it was the rich conservatives who profited most, expropriating the estates of the dead or buying up their holdings for a pittance.

As the death toll mounted, Sulla's own faction was alarmed enough to insist upon a list of the men he had marked for death. He agreed to display a white tablet inscribed with their names. If a man had enough property, covetous Romans killed him, seized his estate and wrote his name on the tablet afterward to justify their crime. Executioners were heard joking that one rich man had been killed by his mansion, another by his lavish gardens. In the turmoil, names were regularly confused, men's throats cut by mistake.

Sulla tried to give a pretense of legality to his rule by reviving the title of dictator for the first time in the 120 years since Hannibal had threatened Rome. And Sulla didn't bind himself to the constitutional six-month limit. He was determined to curtail the power of the people's tribunes so that men like Marius or the Gracchus brothers could never again challenge the senate's authority. He stripped the tribunes of many of their powers, took away the courts from the jurisdiction of the merchant class and restored them exclusively to the senate. The number of senators had fallen to a low of 150; Sulla increased it to 600. Many of the new appointees were his military officers, but he also sponsored a law that let patrician sons pass into the senate more easily.

Sulla was doing everything to turn back the calendar 50 years, to the days when the senate's preeminence had gone unchallenged. But he himself had marched on Rome at the head of an army, and no amount of new legislation could erase his example.

Gluttony distinguished Sulla's rule as much as murder. After centuries of austerity, wealthy Romans had discovered that a meal could be more appetizing than a simple bowl of wheat porridge. Dinner parties now started after an hour or two at a public bath and ended with extended rounds of drinking. Throughout the meal, guests lay on cushions, propped up on an elbow. Because the menu was certain to be rich, Romans excused themselves during a banquet to vomit so they would be able to consume the courses to follow. Purging was considered a polite way to compliment a host.

Appetizers of oysters, eggs and sardines were washed down by wine sweetened with honey. Six or seven main dishes followed: mackerel, mullet, eels and prawns, goose, ostrich, chicken and—if the host could afford it—peacock. The meats might be lamb, suckling pig, hare and wild goat. Desserts included a variety of fruit and honeyed cakes. Ranks of servants stood by to keep the wine glasses filled. To those excesses, Sulla brought his own insatiable appetite. For his banquets, he ordered far more food than his guests could consume, until haunches of uneaten meat were dumped every day into the Tiber along with his enemies' corpses. Sulla uncorked wines more than forty years old for his favorites, including old Metrobius, the transvestite, who was back at the dictator's side.

When Sulla's wife gave birth to twins, he chose names that meant Fortunate and Joyful. But midway through the days of revelry, the new mother fell deathly ill, and priests warned Sulla that her contagion would pollute the entire house. He had her carried away. After she died, his parties grew gaudier.

A few months later, while Sulla was watching gladiators at their games, a beautiful woman named Valeria passed behind him and pulled a tuft of wool from his toga. He wheeled around. The woman said, "There's no reason to be surprised, Dictator. I only want to have a little bit of your good luck for myself."

Soon they were married, but even a new wife couldn't stop Sulla, now 60, from lying all day on his couch and drinking with actors, dancers and former lovers.

III

AURELIA

80–79 B.C.

While Sulla savored life at home, Julius Caesar continued his self-imposed exile, an odd fate for a young man who had grown up wanting so badly to please. Caesar's capacity to charm could arouse suspicions among those older Romans with little tolerance for playfulness or whimsy. But he had learned how to captivate at an early age, and his mother doted on him. Caesar was her only son, her hope for restoring the family's political luster.

Aurelia was admired for respecting two Roman traditions: she had brought to her marriage both money and extremely simple tastes. As other women succumbed to softer fashions from Asia or Greece, Aurelia became known for her austerity.

Gaius Julius Caesar was born three days before the Ides of the summer month of Quintilis in the year 654; Romans calculated time by the years since their city was founded. As the firstborn son, he was named for his father, and as a male child received

Portrait bust of a patrician Roman woman. The Metropolitan Museum of Art, gift of Philip Hofer, 1938.

36

three names. The given, Gaius, came first; the middle, the most important name of the three, identified his gens or clan, the Julians; Caesar was the name of his family within the clan.

All women were called simply by the feminine form of their clan name. Caesar's aunt was Julia, as were his two sisters—Elder Julia and Younger Julia. Had his mother given birth to more girls, they would have been numbered—Julia Three, Julia Four, Julia Five.

Aurelia had married into a clan that boasted of its exalted blood. From the Greeks, the Romans had picked up the habit of claiming to trace their families back to the gods. The Julii Caesares said they had descended from Iulus, son of Aeneas of Troy. Since Aeneas was the son of Venus, that made their heritage divine.

By Caesar's time, speculation over his family name was unresolved. "Caesar" might have been derived from a Punic word for elephant; an ancestor had either killed or been killed by one. But it could have been due just as well to the family's eyes, which were usually blue-gray, although Caesar's were very dark. Or the name might have meant that an infant had once been surgically removed from his mother's womb: *caesus* meant "cut." Growing up, Caesar could decide which legends to believe and which to exploit.

As a Roman aristocrat, Aurelia lived in an ambiguous world of privilege and constraints. Women could not vote or hold property except through their fathers or husbands. They could seem little more than political chattel, and yet the wife in a well-to-do household was far more than an adornment. Through the centuries, the modesty and decorum of the Roman matron had set the tone for society. She was chaste, which reassured her husband that he had sired their children. And she raised those children in drab and honorable ways. Her husband might dally with slave girls, but a Roman matron was expected to resist temptation.

The increasing frequency of divorce had changed much of that, including the handling of dowries. Now a married woman's father often kept control of her money in case her husband later set her aside. If her father died, a divorced woman's dowry passed to a guardian, who was often little more than her employee. Wars and purges, quick divorces and an eroding respect for marriage had created an abundance of unattached, strong-minded women who often became absorbed in politics. Such a woman could be invaluable in promoting the career of a lover—even a former lover, if he had left her smiling.

Caesar's father was responsible for the boy's education— swimming and fencing, along with reading and writing. But it was Aurelia who oversaw his earliest training. Roman children waited on their parents at meals and learned to respect the household gods. They grew up among images of the family's *lares*, figures that represented their ancestors, and *penates*, the smaller images that guarded the pantry. At dawn, children watched their father cast a bit of salted cake onto the hearth, a tribute to Vesta, goddess of fire. Romans had seen too many of their wooden houses burn down, and they respected Vesta's power. Offerings had become more formal over the years until now six aristocratic virgins lived in their own temple in the Forum, stoking Vesta's sacred fire and pledging never to let her flame go out.

When Caesar outgrew his parents' instruction, the family found him a tutor, Antonius Gnipho, a clever and well-traveled Gaul. Conservative families sometimes rejected the hordes of Greek slaves and freedmen ready to teach their own language because of the Greek reputation for decadence, including homo-sexuality. Rome had become more tolerant of that practice, but traditional households often preferred to employ raw-boned, blond-haired Gauls from the north.

Under Antonius' direction, Caesar rose before dawn to wash and dress in a tunic that reached a little below his knees; the female version went to the ankle. Roman boys could look forward to the ceremony at 16 when they were allowed to drape the man's toga over their tunic. The morning routine also had Caesar filling his mouth with water to rub over his teeth before he spat it out. Settled down with his wax tablet, he was given inspirational max-ims to copy out: "A plan is no good if it can't be altered." "A merciful man is always a conqueror." Antonius, versed in Latin and Greek, set Caesar to reading Homer, Hesiod and Menander and writing poems of his own. One honored Hercules, another was based on the legend of Oedipus. Antonius had traveled as far as Egypt's capital at Alexandria, and he turned out to be an ami-able scholar. But he couldn't replace Aurelia in Caesar's heart. Growing up, the boy wanted to please his mother and make her proud.

Since his clan was patrician, Caesar was expected to campaign for a political office and take his place one day in the senate. At nine, he had watched his father seek to become praetor, the position below consul, and learned then that before an election patricians were expected to make a show of their humility and seek support from the poorest citizens. But, in fact, voters were organized according to their wealth. The electorate was based on 35 tribes named originally for the territories they controlled. The Caesars belonged to the ancient tribe of Fabia, one of the 20 that lay either within the city itself or close by, and the tribes were organized into voting units called centuries. The outlying farmers and the city's poor outnumbered the aristocrats, but since a man had to be present in Rome to vote, the system was weighted toward the rich. Elections were sometimes decided without tallying the votes of the poorer centuries at all. Men with money and property considered it proper that critical decisions be entrusted to those with the most to lose.

Rome's strict ladder of succession set out for ambitious young men which rung they could reach for next—quaestor, aedile, then one of the eight positions as praetor, finally as one of two consuls. On election day, members of the Fabian tribe gathered at sunrise in front of Caesar's house in Subura, a residential section northeast of the Forum. Veterans of Marius' army had also come, after their breakfast of a wheat biscuit dipped in honey or wine. When Caesar's father was ready to leave for the polls, his escorts accompanied him to the Campus Martius, the fields outside the city's walls. An official first received assurances that the day's auspices were favorable and then asked, "Among the candidates whose names I hold, who are those you want to make praetors?"

By lot, a century was chosen to lead the voting, and its men set off to cast their ballots, which were wooden tickets painted with their choices. The first bloc's vote was counted quickly and indicated that Caesar's father had been elected praetor. His supporters cheered and followed him back to Subura.

A praetor's duties were demanding. He was expected to receive any Roman who requested an audience, and senators and businessmen came regularly, along with rich plebeians, to ask a favor or plot political strategy. Less prominent men also arrived each morning, looking for jobs, legal advice, a guarantor for their loans. A praetor protected his clientele and pointed them in the direction of money. In return, they provided devotion and votes.

During his year in office, a praetor was accompanied by six aides called lictors, wearing togas hemmed with a purple stripe and carrying *fasces*—bundles of birch rods tied with red cord. Marching ahead of their patron on his way to the Forum, they forced men to step aside with shouts of "Clear the road!"

Caesar was 15 when his father was traveling in Pisa and died from a stroke. Left fatherless and the only male in his immediate family, Caesar was suddenly exposed to the political undercurrents. Aurelia's well-connected family decided to protect him with an appointment as Flamen Dialis, or high priest of Jupiter. It was then that his first engagement had been broken and he was married to Cornelia.

The priesthood's duties were convoluted but not burdensome: Caesar would have been forbidden to ride a horse, look at a corpse or watch an army preparing for battle. A spirited boy might have chafed under those restrictions, but Caesar had obeyed his family and had taken the first two steps toward confirmation before he defied Sulla and lost the priesthood, along with Cornelia's dowry. Sulla had taken his revenge, but he had also set Caesar free to enter politics.

Now, as Caesar evaluated Rome's factions from exile, he was revealing much about his instincts and ambitions. He could have gone to Spain to join Sertorius, a general who had stayed loyal to Marius' cause and represented the last significant challenge to Sulla's dictatorship. Caesar would have been a welcome recruit. But serving in Spain would have meant breaking decisively with the senate. Although Sertorius' cause was honorable, even glorious, it was looking increasingly futile. Caesar protected his future by traveling east instead, to the province called Asia, and becoming an aide to a Sulla appointee, Marcus Thermus. Generals like Thermus collected patrician young men to provide them with amusing company in the provinces.

Before Sulla became Rome's dictator, he had negotiated a lenient truce with Mithridates VI, a long-time enemy in the East. The king of Pontus, Mithridates had watched resentfully for years as Rome picked off territories that his father once conquered. Although he was Persian, Mithridates saw himself as the defender of Greek values against the less-civilized Romans, and until Sulla bought him off, he had been expanding his domain around the Black Sea for a quarter-century. In one notorious episode, he had exploited the widespread hatred of Rome's tax collectors to encourage the slaughter of 80,000 Roman citizens overseas.

Despite the truce, the Greek city of Mytilene was threatening to fight on alone after Mithridates lay down his arms. Rome needed a fleet to lay siege to Mytilene, and the nearest ships belonged to Rome's nominal ally, Nicomedes, the king of Bithynia. But Nicomedes seemed reluctant to commit his navy, and young Caesar was directed to travel to Bithynia to remind the ungrateful king that if Rome hadn't supported him in the past he wouldn't have a crown.

Nicomedes was an urbane monarch and, like most Eastern kings of the time, agreed with Mithridates that their culture was superior to Rome's. Their cities boasted vast theaters; the libraries of Alexandria and Pergamum held hundreds of thousands of volumes, when Romans had to rely on scattered private collections. Bithynia was particularly famed for its excesses, and Nicomedes was well known for his court of handsome young men. When Julius Caesar arrived, Nicomedes offered him the use of his own apartments to bathe and refresh himself. If his guest was tired, the king would extend the honor of his own bed. Since Caesar's mission required his ready charm, he accepted the king's hospitality.

The next day, a group of Roman businessmen visiting Bithynia were shocked to find a new face among the king's stable of boys. Caesar was making himself agreeable, passing the ceremonial cups of wine and giving every appearance of obeisance to Nicomedes.

In Rome, a patrician was not disgraced by having sex with mistresses and slave boys before he was married, and the poems read at his wedding sometimes listed the groom's conquests among both sexes. But the verses ended by observing that the bride's loveliness made any future infidelity unthinkable. For young men who took male lovers, their code demanded that they be the active partner; a Roman citizen must always remain in control. Even lying with a woman, a man should not give pleasure with his tongue. That kind of passivity degraded him, reduced him to the level of a slave. Yet here was Julius Caesar seeming to announce to the world that he had compromised his own honor and Rome's.

Caesar's faith in himself and his luck could make him insouciant, even fatalistic. In Bithynia, far from home, he was indifferent to the impression he might be making on a few Roman traders. And, except for their scandalized reactions, his assignment met with complete success. Nicomedes authorized his ships to sail against Mytilene, and Caesar sailed with them.

As time depleted Mytilene's food supply, the Roman general commanding the siege, Lucius Licinius Lucullus, preyed on the hunger of the townspeople within their fortress. He sent out a raiding party to scale Mytilene's high walls but told them to make a show of failing. In retreat, they were to leave behind mounds of food in plain view. When the starving rebels burst out of their city, Lucullus' men killed hundreds of their soldiers and forced the rest to surrender.

Along on the raid, Caesar had thrown himself into the battle, perhaps to stem any gossip about his behavior in Bithynia. In any event, his valor won him the *corona civica*, a wreath of oak leaves given to a soldier for saving a fellow Roman's life. Back at headquarters, Thermus himself laid the wreath on Caesar's brow. The crown could only be worn on the day it was awarded, but it came with a small badge that allowed the recipient to sit next to the senators at public entertainments. For a 20-year-old who traded on his youthful good looks, the wreath disguised, if only for a day, Caesar's rapidly receding hairline.

IV

CICERO

80–79 B.C.

Since he was no soldier, Cicero knew that his best chance of advancement was his skill as an orator, but to become Rome's best would require sacrifice. He was prepared to renounce sports and hunting and every frivolous pleasure, including the sensual ones. Abstinence would be no hardship. Although Cicero was only 25, no urgent passions intruded on his life.

Soon after he began to plead private cases, Cicero was asked to represent the defendant in a murder trial. It could make his reputation. Or, given the lingering terror in Rome, threaten his life.

The trial would mark Cicero's first appearance in the Forum, the outdoor meeting place down the hill from the Temple of Jupiter on the Capitoline. To early tribes, the expanse of land had been a swamp suitable only for a burial ground. Then the first kings drained off the stagnant rainwater through the sewers of the Cloaca Maxima, and building could begin.

Across the square was the Curia, the senate's meeting

house. Rows of small shops had sprung up to the north and south, and at the Forum's northwest corner was the open space once reserved for the people's assembly. Sixty-five years earlier, those gatherings had been moved into the Forum itself, in front of a stage 80 feet by 40 feet called the rostra.

The Forum's flat natural floor rose to the east toward Palatine Hill. A house and temple for the Vestal Virgins had been built there, just beyond the Forum's limits. Via Sacra, the Sacred Way, was the route through the Forum for religious processions.

As Rome's vital heart, the Forum had often been enlarged and scarred. Here the Gauls had set fire to the city's wooden buildings, and other disastrous fires had swept through shops along the northern edge. When Gaius Gracchus was killed in the Forum, the patrician consul had celebrated by restoring the Temple of Concord. The Forum's first arch had gone up at the same time, to honor a Roman victory in south Gaul. The Temple of Jupiter, most holy of shrines, had been destroyed during the battles between Marius and Sulla, but Sulla ordered it rebuilt. Everywhere Marcus Cicero looked around the square, he could see the history of the Roman republic and monuments to the men and gods who had preserved it.

Cicero was defending the son of a wealthy citizen named Roscius from the town of Ameria, 50 miles from Rome. One of Sulla's early supporters, Roscius should have been safe from the dictator's reprisals, and yet he had been murdered in the street, returning from a dinner party during a visit to Rome. Roscius left a widow and a son past 40, who had been overseeing the family's 13 farms. Two nephews who had been on bad terms with Roscius also lived in Ameria.

On the night of the murder, a friend of the nephews covered the distance from Rome to Ameria in a brisk 10 hours to report the news. Word of the crime also reached Chrysogonus, a former Greek slave who was one of Sulla's favorites. The dictator's proscription lists had already been closed, but Roscius' name was somehow added. His farms were confiscated by the state to be sold for a pittance.

The market value of Roscius' land had been 600,000 sesterces, or nearly 1,600 pounds of silver. But it was sold at public auction for 2,000 sesterces, a little more than 5 pounds of silver. At that bargain rate, one of his nephews took three farms; there were no other bids. Acting for Chrysogonus, the second nephew snatched up the last ten.

The nephews weren't generous in victory. While Roscius' son was arranging his father's funeral, one cousin expelled him from his former property and seized his personal goods. Outraged neighbors in Ameria sent a delegation to protest to Sulla. But it was Chrysogonus who received them. Soon afterward young Roscius began hearing that his own life was in danger. He escaped to Rome, where he learned that, as a last bitter joke, he was being charged with his father's murder.

This would be the first murder trial since the end of Sulla's proscriptions, and heartsore Romans were yearning for a return to the rule of law. Under Sulla's new decrees, a praetor would preside over the trial and the jury would be composed entirely of senators. As Cicero weighed his chances in court, he looked critically at himself. His neck was too stringy, he decided; his entire appearance too young and unprepossessing. But after 10 years of rehearsal, arguing a case in the Forum would give Cicero the stage for his first starring performance.

Parricidium had once referred to all murder; over time, its meaning was restricted to the killing of one's father. To Romans, it was the most abhorrent crime, still punishable by death when other murders were not.

Given a weak case against Roscius, the veteran prosecutor made up in composure what he lacked in evidence. He seemed to be talking to friends in his own home, sitting down in the middle of his speech and pausing to give a casual order to his slave. His manner suggested that whether or not Roscius had killed his father, simply by choosing Cicero he stood convicted of picking a second-rate lawyer.

Cicero rose with two purposes, to prove his client innocent and to suggest who was guilty. He could be sure that attacking the two nephews didn't pose a political threat. No Roman aristocrat would bother defending their bloodstained riches. Cicero laid out the damning facts of the case and then reminded the jury about Longinus, a consul from nearly half a century before, renowned for his integrity. At trials, Longinus always asked one question: "*Cui bono?*" Who has profited?

As Cicero proceeded to offer tentative answers, he took care not to implicate Sulla. To some degree, he could gamble on Sulla's indolence; the dictator had finished his sweeping changes in Rome's government and had voluntarily stepped down. Fond as Sulla might be of Chrysogonus, he was unlikely to interrupt his pleasures in order to punish the insignificant lawyer who abused him. But to be safe, Cicero specifically absolved Sulla from wrongdoing.

He was playing on the resentment of patricians who saw clever former slaves living more lavishly than they. He reminded them that Chrysogonus—the very name derived from the Greek word for gold—had a fine mansion on the Palatine. He also owned a house outside of Rome and a number of fertile farms close to the city. The residence of this former slave was crammed with silver plate, embroidered coverlets, marble statuary, Corinthian bronzes. Cicero claimed that Chrysogonus possessed a new broiler so expensive that when the auctioneer had called out its price, passersby assumed that an entire estate had just changed hands.

Cicero had made a point of coming to the Forum simply dressed. Now he urged the jury to look hard at Chrysogonus: "Take a glance at his curled and scented hair, as he flutters from one end of the Forum to the other."

Cicero indulged in melodrama to keep his audience alert through the labyrinth of fiscal deceit. At one point, he turned on the messenger who had brought the news of Roscius' murder to Ameria: "How do we explain this incredibly rapid journey, this unparalleled speed and hurry? No, I'm not asking who actually did the killing. Don't be frightened, Glaucia! I'm not proposing to shake your clothes, or search you to see if you've got a weapon concealed on your person."

He also broke with custom by speaking as though he were the defendant, not simply his lawyer. "You murdered my father, although he was not proscribed," he said to Roscius' accusers. "After he was killed, you entered his name in the proscription list. You drove me by force out of my home. You possess my patrimony. What more do you want?"

But what roused the crowd to shouts of admiration were Cicero's remarks on the sin of parricide and its grisly punishment. He began by noting that Athens was traditionally considered the wisest state in Greece and Solon its wisest citizen. When men asked him why he had never drawn up a punishment for killing one's father, Solon replied that he simply could not believe that a son would ever do such a thing. But, Cicero continued, Romans were wiser still and knew that nothing was so sacred it couldn't be profaned. "And so, they ordained that anyone guilty of this crime should be sewn alive into a sack and then thrown into a river."

Retribution was even more painful than Cicero described it. The murderer was stripped naked except for his face, which was wrapped in a wolf's skin. He was first beaten, then sewed into a sack with a dog, a monkey, a rooster and a snake. But Cicero was concentrating on metaphorical pain, the way a murderer would never breathe air from the sky, and the sea's waves would toss his bones but never cleanse them. "And at the end," Cicero cried, when murderers are cast up on the shore, "even the rocks do not support their dead bodies to give them rest. That is the enormous crime you are imputing to Sextus Roscius, and that is its horrifying punishment."

No verdict could restore Roscius' inheritance; redress was beyond this court's jurisdiction. But in every other way, the jury's decision was a victory for Cicero. He had won his client's acquittal and a resounding reputation for himself. With times so unsettled, however, he couldn't be sure that his new prominence wasn't more curse than blessing. After he won another case, a challenge to Sulla's right to strip voting rights from the Italian communities that had opposed him, Cicero began to feel the strain of his victories. Never robust, he had lost weight and couldn't hold down food. His voice, still harsh and untrained, had gone shrill from the recent demands on it. Those reasons, physical and political, led Cicero to consider leaving Rome. The decision wasn't easy. He was married now, and his wife, Terentia, had recently given him a daughter.

Cicero's marriage had been advantageous for a new man. Terentia came from an old, rich family and brought a dowry of 120,000 drachmas, an estate outside Tusculum and several houses in Rome itself. His marriage allowed Cicero to remain strict about observing the law that prevented lawyers from accepting pay. But despite his improved fortunes, Cicero decided to leave his new family for a while. Like Caesar two years before him, he went abroad to wait for a less threatening political climate.

V

CAESAR

78–72 B.C.

Julius Caesar, moving on from Mytilene, had barely reached the province of Cilicia in the northeast corner of the Mediterranean when he got news that ended his exile. Sulla was dead. He had declined a third consulship the previous year to retire to his villa in Campania. Departing for the countryside, he had said, "I have lifted the senate into the saddle. Let us see if it can ride."

Sulla wrote his memoirs and persisted in epic indulgences. He developed ulcers of the intestine and knew death was imminent. Still, when a judge refused to pay his debt to the public treasury on the grounds that Sulla would soon be gone, Sulla had the man brought before him and ordered him strangled on the spot. It proved to be a double execution. The strain of shouting commands ruptured a blood vessel, and Sulla bled through the night and died the next day.

Sulla left his twins by Metella and a daughter by Valeria, born after his funeral and called—like other children delivered after their father's death—Postuma.

When his will was opened, it held one surprise. Despite many marks of favor to Pompey, Sulla had left him nothing. Pompey had married Sulla's stepdaughter but when she died and Pompey took a new bride, he and the late dictator were no longer related. Whatever his disappointment, Pompey remained loyal. The body of his own unpopular father had been dragged from its bier and mutilated, and Pompey took precautions to see that Sulla's corpse would not be defiled.

He went to Campania to accompany Sulla's body back to Rome. As dictator, Sulla had ordered Marius' tomb pried open and his bones widely scattered so loyal mourners couldn't collect them. Now Sulla had left instructions for his own corpse to be cremated, a break with his family's tradition but protection against his remains being desecrated. Sulla had also written his own epitaph: "No friend has ever done me a kindness and no enemy a wrong without being fully repaid."

The day of the funeral dawned cloudy, and officials worried that rain would douse the pyre's flames. By 3 P.M., they took a chance and ordered cavalry and trumpeters to lead out the procession, ahead of Sulla's household *fasces* and his golden bier. Senators headed the pallbearers, followed by ranks of priests, judges and throngs of Sulla's veterans. The cities he had favored, the legions he had commanded and the friends he had enriched all sent the same tribute, until more than 2,000 golden crowns followed behind his corpse. Rome's women had contributed enough spices to fill 210 litters and leave enough to shape two large images of Sulla in frankincense and cinnamon. Since Sulla's son was too young to deliver the oration, other speakers praised Sulla on his behalf.

When the pyre was lighted, the crowd watched Sulla's famous luck follow him to the grave. A brisk wind raised a fire that consumed the body. Attendants had just enough time to collect Sulla's bones before heavy rains began to fall.

The senate decreed that the city's women mourn Sulla by wearing black for one year, but by the time Caesar arrived in Rome, Sulla's legislation was already under attack. Lepidus, the new consul, demanded that the senate return to the people's tribunes their former powers. The patricians brought a motion to censure Lepidus, which the full senate rejected. But they forced Lepidus and his co-consul to swear that they would complete their year in office without further provocations; Romans wanted no more severed heads mounted across the Forum. Lepidus ignored his pledge and pushed forward with bills to restore the grain subsidy that Sulla had ended, to pardon political exiles, to pay compensation for confiscated property and to restore all rights to the children of Sulla's victims.

Another civil war seemed to be looming. After his term, Lepidus went north to become governor of Gaul and began re-cruiting an army there. It was reported that he had sent negotia-tors to win over Sertorius in Spain. Stories reached Rome that his ally Marcus Brutus was raising more troops for Lepidus in towns on the Italian side of the Alps.

At home, Catulus, a respected conservative senator, called on his colleagues to defend themselves. But though the senate was back in the saddle, it would not ride. As Lepidus was gath-ering strength, he approached Julius Caesar to join his rebellion. Few young men had more reason to detest Sulla and his patrician supporters, but Caesar held himself aloof. Many others did enlist with Lepidus, however, and when the threat could no longer be ignored, the senate voted for martial law and commanded Catulus and Pompey to save the Republic.

Pompey's troops routed most of Lepidus' rebels, but Mar-cus Brutus had fortified himself in a town in Gaul called Mutina. Mounting a siege tied up Pompey long enough for Lepidus to reach Rome, pitch camp outside the walls and announce that his price for peace would be a second consulship. The sheer number of his supporters panicked the senators, but as they prepared to capitulate, Pompey sent a message that Marcus Brutus had sur-rendered.

Pompey granted Brutus a mounted escort to a town on the Po River. There, a day later, one of Pompey's officers killed him on Pompey's orders. The murder forced Pompey to write again to the senate and retract his earlier account of Brutus' surrender. But Romans found out about Pompey's violation of his pledge of safe conduct and began talking openly about him as "the young butcher."

Brutus' murder caused Lepidus to flee from Italy, and by the time he reached Sardinia his will seemed to have drained away. It was speculated that his depression was caused less by his military defeats than by new evidence that his wife was being unfaithful. When Lepidus died, the senate was free to send Pompey on to Spain, to cope with Sertorius.

In Rome, Marcus Brutus' stately widow, Servilia, prepared to raise her eight-year-old son alone. Named for his father, the young Brutus was a pinched and sullen child, an impressionable pupil for Servilia's lessons that he must never forget Pompey's treachery.

At the age of 23, younger and far less experienced as an orator than Cicero, Julius Caesar argued his first court case, prosecuting Sulla's ally Dolabella. Citizens had come from the province of Macedonia to charge Dolabella with extortion during his term as governor there. The verdict, though, was never in doubt. Conviction would have embarrassed Dolabella's many patrician allies and dishonored Sulla's memory. He was acquitted.

Caesar lost the case but won the people's good will. Dolabella turned out to be a sour winner, and he revived the rumors about Caesar and King Nicomedes. He claimed that in Bithynia Julius Caesar had become "the female rival of Bithynia's queen" and "the bottom half of the royal bed." Other patricians took up the cry. An aristocrat campaigning for the consulship alluded to Caesar's reputation as a philanderer, calling him "every woman's husband and every man's wife." Political candidates had come to expect those accusations. But Caesar was not running for office. The patricians seemed to need to believe that the nature of this young man who had opposed them so actively was essentially passive.

Caesar's popularity might be growing, but Sulla's influence still weighed heavily on Rome a year after his death. The time seemed right for Caesar to sail east once again. King Nicomedes, the one man who knew the truth about Caesar's visit to Bithynia, had died and bequeathed his kingdom to the people of Rome, but Caesar headed instead for Rhodes. Like Cicero, he used the excuse that he was leaving Rome to improve his formal education.

Traveling by sea was always risky, less for the currents than for the pirates. The Romans might own the Mediterranean, but pirates were getting rich from it. They roamed widely, protected by Mithridates and Sertorius, who counted on pirate ships to harass their common enemy. Some were soldiers who had fled their countries after Rome conquered them. Sailing from ports in Asia, Spain and Africa, they formed a loose alliance based in Cilicia, where the forests provided timber for their ships. Roman governors in the provinces seldom suppressed the pirate crews; it was more lucrative to accept regular bribes and pay an occasional ransom. All times of the year were dangerous except the height of winter, when storms kept even the outlaws in port. But as Caesar was crossing the Aegean, pirates braved the rough waters and seized his ship.

Caesar was forced again to ransom his life. This time, the price was 20 talents—more than 1,000 pounds of silver, or 10 times what he had paid Sulla's men. The pirates sent most of Caesar's traveling companions back to the port of Miletus to raise the money, and took Caesar to wait on an island hideaway with his doctor and two servants.

Apart from the expense, being kidnapped was humiliating. Fresh from being mocked in Rome, Caesar knew that the timing of this new indignity made his situation worse. He was being measured constantly against other ambitious Romans—Marcus Crassus, for one, a rich speculator who was aiming at a political career. As the pirates took him into custody, Caesar muttered, "How pleased you will be, Crassus, when you hear that I have been captured."

But when Romans did get word of the incident, the versions they heard described Caesar's reaction as lighthearted and courageous. The stories may have originated with Caesar's doctor—certainly they didn't come from the pirates—and every anecdote was designed to ease the sting of being captured. One account had Caesar annoyed when the pirates demanded only 20 talents to release him. That price was too low, he complained, and volunteered to pay 50 talents instead.

Other stories told of Caesar's composure as he waited on the island for the ransom money. Watching his captors practice with their swords, he was said to have laughed at their ineptitude. And although the pirates wouldn't let Caesar near their weapons, they wrestled and swam with him until he became more their leader than prisoner. Romans heard that when Caesar was sleepy, he demanded that the pirates stop talking. He passed the time writing poems, which he read aloud; if the pirates didn't appreciate his verses, Caesar denounced them jovially as barbarians. Most amusing of all, Caesar often joked with his captors that once he was free, he would see them all hanged. That was how Caesar wanted Rome to believe he had spent his 38 days in captivity.

Caesar had no family fortune to draw on, but his credit was good with the moneylenders, and the ransom was delivered. The pirates had promised to set their victim free, and kept their word. So did Caesar.

Once he was released in Miletus, Caesar hired the merchant ships lying at anchor there. With their crews of mercenaries, he soon captured most of the pirates who had kidnapped him and confiscated their property, including his ransom. Caesar sent them to prison at the Roman base in Pergamum and went to the governor of Asia province to demand that the pirates be punished. The governor, away on a military campaign, answered by letter that the decision would have to await his return. Caesar decided he was stalling until he could think of a way to claim the money for himself. Impatient, Caesar returned to Pergamum and got the prisoners released to him. That done, he ordered them crucified.

Crucifixion was the customary execution for criminals who weren't Roman citizens. Since the pirates had been congenial companions, Caesar wanted to spare them the slow agony of the cross and gave orders that their throats be cut before they were bound to the wooden beams. Caesar might not be able to prevent his kidnapping from setting off a new round of jokes in Rome, but he could show the Romans what Sulla had understood—that an easy manner should not be mistaken for weakness.

Caesar moved on to Rhodes to study with Molon. Most Greek teachers of rhetoric taught only theory, but Molon had argued actual cases in court. He preached austerity, purity, clarity and restraint. Besides rhetoric, Romans were immersed in Greek philosophy. Epicureans, who had accepted the loss of their political liberties to the Macedonians, taught that a man should avoid pain by finding a balance in his private life. Stoics emphasized duty, although their underlying fatalism recognized that a man's destiny was beyond his will to change. The Stoic simply did his best and tried to die well. Cicero's studies in Rhodes stimulated his interest in philosophic questions. Caesar seemed more inclined to live his philosophy than examine it.

Caesar soon had a new excuse for action. Mithridates of Pontus was stirring again and contesting Nicomedes' will, which had left Bithynia to Rome. He marched there, overturned the Roman government and occupied the kingdom. The senate sent out Lucullus to fight, and Caesar gathered together a contingent of Romans living in Rhodes to assist him. They crossed to the mainland, recruited more troops and stopped a rebel band of Sertorius' men from conquering Ephesus and turning the city over to Mithridates. Although the senate was still dominated by Sulla's faction, Caesar was showing again that when Rome was threatened he would stand with his countrymen.

Caesar had punished one band of pirates, but the rogue ships went on creating chaos throughout the Mediterranean. Rome's senators decided they must end the raids and gave the assignment to Marcus Antonius, a pleasant, feckless praetor who had been slipping uneasily among the factions that developed after Sulla's death. Antonius was sent out with the broadest authority, the *imperium infinitum*. Looking on sourly, Cicero said Antonius had been voted so much power because he was too incompetent to abuse it.

Instead of deploying his men wisely or building a secure base, Antonius alienated the Sicilians and Greeks by requisitioning large numbers of ships and then careening aimlessly around the Mediterranean. He was preparing to assault the pirates of Crete when Caesar went to a fishing village in the southern Peloponnesus to join him as an aide.

Caesar discovered that Antonius had been hoarding the funds that Rome had voted for his expedition. He was also extorting so much from local villages that their leaders had to borrow from Roman moneylenders at interest rates of 48 percent. Worse, Antonius showed how badly he underestimated the pirates by loading down his ships with chains for the prisoners he expected to sell to slave dealers along the coast.

Caesar's service with Antonius was cut short by a summons to return to Rome. Antonius sailed without him against the pirates of Cilicia and was defeated ignominiously. The best peace terms he could negotiate were so humiliating that the senate refused to ratify them. But when Antonius died suddenly in Crete, his senate allies moved to salvage his name by bestowing on him posthumously the title of Creticus, conqueror of Crete. He left behind a murky reputation, an ambitious widow and Mark Antony, his handsome son of 11 or 12.

Caesar had been called home by the sudden death of a cousin who had been a pontiff in Rome. Caesar, surprisingly, was selected to replace him. At 26, seven years after Sulla blocked him from becoming high priest of Jupiter, Caesar would hold a religious office.

The College of Pontiffs had been established early in Rome's history to oversee religious rituals. It was free from irksome limitations, and although membership was not overtly political, the current pontiffs had all supported Sulla. Yet their vote for Caesar had been unanimous—a result of the same intense pressures from Caesar's mother that once spared his life.

Caesar rushed home to accept the appointment, recrossing the seas on which he had been captured two years earlier. During the voyage, he thought he saw the masts of pirate ships on the horizon, and he stripped down to escape and strapped a dagger to his side. Before he dove overboard, he saw that the menacing shapes were only the outlines of trees. At least that was another attractively self-deprecating story that followed Caesar back to Rome.

Once at home, Caesar found that Servilia, Marcus Brutus' widow, was opening her large house to men who schemed against the patricians. Caesar was still living in Subura with his mother, wife and daughter, but he showed up often enough at Servilia's gatherings that Romans ignored the chronological evidence and gossiped that he, not Brutus, had sired the serious-minded boy left fatherless by Pompey.

As pontiff, Caesar wanted to extend his reputation. Exploiting his wreath of oak leaves and the recent victory over Sertorius' men, Caesar stood for the unexalted office of military tribune. If Rome were threatened, the appointment guaranteed the command of 1,000 men, but it did not lead automatically to a senate seat. Caesar valued the title chiefly because it was voted on by Rome's citizens, who readily bestowed on him that minor distinction.

VI

SPARTACUS

73–72 B.C.

Near the Appian Way at Capua, south of Rome, a schoolmaster named Batiatus had opened an unusual academy. As pupils, he took only slaves or convicts and housed them in barracks while they attended his classes. Batiatus was training them to die.

Etruscans had introduced the concept of gladiators, ordering slaves to fight each other and provide a human sacrifice at funerals. The Romans embraced and expanded the sport. By Caesar's day, a gladiator might die in a public arena or at a private spectacle in a rich man's house. He might be killed fighting another slave or a wild beast. How he died mattered less than that he died entertainingly.

Romans recognized that all slaves, not just gladiators with a death sentence hanging over them, represented a threat to their own security. An insurrection 30 years earlier in Sicily had set off uprisings as far away as the silver mines of Athens. Rome had required 17,000 soldiers to put down that revolt. The law branded

Bronze group of two men fighting. The Metropolitan Museum of Art, Rogers Fund, 1911.

a runaway slave a thief for stealing his master's property—himself. If a slave murdered his master, every other slave in the household could be put to death as accomplices.

Sometimes slaves were well treated and came to care for their masters. At least in theory, all of them could one day buy their freedom or be set free by a grateful owner. Even the gladiators took defiant pride in being selected for an academy. Romans had witnessed a mortally wounded gladiator looking into the stands for his master's permission to lie down and die.

Batiatus did not inspire that sort of loyalty. When 200 of his gladiators decided to escape from his school, they vowed to fight to the death rather than be recaptured. An informer betrayed the latest plot, and only 78 slaves managed to break out. Their weapons were knives, axes and roasting spits snatched from the cookhouse.

As they fled, they came upon wagons taking arms from Capua to gladiators in another town. They confiscated the lot and headed for a hill they thought they could defend. Once there, they strengthened their position and elected three leaders, one of them a brawny young Thracian named Spartacus. He was as smart as he was strong, and cultured in ways that made him seem more a Greek than the nomad he had been. The slaves first defeated guards sent from Capua to recover them, seized their weapons and threw away the makeshift arms they had taken from Batiatus' kitchen. They would fight as soldiers, not as slaves.

When news of the exploit spread, other slaves began slipping away from farms and villas to swell the ranks. At first, Romans seemed indifferent; the lowness of the slaves' status made them a contemptible foe. But Spartacus outwitted two praetors sent down from the city, and his slave army began to seem more frightening.

Spartacus was not rash or overconfident. Before Rome could marshal its full power against him, he hoped to lead his gladiators through the Alps, where they would scatter and return home to Thrace and Gaul. But not every slave had a home waiting for him. For many of them, the excitement, plunder and revenge of battle had become too exhilarating to give up. They overruled Spartacus and insisted on staying on the offensive throughout Italy. The revolt was threatening the survival of the state, and both consuls were dispatched from Rome to end it.

One consul surprised and destroyed a group of German

slaves. But Spartacus' main force defeated Rome's soldiers and again seized their equipment. As Spartacus moved toward the Alps, he defeated 10,000 troops led by the governor of Cisalpine Gaul, who barely escaped alive. The senate panicked and sent its inept consuls back to civilian life.

Rome's two best generals were far away—Pompey fighting Sertorius in Spain, Lucullus pursuing Mithridates. When Lucullus sank the enemy fleet, the senate told him to offer the same easy terms to Mithridates that Sulla had once negotiated. Lucullus ignored those instructions and led his troops on the attack. He became Rome's first general to disobey the senate's direct order.

Rome's senators gave temporary command in the war against Spartacus to Marcus Crassus, a newly reelected praetor known to be the greediest man in Rome. Although his father had once been honored with a triumph for military success in Spain, Crassus grew up with his two married brothers and their wives in a cramped house. When one brother died, Crassus married his widow to keep the dowry in the family.

In his youth, Crassus had started speculating and found he could profit from other men's disasters. Sulla's proscriptions let him pay low prices for the estates of condemned men. And Crassus learned how to exploit Rome's many fires. With no fire department, the city's rows of wooden shops and tenements often went up in flames. Crassus bought slaves who could design and construct buildings. He supplied others with pails of water and turned them into a fire brigade. When a house ignited, Crassus rushed to the scene and began negotiating with its owner. After he had bargained to the lowest price, Crassus salvaged what he could of his new property and set his slaves to restoring it. By the time he was appointed to lead the war against Spartacus, his wealth was immense. In land alone, his holdings were estimated at 200 million sesterces—50,000 pounds of gold.

Crassus wasn't tempted to build extravagant houses to flaunt his wealth; he regarded those estates as a foolish display. His slaves were known as the best-educated secretaries, the sharpest-eyed stewards, the most gifted silversmiths, and Crassus considered them his greatest treasure.

His father and brother had been killed during Marius' reprisals, and Crassus himself had escaped with a few friends and

10 servants to Spain, where a political ally hid the young man in a cave and sent him food each day. To pass the time, his host also supplied two attractive women. Some months later, Crassus emerged to become one of Sulla's commanders. He proved himself an effective organizer, and during the climactic battle for Rome, Crassus' charge against the enemy line assured Sulla's victory. It galled him afterward that the dictator so clearly favored young Pompey over him.

It was more Crassus' personal fortune than his military experience that qualified him to lead the war against Spartacus. Rome's treasury was depleted, and Crassus defined true wealth as a man's ability to support an army out of his own pocket, a test he could meet. For him, the call was providential. In his middle forties, he didn't need more money. He had studied rhetoric and could speak well in public, but Cicero was becoming the noted orator. Pompey was already a famous soldier, and Caesar was showing adroit political skills. Although Crassus was rich, aristocrats considered a life in trade improper for a senator; farmland was the only respectable investment. To play a leading role, Crassus needed both his wealth and an army loyal to him. Now that he had been given this command against the slaves, he wanted to marshal his troops before Pompey returned from Spain more arrogant than ever.

The senate bestowed on Crassus a proconsul's imperium, and he quickly raised more than 40,000 men. His first goal was to protect Rome by fortifying the area south of Capua. Before engaging his troops, he wanted to gather intelligence by observing the slaves, not fighting them. One commander, however, couldn't resist a chance for glory and disregarded his orders. When he was badly beaten, the rest of his men threw down their weapons and ran away.

To punish their cowardice, Crassus revived a practice that the Roman army hadn't used for years, beating to death soldiers from each squad while the entire army looked on.

That horror braced the survivors for action, and Crassus led them against the slaves. Spartacus slipped away and tried to hire pirate ships that would transport his men to Sicily, where he hoped to fan the embers of earlier slave revolts. The pirates took his money and sailed without him. Spartacus marched his men back from the sea to the peninsula of Rhegium.

When Crassus caught up with him, the Roman merchant drew upon the shrewdness that had made his fortune. He set his men to digging a ditch, long and wide. Above it, they built an immense wall. He had isolated the slaves at the edge of the peninsula without supplies or reinforcements.

Spartacus built rafts, hoping to reach Sicily. But there were notorious currents between Scylla and Charybdis, and his attempt failed. Provisions had run low, winter storms were raging along the coast, and Crassus' barricade held against every attempt to breach it. Once Spartacus tried to steel his men by crucifying a Roman prisoner at the edge of the ditch, a reminder of their own fate if they were to give up.

Crassus may have devised a winning strategy, but Rome's senators were impatient for victory and the long siege looked like a stalemate. Pompey's supporters collected enough votes to bring him home to conquer Spartacus.

VII

POMPEY

76–71 B.C.

In Spain, Pompey's mission had begun badly. Sertorius had moved his troops near Lauro, a rich farming community on the east coast, but Pompey's reputation had frightened the towns-people, and they sent word to him that any past allegiance to Sertorius was over. When both commanders marched on Lauro, Sertorius sprang a trap one summer morning that killed or wounded one-third of Pompey's forces. For Pompey, losing this war was unthinkable. He urged the people of Lauro to remain cheerful and invited them to take seats along the town wall to watch him lay siege to Sertorius' camp.

But Sertorius hadn't exhausted his tricks. At 47, he had been a soldier almost as long as Pompey had been alive. Told of Pompey's boasting, he laughed and promised to teach Sulla's pupil a lesson. "A general," Sertorius said, "must look to the rear rather than to the front."

With that, he revealed the 6,000 heavy infantry he had brought up behind Pompey. Lauro's citizens weighed Pompey's past reputation against the present reality and surrendered to Sertorius, who plundered the town and burned it to the ground.

Had Pompey ever been tempted to join with Sertorius, that was the moment. Every distinction Pompey had received in Rome had come grudgingly from the patricians. With the armies of Sertorius and Pompey joined, no force in Rome could have stopped them. Pompey had remained loyal before, and he didn't waver in Spain. And yet once again his enemy was a fellow Roman citizen. On the brink of turning 30, having held none of the high offices to justify this command, he had become Pompey the Great for leading his army against his own countrymen.

Sertorius harassed Pompey continually, cutting off his supply of grain and driving him farther into hostile territory. At the height of a bleak winter, Pompey wrote an angry letter to the senate. Privation made him bold, but his frustrations produced a protracted whining. No actions the senators might take against him, Pompey wrote, could be worse than what they had done through their neglect: "Having exposed me, in spite of my youth, to a most cruel war, you have, so far as you could, destroyed me and a faithful army by starvation, the most wretched of all deaths."

Pompey boasted of his victories—leaving out his rout at Lauro—and concluded with a naked threat: "I myself have exhausted not only my money but even my credit. You are our only resource. Unless you come to our rescue—against my will, but not without warning from me—our army will pass over into Italy, bringing with it all the war in Spain."

Lucullus, for one, took Pompey's threat seriously. His command against Mithridates depended on keeping Pompey in Spain. At his instigation, the senate put together two more legions and sent them to Pompey, along with substantial money. Those reinforcements turned Rome's fortunes. Over the next two years, Pompey forced Sertorius into guerrilla tactics of harassment, while he and the commander of Rome's fresh troops conducted a war of attrition. Sertorius' support dwindled; his loyal Spanish cities defected one by one to Rome. On occasion, Sertorius' troops would rouse themselves and deal Pompey a defeat. But two winters after his fretful letter to the senate, Pompey could consider the war won. To return in triumph, however, he had to capture Sertorius or kill him.

■

Marcus Perperna spared Pompey that chore. Sertorius' second-in-command, Perperna had been whispering against his chief for at least a year and finally arranged for his murder. But when he assumed the rebel command, Perperna proved no match for Pompey. During the next battle, he fled to a thicket, where a mule-skinner recognized him and delivered him to Pompey. Perperna bargained for his life with a packet of letters he claimed would demonstrate that for years a group of treasonous senators in Rome had been dealing secretly with Sertorius. Pompey executed Perperna and sent word back to reassure the senate that he had burned the letters unread.

Pompey spent the better part of the next year putting down the pockets of resistance before he set off for Italy to take command of the war against Spartacus. At the top of the Pyrenees, he paused to erect a monument with his statue and accomplishments. The inscription read, "876 towns brought into subjection from the Alps to the limits of Farther Spain."

It made no reference to Sertorius. Let posterity believe that Pompey the Great fought only against foreigners.

The prospect of Pompey sharing in the defeat of Spartacus had goaded Crassus to take new risks. In the bloodiest battle of the war, he claimed to have killed more than 12,000 slaves. Spartacus led his survivors to the mountains of Petelia with Crassus' officers chasing after them. Discipline within the slave army had been destroyed, and they disregarded their officers' advice to avoid another confrontation. A captive to his men's misguided confidence, Spartacus threw his entire force into the battle.

He hadn't lost his bravura. When his horse was brought to him, Spartacus killed it with his sword. If he won today, he said, he could choose from the enemy's horses. If he lost, what would he need with one? Spotting Crassus through the fray, Spartacus flew at him, cutting down two centurions in his path. But the slaves saw they had provoked a battle they couldn't win and ran from the field. Spartacus stayed, fighting until he was cut down. Amid the mounds of corpses, his body was never found.

Pompey had come to the battle too late for its climax but in time to chase after the retreating slaves. He annihilated them—as many as 5,000—and wrote at once to the senate to magnify his contribution. Crassus may have conquered the slaves in combat,

Pompey said, but it was he, Magnus, who had torn up the rebellion by its very roots.

Back in Rome, Pompey demanded a second triumph for his services in Spain. He still had no more official claim to the honor than when he had pried one from Sulla. The senate bristled with envy and dislike but had to agree. Crassus' men believed that defeating Spartacus had eliminated a far greater risk to Rome than Sertorius, and yet they wouldn't argue for a triumph for Crassus since he had put down an insurrection of mere slaves. He was accorded a lesser honor called an ovation. But Crassus had devised another method of impressing Rome, a spectacle more memorable than any parade.

Via Appia was the achievement of a stubborn old Roman some two centuries before Caesar's birth. Appius Caecus had ordered a road built to the south, even though other Romans feared that it would connect them with the Samnites, their most bellicose neighbors. Near Rome itself, Appius built the road with blocks of gray basalt, but as it wound past cypress and pine trees and across the Pontine marshes, his road became only gravel and, at its farthest points, it was no more than a dirt footpath amid weeds and flowers. Appius lived to open the first length between Rome and Capua. As Rome's sway expanded during the next decades, Via Appia unrolled down the peninsula, scaling up hills and swerving around lakes, until it ran the 360 miles to the tip of Italy's boot.

Along that road from Rome to Capua—where the slave rebellion had begun—Crassus ordered his captives whipped and then forced to carry crossbeams to a spot where matching stakes had already been pounded into the ground. Each slave was stripped and fastened with cords to a crossbeam, which was then hoisted by ropes until the prisoner's feet were off the ground. When the beams had been fastened to the stakes, men hung there to die of thirst and exhaustion. Spartacus and his army had known from the start that crucifixion would be the price of their rebellion and that no one would do them the kindness of slitting their throats.

For more than a hundred miles, along Roman's grandest road, Crassus crucified 6,000 slaves.

VIII

CICERO

76–69 B.C.

Two years abroad had transformed Cicero. He had strengthened his lungs and put on weight. Comparing his speaking style to a river, he said that he had learned to prevent his rhetoric from overflowing its banks. But while Cicero might see himself as a new man in the best sense, he knew that Rome's aristocrats still regarded him as just another *novus homo*, doomed to scheming and scraping for the status they had inherited at birth. Senators from old families would expect him to do a hundred favors to build a network of loyalty and support—and then despise him for it.

At Delphi, Cicero had asked the oracle to chart his future. The priestess sensed the strident ambition in this young man not yet 30. She warned him not to take public favor as his guide in life. Be led by your own nature, she said.

But Cicero's nature was not always a reliable guide. Even as he tried to ingratiate himself with the patricians, he could not

Wall painting from the Villa near Boscoreale. The Metropolitan Museum of Art, Rogers Fund, 1903.

conceal his wide streak of independence. Caesar's ready charm
rested on an absolute self-assurance, but Cicero's wit masked an
anger that could erupt and offend even the listeners he hoped to
please. Cicero wanted to be more easygoing, but the men loitering
around the Forum soon discovered that he was somewhat stuffy.
They mocked him as "the Greek" and "the scholar."

Once Cicero resumed taking law cases, his learning quickly
distinguished him. Still dissatisfied with his physical limitations,
he tried to make a virtue of them. Since he couldn't bellow his
speeches like most popular orators, Cicero accused those competitors of shouting because they didn't know how to speak natu-
rally. Lame men, he called them; they rode horseback because
they couldn't walk.

Cicero sought out only cases that would gild his reputation.
Since Rome's prosecutors were lawyers hired privately by the injured party, he was free to pick which side to represent. Caesar
had chosen to be a prosecutor and lose cases while gaining in
popularity. But Cicero had been a defense lawyer before he went
to Greece and wanted to continue representing defendants. A
lawyer made fewer enemies that way.

In the year an ambitious Roman turned 30, he could aspire to a
low rung on the civic ladder, the office of quaestor, or treasurer.
Cicero reached the qualifying age, offered himself for one of the 20
positions and was pleased to be the first candidate elected.
Quaestors served throughout the provinces, and when Cicero
drew lots for his assignment he was posted to Lilybeum, one of
the two provinces in Sicily. He regarded his new job as a public
performance that the entire world would be watching. It was a
grandiose reading of a relatively minor role, but Cicero's year
abroad did turn out to be critical.

Along with Africa and Sardinia, Sicily was considered the
Republic's granary. From the time of the Gracchus brothers, grain
had remained a political issue, and a quaestor's first duty was to
keep Rome well supplied. In Cicero's year, Romans expected
about three pounds each day, but the supply was low. Civil peace
depended on getting quantities of wheat to Rome quickly, and yet
Cicero couldn't ship out so much that the Sicilians went hungry.

The crisis was a test of efficiency and fairness, and Cicero
passed it. Roman administrators were seldom popular in the prov-

inces, but the people drew a distinction between greater and lesser evils, and when Cicero's year was up the Sicilians fêted him.

On his way home, Cicero went to Syracuse to visit the tomb of Archimedes. When he found the sepulcher forgotten and covered with brambles, Cicero asked himself what that said about contemporary fame. He soon found out. Pausing at Puteoli, a fashionable spa, Cicero met an acquaintance from Rome and preened himself for congratulations on the fine job he had done for his country. Instead, the fellow asked how long it was since Cicero had been in Rome and what news he had from there.

"I have just come from my province," Cicero replied.

His stiff answer jogged the other man's memory. "Oh, yes," he said. "From Africa, I believe."

A man might go abroad and work conscientiously for the public good, believing that his efforts were being admired in Rome. In fact, Cicero learned, all Romans cared about was what they saw in front of them. From that time on, Cicero was determined not to drop from sight.

With his political apprenticeship behind him, Cicero felt it was time to break away from the pack of other ambitious men his age. To become better known, he vowed to remember the names of every Roman he met. Since there were more than 900,000 voting citizens, however, Roman politicians usually traveled with a slave who could whisper identifications in their ear. Publicly, Cicero ridiculed that practice, but he kept his own well-versed slave close at hand.

Cicero's estate remained comparatively modest but sufficient for his needs, and defending men in court was increasing his political capital. Cicero's term as quaestor automatically admitted him to the senate, but the seniority system didn't allow him to speak, and he was relegated with the other newcomers to the minor committees that heard tax protests. To be more visible, Cicero needed a new title, and he weighed two options. He could become a people's tribune, but that would alienate the patricians he had been courting, although so far with little success. "They withhold their interest and sympathy from us," Cicero complained, "as completely as if we and they were different breeds of men."

The alternative was to become an aedile, a caretaker's job.

Aediles were charged with running the city, with overseeing the food supply and—vital for a man seeking greater popularity—with staging Rome's games on festival days. There were 10 tribunes and only four aediles; that made the odds longer. But after waiting the traditional five years between posts, Cicero became a candidate.

Pompey was not observing the niceties. Even before he entered Rome for his latest triumph, the senate had been cowed again by his popularity, had waived all requirements to permit his candidacy, and Pompey had become consul. The same age as Cicero, he now held Rome's highest office, although he knew so little about governing that he asked a friend to prepare a memorandum on a consul's duties. Marcus Crassus had choked back his resentment at the Spartacus affair and bought the votes to be Pompey's co-consul.

While Cicero found Pompey's politics inconsistent, he looked for ways to use the new consul's power to boost his own career. Crassus' election, however, simply outraged him. As a noble, Crassus should be setting the highest example, upholding the standards from those glorious years when—as Cicero read history—being a Roman senator meant unassailable honor. Instead, Crassus was only a thief. Rich, but a thief. Cicero hated him.

Cicero's support from the patricians was indifferent, but he seemed headed for victory as aedile. Then, before the election, an impediment arose that threatened to jeopardize everything he had been planning so methodically.

Gaius Verres had gone to Sicily as governor the year after Cicero left. During his three-year term, Verres had stolen everything he could cart away. He imposed new and impossible taxes and pocketed the profit. He robbed temples and private houses of their art—a marble Cupid by Praxiteles was his most notable theft—and pretended that he had paid the owners.

Indignation mounted with Verres' crimes, until his term expired and he could be called to account. A delegation from Sicily's largest cities came to Rome to find a prosecutor. Their logical choice was Cicero; he had served the province honestly and knew it well. Although Cicero still believed that self-interest called for him to avoid all prosecutions, his sense of duty prevailed, and he agreed to represent the Sicilians. Verres had chosen Hortensius, who was running to succeed Pompey as consul.

Verres' allies quickly made overtures to Cicero. When he refused their bribes to withdraw from the case, they tried to get their own incompetent man appointed prosecutor. The jury declared Cicero the better choice, and he asked for 110 days to gather evidence. But Verres had reason to delay the trial beyond that, since the officials for the coming year looked more favorable to him.

Cicero's ambition, principles and vanity were all engaged, and he was determined to see the trial begin during the current administrative year. It had already been delayed until the last month before Rome's festivals would begin and serious business suspended until the next term. Cicero hurried to Sicily and set to work. With his cousin Lucius, he traveled across the island, interviewing citizens in towns and farmers in their huts.

The investigation took them to scenes of mourning and loss. One night at Heraclea, a woman led out a procession of widows and bereaved daughters and sisters, all carrying torches. Falling at Cicero's feet, she murmured the name of her son, murdered by Verres.

Despite interference, Cicero returned to Rome with stacks of public records, affidavits and many witnesses who had sailed with him to testify in person. He risked drowning or kidnapping by taking a small boat that got him home faster.

Cicero had used 50 of the 110 days he'd requested for preparing his evidence. When he arrived in Rome, voting was already under way for the next year, and Verres' defender Hortensius won the consulship as expected. One of Verres' friends heard the result, embraced him and shouted, "With this election, you have been acquitted!"

Cicero and the other candidates for aedile faced the voters next. Verres' effort to bribe the voters foundered, and Cicero was once again the first man chosen. All the same, further delays in Verres' trial—and presumed acquittal—seemed certain. Standard legal procedure called for Cicero's opening speech to go on for several days, which would allow Hortensius to stretch out his rebuttal until a recess was assured.

The court met on the seventh day of Sextilis, the eighth month, in the lofty Temple of Castor, more than 400 years old.

Cicero was tense with anticipation but exhilarated by the swelling crowd. He saw delegations from every market town of Sicily, from Greece, the Black Sea and islands in the Aegean, all demanding punishment. They jammed the porticos and steps of the temple, spilling out to cover the Forum. When the ground was filled, they climbed onto colonnades and rooftops.

Cicero trusted the honesty of the praetor who was presiding, and he began his speech by flattering the jury as excellent men who were above reproach. Then he surprised the court with a risky gambit: he would offer no opening indictment beyond a brief introduction. That prevented Hortensius from making a prolonged response. "We say," Cicero told the jurors, "that Caius Verres, while he has often acted rapaciously and cruelly toward Roman citizens and our allies, and nefariously toward gods and men, has also carried off illegally from Sicily 40 million sesterces."

Cicero's vast audience was disappointed, and even suspected that he had been bribed. At a preliminary hearing, he had estimated the losses at twice that figure. But Cicero was claiming only what his documentation could prove, and during the next nine days of testimony his aggressiveness reassured the onlookers. Hortensius had been thrown off guard by Cicero's maneuver, and his cross-examination of witnesses soon became desultory.

As Cicero called more witnesses, Hortensius objected to the tone of the proceedings. Certainly the crowd in the Forum was aroused. Following testimony about a particularly savage abuse, the judge had to call a recess to let the audience calm down.

Verres saw the guilty verdict looming and exercised an attractive option granted to former Roman governors. Even in mid-trial, an accused official could chose voluntary exile before the court pronounced on him. Gathering up his spoils on short notice, Verres went to live among his statuary and bronze plate in Gaul.

The court confirmed Verres' exile and ordered that everything he had left behind be offered at a public sale.

Afterward, critics said that Cicero had won his greatest case without having to speak; so he arranged to have copies made of the five speeches he would have given if Verres hadn't decamped. They set forth the former governor's crimes in compelling detail. After describing a factory devoted exclusively to making gold vases for Verres' private use, Cicero lamented, "O tempora, o mores!"

Circulating the speeches consolidated Cicero's reputation as Rome's leading advocate, and there was a second happy outcome to the trial. Since aediles were expected to stage the city's games, men often went deeply in debt to guarantee their magnificence. Cicero was too thrifty to fall into that trap. Instead, when appreciative Sicilians loaded him down with gifts, he avoided any sign of impropriety by giving them away. The cattle went to the poor, to improve their diet. But he sent the wild animals to circuses, to give the people—at no cost to himself—the spectacles they demanded.

IX

CAESAR

69 B.C.

Surveying his political competition could dishearten Julius Caesar. Cicero was already considered a master orator, and Pompey was called "Magnus." And yet the mood in Rome was favoring the people's cause. Pompey had restored the tribunes' power unconditionally and pared away Sulla's other boons to the senate's patricians; Caesar had played a minor role in those reforms. As a sop to his opponents, Pompey was promising not to seek another consulship. At the end of his term, he would follow tradition by leading his horse into the Forum and receiving his military discharge. Then, not yet 36, he would retire to civilian life.

By the time Pompey and Crassus were due to step down as consuls, their relations had become so strained that they couldn't bear to look at each other. They had been competing for popularity—Pompey with lavish games, Crassus with a three-month ration of grain. At their final joint appearance, a man took the speaker's platform to announce that Jupiter had told him in a dream that the consuls must not leave office without reconciling.

As the crowd waited, Pompey refused to move. But Crassus reached over, took Pompey's hand, murmured to him and told the audience that he did not think he was demeaning himself by taking the initiative. Pompey's political instincts may not have been keen, but he recognized that further churlishness was impossible and joined in the reconciliation.

The outgoing consuls had been so engrossed in their feud that they had neglected to build a foundation beneath their reforms, which explained why Hortensius and Metellus, with their well-known ties to Sulla, had been able to replace them. But Cicero sensed that opinion in Rome was shifting toward men like Caesar, aristocrats who also ranked high with the people. Cicero watched Caesar moving through the city, so gracious and yet, Cicero suspected, aiming every affable gesture toward his goal of absolute power. Or were Cicero's misgivings another sign of his resentment of men who had been born into the class he was struggling to join?

In either event, Caesar's concern for his grooming opened him to ridicule from Cicero, ever alert to foppish behavior. He jeered at the way men let a *tonsor*, or hairdresser, dye and perfume their curls, spread makeup cream over their cheeks, paste on small patches of cloth to cover imperfections in their skin. Cicero couldn't charge Caesar with those extreme practices, but he did observe: "When I notice how carefully arranged his hair is, and when I watch him adjusting its part with one finger, I cannot imagine that this man could conceive of such a wicked thing as to destroy the Roman constitution."

Moving along the recognized stations to power, Caesar put himself forward as quaestor. As Cicero had learned, the job meant a year abroad, and Caesar would be departing without so much as a recent lawsuit to keep his memory alive. But before he left Rome for his assignment in Spain, Caesar's aunt Julia died.

Even without Caesar's participation, Julia's funeral would have been an extraordinary event. She had been widowed for 15 years, but Marius' allies and their sons had recently come back from exile and were certain to turn out for the ceremony. Rome's population—including women, slaves and foreigners—ran between 800,000 and a million people, and registering Italians as citizens had nearly doubled the voting population, from 463,000 to

910,000. Those new citizens remembered who had fought to give them their rights; they would want to honor Julia. Even Sulla's senate faction would feel compelled to attend.

Caesar staged the ritual with great flair, including in the procession, to the crowd's amazement, large images of Marius. His portrait hadn't been seen in Rome since Sulla banned any likeness of him. Conservative voices shouted against the outrage but were drowned out. It was as though Caesar had plucked Marius back from Sulla's hell.

In his oration for Julia, Caesar went further still to stake his claim for leadership of the people's faction. Whatever he might believe about the divinity of his family—whatever any educated Roman truly believed—Caesar described his heritage as one impossible to improve upon.

"The family of my aunt Julia is descended by her mother from kings," Caesar said, and he reminded the audience that Julia had descended from Venus. "That means," he concluded, in case anyone had missed the sweep to his boast, "our stock can claim both the sanctity of kings, who reign supreme among mortal men, and the reverence due to the gods, who hold power over even kings themselves."

Caesar was presenting his qualifications for leading a mixed constituency of Marius' veterans, Rome's former slaves and those Italians who had only lately won the right to vote. And he was doing it as the noblest of Romans—half god, half king.

That same year, Caesar suffered a second and far more painful loss when Cornelia died. Fidelity might not have been one of his virtues, but he had defied a tyrant to keep her. Julia had been a distinguished woman who deserved the recognition of a public funeral. But Caesar insisted on a second grand ceremony for young Cornelia. Rumors about his promiscuity or the indiscretion at Bithynia might never fade. But Cornelia's funeral gave Caesar the chance to remind Rome that he had adored his wife, the mother of his only child. After Rome's years of savagery, Caesar's tender speech of mourning touched a chord and won him respect for his warm heart.

X

CLEOPATRA

69 B.C.

While the new generation of politicians vied for power in Rome, a female child was born in Egypt to an ancient royal family. Under the Pharaohs, Egypt had been a nation for 3,000 years, and its monuments mocked the pretensions of both Greece and Rome. "Everything fears time," Egyptians said, "but time fears the Pyramids."

But now their dynasty ruled only with Rome's consent. Like Caesar, Egypt's rulers claimed divine ancestry, but more practically they owed their throne to Alexander the Great. After Alexander's death, fighting had broken out among his generals. One, a Macedonian nobleman named Ptolemaios, let his rivals compete for the territories of Persia, Syria and the rest of Asia Minor. Ptolemy settled for control of Egypt, which was somewhat isolated but rich in grain. Knowing something of the nature of his new subjects, the farmers who watched every summer as the Nile

A relief of Cleopatra and her son Caesarion as Isis and Osiris from the Temple of Hathor at Dendera. The Ancient Art and Architecture Collection, London.

flooded its banks and left behind fertile land for the planting of wheat and barley, he presented himself as divine. Before swearing their allegiance, the Egyptians wanted to be sure the cycle of their life would not be disrupted, and they asked little more from Ptolemy than assurance that he had descended from the Pharaohs they once worshiped.

Except for a few cheerful influences absorbed from Greece, the Egyptian religion was glum and shot through with mysteries. Veneration of animals had produced drawings and statues that were half man, half beast, and although the Sphinx was the most awe-inspiring, it was hardly unique. Ptolemy and his successors accommodated the conservative Egyptian character, even to embracing the Pharaohs' marriage code. Since the Ptolemies had become the sons and daughters of gods, they couldn't mate with mortals, only with each other. Sometimes, they consummated their incestuous marriages. More often, a Ptolemy king or queen took lovers and passed on the throne to children from those affairs.

The Ptolemies had adapted well to their new nation in most respects, but were too proud of their Macedonian heritage to bother learning the Egyptian language. Despite that obstacle, the country flourished. Two years before he died at the age of 84, Ptolemy had handed over the dynasty to his son, who doubled the library at Alexandria to 400,000 volumes. Ptolemy II also established diplomatic relations with Rome, although his own courtiers were far more intellectual and worldly than most Roman aristocrats. In Alexandria, Euclid was pursuing geometry; the physician Herophilos was dissecting corpses; and a student from Ephesus named Zenodotus had become the first Homer scholar, devoting his life to bringing out editions of the *Iliad* and the *Odyssey*.

The first two Ptolemies had also stimulated agriculture, their nation's great asset, by leasing land to selected peasants and taking their rent payments in grain. Egyptians learned to rotate crops and enjoy two harvests a year. Ptolemy III sent an army into the eastern sector of Alexander's former realm to bring back Egyptian statuary that the Persians had carried off. Rome offered assistance in that campaign, but Ptolemy worried about Roman domination and refused it.

Some 120 years before Caesar's birth, Egypt slid into decline. Ptolemy IV was said to have murdered his father to get the throne, then murdered his mother to keep it. Ptolemy V took the throne at five and grew up to be equally cruel. His successor was taken prisoner by the king of Syria, who invaded Egypt and stayed until Romans arrived to demand he leave Alexandria. From that day, Egypt would become Rome's property whenever Romans chose to foreclose on it.

As Egypt's independence waned, murder continued to be the usual route to power. Ptolemy VII killed his nephew, the true heir, and strove for legitimacy by marrying Cleopatra, the boy's mother. A later Cleopatra drove her eldest son from the throne to install his more obedient younger brother.

By the time of Sulla's dictatorship, Roman generals who called into port at Alexandria recognized that it was the world's most sophisticated city in the world's richest nation. Its library was immense; nearby, a museum of science and art was staffed by the finest scholars from around the Mediterranean, all living at state expense as they delved into Greek literature, history, medicine and geography.

If Alexandria was dazzling, it was also clerk-ridden and corrupt. Everything in Egypt was controlled by the royal family, under a decree that "no one has the right to do what he wishes, but everything is organized for the best." Farmers of the fertile Nile delta might be blessed with high yields, but their land belonged to the Ptolemies. City merchants required a royal license to manufacture anything—linen, perfume, glass, wool and papyrus, which was a leading export.

The Ptolemies tolerated Egypt's priests, with their shaved heads and white robes, so long as they paid tax on the goods made at their temples. But true power in Alexandria lay with the Ptolemies' court, which was formally divided into the Friends, First Friends and Kinsmen. The prime minister came from the Kinsmen and for the last century had often been a eunuch. A dynasty that encouraged incestuous but sexless marriages took comfort in knowing that their prime ministers were not going to impregnate a princess. And since Egyptians laughed at eunuchs, they were unlikely to seize power for themselves.

So long as the Ptolemies were deferential, Rome had been pleased to let them keep their throne. But Sulla had indulged his penchant for arranging marriages by forcing Queen Berenice, an elderly widow who had governed Egypt successfully for 20 years, to marry his Egyptian protégé. The Alexandrians were furious when the new king, Ptolemy XI, had his bride murdered 19 days after the wedding. In revenge, they stormed his palace and killed him. Ptolemy XII was afraid he might not have a kingdom; perhaps Sulla would be too enraged by the death of his favorite to recognize a successor.

But Sulla was preoccupied in Rome and looking toward retirement. He did not intervene. Conservative senators were already dismayed at the way Rome's provinces were expanding. They saw their power being diluted as the new territories permitted the rise of far-flung generals difficult to control. If this latest Egyptian king knew his place, he could keep his crown.

Ptolemy XII wasn't inclined to cause trouble. For a start, he was illegitimate, the son of a previous king by a concubine. But since no other contender could claim any Ptolemaic blood at all, and since Alexandrians were eager to put a body on the throne, they accepted him. Officially, he became "the God, Lover of his Father, Lover of his Sister, the New Dionysus," but Egyptians gave their kings earthier nicknames than that. In the streets, Ptolemy VIII had been called Physkon, "Potbelly," and now the latest Ptolemy was first called Nothos, "the Bastard," and then Auletes, "the Flute Player."

The mildness of that name indicated how his people saw him—as a weak and drunken man who wanted simply to be left alone with his music. Only his marriage arrangements recalled the age of the Pharaohs. He wed his sister, Cleopatra, and had two daughters, Cleopatra VI and Berenice. When he married again, he fathered a third daughter, Cleopatra VII.

That infant's features were Greek and not at all Egyptian, but her lush coloring was olive and the effect, if not beautiful, promised to be striking. She was less than a year old when Caesar went as a quaestor to Spain. In Rome and Egypt, this seventh Cleopatra seemed destined to be one more brief entry in the increasingly irrelevant chronicle of the Ptolemies.

XI

CAESAR AND CICERO

68 B.C.

Julius Caesar arrived as quaestor in Spain to find the province still recovering from Sertorius' rebellion. Romans had been occupying Spain for 150 years and had divided it into two administrative provinces—Nearer Spain and Farther Spain, which included the seaport of Gades, where Caesar was posted.

Despite the confused loyalties that Sertorius had stirred up, Spain was more like Rome than any other province. Its hills were browner, its air drier, but Latin had become the ready language of culture and commerce. Thanks to Pompey, Roman citizenship had been widely conferred, and since land was more plentiful in Spain than near Rome, legionaries sent to pacify the provinces often stayed on. In Córdoba, the capital of Farther Spain, the Spanish aristocracy spoke Greek as well as Latin and used their slaves to mine a treasury of metals—gold and silver, but also iron, copper, tin and mercury.

Rebel tribes controlled pockets of northern Spain, and they were the ones who felt the harshness of Rome's overseas policy.

Romans relocated whole towns and exterminated or took as slaves all the young men who might later fight against them. Slaves were sent into the mines or put to work on farms along the Baetis River, which yielded the Mediterranean's best olive oil. The farms also produced cattle. Since Romans ate little red meat, beef could appear regularly on Spanish tables. Ships from Spain carried grain and salted fish to the Roman port at Ostia in seven days.

Caesar rode the judicial circuit around the province, settling minor disputes over property lines and runaway slaves, winning friends among Spain's leading families. He became especially close to a millionaire named Cornelius Balbus.

A few miles from Gades stood the Temple of Melkant, which contained a bust of Alexander. His companions on one excursion said that when Caesar saw the statue, he had given an eloquent sigh before going back to adjudicating petty provincial disputes.

While Caesar chafed at being rusticated, Cicero was ending a successful year as aedile. His service had added a purple border to his toga and given him permanent use of an ivory chair in the senate. It had also elevated his rank. His son—should he have one—could someday put Cicero's bust in his entrance hall, although a single ancestor might look forlorn there. But a new man had to make a beginning. Cicero was supporting his brother's campaign for quaestor and was now established enough to guarantee that Quintus would be elected. Privately, however, Cicero considered one orator quite enough for a family, perhaps for an entire city.

Cicero also found his brother a wife—Pomponia, the sister of Cicero's dearest friend, Titus Pomponius, who had retreated to Athens from the hazards of Sulla's dictatorship and seldom came back. Friends called him Atticus, and he had cultivated the Epicurean ideal of a tranquil life while he rolled up a substantial fortune. Atticus appreciated fine writing, and Cicero found him a responsive correspondent.

Problems quickly arose with Pomponia, who was older and richer than Cicero's brother. It fell to Cicero to keep the peace and see that the marriage at least survived Pomponia's pregnancy. Cicero turned over to Quintus the house their father had bought when he first launched his sons in Rome and moved to a villa in the fashionable Palatine neighborhood.

Cicero complained that his supporters made as many demands on his time as if he were as rich as Crassus. Even Pompey came by for political advice. To Cicero, his busy schedule justified close attention to his health—no meals during the day, regular walks for exercise, massages to keep him fit.

It was rumored that Caesar had received a prophecy in Spain the night after he reproached himself in front of Alexander's statue. He was supposed to have dreamed that he raped his mother. It was not an uncommon dream among Romans, but still disturbing to the men who dreamt it. Caesar's love for his mother was intense enough for others to have remarked on it.

Aurelia had not remarried after her husband's death, although her political connections made her highly eligible. Instead, she and her family had devoted themselves to advancing Caesar's career. Far away in Spain, himself recently a widower, the years passing with no real achievement, Caesar may have felt he had failed his mother, but that was far different from defiling her. Since Rome's gossip was inventive, the story of his dream might have been fabricated. But if Caesar had indeed dreamed of incest, he had soothsayers at hand to relieve his guilt. They could assure him that no, the woman had not literally been his mother. The figure Caesar had mounted was the universal mother, the earth itself. His dream meant that he was destined to conquer the world.

Romans seemed to need a symbol, a turning point—the bust of Alexander, a prophetic dream—to explain the change they saw come over Caesar in Spain. Before his term as quaestor ended, he petitioned the governor for permission to return to Rome. That was unusual. Most men milked an overseas position until the day they had to surrender it to their successor.

Caesar returned by way of a Latin colony in Cisalpine Gaul, which took in territory from the Alps to the Adriatic. Romans had set up colonies along the Po River from the time of the war against Hannibal but had never conferred full citizenship on them, and those Latins were on the verge of revolt. They had expected Pompey to champion their cause. But Pompey's term as consul had come and gone, and wealthy farmers and traders along the Po still couldn't launch their sons in Rome.

Cisalpine Gaul was not entirely strange to Caesar. His tutor had been a native, and the region was becoming known for its spirited young poets, among them a teenage boy from Verona named Catullus. Arriving at the Po, Caesar met with the local leaders and sympathized with their grievances. When the consuls in Rome heard that the discontent might be turning to resistance, they sent up enough legionaries to discourage an uprising. Caesar continued homeward, leaving behind another bloc of potential support. His instinct for injustice was becoming sharp. If he promoted his own fortunes while addressing an obvious wrong, who in the people's faction could object to that?

Back in Rome, Caesar needed a job and a wife. It would be two years before he was eligible to campaign as aedile, and renouncing his heritage to become a people's tribune was out of the question. Instead, he won a post as curator of the Appian Way. It remained Rome's route to Italy's large port at Puteoli, and grain and pottery from the south were still hauled over its ancient bricks. Caesar did not view the job as a sinecure. From Rome's engineers, he learned to calculate elevations and design a sturdy bridge. Repairing the road at his own expense, Caesar was spending money he didn't have, but he saw his mounting debt as one more investment in his future.

As for a wife, Caesar, with no fortune of his own, required a dowry. And now that he seemed resolved to grasp at Rome's highest prizes, he needed a wife with connections. Caesar picked Sulla's granddaughter Pompeia, even though much family history had to be forgiven on both sides. The girl's mother, Cornelia, was Sulla's daughter, now one of the richest women in Rome. She parted with money reluctantly, but her fortune would be seen as backing Caesar.

Politically, Pompeia's link to Sulla offered no obvious advantage to a man carving out his following among the people. But, as her name suggested, the bride was also a cousin of Rome's great hero. Pompey himself seemed restless in retirement. If he was ready to take on a new command, he would again become the most powerful man in the Republic, and Caesar was forging a claim to kinship.

XII

POMPEY

67 B.C.

With Sertorius dead in Spain and Mithridates stalemated in the East, the greatest threats to Rome's serenity these days were the pirate fleets menacing the seas. Their armadas had grown to more than 1,000 ships, and the pirates' impudence surpassed their strength. Romans were outraged by their brazen raids and by the opulence of their navy. Far from being wretched highwaymen of the seas, a new generation of pirates was recruiting the sons of good families and behaving like a larcenous nobility.

The pirates sailed in expensive ships with silver-plated oars and purple awnings. When they put in at port, their drunkenness and loud music were a calculated affront to Roman dignity. At city after city—some said 400 had been hit—they hijacked cargo and kidnapped officials for ransom. With the pirates intercepting shipments of grain, traders became reluctant to leave port in Sicily, Sardinia, even Africa. Shortages had sent the price of wheat soaring, and Romans foresaw famine and riots.

The pirates had given every country around the Mediterranean reason to fear them, but they singled out Romans for particular humiliation. When a victim invoked the customary protection—"I am a Roman citizen"—his captors made a show of being petrified with fear, slapping their thighs at their stupidity, falling at his feet and begging for mercy. The pirates next brought out a toga and Roman boots and explained that they were dressing him appropriately so their mistake could never happen again. Then, far out on the water, they dropped a ladder and told him that as a Roman citizen he was free to go. When he declined the invitation, they threw him overboard.

After pirates had kidnapped two praetors and a dozen aides, Romans began to clamor for the service of their best general. Patricians in the senate feared Pompey more than they feared the pirates, but now that the full powers of the tribunes had been restored, the people could outmaneuver them. A tribune named Gabinius was a protégé of Pompey, and he circulated a proposal urging the people's assembly to choose one of the recent consuls to head a unified offensive against pirates everywhere. Gabinius did not mention a candidate for the new command, which would extend through the entire Mediterranean, the Black Sea and—since pirates were sacking Roman country estates on the peninsula itself—inland about 50 miles along the Italian coast. The commander would be given unlimited access to the public treasury to raise a fleet of 200 ships, along with however many sailors and legionaries he thought were necessary. The command would last three years.

Gabinius carefully avoided the word "dictator," although the new commander would hold powers almost equal to those Sulla had seized for himself. Gabinius claimed that his measure didn't require senate debate, but the patricians demanded to be heard. As senators, they would be surrendering more specific powers than those held by the assembly, and they had distrusted Pompey for years. Decorum vanished in that charged atmosphere as senators rose to denounce Gabinius. One consul threatened his life.

If Caesar wanted to confirm his role as the people's leader, this was the time, and he would also be strengthening his alliance with Pompey. Caesar first spoke for Gabinius and then had to defend him when senators leaped from their seats, ready to strangle him. Caesar stayed at Gabinius' side and got him out of the chamber. On the street, Romans were outraged and ready to attack the senate. Most senators quickly withdrew.

Gabinius returned to the people's assembly to nominate Pompey for the command against the pirates. Two other tribunes had been recruited to argue against the motion, and their speeches showed Pompey that his nomination would not ride through on a wave of popular acclaim. Pompey's craving for honors and applause ran deep, as though he thought his own popularity could finally erase the loathing his father had inspired.

When Gabinius invited him to the platform, Pompey went forward and refused the command. He explained that he shouldn't always be the one to hold powerful positions since new authority would only excite fresh envy among his enemies. "Surely, I am not the only one who loves you, and I am not the only one skilled in warfare."

The people shouted down his attempt at modesty. Gabinius reminded them that they must vote to benefit the Republic, not to please Pompey. An opposition tribune tried to veto the proposal but was booed. When a crow dropped from the sky, onlookers found it easy to believe that their shouts had stunned the bird and brought it down.

With his victory assured, Gabinius made a conciliatory gesture to the senators by permitting Catulus to come to the rostra. A former consul and distinguished conservative, Catulus was politely received as he argued that if the emergency required a dictator, that man should be restricted to the traditional six months.

At the sound of the word "dictator," the crowd remembered Catulus' allegiance during the purges and shouted back at him, "Sulla!"

Catulus pressed on, praising Pompey's talents as a general. In fact, he said, Pompey was so essential to Rome's security that he should not be exposed recklessly to every passing danger. "If you lost Pompey," Catulus asked, "what other man could you find to take his place?"

Someone in the crowd yelled, "You!"

That triggered memories of Catulus' failure of nerve during past showdowns, and men took up the derisive chant "You! You! We would have you!"

Gabinius delayed the final vote to let Pompey leave for his house outside Rome and avoid accusations that he was influencing the outcome. When word arrived that the new powers had been granted to him by acclamation, Pompey remained cautious and waited for nightfall to return to the city. He wanted no jubilant welcome that would fan the senate's resentment. But by the time he appeared the next day to offer a sacrifice for victory, Pompey had resolved any doubts about the assignment. He asked for an even greater force than Gabinius had won for him—500 ships, not 200, and an army of 120,000 infantry and 5,000 cavalry. As his lieutenants, Pompey drafted two dozen senators who had either commanded an army or had served as praetor or quaestor.

As reports of Pompey's new command filtered to the outlying ports, confidence was renewed and traders started shipping grain to Rome again. With supplies increasing, prices dropped. Pompey's boosters claimed that his very name had put an end to piracy.

The pirates had been operating as guerrillas, picking off easy targets and sailing away before Rome could catch up with them. While past commanders might overpower a single pirate band in Crete, dozens of other raids were terrorizing Romans in Sicily or Sardinia. Pompey spent the winter laying his plans and rounding up ships and manpower.

He prepared one massive coordinated strike. Dividing the seas that reached from Farther Spain to Syria into 13 districts, he assigned one of his best generals to each. Commanders were told to patrol the seas and attack all pirate bases. Metellus Nepos, for example, was ordered to keep the enemy out of the sheltering coves along the Cilician coast. When a pirate ship put into a harbor there, Nepos was to blockade it until troops could arrive to finish off its crew.

Pompey himself took a fleet of 60 ships in a circle around the Mediterranean, first clearing the port at Ostia, then moving on to Sicily and along the coast of Africa to Sardinia. He sailed to Farther and Nearer Spain until he came to the coastline of Transalpine Gaul between Spain and Italy. There he hit an obstacle. The governor had opposed the entire mission and was prematurely releasing the crews that Pompey had recruited. Pompey was forced to return to Rome and enlist Gabinius' aid in having the man recalled.

As Rome scattered the pirates, they often slipped back to civilian life in their hometowns. The stubbornest bands retreated with their loot and families to fortresses in the Taurus mountains of Cilicia and prepared for a climactic battle. Pompey defeated the last remnants at sea, then launched a siege against the strongholds until the pirates surrendered unconditionally.

The youthful butcher of past years might have condemned them to death. But Pompey was now 39, and he acted differently. While 20,000 prisoners from 90 warships were laying down their arms, he resolved not to kill or release them. Finding that many of his captives knew no trade but piracy, Pompey dispersed them among the smaller communities of Cilicia with a decree that gave them citizenship and plots of land to farm.

Romans had voted their commander three years to rid them of pirates. Pompey the Great had done it in three months.

XIII

CICERO

66 B.C.

Cicero was harboring an unlikely fantasy as he went off to make his first speech before the people's assembly. He was prepared to alienate aristocrats like Catulus in exchange for impressing enough of the people that they would elect him consul one day. Cicero intended to endorse legislation that would remove Lucullus as Rome's general against Mithridates and replace him with Pompey.

Although Cicero still saw Rome's senate as the bastion of the Republic, self-interest was persuading him to argue for this assault against its authority. Enough senators were intimidated by Pompey's vast popularity that they might mutter among themselves but only a few would oppose it. Hortensius was one, and Catulus was crying that Romans should go to some mountain or isolated rock and preserve their liberty there. Because if they granted Pompey this power, Rome's freedoms were ended.

To no one's surprise, Caesar endorsed the bill, but during

Bust of Marcus Tullius Cicero. Alinari/Art Resource.

the earlier debate over the command against the pirates, Cicero had taken no position. Now, standing at the rostra, he felt compelled to explain why he was making his first appearance before the assembly. At an earlier stage of his life, he said, "I was too young to intrude on this imposing place." He had felt then that he should give his time exclusively to friends who needed him in court. Cicero deprecated his oratory but claimed that since his subject today was Pompey, anyone would be stirred to eloquence. "A speech on such a subject," Cicero said gracefully, "is harder to stop than to start."

He reviewed the history of Rome's war with Mithridates. Nineteen years had passed since Sulla, in his eagerness to get back to Rome, had signed a hasty treaty and eight years since Rome sent Lucullus to fight for control of Bithynia. Despite his early losses, Mithridates at 54 remained powerful throughout Asia. Cicero reminded them that the king had never been made to pay for the infamous day he ordered the massacre of 80,000 Italians in Asia—not merely the Roman tax collectors but also their wives and children. After assuring the crowd that he would not disparage Lucullus, Cicero immediately referred to his bad luck. As he knew, Roman audiences preferred their generals to be venal or greedy than unlucky.

Businessmen who had invested in Asia—paying Rome for the exclusive right to collect taxes over a five-year period—were facing ruin. Cicero had to explain to this crowd of the urban poor why the reverses of middle-class speculators should matter to them. He said that Rome's whole system of credit and finance was directly bound up with money invested in Asia: "If that is lost, then our Roman finances, too, are inevitably involved in the same process of upheaval and collapse."

Having impressed his audience with the many dimensions of the war in the East, Cicero outlined the qualities of an ideal general and said Pompey possessed them all. "He has waged more wars than other people have read about, held more public offices than anyone else has even dreamed about."

When the tribes met to approve a new commander for the war against Mithridates, they chose Pompey unanimously.

XIV

POMPEY

66–63 B.C.

When letters reached Pompey in Cilicia with news of his expanded powers, his friends swarmed to congratulate him. But Pompey furrowed his brow, pounded angrily on his thigh and said, in a voice rich with self-pity, "How sad it makes me, this endless succession of duties! If I am never to have any relief from military service, I would really rather be one of those men no one has ever heard of." All he wanted, Pompey added, was to live quietly in the country with his wife.

The lament bored even Pompey's friends. They knew that Pompey was delighted to see the senate embarrass Lucullus, and they understood that Pompey's need for approval, for being preeminent in Rome, made this a great day for him.

Pompey's actions soon revealed the satisfaction his weary words couldn't disguise. In proclamations and interviews with princes and kings, Pompey overruled most of the decrees Lucullus had made, until the humiliated former commander demanded that they meet at a town in Galatia.

Lucullus could claim a number of victories against Mithridates, and once his men had wounded the king under his eye with a poisoned dart that took a remedy of snake venom to cure. But when Pompey accused Lucullus of greed, it was hard to refute. Lucullus' military command had been most remarkable for its epic looting—temples, stores, private houses. He had waged war on harmless towns because their wealth stirred his envy, until at last a mutiny had been mounted by his brother-in-law, a patrician hothead named Clodius Pulcher. Joining Clodius were legionaries who resented the callous way Lucullus had left his dead where they fell, unwilling to give them a proper burial. The disaffection in his ranks had kept Lucullus on the defensive for the two years before Pompey arrived to replace him.

But Lucullus' accusations were equally stinging: that Pompey had come here in the same spirit as when he had marched against Lepidus, Sertorius and Spartacus—arriving only after better generals had already broken the enemy's back. In Asia, Pompey was following his usual practice of swooping down—Lucullus compared him to a lazy carrion crow—on bodies that others had killed. The wars of Pontus and Armenia were all but over, and yet Pompey was sure to claim the victories. What else could one expect from a man who had extorted a triumph for beating a pack of runaway slaves?

At that point, aides had to step in and separate the two generals.

Pompey had to kill or capture Mithridates. Nothing less would satisfy Rome. He had been stalling for time by offering Mithridates empty peace terms, but when he persuaded the king's ally, Phraates III of Parthia, not to go to war against Rome, Mithridates agreed to make peace after all. By then, however, Pompey had no incentive to sign a treaty. Lucullus and his circle would jeer if he settled the war without more combat.

Mithridates commanded a force of 30,000 infantry and another 2,000 cavalry, but his superior numbers couldn't defeat Pompey's men. Pompey laid siege to the enemy camp, and after 45 days Mithridates killed his sick and wounded and slipped away. Pompey forced his soldiers to trail him under the hot sun, until they reached the banks of the Euphrates. By that time, it was midnight. Pompey considered the terrain too confining for a night battle, but his officers persuaded him to attack by moonlight. At dawn, 10,000 of Mithridates' men lay dead in their camp, along with their women and animals. Another 10,000 were captured.

Mithridates escaped with 800 cavalry. When they too scattered, the king was left with three companions, one of them a brave and boyish mistress who had dressed as a Persian soldier. They were joined by a number of mercenaries who escorted the king to safety at his fortress in Sinora, where he had stored his money in bronze vessels bound with iron. He drew on that treasury to reward those who had stood by him and provided poison for senior officers who might prefer suicide to being taken prisoner. Although his situation looked hopeless, the king was not ready to end his life. He saw himself carrying on a great Eastern tradition; in his youth, he had worn a lion's-head helmet in the style of Alexander the Great.

Leaving Sinora, Mithridates hoped to find greater security in Armenia. But King Tigranes was having trouble with his rebellious son and needed peace with the Romans to hold his own throne. He forbade Mithridates to come and underscored the warning by setting a price of 100 talents on his head. Pompey rewarded Tigranes by putting his son in chains and assuring the king he could keep his crown. Pursuing Mithridates through Albania, Pompey had to beat back local tribes who attacked while the Romans were celebrating Saturnalia.

By the following autumn, Mithridates was in hiding, the Albanians had reneged on their peace treaty, and Pompey was crossing and recrossing the Cyrus River to maintain his hold over a dry and treacherous terrain. In one battle, the legendary Amazons were reported seen fighting, but when the corpses were stripped no women's bodies were found. After finally beating the Albanians, Pompey was curious to explore further and struck out toward the Caspian Sea, the farthest boundary of Rome's known world. Three days from the Caspian, however, the army came upon a plague of poisonous snakes that forced Pompey to turn back.

As Mithridates continued to flee, his discarded mistresses were brought to Pompey, who sent them back to their families. Stratonice, Mithridates' favorite, offered her castle and its treasures, and Pompey took what he could ship to temples in Rome, along with art and gold to enhance a triumph that was becoming inevitable.

At one of Mithridates' fortresses, Pompey was amused to find secret documents that revealed that the king had poisoned many rivals, including his own son. One hapless man died solely because his racehorse had beaten one the king owned. Pompey also found interpretations of dreams carefully preserved and a set of lewd letters between Mithridates and another of his mistresses.

Both sides understood that their war had ended on the night of Pompey's moonlit battle. Mithridates still held pockets of strength, but his allies continued to desert him. With his own food in short supply, Pompey sent his fleet to blockade the Bosporus and announced that he was leaving Mithridates to confront inevitable famine, a stronger challenge than any the Romans posed.

Marching overland to Syria, Pompey moved on toward Palestine, where the kingdom of Judaea was being wracked by a civil war between two princes, Hyrcanus and Aristobulus. Palestinians had lived under many masters—the Persians, then Alexander, the Ptolemies, the Seleucids. But more than a hundred years earlier, Judas Maccabaeus had led priests of the house of Hashmon in a resistance that had given his people a troubled independence. To Pompey, the people of Judaea, called Jews, represented only one more minor kingdom to be pacified in a way that served Rome's interests.

At Damascus, Hyrcanus appeared before Pompey with a subdued delegation of a thousand elders and argued for his rights as the firstborn of the two princes. When Aristobulus arrived with a more magnificent court, he saw that Pompey already favored his brother and rushed back to his stronghold in Judaea to resist a Roman onslaught. He soon had second thoughts, came out of his redoubt to discuss peace terms and finally agreed to turn over Jerusalem to the Romans. But by then Aristobulus could no longer control his officers, and they refused to obey him. Pompey took the prince prisoner and prepared to attack.

The Palestinians had barricaded themselves inside the city's temple. In Rome, Jews were treated like all outsiders, free to pursue their own worship and customs, although Romans found it odd that they honored only one god and permitted no statues of it. Jews were often taken for Syrians, a confusion that carried a degree of contempt since "Syri" was the dismissive word for men with no appetite for war. As Pompey was learning, the Jews were not pacifists. But their strict observance of holy days extended

even to wartime. Although the Jerusalem temple was well fortified, Pompey saw that each week, on the day the Romans had
named for Saturn, the Jews under siege would not fight back,
doing little more than fend off the Roman attacks.

Over the next three months, Pompey used the weekly day
of worship to batter at the north side of the temple walls. At last
came a seventh day when defenses could be breached. The Romans poured inside, where they found priests going on with the
Sabbath ritual. Their piety did not move Pompey's men, who were
angered by the long resistance. That day, the Romans slaughtered
12,000 Jews.

Pompey stepped inside the temple, the first Roman general
to enter in conquest. The vanquished worshipers considered him
a defiler, and friendly Palestinians warned him that he would be
committing an even more unpardonable sacrilege if he pushed on
to the temple's sanctuary. Pride and curiosity demanded that Pompey enter. He found an empty room. Returning outside, he tried
to make amends by leaving behind the temple's furnishings and
its treasury of 2,000 talents. He also installed Hyrcanus as high
priest of a land that had become one more Roman dependency.

As Pompey's soldiers were marching south from Jerusalem, messengers rode up from Pontus. Soldiers always knew when couri-
ers brought good news by the laurel leaves they wrapped around
the tip of their spears. Seeing the green sprigs, Pompey's men
took the messengers to a spot where their general was exercising
his horse. Pompey intended to finish his workout and ignored
them. But his men clamored for him to stop and read the dispatches.

Pompey led the way back to camp, which was so newly
settled he had to climb on a mound of saddle bags to read the
announcement: Mithridates was dead.

When he had learned that his army officers had united with
his son against him, Mithridates said that he had always taken
care against poison in his food but had not made any provision
against the most deadly poisons in a royal household—princes
and armies. To spare himself further indignity, Mithridates poisoned his wives and two loyal daughters and swallowed what was
left in the cup. But a lifetime of precautions against poisoning had
inured his system. He tried next to run himself through with his

sword, but the poison that failed to kill him had left his hand too weak, and it took his son Pharnaces' soldiers to finish the job. Pharnaces had the king's body embalmed and sent to Pompey as a show of his future loyalty.

When it arrived, the Romans found that the men who had prepared the corpse had not removed the king's brain, and the swollen face had become unrecognizable. Pompey refused to look at it, but the body could be identified by its scars.

Pompey's campaign had taken three years. When he set out, the province called Asia had been the eastern border of Rome's holdings. Now he had extended Rome's dominion south from the Black Sea into Pontus, Cilicia and Syria. Pompey had placed on the throne a host of client kings in lands too trouble-some for Rome to rule directly.

The campaigns had also left Pompey the richest man in Rome, and his supporters at home guaranteed that the scope of his victories would be widely heralded. When news that the Mith-ridatic war had ended reached Cicero, he won senate approval to honor Pompey with 10 days of thanksgiving.

Pompey headed home at a regal pace. He granted freedom to Mytilene on the isle of Lesbos for the sake of a native son whom Pompey intended to make the historian of his glorious adventures in the East. The poets of Mitylene held their annual competition in Pompey's presence, their theme the grandeur of his exploits. Mi-tylene's theater struck Pompey's fancy, and he ordered sketches made so that he could construct a larger and more magnificent version at home.

When Pompey reached Rhodes, the local pedagogues each addressed a discourse to him. Never a scholar, Pompey heard them out and distributed a gift of one talent each. At Athens, he offered the same prize for its philosophers, along with a bequest of 50 talents to help restore the city. As the procession continued west, trailing money and favors, Pompey was feted as the most brilliant commander of the age. This time, surely, his homecoming in Rome would be equally generous and warmhearted.

XV

CICERO

64 B.C.

In Pompey's absence, Cicero had been waging his own skirmishes. Sometimes he seemed to consider his victories in Rome's political wars as the equal of anything Pompey was accomplishing on the battlefield. From experience, he knew how dangerous a prolonged absence from the Forum could be, and he turned down the chance to govern a province, which should have been his reward for the year as praetor. Instead, Cicero stayed in Rome, charting his campaign to become consul.

He understood the odds. If he should succeed, Cicero would be one of only 15 new men to be elected consul in the last three centuries, the first since Marius 40 years earlier.

Cicero knew he had to learn to control his tongue. His wit was as sharp as any soldier's sword. He could be generous and at times poetic—though usually when he was talking about a dead man. He called Aristotle's writing a river of flowing gold and said that if the gods chose to talk in human words they would sound like Plato's dialogues. Asked which was the best of Demosthenes' speeches, Cicero replied, "The longest one."

But living men were dissected with deadly precision, and once Cicero had sharpened a barb he couldn't resist slipping it between an opponent's ribs. As a political candidate, he would have to neutralize the bad feelings he had provoked.

A young lawyer named Appius, for example, had opened his plea in court with the disarming remark that a friend had urged him to display care, eloquence and integrity. Cicero interrupted him: "Then how can you be so hard-hearted as to not exhibit a single one of the qualities your friend demanded?"

Cicero would attack a man's character, his appearance, even his background if it was humbler than his own. A man called Octavius, who was suspected of having African blood, complained in court that he couldn't hear what Cicero was saying. Cicero struck back with an insinuation that Octavius had been a slave: "That's odd," he said, "considering that your ears have been pierced."

Cicero's line of questioning angered a defendant accused of giving his father a poisoned cake, and he threatened to give Cicero a piece of his mind. "I'd rather have that," Cicero replied, "than a piece of your cake."

In letters, Cicero delighted in imagining the details of the scene when a young Caesar had visited Nicomedes' bedchamber in Bithynia. Caesar "lay on a golden couch," Cicero wrote, "dressed in a purple shift." The episode provided Cicero with an irresistible opening when Caesar rose in the senate to promote the fortunes of Nicomedes' daughter. As Caesar was listing his obligations to the king, Cicero interrupted: "Enough of that, if you please! We all know what he gave you, and what you gave him in return."

Cicero would have to muffle that sharpness during his campaign. His brother was taking an avid interest in Cicero's race, and much later an 8,000-word letter appeared, attributed to Quintus and filled with useful advice about the process Romans called *prensatio*—handshaking. Whether or not the document was genuine, it reflected Cicero's strategy. He knew that he would be depending on support from men he had defended in legal cases, and the letter noted that "since you have never importuned any of them in any matter, you should make them realize that you have saved up for this moment all the debts that you think they owe you."

The letter recalled approvingly the times Cicero had sided

with the people and added that he must build upon that popular backing and yet remember that no one had ever won the consulship without the support of Rome's leading citizens. The letter noted that, in a campaign, image mattered more than reality: although Cicero was praising Pompey regularly these days, Pompey was occupied in the East and not likely to intervene next year on Cicero's behalf. No matter. "You must also make sure that everyone knows that Pompey is extremely well-disposed to you and is vitally interested in your success."

Besides receiving advice from Quintus, Cicero consulted with Atticus on his every move. He had already identified most of his potential rivals and dismissed them. Only two candidates seemed serious: Catiline and Antonius, an uncle of Mark Antony, the fatherless boy who had grown into an idle 19-year-old. Antonius was handicapped by a public disgrace five years earlier when his bad character led Rome's censors to erase his name from the senate list. He hoped to rehabilitate his reputation by being elected consul.

Cicero had been in his teens when his path first crossed Catiline's. Both had served on the staff of Pompey's father during the war between Rome and its Italian allies, and then Catiline had benefited richly from Sulla's proscriptions. Descended from an old family, Catiline exuded a confidence that had always drawn men to him, first when he entered Roman life as a reactionary, now more than ever that he was campaigning as a champion of the people. After serving as governor in Africa the year Pompey took over the command against Mithridates, Catiline had returned to Rome, expecting to run for the consulship. But charges of corruption trailed him across the sea, and the official who drew up the candidate list had refused to enter his name. Catiline's backers were said to include Crassus and Caesar, who seemed to be working closely together these days. When Catiline indicated for a second time that he intended to stand for consul, his conservative opponents again brought charges to disqualify him. That trial was approaching and, as Cicero predicted to Atticus, the jurors would surely find Catiline guilty, unless they also found that "the sun does not shine at noon."

And yet soon afterward, Cicero was weighing how Catiline's trial might affect his own candidacy. In what began as a casual letter to Atticus about Cicero's new son, he turned to a more serious matter: "At the moment, I am thinking about defending my fellow candidate Catiline. We can have any jury we want, with full cooperation from the prosecution."

That cooperative prosecutor was Clodius Pulcher, the sort of stormy young man Cicero would have shunned in an off-election year. If Catiline was acquitted, "I hope he will be more inclined to work with me in the campaign," Cicero told Atticus. "But should it go otherwise, I shall bear it philosophically."

The trial opened, but without Cicero, after all. And when Catiline was duly acquitted, he didn't join Cicero's campaign. The next time the two men confronted each other, nothing about Cicero's behavior was philosophical.

XVI

CAESAR AND CICERO

65–63 B.C.

Because Caesar was six years younger, he seemed destined to remain one rung behind Cicero on Rome's ladder of honors. While Cicero maneuvered to be consul, Caesar, at 34, was campaigning for one of the curule aediles—the city's caretakers who also had the demanding job staging spectacles to honor the gods. The festivals took up most of April, eight days in the summer, fifteen days in September and a final week in December.

Besides handshaking, a campaign involved seeking endorsements from Rome's many workingmen's guilds and clubs, like the funeral syndicates, which had been set up to guarantee their members enough money and mourners for a decent burial. Caesar also had signs painted throughout the city and along the Appian Way. Merchants were encouraged to post a notice in their shops with a campaign slogan: "Make Caesar aedile and he will make you one." Three and a half weeks before the election, Caesar officially put on a toga whitened with chalk—the word "candidate" meant "pure white."

Traditionally, many men bought their positions. Cicero had never resorted to bribery, because of his principles, his frugality or his need to know that his virtues were appreciated. Caesar, already in debt from his stewardship of the Appian Way, made lavish pledges of entertainment.

Once elected, Caesar had to borrow still further to meet his campaign promises. He turned to Crassus, who was rankling at Pompey's fresh successes in Asia and happy to promote the career of a young ally. The showmanship required of an aedile came easily to Caesar. Popularity depended on excess, and he unleashed his exuberant imagination. His fellow aedile, an older and richer conservative named Bibulus, had none of Caesar's flair for self-promotion, but Caesar pressured him into putting up half the money for a series of extravaganzas. Bibulus soon found, however, that no one was cheering him in the streets. He told friends he had considered changing his name to Pollux: "In the Forum, the Temple of Castor and Pollux is always simply called Castor's. That's the way it is when Caesar and I give a public entertainment."

By September, some senators were growing nervous about the number of gladiators Caesar planned to import for his games. Remembering Spartacus' revolt six years earlier, senators limited the size of the contingent that could be brought into the city. Caesar yielded to the restriction and still provided the most magnificent shows in Rome's memory. First came lavish public banquets. Then, ignoring Bibulus, Caesar announced that the games would be held in honor of the twentieth anniversary of his father's death, with Aurelia on hand to share in the tribute.

Caesar had ringed the Forum with handsome colonnades and erected bleachers. Crowds overflowed the stands and climbed to the rooftops. Cages of animals were rolled in, the bars gleaming with silver. Next came 320 pairs of gladiators, all stripped to loincloths and carrying silver shields and polished swords. When the days of splendor seemed to have reached their peak, a morning dawned when Romans looked up at the roof of the Capitol to find huge images of Marius carrying the trophies that Sulla had ordered destroyed. Three years earlier, Caesar had added symbols of Marius to a funeral procession, but his challenge on this day was far bolder.

Patricians heard the people's cheers, saw their tears of joy, and shuddered at the shouts that Caesar was a man worthy of his famous uncle. When the senate met to discuss the display, Catulus led the attack: "You are no longer operating underground," he warned Caesar. "Your artillery is planted in the open, and it is there to capture the state."

Caesar assumed his most ingratiating manner. He assured the senators that they were misjudging him, that it was time to put aside old hatreds. Soothing and cajoling, he may not have convinced every listener but he avoided a formal vote of censure.

As Caesar expanded his influence, Crassus was learning that hostility to Pompey did not ensure acceptance from the patricians. When he endorsed Roman citizenship for Transalpine Gaul, a region from which Caesar and Pompey drew support, Catulus headed a successful resistance. The patricians were afraid of any one of the three increasing his strength among potential voters there.

Crassus turned to a more tantalizing prize. Egypt's King Ptolemy Auletes was unpopular with the Alexandrians, but his four-year-old daughter Cleopatra was too young to succeed him. Since the previous Egyptian king had reportedly bequeathed his nation to the Roman state, Crassus recommended annexing Egypt and appointing a governor-general there. Caesar lobbied the tribunes on behalf of the plan. Caesar's goal was ambiguous. Crassus would benefit if Pompey's impact throughout the East were blunted by sending a new governor to Egypt. But if Pompey won the post, that would extend his domain. Asia's sophistication had charmed Caesar once, and he would stand to gain great prestige by heading a mission to Egypt.

Cicero thought he knew Caesar's motives well enough to distrust them. But he also hoped Caesar's friendship with Pompey might help him win the consulship. In his speech against annexation, Cicero singled out Crassus, not Caesar. Crassus was known to be Pompey's enemy, and Cicero was safe in denouncing him as the greedy hand behind the proposed takeover. The senate made the same decision it had made under Sulla: Egypt was a greater threat as a province with an ambitious Roman governor than as an enfeebled dependency with a grateful Egyptian king.

Cicero had been diligent in heeding this campaign advice: "Every day, as you go down to the Forum, you must repeat to yourself: I am 'new.' I seek the consulship. This is Rome."

Atticus had come back to Rome to support his friend. He moved among the nobility, offering assurances of Cicero's reliability. Senators must understand that Cicero was only trying to stop Pompey from backing an opposition candidate. Conservatives were assured they could count on Cicero—once safely elected—to uphold their authority. Businessmen and middleclass merchants should consider Cicero devoted to a harmony between their class and the aristocrats.

But campaigns were not conducted solely on the high road. When a tribune claimed that Cicero's undistinguished birth made him unfit to be consul, Cicero seized his chance. Dressed in the candidate's spotless white toga, he declined to defend himself but accused Catiline and Antonius of meeting the previous night with agents they were paying to bribe the voters. They had gathered, Cicero continued, at the house of a high-ranking man notorious for that sort of corruption. Cicero seemed to be implicating Crassus but, if they preferred, his listeners could read in Caesar's name.

Even by the jabbing standard of Roman campaigning, it was a notably rough speech. Cicero raked up every charge made against Catiline, reviving rumors of murder, incest, of defiling a Vestal Virgin, although here Cicero had to tread cautiously since the woman was Terentia's half-sister. Cicero noted that Catiline's usual behavior led to presumptions of guilt even when no wrongdoing had occurred. Beneath the surface of his speech ran a warning that a man like Catiline wouldn't stop with tainted votes but was capable of subversion.

Catiline tried to defend himself. A new man, he said baldly, had no right to question an aristocrat. But Cicero seemed the clear winner. When electors met a few days later in the Campus Martius, they refused to cast ballots and unanimously shouted in Cicero as consul. As the voting resumed, Antonius edged out Catiline for the second spot. Cicero had fulfilled a new man's highest dream: on the first day of January, he would hold the title of consul.

Cicero's inaugural took place two days before his forty-third birthday. His fretting over his appearance and his voice had ended when middle age added a more solid veneer. His features had coarsened, and these days his mouth was set in an expression of slight disdain. His hair had receded more frankly than Caesar's, and he didn't rely on tricks to disguise its loss. Cicero had become a commanding public figure.

He launched his term with a high-minded speech. "I will conduct myself in this office," he pledged to a packed senate, "in such a way that I can chastise the tribunes if they oppose the Republic and despise them if they oppose me."

The challenge was clear. Cicero would make good on his private reassurances to the patricians by keeping the people and their tribunes in their place. He had already assured himself substantial control over his consulship by making a deal with Antonius over which provinces they would govern when their year was out. On inauguration day the two consuls traditionally drew lots for that post, since it would be their chief reward for their service. But before the draw, Cicero agreed that if he got a richer province than Antonius did, he would cede it to him. When he drew the highly exploitable Macedonia, he kept his word and traded it to Antonius for Cisalpine Gaul.

That was no sacrifice. Cicero was determined never to go abroad again. He intended to be an exemplary consul and then move securely into the role of trusted confidant and backstage manipulator.

The economy Cicero inherited was dangerously sick. Pompey's victories, while gratifying, had disrupted Eastern trade, and the veterans that Sulla had settled on farms were struggling to keep their land. Many men were out of work, and only *frumentatio*, the dole of subsidized wheat, kept the urban poor from starving. Money was so scarce that Jews living in Rome were forbidden to send their usual donations to Jerusalem.

Before Cicero took office, he heard that the tribunes elected with him were preparing a sweeping bill to relieve farmers and move Rome's poor to homesteads where they could support themselves; Caesar's influence was detected in the reforms. Cicero volunteered to review a draft of the law. If he thought it would help the mass of Romans, he said, he would back it with his prestige as consul. The tribunes rejected his offer with an insult.

Twenty days before Cicero's inauguration, the tribunes were sworn in, and one of them, a popular leader named Rullus, read out the 40 clauses of their farm law. Cicero noted that Rullus read monotonously but could take no other satisfaction in the performance. Rullus called for 10 commissioners to be elected for five years and given unchecked power. They could set up new colonies on almost any site they chose. To defray costs, they could sell public holdings throughout Italy, including the rich properties in Campania, where the rents from Rome's last publicly owned farmland were the foundation for the state's annual revenues. Although neither the lands already allotted by Sulla nor other private property would be confiscated, they could commandeer newly conquered farms from any general, except Pompey.

Almost 70 years had passed since the first attempts at reform, and this latest bill was far from radical. With Pompey's veterans returning one day to Rome, the patricians worried that he might use force to impose one-man rule. Here was their chance to defuse social unrest and make Pompey's homecoming peaceful. But given Rome's recent history, the senate was skeptical. Could the average Roman, scuffling for a living in the city, be transformed suddenly into a contented farmer? The experiment had been tried with Sulla's veterans, and as their farms failed they had begun looking for other armies to join.

Cicero based his opposition on the power given to the 10 commissioners over most of Rome's wealth. Liberally interpreted, the law could be stretched to allow annexing Egypt and setting up a new army of pacification under the command of the commissioners. Cicero had not sought Rome's supreme office to see its powers fragmented.

To thwart the plan, Cicero called a public meeting in the Forum. Even a mind as nimble as his seemed to face an impossible challenge: How could he persuade an audience of poor men that it was not in their interest to accept free land from the state?

Cicero's solution was to appeal to their better natures, even if he doubted privately that such natures existed. He spoke from the rostra as though each of his listeners exemplified the Roman tradition of restraint and self-sacrifice, taking apart the law that Rullus had mumbled his way through. Cicero had denounced the measure to the senators for jeopardizing their privileges. Now, without offering evidence, he told his mass audience that Pompey was the bill's true target, although Pompey and his plunder had been specifically exempted. Cicero pretended to speak for the absent general: "Pompey rejects Rullus' offer."

Cicero managed to suggest that he himself was from the

people's faction. He lamented the games and festivals of urban life
that poor families would be missing if they were resettled. Facing
a mass meeting, Cicero fell back on arguments he would have
ridiculed in the senate. Trying to outdo Rullus in promises, he
demanded to know why, if the plebeians were to have land, they
shouldn't have plowed land? Why expect them to do that hard
work themselves?

Cicero's gamble seemed to succeed; his evasions clouded
the crowd's mind until men were turning against the bill. A little
later, however, his spell lifted and the assembly came back to the
virtues in Rullus' proposals. Cicero was summoned again to the
rostra, and this time he faced clamorous men on guard against
being duped. He calmed the din and imagined for them the insulting letter that Rullus would send to Pompey. Swollen with his
new authority as a commissioner, the tribune would first omit the
word "Magnus" from Pompey's name. Then Rullus would say
curtly, "Meet me at Sinope and help me out while I, acting under
my law, sell the land that you have won with your labors."

Cicero knew his listeners better than they knew themselves.
Flattery from this consul—who they thought scorned them—was
sweeter than any words from the tribunes they had elected. Cicero
assured the people that he was not opposed to all land reform,
only to this particular bill.

In a coda to the debate, Rullus offered increasingly legalistic
rebuttals, to which Cicero made perfunctory replies. But the new
consul had won his first challenge; the bill was rejected. Cicero
had met its sponsors—including Crassus and Caesar—on the field
most hostile to him and had prevailed.

The people's leaders next moved to restore the voting rights
of Sulla's enemies, along with those of their children. Patricians
saw the measure as one more attempt to undermine their authority. If the families of Sulla's victims could enter politics again, they
would be sure to press for return of their confiscated estates. But
Cicero spoke against amnesty, and it was defeated.

The people's faction needed a victory. Caesar and his allies concocted a court case meant to warn Cicero and the patricians that
Romans would never again permit the terrors of Sulla's reign. The
outcome of the trial—which involved a 37-year-old murder committed during a time of the senate's ultimate decree—was clearly

less important than the opportunity it provided Caesar's party to remind citizens of the way the aristocrats had once abused their power.

Cicero met the challenge directly. Appearing for the defense, he praised the decree, the *senatus consultum ultimum*, for allowing extraordinary measures to preserve liberty. Cicero also extolled the accused murderer for having rid Rome of a potential tyrant and vowed that, facing the same challenge, he would not shrink from enforcing the decree. "And never," he added, "use your votes to prevent me, as consul, from having recourse to it!"

That was Cicero's warning. Any popular leader who threatened the state could expect his retribution.

XVII

CATILINE

63 B.C.

Rome's chief pontiff died, and the scramble to replace him gave Julius Caesar a new chance to test his growing popularity. Catulus and another patrician were campaigning for the position, and since both men had already served as consul, they considered Caesar's challenge an impertinence.

Catulus knew that his age and rank alone wouldn't guarantee success. Calculating the debts Caesar had amassed as aedile, he made a tempting offer. If Caesar would withdraw, Catulus would pay off all his obligations. Caesar was confident enough to reject the bribe and rash enough to pledge that to win he would plunge even further in debt. He would spend even more, he said, than Catulus had just offered him.

Caesar's mother understood the desperation behind his gamble. Without the rewards of being high priest, Caesar would be a bankrupt and probably forced to flee the country. On the day

Banquet scene from Herculaneum. Lauros-Giraudon.

of the election, Aurelia followed him to the door with tears in her eyes. Caesar acknowledged the stakes as he kissed her goodbye. "Today, Mother, you will see your son either Pontifex Maximus or an exile."

The people repaid Caesar's confidence. Even in his opponents' strongholds, he drew more votes than both of them combined. Returning home, Caesar could tell Aurelia to begin the move from Subura to Domus Publica, the official residence of Rome's high priest.

The Caesars had another reason to celebrate these days: Aurelia became a great-grandmother. Octavius, the infant's father, was not a patrician but he came from a wealthy and prominent family of businessmen, and Caesar's sister Julia had decided he was suitable for her daughter, Atia. Now Atia had delivered their first son, and the infant, Octavian, could be assured of fond interest from his great-uncle, the new high priest.

Entering the second half of his consulship, Cicero made a list of the types of Romans who opposed him. Alarmingly, most were attracted to Catiline, whose followers seemed to be multiplying fast enough to offset his loss of support from Crassus and from Caesar, who preferred to wait for Pompey's return rather than cast his lot with a man as erratic and indiscreet as Catiline. To Cicero, Catiline's backers were the bankrupts, the criminals, the malcontents, the failed farmers and the lazy urban poor. And worst of all were the city's elegant but reckless young men with their tunics too long and their faces too carefully made up. That sort of aristocratic idler had always repulsed Cicero. Caesar in his teenage years might have fitted in and, in his mid-thirties, he didn't underestimate them. A long sleeve might look effeminate, but it was a good place to hide a dagger.

Such were the men Cicero saw threatening him and the Republic, and joining their ranks was a certain class of Rome's women, among them Gaius Gracchus' daughter Sempronia. Though nobly born and a consul's widow, with the wit and beauty Cicero admired in an aristocrat, Sempronia was heavily mortgaged and looking for relief from debt.

Cicero couldn't ignore the numbers. Catiline again was standing for consul and might well be elected. He endorsed *tabulae novae*—clean slates that would cancel all debts—and could invoke precedents for the proposal. Nearly a quarter of a century earlier, a law had reduced debts by 75 percent. That had hurt the patricians badly, and now Catiline was urging an even greater redistribution of Rome's wealth.

To Cicero, the clean slate was a swindle, and he considered any attempt to ease the existing debts to be immoral. "What is the meaning of an abolition of debt except that you buy a farm with my money and you have the farm and I do not have my money."

To men with encumbered estates, Cicero suggested they cancel their debts "by the auctioneer." They had the option of selling their properties, just as Sulla's veterans could give up their pretentious scale of living and try harder to make a success of their farms. Cicero certainly wouldn't challenge the unyielding judge who was presiding over bankruptcy cases and reviving a practice that let creditors send a defaulter to debtors' prison. From early in Cicero's term, impoverished men had been pleading with the senate for help, and the prevailing despair explained why some Romans had turned to a champion like Catiline, even though he had been disqualified or lost the consulship three times.

Cicero wasn't the only one alarmed by the tone of Catiline's campaign. As his language grew more incendiary, Crassus and Caesar continued to distance themselves from his candidacy. He was quoted as saying that the poor and miserable should not put their faith in smug and prosperous leaders but in a man as wretched as themselves. Only he could be fearless, because only he had nothing to lose.

Voters from outside Rome began flocking to the city to accompany Catiline on his daily rounds. The result was a roiling mass of strangers in the Forum, shouting insults and picking fights. A large number had come from Faesulae to the north, where the townspeople were rumored to favor outright revolution. When the senators passed a law to prevent candidates from hiring gangs to escort them, everyone knew the target was Catiline. But he hardly needed to hire the crowds at his side.

Catiline began to act as though he were already consul. Even if the senate thwarted him again, he had appealed directly to the people and taken their verdict. Cicero heard enough threats from desperate men to believe that his own life might be in danger. On the summer day before the election for consul, he persuaded the senators to delay the voting briefly until they could hear the latest accusations against Catiline.

Despite open hostility in the senate, Catiline had been showing up whenever he wished, claiming the seat he had won as praetor five years earlier. On the day charges were to be brought against him, Catiline was in his place, looking not at all abashed.

Rising, he explained to the senators that the aristocrats might have brains but their numbers were few. The people, on the other hand, needed his leadership. "I see two bodies in the state— one thin and wasted but with a head. The other is headless but large and powerful. What is so dreadful about my becoming the head of the body that needs one?"

The senators groaned with displeasure but took no action against him, and Catiline left the senate in triumph.

Cicero was sure that Catiline planned to have him assassinated during the confusion of voting. When election day arrived, he took a throng of bodyguards to the Campus Martius. Once there, Cicero flung off his cape to reveal a shining breastplate. Since he was no warrior, the armor was clearly for self-defense, a reminder of the rumored threats against his life. When the voting began, Lucullus' band of veterans, back from the war against Mithridates and disturbed by the chaos in Rome, carried the day and defeated Catiline.

Four times Catiline had reached for the consulship and four times he had lost. Jubilant, Cicero boasted about his role in denying him the prize. The attention given to Catiline's loss overshadowed Julius Caesar's victory in the elections for praetor.

Rumors spread quickly of a conspiracy by Catiline to take by force what he couldn't win legally. Property values fell, creditors began dunning for their money even more insistently. The political uncertainty became intolerable.

From Faesulae, Catiline's ally Gaius Manlius was reported to be urging men to take up arms. Agitation seemed to be spreading among the failed farmers in other Italian towns. Revolts against the Roman nobility went back at least 400 years, but this time Italy's discontented seemed to be organizing an insurrection that might be impossible to put down.

■

On the night of October 18, about three months after the election, an unidentified messenger brought three scrolls to the door of Marcus Crassus, each sealed and addressed to a different man. Crassus claimed afterward that he opened and read only the one with his name before he sent slaves to the two other senators. He instructed them to join him at once at Cicero's house, and they assembled shortly before midnight. When Cicero had his guests ushered in, they told him the story.

Crassus' scroll warned him to flee from Rome because Catiline was plotting a massive slaughter. Since his past friendship with Catiline was well known, Crassus had come at once to the consul to clear himself of suspicion. Cicero was less amazed by the scrolls than Crassus expected. He had developed a network of informers that included Fulvia, the mistress of a member of Catiline's circle, and Cicero took her gossip seriously.

Cicero convened the senate at dawn. Many senators had hung back when he had claimed earlier that his own life was at risk and had sniggered when he began each accusation with "I have been informed . . ." But given these scrolls, the patricians would have to act. Cicero had already warned Romans that he wouldn't hesitate to seek the ultimate decree that provided for martial law. Now he would demand it.

When the senate was seated, Cicero asked the other two senators to break the seals and read aloud the scrolls left for them with Crassus. The readings were dramatic, but the impact was ambiguous. Even though the scrolls warned of a conspiracy, most senators decided they didn't provide enough detail to ensure a conviction. They agreed only to investigate further, and Cicero was forced to wait for more evidence. But not long. A day or two later, a report reached the senate that the roving bands in Etruria seemed to be forming into an army. Catiline's ally Manlius was said to be ready to march on Rome. As tension rose hour by hour, the senate voted Cicero and his co-consul full powers to protect the city and save them from Catiline.

The senate also dispatched a contingent of soldiers to the north to put down any incipient revolt. Manlius refused to lay down his arms until the senate took action against the moneylenders who were driving his followers from their land. Cicero took that response as a threat, and new rumors circulated: Catiline was being urged to recruit slaves for his movement. His defenders admitted that he was being pressured but said he had refused. Catiline's conspirators were sealing their pact by drinking a mixture of wine and human blood. They had sacrificed a young boy and eaten his entrails. Romans recognized those hoary attempts to defame an enemy, and yet they observed the misery seething throughout Italy and wondered how long before there was an open rebellion. Whatever his inclinations, Catiline was being maneuvered into the role of traitor to his country.

One of Catiline's allies hoped to clear his name by trying an odd ploy to diffuse the tension. He indicted Catiline on charges of plotting violence against the Republic in order to give him a chance to challenge Cicero's accusations in court. For Catiline, there would be a second benefit: as the defendant in a current trial, he couldn't be exiled under the ultimate decree. Catiline went along with the plan and volunteered to live under Cicero's roof during the trial so that the consul could monitor his movements. But the charges were dropped.

The political stakes were rising sharply. Word spread that a mob from Faesulae would be reaching Rome on October 27, less than a week away. Others said that a second band of revolutionaries intended to seize Praeneste, south of Rome, on November 1.

October 27 passed without an assault on Rome. November 1 came and went, and Catiline's men had not seized Praeneste. Had the ultimate decree delayed the rebellion or even ended it? Or had there never been a conspiracy? Was there instead a widespread misery that Cicero was unable or unwilling to confront and preferred to treat simply as a lunge for power?

On November 8, Cicero called another emergency session of the senate. He wanted a site that was easier to defend than the senate chambers and chose the Temple of Jupiter Stator, near the beginning of the Via Sacra. He let the senators know that an informant—it was Fulvia—had warned of a new plan to assassinate him. Meeting at a house on the Street of the Scythemakers, Catiline had supposedly recruited two men to go to Cicero's house at daybreak as though they were paying their respects. When Cicero appeared, they were to draw their swords and run him through.

Exactly as his spy predicted, two men had appeared, and when Cicero's servants refused to let them in, their surly and abusive manners confirmed the plot, at least to Cicero.

Guilty or not, Catiline knew of the charges before the senate convened. He came to the temple to answer them, but as he
took his seat many of the senators shrank away and moved to sit
far from his side. Although Catiline's defenders had not been able
to arrange a public trial, the senate seemed to have tried Catiline
and found him guilty.

Cicero hadn't expected Catiline to attend his own unmask-
ing and was astonished to find his enemy seated in front of him.
The sight of Catiline unnerved him, but it also sent adrenaline
through his body. Cicero was fighting back hysteria as he launched
into his indictment:

"How long, Catiline, will you abuse our patience? How
long will that madness of yours mock us? To what length will your
unbridled audacity go?

"Are you not at all impressed that there is a guard each
night at the Palatine? That there are patrols throughout the city?
That the people are in a panic? That all honest citizens are rallying
together? That the senate is meeting here in this stronghold? That
you can see looks of horror on the faces all around you?

"Do you not realize that your plans have been discovered?
Do you not see that your conspiracy is known to everyone here?
Do you think that there is a man among us ignorant of what you
did last night, and the night before—where you were, the men
you called to your meeting, the decision you reached? O tempora,
o mores!"

With that, Cicero demanded that Catiline pay for crimes of
which he had been only accused:

"The senate knows it all, the consul sees it and yet—this
man is still alive! Alive? Yes, and even come to the senate, takes
part in our debates, singles us out one by one for his slaughter.

"You, Catiline, should have been led to your death long
ago, and on a consul's orders. On your head should have fallen
the destruction you have been planning so long against us all."

Cicero outlined the meeting Catiline was accused of attending, the attempt on his own life and the insurrection being fo-
mented in Etruria. He wheeled scornfully on those colleagues who
had prided themselves on avoiding a showdown. Then he stared
at individual senators and claimed to be able to identify the other
conspirators among them. Cicero recalled that previous consuls,
armed with the senate's ultimate decree, had immediately exe-

cuted Rome's enemies. But he admitted to worrying that even now some men might say he was acting too harshly.

"In these circumstances, Catiline, finish the journey you have begun. At long last, leave the city. The gates are open. Be on your way."

If Cicero could persuade Catiline to go to Manlius' armed camp, he would be proving that the charges against him had been valid. Cicero urged him to go and take his troublemakers with him. "Cleanse the city," Cicero implored. "You will free me from my great fear, once there is a wall between us. You cannot remain among us any longer. I cannot—I will not—I must not permit it."

But as Cicero went on speaking, his furious indignation began to fade, along with his resolve. He began to plead. Catiline should look around him, Cicero said. No one supported him. As proof, he observed that since no one had raised his voice in Catiline's support, the senators had convicted him with their silence.

"What sort of life are you living?" Cicero asked. "I speak to you now to show that I do not feel the hatred I ought to feel but instead a pity that you do not at all deserve."

When Cicero finished, Catiline rose in rebuttal. He traced his own lineage, sneered at Cicero for being a mere tenant in the House of Rome and called for a vote on whether he should leave the city. "Put the proposal to the senate," he challenged Cicero. If the result went against him, he would leave for exile voluntarily.

Cicero would not accept the dare. He had been trusting to his eloquence to hound Catiline into leaving Rome on his own. The senate was not a judicial body, and any vote on Catiline would be moved to a less reliable court. Cicero wouldn't even seek symbolic support from the senate. His evidence had never been overwhelming. If pressed, some senators might support a patrician blackguard against a consul who remained irredeemably new.

But that night, Catiline obliged Cicero by going from Rome to Faesulae and joining Manlius. As he left, he sent Catulus a statement in his defense that he said he had been too proud to offer to Cicero. Catiline wrote that he would only explain to a friend, who would understand that he was not speaking from guilt. He admitted that he had been maddened by the slights and wrongs done him and at the way he had been robbed of the position he felt he deserved. All the same, "I followed my usual custom and took up the cause of the unfortunate." But as he watched unworthy men elevated to high honors, Catiline wrote, "I realized that I was an outcast because of baseless suspicion." He believed that he, not Cicero, was being threatened with violence. As he prepared to flee, Catiline asked Catulus to look after his wife.

The next day, Cicero appeared before the people to claim victory. His forum was a public meeting that was open to women, foreigners, even slaves; it was not an assembly for voting. Without his enemy staring back at him, Cicero spoke passionately, though he began with a grudging admission that Catiline had left the city voluntarily.

"At long last, citizens, we have expelled Lucius Catiline. Or, if you prefer, sent him off. Or followed him on his way with our farewells as he left Rome of his own accord, roused to a frenzy of audacity, breathing crime, foully plotting the destruction of his country and ceaselessly threatening you and this city with fire and sword."

Repeating his call for Catiline to be put to death, Cicero explained why he had shrunk from doing it. "I saw that, if I had inflicted the death penalty that he deserved, the unpopularity of that action would have prevented me from tackling his confidantes." In an aside, Cicero gave thanks that Catiline had taken away a few followers. "But the men he has left behind! What debts they have! What power! What distinguished birth!"

Those were the men Cicero intended to confront one day soon. But he had to wait until he could be sure that Rome would support his drastic measures.

With events moving toward a climax, Cicero was irritated and distracted by an irrelevant lawsuit brought by Marcus Porcius Cato, great-grandson of the famed Roman censor. The present-day Cato complained as bitterly as Cicero about the low morality of the age but with less wit. Slow to smile, slower still to change his mind, Cato, at 32, seemed caught in the world of his distinguished ancestor, who had been consul a hundred years before his birth. The young man cultivated a number of quirks to show his disdain for modern customs—going barefoot, dressing in dark colors when light purple was the fashion, refusing to wear a hat during the steamy summers. As a young officer, Cato had forbidden his troops to plunder; as a civil official, he fired underlings for any hint of embezzlement or profiteering. His reputation was impeccable.

Cicero had to admit that Cato was free of the contemporary vices but considered him a maladroit politician. In the midst of Rome's turmoil, Cato was bringing suit against Lucius Murena, even though Murena had done the patricians the favor of defeating Catiline for the consulship. Acting on behalf of another candidate, Servius Supilcus, Cato invoked an old law against corrupting elections. These days, thanks to the measures meant to warn off Catiline, the penalty for corruption had become exile for 10 years, rather than one year. Even though Rome's civil peace depended on stability, Cato was proposing to eliminate one of next year's consuls.

Sulpicus was Cicero's friend, too, but Cicero considered himself engaged in averting "the destruction of the entire world," and he joined Murena's defense. The prosecution's case opened with Sulpicus claiming that the triumph of a new man like Murena over an aristocrat like himself was, on its face, proof of corruption. Cicero could hardly accept that argument. He had worked all night on his speech and, given the other strains on his nerves, he seemed exhausted when his turn came. Since Murena had undeniably bribed his way to victory, Cicero didn't try to defend him. Instead, he attacked his accusers, starting with Cato.

In waves of excessive language, he lauded Cato's integrity, serious-mindedness, self-control, strength of character, sense of justice. "In short," Cicero said, Cato was "a paragon of every virtue."

From the laughter around him, even Cato knew he was being mocked. He forced a smile and muttered to the men at his side, "My friends, what a droll fellow our consul is."

But Cato was only a diversion. To clinch his case, Cicero was willing to betray his deepest convictions by arguing that a soldier was far more admirable than either an orator or a scholar of the law. "Servius," Cicero said slightingly of his old friend, "soldiered with me here at Rome, giving opinions, copying public documents and securing loans. A life full of worry and vexation. He became an expert in civil law, worked long hours, spared no efforts, readily helped his many clients, put up with their stupidity, endured their arrogance and stomached those who were hard to please."

In other words, Sulpicus had pursued a career identical to Cicero's own, and it was only to win this case that Cicero would pretend to find their lives fusty and pedestrian. Sulpicus was proud of being a lawyer? "Your profession, as I have already said, has never conferred the prestige, much less the public support, required for the consulship, for it consists of nothing but fabrication and deceit."

Cicero was aware that Romans were bored by theory, thrilled by action, and he laid out for his audience the glamorous life of Murena: "In his command, he led an army, fought pitched battles, engaged in hand-to-hand fighting, routed strong forces of the enemy, took cities—some by storm, some after a siege— crossed the face of that Asia of yours, so crammed with wealth and luxury, and yet left behind in it not a trace of acquisitiveness or extravagant living."

"That Asia of yours" was Cicero's reminder of the glory that defeating Mithridates had brought to every Roman. "In truth," Cicero said, "there is no doubt—for I must speak my mind—that success in a military career counts for more than any other."

Then Cicero swept away the charges against Murena and got to the nub of his argument: "It is vital, gentlemen, that there are two consuls in the State on the first of January and that is what, in the face of strong opposition, I have worked so hard to achieve."

He reminded the court that Catiline presented a threat more dire than this case of routine bribery. "Plans have been laid in this state, gentlemen, to destroy the city, slaughter the citizens and obliterate the name of Rome," cried Cicero—and Murena was acquitted.

By the end of November, with only a month left of his consulship, Cicero faced the prospect of leaving office with Catiline and his allies at large and unpunished. He wanted his co-consul Antonius to move troops against the makeshift army that seemed to be gathering outside of Rome. One report had 12,000 men joining the rebels, a quarter of them with weapons. But so far Antonius would not march. Cicero needed a piece of conclusive evidence to galvanize the city. In early December he got it.

Two delegates from the Allobroges tribe in the foothills of

Transalpine Gaul had come to Rome to complain about the harshness of their governor. A group allied with Catiline sent an agent to meet them, express sympathy and try to recruit them for the rebellion. Instead, the Gauls notified their Roman patron about the approach, and when Cicero heard, he urged them to get enough tangible proof to convince the most skeptical senator.

The Gauls agreed to meet their contact at night and leave Rome along the Flaminian Way. Two miles north of the city, at a stone bridge over the Tiber, they were seized by Cicero's praetors and escorted back to Rome to appear as witnesses. The soldiers also confiscated letters from four prominent Romans, including the senators Lentulus and Cethegus. A former consul, Lentulus was Mark Antony's stepfather.

The correspondence was turned over to Cicero, who summoned the senators to another emergency meeting, this time at the Temple of Concord. He also sent messengers to invite the four suspects to come first to his house. All obeyed the summons without knowing of the evidence against them. Cicero's friends urged him to open the letters before he took them to the senate, in case they were innocuous and made him look foolish. But Cicero had pieced together enough elements of the plot to be sure that swords and other weapons were hidden at Cethegus' house. He believed that Lentulus had devised a plan to kill the entire senate and take Pompey's children hostage as a bargaining chip against the day the general returned. Cicero had also been informed that the plotters had assigned 100 recruits to set fires in different sectors of Rome so that, during the Saturnalia, arson and killing would sweep through the city.

At dawn on December 3, the senators were in their places, impatient for Cicero to arrive. At other times, many of the 600 senators were away from Rome, serving the state or attending to their own business, but this morning the temple was packed. Cicero appeared, surrounded by his lictors and a guard of citizens. He was leading Lentulus by the hand, a mark of favor Cicero felt he owed him as a praetor. The other accused men had been brought by praetors and their retinues. Lentulus and Cethegus were the first to be ushered inside the temple, then the other Romans and their go-between.

Cicero laid out his case with drama and precision. First, he produced the messenger who had been arrested with the Gauls the previous night. Acting for the senate, Cicero coaxed him to tell what he knew in exchange for a full pardon. The man confessed that Lentulus had given him instructions to take to Catiline; they concerned the need to surround the city walls in order to cut off anyone who tried to escape from the slaughter he planned. The Gauls confirmed the story.

In an effective bit of stagecraft, Cicero produced the confiscated letters. Cethegus, he asked, is this your seal? The senator admitted it was. Cicero cut through the string binding the scroll and read its contents. In his own hand, Cethegus had assured the Allobroges that he would support their cause and asked in return that they obey certain instructions. The language was vague enough to raise doubts, but Cicero had already sent men to Cethegus' house, where they found a cache of weapons. Cethegus had tried to bluff by saying that he had always been an avid collector of arms. But hearing his letter read aloud, he found nothing more to say.

The charade was repeated with a plotter named Statilius. He was forced to admit that the seal was genuine, then his scroll was read to the senate. When Lentulus' turn came, Cicero used the senator's illustrious birth to intensify his shame. Lentulus' seal included a portrait of his grandfather, a famous patriot. "Surely this seal, even though it cannot speak, should have called you back from so heinous a crime," Cicero said.

Lentulus challenged the Gauls' testimony, but as the witnesses against him stuck coolly to their story, he began to falter. When his letter to Catiline was entered as evidence, even its indirection made the contents damning: "You know who I am from the man whom I have sent to you. Be resolute and take stock of your position. See what you must now do and take care that you get the support of everyone, even the lowest."

Last came the fourth of the accused, Gabinius, whose bluster ended in a confession to every charge.

Cicero's vindication was complete. Senators had derided his warnings and laughed at his putting on armor and traveling with bodyguards to dramatize the peril. For months, Catiline's high birth had seemed to count for more than Cicero's dedication to the Republic. Now doubt was impossible, and Cicero demanded to know what action the senators were ready to take.

But under the ultimate decree, the decision rested with him as consul, not with the senators. If Cicero risked a trial and won the death sentence, the defendants would have the right to appeal to the people. And any time during the three and a half weeks before execution could be carried out, they could choose exile. But if Cicero meted out the punishments on his own authority, he wanted to be sure he enjoyed wide backing. He would be leaving the consulship in less than a month and open then to criminal prosecution for any misdeeds in office. The senate supported him to the extent of voting that Lentulus resign his praetorship, remove his purple-edged toga and go into custody with his three other conspirators. They also decreed that the freedman who had first introduced the Gauls to Gabinius be arrested.

The danger had suggested the dimensions of a revolution, not a simple cabal. Cicero knew that every one of Catiline's sympathizers could not be arrested. But some patricians pressed him to implicate at least Crassus and Caesar. Both men had certainly backed Catiline in the past and shared the support of many of the same popular factions. Catulus was unforgiving over his loss as Pontifex Maximus and urged Cicero to act on his suspicions and not demand strict evidence. Privately, Cicero agreed that both Caesar and Crassus had contributed to the present crisis by encouraging Catiline. But he resisted stretching the evidence and instead let Crassus and Caesar be among the senators entrusted with taking the conspirators into custody. If either man let his prisoner escape, he would be signing his own confession.

The senate hearing had lasted until dusk. Cicero emerged from the Temple of Concord to find Romans crowding into the Forum for his report on the day's extraordinary events. He was happy to recount for them the highlights, especially since the session had ended with an unparalleled honor for him. The senate had voted a thanksgiving in his name, the first time a consul had been honored for civilian service to Rome rather than a military conquest.

Cicero told the throng that only his actions had saved them all. But for his valor he wanted no reward, no monuments. He asked only that this day be remembered for all time.

Cicero left the crowd and went with his brother and a few close friends to a house near his own. On this, the greatest night of his life, he couldn't go home because Terentia was hostess to a gathering made up exclusively of women. They were honoring Bona Dea, the Good Goddess, who oversaw the fruitfulness of marriage. Meeting at the home of a high official, Rome's leading matrons and the Vestal Virgins conducted secret rituals, and they excluded men so thoroughly that every statue or painting of a male figure was draped with veils. Had Cicero crossed his own threshold that night, he would have committed a sacrilege; according to the superstition, perhaps been struck blind.

As Cicero brooded over what punishments to impose, Terentia appeared unexpectedly. Cicero had complained in the past that his wife was more likely to insist on a share in his public life than to give him a voice in running her household. Now she had come to tell him about a ritual the women had just performed.

When the women had gathered around an altar covered with dead ashes, a bright flame had burst from the charred wood. As the women shrunk back, the Vestal Virgins told Terentia to hurry to her husband and assure him that the flash of light had come from the Good Goddess, promising Cicero safety and glory.

The next morning, the senate met to reward the Allobrogan delegates and the messenger for their testimony. Cicero had heard that Lentulus' clients were urging slaves and workingmen to rescue him from confinement and that Cethegus was also appealing to his slaves to free him. Cicero ordered the praetors to swear in Rome's entire male population as soldiers in case actual warfare broke out. At the same time, however, he persuaded the senate to reject a new accusation against Crassus. It was a question of motive. Crassus might still hate Pompey and dread his return to Rome, but would the city's richest man be likely to join in a movement that threatened his vast properties?

On the Nones, or fifth day, of December, Cicero convened the senate again. As he asked for recommendations for a proper punishment for the conspirators, he still seemed undecided. One of the newly elected consuls spoke first and said that those implicated in the plot deserved "the extreme penalty." Murena and 14 other senators who had once been consul were on hand for the debate, and they all agreed on death.

The current praetors were next to be polled, then the men who would be assuming the praetorship in less than a month.

When his turn came, Caesar's speech was sure to affect his future ambitions. The senators heard a growing tumult from outside the temple, but Caesar began calmly.

"Men who deliberate on difficult questions ought to be free from hatred and friendship, anger and pity," he said. "When those feelings stand in the way, the mind cannot easily discern the truth, and no mortal man has ever served his passions and his best interests. When you apply your intellect, it prevails. If passion possesses you, it holds sway and the mind is impotent."

Caesar argued that reason dictated that the prisoners should not be executed without a trial. The ultimate decree gave the consul the power to impose death, but only if the traitors were captured in an armed uprising. Did the weapons found at Cethegus' house fulfill that condition? Could the vague wording of the plotters' letters support a charge of treason in an actual trial? Cicero had persuaded many Romans that the accused men were guilty. Caesar, by as much as hinting that they might be innocent, could be ending his career. He couldn't make a direct plea for their lives; he could only argue on behalf of Rome's future.

"All bad precedents have originated in cases that were good," Caesar said. "But when control of the government falls into the hands of incompetent or bad men, your precedent may be wrongly applied, and men blameless and not guilty may suffer." He gave a tactful nod to Cicero: "I have no fear of this with Marcus Tullius, but with this precedent established, what might happen to innocent men at the hands of another, less scrupulous consul?"

Caesar made a counterproposal. He said that the existing law was wise in permitting a Roman to choose exile as an alternative to death. He recommended sending each conspirator to a different town around Italy. A town that allowed the prisoner to escape would lose its privileges and become Rome's enemy. As further punishment, the conspirators' estates should be confiscated, and they should not be allowed to appeal their sentences.

In an hour, Caesar's rational and humane argument had broken the fever that Cicero and the patricians had been stoking for months. Senators who had arrived that morning calling for blood were reminded that great numbers of people throughout Italy favored the reforms Catiline had advocated, and his followers might exact vengeance later for what was being done today. The consul-elect took the floor again to explain that he had certainly never suggested death; of course, he said, the "extreme penalty" he had proposed was imprisonment. Cicero's own brother rose to agree with Caesar, and the conspirators' lives seemed spared.

But Cicero could see the loopholes Caesar had woven. From the safety of exile, the accused men would surely demand a trial. As tempers cooled, the evidence against them might look even more dubious. Whatever lifetime guarantee against pardons Caesar was proposing today a tribune could overturn next year or the year after. When Cicero spoke, however, he went on playing the role of an impartial judge. He had been genuinely impressed with Caesar's speech, but he found a way to turn Caesar's very mercy against him. Describing Caesar as the kindest and gentlest of men, Cicero claimed that a life sentence without the possibility of parole was actually a more hideous punishment than execution. And by making it illegal to appeal the sentences, Caesar was removing "even hope, the one consolation of men in their misfortune."

Two days earlier, Cicero's pride had come close to bursting, and it hadn't noticeably deflated since then. He first urged the senators to forget his safety and think only of Rome. But soon he was letting them know that his dear brother was anguished by the possibility of retribution that Catiline's faction might inflict, that Terentia was terror-stricken and his 13-year-old daughter was prostrate with fear.

And yet, Cicero continued, let the senate vote the death sentence and he would brave the consequences, because he saw a vision far worse than anything that might happen to him alone: "There passes before my eyes the sight of Cethegus as he prances upon your corpses in his frenzied revels." Cicero did not ask the senate to vote outright for the death penalty, merely show its preference for it.

Cato arose, determined to settle the matter. He too praised Caesar's speech as eloquent. But his assault was ferocious. Legends soon sprang up about this session, as they did whenever Caesar was involved. And as usual, the stories were favorable to him. During Cato's speech, a messenger was supposed to have delivered a note to Caesar. Cato broke off and accused Caesar of receiving correspondence from the conspirators. He demanded that Caesar read the message aloud. Instead, Caesar passed it over to him. It was a love letter from Servilia, Cato's favorite stepsister.

Enraged, Cato reportedly threw it back at Caesar, snarling, "Take it, you drunkard!"

The anecdote had the virtues of embarrassing Cato and reminding Romans that, in fact, Caesar drank sparingly.

When Cato resumed his speech, he defined the issue simply: there were rich men, and there were men who wanted to take away those riches. "You have always valued your houses, villas, statues and paintings more highly than your country," Cato told his fellow senators contemptuously. "If you wish to hold on to the treasure to which you cling, arouse yourself to take charge of the state!"

He called for death, immediately.

Cicero polled the senate, instructing the senators to move to the side of the temple that would reflect their vote.

Caesar attempted to withdraw his recommendation that the estates of the accused men be confiscated. Since the senators were rejecting his plea for clemency, they shouldn't retain only the part of his proposal that would punish innocent families. But he seemed to be arguing more openly for the prisoners, and was shouted down. Tempers grew feverish. Caesar tried to leave the temple but was assailed by the young men Cicero had recruited as guards. They might have run him through with their swords if Cicero hadn't signaled to Atticus that Caesar should be escorted from the building. Caesar's allies wondered whether Cicero intervened because he truly opposed illegal killing or because he feared the riot that would occur if another popular leader were murdered. Whatever his motive, Cicero approved Caesar's appeal and spared the prisoners' property.

But not their lives. That same evening, Cicero ordered the praetors to bring out the other condemned men while he went himself to the house on the Palatine where Lentulus was being held. The prisoners were led to the northeast corner of the Forum where two dungeons lay beneath the Capitol. The prison, which dated from Etruscan times, was named the Tullianum for the king who had enlarged it. There were no stairs. Prisoners were let down through a hole in the roof. When Jugurtha, king of Numidia, had been lowered to the dungeon to starve to death, he had called back on his way down, "How cold, Romans, is this bath of yours!"

Mobs were lining the Via Sacra to hear the fate of Lentulus

and the others. Cicero waited for each of the accused conspirators to be let down through the hole and strangled by the prison's executioner. When the last man had been killed, Cicero made an announcement to the crowd. At such times, Romans avoided the bad luck of the word "death" and used instead the eloquent past tense.

"Vixere!" Cicero cried. They have lived.

XVIII

CATO

62 B.C.

In his inaugural speech eleven months earlier, Cicero had promised the senate's aristocrats that he would restore their authority and bring harmony among the social classes. The triumphant crowds lighting his way home with torches that evening proved that he had fulfilled his vow. Catiline was hiding in the Apennines mountains of Etruria, hoping to hear of new waves of popular support in Rome. Cicero could assume that the swift executions would discourage further uprisings. At a small price in human life, Rome seemed about to enter upon an era of harmony.

Five days later, Cicero's dream came crashing down. On December 10, two of the newly elected tribunes attacked him before the people, one for hounding Catiline into exile, the other for executing Roman citizens without a trial. The second charge was particularly galling since it came from Metellus Nepos, and Cicero had just passed along his own province for the coming year to one of his relatives. Now Nepos was proposing a bill to bring Pompey back quickly to Italy and ward off more executions of Romans without a trial. Behind the scenes, Cicero worked against the measure, but Cato, just elected tribune, moved more skillfully. He recognized that men must eat and that the surest way to undercut Catiline's alliance with the city's poor was to increase the number of men eligible for cheap grain.

That was a defensive measure. On the attack, Cato remained the most unbending aristocrat against Pompey. He tried to win Metellus Nepos over with reminders that the Metelli had always sided with the patricians. Nepos took his overtures as weakness and became insolent. That led Cato to drop the mask of civility and vow that as long as he lived, Pompey would never come into Rome with an army.

Rather than ushering in an age of concord, Cicero was leaving a legacy of ill will. On the last day of the year, Nepos and his allies moved their benches to block Cicero's way to the rostra and stop him from giving the customary review of his year as consul. Nepos maintained that no man who had punished others without a trial should be allowed to speak. At most, he would allow Cicero to mount the platform and recite the brief oath that relinquished his office.

If Cicero hadn't been pumped up with pride, he might have understood that inadvertently Nepos had done him a favor by muzzling him. Romans were already growing tired of Cicero's constant boasting. Even his supporters deplored the way he kept extolling his performance in the Catiline affair. As he prepared to leave office, Cicero took his place at the rostra, waited for the audience to become quiet and then delivered his own version of the oath.

"I swear in the very truth—" he began traditionally, but then substituted his own words, "—that I have saved my country and maintained her supremacy."

Enough of the crowd cheered wildly that, for a time, Cicero was reassured. When Cato praised him as the father of the fatherland, Cicero ignored Cato's political motives and accepted the title as his due. He also found a chance to revenge himself on Nepos during a senate debate when the nobly born tribune tried to humble Cicero by repeating, "Who is *your* father?"

"I can scarcely ask the same question," Cicero responded, "since your mother has made it rather hard to answer."

Befitting his new status, Cicero bought from Crassus a splendid villa overlooking the Forum. He had to borrow almost two-thirds of the price, but he reveled in its fashionable location. Rumors arose that he was taking kickbacks from Antonius, who had been installed as governor of Macedonia. Cicero shrugged them off with a joke. He was so far in debt these days, he told friends, that he was ready to join a conspiracy himself.

Julius Caesar had shown himself at 38 to be fearless but not fool-hardy. After his unsettling skirmish with Cicero's bodyguards, he stayed away from the senate for the rest of the year. Once installed as praetor, though, Caesar wasted no time in declaring war on the patricians and trying to pull Pompey into the popular camp.

On January 1, Caesar made a serious charge against the man he had defeated as high priest. He demanded that Catulus appear before the assembly to explain why restoring the Capitol was taking so long. Implied was an accusation of embezzlement. Caesar added that the restoration should be taken away from Catulus and given instead to Pompey when he came back to Rome.

As Pompey's return approached, the jockeying for his support had become strenuous. After the execution of the conspirators, Cicero had sent Pompey a breathless account of the way he had saved Rome. It didn't occur to him that Pompey might be annoyed by the suggestion that they were now equals in their service to the Republic, and Cicero was puzzled by Pompey's cool response.

Cicero had left himself without a governorship to protect him when he returned to the senate, and he felt nervous about Nepos' increasing hostility. He sponsored further honors for Pompey in the senate and sent him a second letter. This time, Cicero wrote candidly about feeling hurt by Pompey's lack of appreciation for his handling of Catiline and went on to compound the insensitivity of his first message: "My achievements were such that I looked in your letter for some congratulations due both to our relationship"—until elected consul, Cicero had never dared to claim a special bond with Pompey the Great—"and to the public interest. I believe that you omitted this for fear of offending certain people."

But Cicero's mild overtures didn't match Caesar's vigorous efforts to link himself to Pompey through Nepos. After Cato persuaded the senate to reject Nepos' bill to bring Pompey and his army back to save Rome, Nepos took his case to the people. He packed the Forum with poor men who couldn't be sure that Pompey was their savior but, with Catiline gone, had decided he was their best hope. When the patricians saw Caesar adding his followers to that movement, most ducked their heads and hoped the popular outcry would pass.

Not Cato. The night before the meeting, he slept soundly while his friends stayed up comforting his weeping wife and sister. At dawn, Cato set out for the Forum with a small group. On the route, his admirers stopped him often with warnings to turn back.

The speeches had been scheduled in front of the Temple of Castor and Pollux. Cato arrived to find the steps ringed with the unfriendly gladiators. At the top of the stairs, Nepos and Caesar were side by side, Caesar in his official praetor's seat, Nepos on a tribune's bench.

"Look at that flagrant coward!" Cato shouted, gesturing to Nepos. "Calling up a regiment of soldiers against one naked unarmed man!"

Guards tried to stop Cato from climbing the steps with another tribune. Cato took his ally by the hand and succeeded in dragging him through the crowd. When they reached the platform, Cato marched to Nepos and sat between him and Caesar, to stop their whispering together. The two men's obvious discomfort delighted Cato's followers, and they shouted praise for his courage.

A clerk prepared to read Nepos' bill aloud, but Cato stopped him. Nepos took the bill and prepared to read it himself. Cato snatched it away. Nepos knew his legislation by heart and began to recite it. Cato's ally stepped up and put his hand over Nepos' mouth.

Romans might have taken the spectacle as comedy or drama, but Cato's bravery swayed enough of them that Nepos sent for more armed men. When fighting broke out between the two factions, Murena as consul led troops to the Forum, where he found Cato in clear danger. Forgiving last year's prosecution, Murena held out his consular robe to shield Cato from sticks and rocks. Caesar also withdrew. That afternoon, senators met in the Temple of Concord and gave the consuls absolute power to impose order. They also barred anyone from challenging the legality of Cicero's executions and suspended both Nepos and Caesar from office.

Nepos hurried to the rostra to announce that he was leaving immediately for the East to tell Pompey of that outrageous behavior. Caesar took a different tack. Defying the suspension, he convened his praetorian court. Then, his point made, he dismissed them, returned to his house and sent lieutenants to organize throughout the night. At daybreak, Rome's workingmen and shopkeepers, freedmen and slaves marched to Caesar's door, shouting his title of praetor. They left no doubt they were ready to restore him to office by force.

Caesar appeared and thanked the multitudes for their endorsement. But, he said, this was no time for more violence. They should go home peacefully. Enough senators were grateful for Caesar's restraint to vote him back as praetor. As for Caesar, so long as he could protect his dignity, he had been willing to respect the Republic.

Each report about Catiline's stalled rebellion was cooling the city's political temperature. Antonius had no heart for fighting an old ally and had left prosecution of the war to Nepos' conservative brother, Metellus Celer. In Etruria, Catiline and Manlius had amassed 20,000 rebels beneath a standard with a silver eagle. That trophy, which dated from Marius' day, was their glistening assertion that the revolt was as honorable as any led by Caesar's uncle.

But the executions in Rome had caused enough men to desert so that Catiline took the remainder of his troops north into Gaul rather than south into Rome. Moving fast, Celer caught him between two Roman forces. When Catiline tried to move west across the Apennines, legionaries blocked his way. Antonius had developed a convenient gout that kept him out of the climactic battle. Catiline hurled himself into the fray far ahead of his troops, and they were inspired by his bravery and fought until the last man fell.

When Catiline's body was found, covered with slashing wounds, his strong chest was still heaving but his life was over. He was buried in the Arno valley near Pistoria. Even his enemies admitted that Catiline's death would have been glorious if only he had been fighting for his country.

■

Pompey returned at last to Italy in a style both magnanimous and foolish. As a young man, he had insisted on premature triumphs, but he also revered stories from the Republic's early days, when heroes had acted from their love of Rome. He was aware that the senators who already feared him were dreading his return, and Crassus added to the panic by leaving the city and taking his children and all the money he could carry.

But when Pompey reached Brundisium from Greece, he astonished foes and friends by calling together his soldiers to offer his heartfelt thanks and disband them. Go to your homes now, Pompey said; later, be sure to come to Rome to march in my triumph. When his men had scattered, Pompey headed west accompanied by a small band of friends. The effect on farmers and villagers was galvanizing. They came rushing out to cheer his progress, and he reached Rome with more people trailing after him than if he had brought his army.

Disbanding his troops was the grandest gesture Pompey could make to show that he had returned in peace. He soon found, however, that he had been too convincing; senators who had feared him now felt free to show their scorn. Pitching camp outside the walls, Pompey sent a messenger to the senate with a modest request. The election would soon be under way. Although Pompey didn't intend to be a candidate for consul himself, he wanted to be on hand to back his choice. He asked the senate to waive the rule that a general could not enter the city before his triumph. With Cato leading the patricians, the senate rebuffed him. If Pompey wanted his triumph, he would have to abide by the rules.

Pompey's grasp of the intricacies of Roman politics had never been keen, but he realized that as a general without an army he had to cultivate alliances with those politicians who had stayed home while he was off becoming the new Alexander. He sought out Cicero, who was less flattered by the attention than he might have been before his consulship. Pompey also thought he saw a way to win over Cato.

As he returned from the East, Pompey had imagined the joy of his wife, Mucia, and their three children at having him home again. He had been too busy in Syria and Judaea to fret over rumors that Mucia was being unfaithful. Once he reached Greece, however, he couldn't ignore those infidelities any longer, and his first act upon arriving in Italy was to divorce her.

Although Pompey lacked Caesar's adroitness with women, he needed to be married. When he saw that Cato's integrity and patrician views had made him a power in the senate, Pompey purposed a double merger of their families. He himself, in his mid-forties, would marry one of Cato's nieces; Pompey's teenage son would marry her younger sister. Conquering generals traditionally had their pick of brides, and since both young women embraced the plan, Cato was bound to be flattered and neutralized.

But Cato remained unpredictable. "Go," he told Pompey's emissary, "and tell Pompey that Cato cannot be conquered through the women's quarters." He added that as long as Pompey behaved honorably, Cato could promise him a friendship stronger than any marriage tie.

The senate gave Pompey permission to delay his third triumph for 20 months so it would coincide with his forty-fifth birthday. Meantime, every day brought reminders that while he had been abroad, power in Rome had shifted drastically. Pompey's role in repealing Sulla's legislation when he was consul had seemed daring, but the past decade had brought even greater gains to the popular movement.

XIX

POMPEIA

62 B.C.

To his dismay, Caesar found himself embroiled in a new sexual scandal. His praetorship had been unrolling smoothly, but he was threatened once again with becoming the butt of Rome's ridicule.

Because the latest Bona Dea ritual was being held at his house, Caesar had been banished for the night while his mother and wife served as hostesses to the Vestals and Rome's other noble women. The proceedings were strictly guarded, but Roman men guessed at what went on when their wives and sisters were left unobserved, and each man's conclusions reflected the fervor of his imagination. Trusting husbands saw the evening as nothing more than a tribute to the mother of Bacchus. Adopting a Greek ritual, Roman women covered the floor with branches while they performed their ceremony; in earlier times, it had involved sacrificing a pregnant sow.

The fantasies of other men were less chaste. They remem-

The Temple of Vesta. Art Resource.

bered that 120 years earlier the senate had banned men from the Bacchanalia because the night had become a flagrant orgy. And reports suggested that those days were not entirely past. The hostess apparently served wine, which was called "milk." Music played continuously while the women faced many nighttime hours alone. Men traded stories of women in whirling abandon as they howled songs of pent-up lust to the goddess of fertility. In the most ribald versions, women tore off their gowns and ground their hips against each other, desperate for release.

Only the women knew which version was true, but one man was determined to find out. Clodius Pulcher had already been involved in many scrapes, but so far his family connections had smoothed them over. He had prosecuted Catiline for adultery with a Vestal and had raised a mutiny against Lucullus. In his second prosecution of Catiline, Clodius had accepted a bribe to lose the case. Cicero had never taken him seriously and called him "Pretty Boy," punning on his name, Pulcher.

Clodius had been born to the arrogant Claudian family that had given Rome the Appian Way, but he had thrown in his lot with the popular movement. He wanted to be adopted into a plebeian family so that he could become one of the people's tribunes.

His sister Clodia matched him in wildness. She had married well—first Lucullus, then Metellus Celer—but Lucullus claimed that she and Clodius had indulged in incestuous sex. Around the Forum, men called her Quadrantaria because she went regularly to the public baths, and a quadrans was the small coin of admittance. Rome's women saw a more obvious significance to the nickname.

Cicero detested Clodia. Or at least he had to condemn her loudly at home because Terentia was jealous of the young woman. Clodia was as free with her body as Cicero was parsimonious with his, and yet mischievous rumors about the two of them persisted. A bold young poet, Valerius Catullus, was ensnared in Clodia's net. He had translated Sappho from the Greek, and he addressed his love poems to Clodia as "Lesbia." Capricious and fickle, she tormented Catullus with her faithlessness.

"Odi et amo," he began a two-line verse:

> I hate her and I love her. Don't ask me why.
> It's the way I feel, that's all, and it hurts.

Clodius at 30 had retained his appealing youthful looks, and his beard was light. On the night of the ceremony, he put on women's clothes and waited for darkness. Romans lived by daylight, their days beginning with cock's crow and ending with the evening star. It was *concubium*—bedtime—before Clodius could set out for Caesar's house.

Had more than his curiosity brought him? Pompeia was a neglected wife with a vigilant mother-in-law. If Clodius had begun a flirtation with her, what more daring adventure than to possess her on the most unlikely night in the chief priest's own house?

From the time Clodius stepped inside, accounts about his behavior depended on who was telling the story:

One of Pompeia's maids, in on the plot, had hurried to tell her mistress.

No, that wasn't right. Clodius had only crept about in a darkened room until one of Aurelia's attendants approached him. She thought he was a girl and invited him to join the ritual.

No, that wasn't it, either. She had asked Clodius to play with her, whatever that might mean.

Several rumors agreed that when Clodius spoke, his voice betrayed him and the maid had run to her mistress. Aurelia was as alert to the damaging effects of scandal as her son. She located Clodius and tried to let him escape undetected.

Or was that wrong? Didn't the virtuous matron instantly organize a search that found the intruder and expelled him?

Perhaps so. But hadn't the outraged women torn his disguise to shreds?

Whatever happened, the ceremony had been hopelessly defiled. Each woman returned home to regale her husband with the night's excitement. The next day Cicero reported to Atticus, "The affair is causing an immense scandal." The Vestal Virgins scheduled another night to perform the rites properly, but their piety couldn't stanch the gossip.

Caesar had a choice. He could follow the example of Cipius, whose name had become a Roman joke. Cipius' wife often strayed from their bed and, to salvage a little of his honor, he pretended to be asleep whenever she slipped away. One night, a slave saw Cipius' eyes close and moved to steal a cup. Bolting up in bed, Cipius announced, "I do not sleep for everybody!"

With Pompeia, Caesar had reasons—including a profound

lack of interest—to feign sleep now. But he couldn't allow gossip to besmirch his dignity, and he sent Pompeia a letter of divorce.

What had begun as Clodius' romp had turned deadly serious. For the remaining months of Caesar's praetorship and some time afterward, the senate's patricians demanded that Clodius be brought before a special court on charges of sacrilege. Hoping to avoid bribery and intimidation, the senators appointed jurors instead of drawing them by lot. They wanted Clodius convicted.

Clodius had demonstrated his political flexibility by serving as one of Cicero's bodyguards in the Catiline affair. Now he expected Cicero to return the favor. He wanted him to swear that Clodius couldn't have infiltrated the Bona Dea ceremony because he had been traveling outside of Rome. But when Cicero was called as a witness, he testified that on the morning of the ceremony Clodius had come to his house for legal advice.

Clodius struck back by mocking Cicero's rhetorical device in his four orations against Catiline. Then, Cicero had begun many sentences, "I have discovered . . ." Now, playing to Catiline's former faction, Clodius repeated, "I have discovered . . ." until he succeeded in making Cicero a laughingstock. Even Caesar joined in. He was determined to maintain his ties to Clodius and his young cronies, and when he testified, he said that in the Bona Dea affair, he had "discovered nothing."

Unruly factions on both sides were keeping passions inflamed. The senate had to send armed guards to protect the jury while deliberating, since a vote to convict Clodius would expose the jurors to violence from the people and acquitting him could mean reprisals by the patricians. Each juror disguised his handwriting as he handed in his verdict.

When the vote was announced, 31 jurors, a majority, found Clodius innocent. The verdict had cost him 300,000 or 400,000 sesterces for each juror who acquitted him.

When Caesar was asked why he had divorced Pompeia since he had found no evidence against her, his reply was pompous, hypocritical and imperishable. Caesar's wife, he said, must be above suspicion.

XX

CAESAR

61–59 B.C.

Caesar had done what he could to separate himself from the Bona Dea scandal, and the end of his term as praetor gave him an excuse to leave Rome while Clodius' trial was still wearing on. As his province, Caesar had drawn Farther Spain, where he had served as quaestor eight years earlier. He planned to spend the year among friends and return solvent. But shortsighted creditors were hounding Caesar to pay his mountain of debts and vowing to keep him in Rome until he did.

His obligations would have sunk a less resourceful man. Caesar joked that he needed 25 million sesterces simply to have no money at all. But he could afford to be blithe: Crassus had personally guaranteed 80 percent of his debts, and Caesar was free to depart.

Given a choice, Romans preferred to travel overland than by sea, and Caesar chose to reach Spain by crossing the Alps. One story that filtered back to Rome told of his party passing through a wretched village of a few tumbledown shacks. Caesar's companions, fresh from the intrigues in Rome, laughed about the desolate spot. "No doubt," one said, "even these people are pushing for rank and position. Here, too, there are jealous rivals among the local great men, and struggles to get to first place."

If Caesar's reply had an ironic edge, it was lost by the time the anecdote reached Rome. "As far as I am concerned," Caesar was quoted as saying, "I would rather be the first man here than the second in Rome."

When Pompey's third triumph finally opened on September 28, its excesses were more than Rome could accommodate. His lieutenants had collected so many prisoners, so much treasure, so many partisans waving placards that at the end of an unprecedented second day, one-third of the march still remained outside the city gates and had to be disbanded. Pompey boasted that each of his three triumphs had represented a different continent—first Africa, then Europe after the defeat of Sertorius, now Asia. Banners proclaimed the 14 different Asian nations he had conquered—among them Pontus, Armenia, Mesopotamia and Judaea—and the 800 pirate ships he had captured or sunk. The statistics alone were intended to awe the opposition into silence: Pompey had taken nearly 900 cities and founded another 39. Taxes from the new territory would nearly triple Rome's revenue. In gold and silver coins, Pompey was delivering to the city 20,000 talents, each talent worth 24,000 sesterces. That gift was in addition to the spoils he had already distributed among his soldiers. His lowest-ranking man had received 6,000 sesterces.

The triumph included noble hostages and prisoners from each vanquished nation. Pompey had decided against marching them through the Forum in demeaning chains. Their high rank—and his glory in capturing them—was better shown by displaying them in their dazzling robes. Five children of Mithridates were on parade, and Aristobulus, once king of the Jews, marched along with hundreds of other Jews captured at the temple in Jerusalem.

Paintings and sculpture rolled down the Via Sacra, depicting Pompey's great battles. One statue of Mithridates was more than twice life size and made of solid gold. In its wake came two silver statues of the king, along with his actual scepter and throne. The booty included astonishing treasures—cups and bowls of murrine, for example, an agate that Romans had never seen. A portrait of Pompey composed entirely of pearls showed a curl sweeping down his forehead. But nothing could compare with the largest trophy, a giant float representing all of the inhabited world that now belonged to Rome.

Pompey had refused to add more surnames taken from the nations he had conquered. "Magnus" stood better alone. But he didn't correct anyone who hailed him as being the same age as Alexander when he conquered the world at 33; on the triumph's second day, Pompey had turned 45. He appeared in a chariot pulled by four white horses, and he wore a cloak he claimed once belonged to Alexander. It had somehow survived intact for nearly 300 years.

Sinking pirate ships, Pompey had spared the crews' lives. Now as the procession ended, he sent home all the commoners he had taken prisoner but kept their kings in Rome, as a safeguard against future insurrections. Aristobulus was the only monarch taken to the prison.

The patricians were indulging Pompey's ostentation, but his conciliatory words hadn't won them over. He could lead a grand parade, plan to build the largest theater Rome had ever seen and still lack the influence to provide for his veterans. Despite Cicero's irritating vanity, he had begun to seem indispensable to Pompey. Cicero was gratified by Pompey's advances but no longer flattered by them. He confided to Atticus: "Your friend—you know whom I mean, the man who, you say, began to praise me as soon as he feared to blame me—is now parading his affection for me openly and ostentatiously. But in his heart of hearts he is envious, and he does not disguise it very well."

Younger popular leaders hoped to cause a rift between the two by taunting Pompey as "Gnaeus Cicero." Pompey ignored their gibes. Clodius, however, hadn't forgiven Cicero for his betrayal in the Bona Dea trial, and his attacks were growing more intemperate. But with Pompey at his side, Cicero saw no reason to fear. He even enjoyed the thrust and parry in the senate, confident that his wit would crush his opponents.

When Clodius said that the judges in his trial had not believed Cicero under oath, Cicero shot back: "Twenty-five of them gave me credit. The other thirty-one wouldn't give credit to you. They made you pay your money beforehand."

Two years after his return, Pompey was still finding it impossible to get senate approval for his soldiers' bonuses. Metellus Celer was one of the year's consuls and had family reasons for opposing Pompey. To elect a friendly co-consul had cost Pompey extensive bribes, and then he found out that the man had no influence with the patricians. Turning to the people, Pompey got a tribune named Flavius to introduce yet another farm bill to provide land for his men.

This time Lucullus joined the opposition; he was still incensed about being shouldered aside in Asia. Pompey insisted that the benefits for his troops be approved as one package. Lucullus demanded an item-by-item accounting. And when Celer's opposition became strident, Flavius invoked his powers as tribune to have him arrested. He had thought he was acting in Pompey's interest, but he had embarrassed the general. Pompey ordered Celer freed and let the farm bill die once again.

Cicero was relieved to see the latest threat to the aristocrats fail. "As you know," he reminded Atticus, "the strength of our party rests in the rich landed gentry." And Cicero was smugly sure that "the dislike that had been aroused against me among our dissipated and dandified youth has been smoothed away by my affability."

Caesar hadn't been in Spain long before a surprising reversal of roles took place. Pompey was now the politician in Rome—and not proving very adept—while Caesar was emerging as a gifted commander. His uncle Marius had once held this same governorship, and Caesar came to Spain primed for action. Although there was no apparent threat in the province, Caesar was determined to provoke enough fighting to establish a military reputation.

For years, Romans had ignored a persistent resistance in the north of Spain. Caesar targeted those tribes even though they had remained Marius' last remnant of support against Sulla. At Gades, he took over a Roman force of 10,000 men and quickly raised another 5,000. Then he sent a warning to the two northern tribes: they must settle down as farmers and stop rushing from the mountains to plunder towns on the plains.

When the tribes rejected his demand, Caesar marched his troops to the plains south of the Tagus River. He had picked no easy foe. The tribes slept on the ground and lived off acorns and goat meat, and rather than take slaves they stoned their prisoners to death. Caesar tried to demoralize them by launching a rumor that his miraculous horse had hooves that separated into toes. But Caesar's victory came from Roman training and tactics, not from his propaganda.

With a fleet from Gades, Caesar next chased a band of pirates to their island base, attacked tribes at Brigantium and conquered the last holdouts. Along the route, he collected enough gold and valuables to pay off his debts. It was also legal for his Roman and Spanish troops to share in the booty so long as they took their reward before the money was assigned to Rome's treasury. Impressed with his military acumen, legionaries began saluting Caesar with their highest tribute. "Imperator!" they shouted. With each victory, Caesar had staked his claim for a triumph that his enemies would find hard to refuse.

Caesar strengthened the province's loyalty by persuading the Roman senate to cut the punishing taxes on towns that had backed Sertorius. As his adjutant, Caesar named Cornelius Balbus, the wealthy merchant Pompey had already made a Roman citizen. Together they traveled the province, redressing wrongs, rewriting laws and building up reserves of good will for Caesar. When they reduced debts, they did it modestly enough not to antagonize Rome's bankers.

Caesar had hurried to his Spanish governorship before the senate could officially confirm him. Now, after less than a year, he rushed away from Gades before his replacement had arrived. Caesar wanted to ride the crest of his recent victories to become next year's consul.

When he reached Rome in early June of his fortieth year, Caesar found that his haste had been pointless. Three years earlier, senators had voted to protect themselves against ambitious generals by resurrecting a rule that candidates for consul had to come to Rome in person. The regulation caught Caesar in a bind since a far older restriction forced a returning governor to yield his command as he crossed the sacred circle of the Pomoerium. The election date had already been set, and there was no time beforehand for Caesar's triumph. He had to choose between running for consul and riding down the Via Sacra.

He wanted to do both, and when he asked the senators to waive the more recent rule, most were willing to let Caesar remain outside the walls and yet offer his name for consul. Only Cato protested. Cicero was annoyed by Cato's objections since he himself had already backed Caesar's request. By giving way on these minor points, Cicero believed that he was serving the aristocrats more effectively. He hoped to make Caesar what he termed "a better citizen," and Cato was jeopardizing that strategy.

In the senate, Cato spoke and spoke until night fell and the debate was adjourned. His delaying tactic forced the decision back to Caesar, who didn't hesitate. He sacrificed his triumph and crossed the Pomoerium. Voters would know that he had earned his parade, that it had been denied him by a few patricians, and then on a technicality.

Caesar had struggled out of debt into prosperity, but he didn't have a fortune like Crassus' for his campaign, or a reputation like Cicero's. To win the consulship, he went to a wealthier candidate and suggested they combine forces. Caesar's enemies heard of the deal and pledged to raise sufficient bribes to elect one of their own. They chose Bibulus, who had already served his anonymous aedileship with Caesar. Cato, married to Bibulus' daughter, readily set aside his scruples and consented to the bribery. Corruption was excusable, Cato explained, when it was the only way to preserve the constitution.

By tending to Pompey's interests diligently while he was fighting in Asia, Caesar had remained on cordial terms with the general. Now Caesar was working to reconcile Pompey with Crassus. Meantime, Crassus was moving closer to Cicero in the senate, playing on his vanity with a chorus of praise. He had also lent Cicero money on very advantageous terms for his new house. In the election, Caesar drew support from every faction except Cato's adamant conservatives. He was elected consul easily, although Bibulus defeated Caesar's candidate for the second spot. It hardly mattered. Caesar didn't intend to let another man share his fame.

Caesar's inaugural address was low-keyed and reassuring. Four years earlier, Cicero had pledged to be consul for the plebeians. Caesar promised hostile senators that he would propose nothing for the people that wouldn't also benefit the patricians.

As the consul elected first, Caesar announced ceremonial courtesies that he was extending to Bibulus. He also decreed that the senate's daily actions be posted throughout the city, along with a listing of public events. Those minutes would be sent by messenger to officials and citizens of Rome throughout the provinces. Caesar was making the senate's deliberations known to the world.

After that lulling preamble, Caesar delivered the less welcome news that he'd be pressing again for land reform. But he would not take his law to the people unless the senate had already approved it. Caesar's new legislation borrowed from both Rullus' bill and Pompey's recent measures—giving Pompey's veterans bonuses of land and resettling Rome's poor and unemployed on farms. He would recommend meting out almost all of Italy's public land and allowing Sulla's bankrupt veterans to get out of debt by selling their land back to Rome. Caesar's plan called for a board of 20 overseers; he specified that he would not be one of them. In closing, Caesar said he would welcome the senate's amendments.

To launch the debate, Caesar called first on Crassus, then on Pompey, by inches drawing the old enemies closer. He hoped to entice Cicero into the same loose partnership—four men working behind the scenes to manipulate the senate. But Cicero would be hard to recruit. Although he might rail privately against an indolent or selfish senator, he wasn't inclined to blame the patricians for Rome's troubles. Cicero was convinced that the street theater of recent years—roving gangs that jeered, threatened and threw rocks and filth from the gutters—had paralyzed the city and interfered with his attempts to restore harmony. Cicero's ideal of harmony envisioned the senate firmly in control, the prosperous businessmen tending to their investments and Rome's freedmen and slaves leaving politics to the philosophers who understood it.

Cicero outlined his options to Atticus: He could resist the new farm bill; that would mean a senate fight but also renewed prestige among the only men he cared to impress. Or he could keep silent, which would be like being banished from Rome. Or he could support the measure and accept Caesar's offer of a share in power that would be covert but very real. "Balbus assured me that Caesar will take my own and Pompey's opinion on everything," Cicero told Atticus, "and that he will make an effort to reconcile Pompey and Crassus."

Cicero had asked to reserve his decision. He had never cared much for Caesar, but he acknowledged Caesar's hold over masses of men he himself could not reach. Troublemakers were trying to grind Cicero's achievements to dust, and Caesar could stop them. But echoing in his ears, Cicero heard lines of poetry that urged him to do his duty, and those lofty sentiments kept coming back again and again. With a trace of embarrassment, Cicero confessed to Atticus that he recognized the source of the inspiring verses: they came from a poem he himself had written as a young man.

Not many senators had been won over by Caesar's show of moderation, but they worried that his affable manner and the cleverly drawn land bill had gained him wide support. Opposing the measure could be dangerous. Lucullus was against it; but it was hard to imagine any bill favored by Pompey that he would support. Like the others, however, Lucullus kept quiet. Only Cato took a loud, unwavering stand. He defended Rome's existing distribution of power and vowed never to permit any dangerous changes. He tried again to defeat the bill through sheer endurance, intending to go on speaking until its supporters lost heart. But that was the tactic that had cheated Caesar of his triumph, and he wouldn't let it succeed a second time.

From his consul's chair, Caesar told Cato to keep quiet. Cato ignored him and went on talking. At that, Caesar ordered a guard to take Cato to jail. It was an uncharacteristic show of temper, and Caesar soon regretted it. Seeing their spokesman taken away, the patricians agreed that they had been right in doubting Caesar's promises. As they rose and followed Cato out, even a praetor loyal to Pompey joined them. Caesar asked where he was going.

"I prefer to be with Cato in prison, Caesar," the man answered, "than to be here with you."

Caesar ordered Cato released, with a warning to the aristocrats that he had given them their chance. Now he would take his farm bill to the people. Caesar stalked out to speak to the assembly, Bibulus trailing after him. Before a crowd of Romans, Caesar demanded that Bibulus state his objections to the bill publicly.

Bibulus made a sweeping reply. He would tolerate no innovations at all during his year in office, he said.

Caesar urged the audience to join him in changing Bibulus'

mind. "You can have this law," Caesar told the crowd, "only if he wishes it."

Above the roar, Bibulus shouted, "You shall not have this law this year, even if all of you wish it!"

He left the rostra amid booing and jeers. Caesar turned to two men who held no official position. His efforts to reconcile Crassus and Pompey had been successful, and Romans were impressed to see them united in support of Caesar's bill. Pompey spoke on behalf of his soldiers and other veterans of past wars who had been denied their rewards when Rome was poor. "But, at present," he said, "since Rome has become exceedingly rich through my efforts, it is only right that the promise made to the soldiers be fulfilled."

Caesar's sense of drama prompted him to ask whether Pompey's speech meant he would fight the men opposing the measure.

Caught up in the moment, Pompey spoke again, long and ponderously but ending with an oath that undercut his standing with the senate's conservatives. "If anyone dares to raise a sword," Pompey swore boldly, "I too will snatch up my sword! And my shield!"

Crassus joined in the tumultuous applause.

Over the next days, Bibulus persuaded three tribunes to denounce the land bill, but Caesar was proceeding inexorably toward its passage. Bibulus next proclaimed the entire remainder of the year to be a holy period. Normally that would have prevented the assembly from meeting, but Caesar ignored the decree and set the date for the land bill to become law.

By now, the city was in turmoil. The night before the scheduled announcement, Romans camped out in the Forum for a chance to hear Caesar thwart the patricians and proclaim a law that would improve their lives.

But Bibulus resembled Cato in physical courage. At dawn, he rounded up his followers and the friendly tribunes. At the Forum, they elbowed their way to the steps of the Temple of Castor, where Caesar had already begun to speak. Bibulus climbed to a stair above him and tried to drown him out. At that, Caesar's men rushed Bibulus, pushed him down the steps and broke his lictors' ceremonial *fasces*. The tribunes hostile to Caesar were scratched and punched. As Bibulus and the others were fighting to escape, Caesar polled the assembly and announced that the bill had passed.

The next day, Bibulus appeared in the senate to demand that Caesar be censured. The senators had heard blood in yesterday's cries and were afraid to rebuke the man who played a mob so masterfully. Denied his revenge, Bibulus went home and didn't emerge for the rest of the year. He justified his retreat by issuing occasional announcements about unfavorable omens in the sky. In all other years, Romans had dated their documents with the name of their two consuls. But instead of "During the consulship of Caesar and Bibulus," a parody was circulating that began, "During the consulship of Julius and Caesar."

Cato, Metellus Celer and a third senator announced that they would not take the oath to uphold the new farm law. But when the deadline came and disobedience would have cost them a fine, they backed down. Caesar appointed the 20 commissioners to administer the law and kept his word not to name himself. He did include his brother-in-law, however, and Pompey and Crassus.

XXI

CICERO

59 B.C.

The agreement that Caesar had cobbled together between Pompey and Crassus involved no far-reaching program. Men who learned later about their pact called it a triumvirate, which suggested a formal treaty for governing Rome. But Caesar, Pompey and Crassus had simply made one solemn promise: if any of the three opposed a piece of legislation, the other two would join in blocking it.

Caesar's strategy showed his growing impatience with traditional Roman politics. Dictators had been openly chosen in the past, but their terms had been limited. Caesar's secret attempt to rule the senate could last as long as he kept his two partners in harness. It suited Caesar if Pompey imagined himself first among equals since Crassus was merely rich and Caesar was junior in prestige. Yet Caesar was this year's consul, and to expand his powers he pulled one praetor into his orbit and enlisted a tribune

The twins Romulus and Remus suckled by the wolf, on a Roman coin. The New York Public Library Picture Collection.

148

named Vatinius. But that took cash. Vatinius' price for carrying out orders came so high that Caesar complained afterward, "Vatinius did nothing gratis."

From that hidden strength, Caesar could address other items on the popular agenda. He revived a plan to relieve the debts of tax collectors in Asia, the cause dear to Crassus and frustrated by Cato. Cutting their obligations by one-third, Caesar warned them to make their bids for state contracts more realistic in the future. Caesar had first withheld distributing the fertile public territories in Campania and the Stellas plains. Now he had them partitioned into farms and, rather than assigning them by lot, awarded them to men with three or more children.

When a request could be granted easily, Caesar was obliging, although he remained alert to the stirrings among his opponents. Cicero had dealt himself out of Caesar's game, but he counted on Pompey's patronage and his own reputation to protect him from Clodius. All the same, Cicero thought it might be time to pay a visit to Alexandria. "And also to get away from here," he told Atticus candidly, "where people are sick of seeing me, and then return when they're missing me a little."

Cicero misread the city's mood. He believed he had been lying low, when in fact he had made himself a highly visible target. Defending his former co-consul against charges of misconduct, Cicero once again deplored the woeful conditions in Rome. "*O tempora, o mores*" had been effective before, but this time Caesar was consul and took Cicero's complaint as a personal affront. His revenge was quick and cunning.

Cicero spoke in the morning. By noon, his lament had been reported to Caesar. Three hours later, Caesar had decided on Cicero's punishment: Clodius Pulcher was granted the wish he had been denied for months, to be adopted by a plebeian family. Clodius had chosen a 20-year-old plebeian as his new father, and the young man had agreed to release him immediately so Clodius wouldn't have to change his name.

Clodius' scheme was a blatant evasion of the law, and Caesar as consul had been withholding his consent. Clodius had been a useful tool, but undependable and a potential rival. When Cicero's speech tipped the balance, Caesar had cleared the way for Clodius to become a people's tribune.

∎

Crassus was a solid ally, but Pompey required Caesar's constant attention. From the day he returned from Asia, Pompey's mild behavior had proved his devotion to the Republic, and he seemed to regard the rebuffs and outright contempt from conservative senators as the price of winning their approval. For now, however, he looked on silently as Caesar usurped the senate's powers. Cicero was indignant at how deftly it was being done.

"If the senate's power was hateful," he asked Atticus in the middle of April, "what do you think the situation will be now that power has been concentrated in the hands of three unfettered individuals?"

Cicero wondered what Pompey—whom he mocked as "the Pasha"—would do when he realized that Romans blamed him for Caesar's excesses. Romans cherished the balanced government that had preserved their freedoms, and not only the patricians resented the way one consul was ruling alone. Bibulus might be a laughingstock, but Caesar's reforms were decidedly high-handed. Bibulus tried striking back with powerless jabs. Reviving memories of Bithynia, he said, "Pompey is the king of Rome, and Caesar is his queen." And then: "Caesar was once in love with a king but now he is in love with kingship."

Cato would have shrugged off popularity if it had been thrust upon him, and that temperament stopped him from building an effective opposition to Caesar. Curio, a young patrician who was one of Cicero's protégés, took up the cause, repeating the stream of abuse against Caesar. Cicero was delighted when Curio was cheered in the Forum each day, while a praetor friendly to Caesar was hissed. And at the games for Apollo, Caesar had been greeted tepidly.

Caesar countered his declining public support by seeking closer ties to Pompey. Several days before Caesar's daughter was to marry a young Roman, Caesar bestowed her on Pompey instead. Pompey was 47, Julia less than half his age. Caesar neatly tied up the loose ends by offering Julia's former fiancé to Pompey's daughter, whose second husband had just died.

Julia had been raised by a father who paid in charm what he couldn't always afford in money, and she had inherited his agreeable ways. In Pompey, nature had produced a man destined to be a husband. Caesar had brokered a happy marriage.

Next, Caesar had to pick his and Bibulus' replacements as

consul. For one candidate, he turned to Gabinius, who had won Pompey the command against the pirates. Caesar's other choice, Lucius Calpurnius Piso, had a young daughter, Calpurnia. Caesar wasn't so uxorious as Pompey, but more than two years had passed since he divorced Pompeia, and Caesar knew he, too, should have a wife.

For years Cato's half-sister Servilia had offered Caesar a comfortable retreat. But with her son, Marcus Brutus, already in his mid-twenties, Servilia wouldn't be providing Caesar with an heir. Parting from her, Caesar gave Servilia a huge pearl said to have cost 6 million sesterces—a year's rent for 3,000 Roman tenants. Having provided Servilia with tangible evidence of his gratitude, Caesar married Calpurnia.

XXII

CAESAR

59 B.C.

Caesar had been prevented from exploiting Egypt, but recent events in that exotic land had enriched him in other ways. Ptolemy the Flute Player was paying immense bribes to get Rome to recognize him and his heirs, including his daughter Cleopatra, now 10 years old. Rumors had Ptolemy giving Caesar and Pompey each about 36 million sesterces for their help. The bribe represented Egypt's entire revenues for at least six months, and Ptolemy had to borrow it from a Roman moneylender. For the money, Caesar publicly endorsed the Flute Player as "the friend and ally of the Roman people."

Looking ahead to the end of his consulship, Caesar needed an option to keep him safe. His enemies were waiting to charge him with acting illegally during his term, and his best protection would be the command of a powerful province. But instead the senate allotted him minor administrative duties that were not only insulting but would keep him in Italy. Caesar was unwilling to be trapped that way and cast a shrewd eye around the world for the most promising province. The answer seemed to be Gaul. But the current governor claimed he had subdued any danger there.

In May, with his consulship not yet half over, Caesar sent Vatinius, his paid tribune, to the people with a measure giving Caesar immediate command of Cisalpine Gaul, the province closest to Italy, along with a coastal strip east of the Adriatic. Vatinius also proposed giving Caesar three legions and the funds to maintain them. To Caesar, the most appealing feature was the length of the command in Gaul—almost five years. The senate had been reluctant to give Pompey three years to quell the pirates.

The grumbling after Caesar had been voted the governorship provoked him, and he lost his customary detachment. To a packed session, Caesar boasted that he had got what he wanted despite the patricians' concerted effort to keep him from it. He was ready, Caesar added, to use his new authority to "stomp on their heads."

A heckler tried to shame him by shouting that to crush this body of *men* would not be an easy feat for a *woman* to accomplish.

Caesar took the resurrecting of that old charge as a sign of their desperation. Smiling, he replied, "Why not? Semiramis was supreme in Syria"—citing the legendary Greek goddess who built Babylon. "And the Amazons once ruled over a large part of Asia."

A peculiar episode soon afterward caused his opponents to ask whether Caesar had more sinister plans for them. Vettius, an informant Caesar had once sent to jail, was out of prison and tried to enlist Curio, Cicero's protégé, in a plot to assassinate Pompey. Curio reported the overture to the authorities, and the senate ordered Vettius to appear, promising him immunity if he would name the other men in the plot. When Vettius tried to implicate Bibulus, his testimony was discredited. But the next day, Caesar took him to speak from the rostra. As Cicero noted sourly to Atticus, that was more exposure than Bibulus could hope for these days.

Caesar called on Vettius to repeat his charges to the people. This time, his list of conspirators included many new names. All were Caesar's enemies, including two who were strong candidates in the coming election. Vettius didn't cite Cicero but did implicate a young patrician engaged to Cicero's daughter. Vettius also left out a name that he had given to the senate earlier—

Marcus Brutus, Servilia's son. For Cicero, the omission was proof
that Caesar was the architect of a transparent revenge.

Catullus, the brash poet, captured the mood among the
aristocrats. Barely changing Vettius' name, he wrote, "Victius,
always full of shit and running off at the mouth."

Vettius convinced few listeners and was returned to prison
to await the trials at which he would be the prosecution's star
witness. Before those proceedings could begin, however, he was
found strangled in his cell. Caesar's detractors believed he had
given the order.

Cicero still considered himself safe in Pompey's friendship,
despite constant murmurings about Clodius' campaign against
him. And yet he confided to Atticus, "I am sick of life. The whole
world is out of joint."

Amid the sniping and physical threats by Clodius' hired gangs,
Rome's government lurched forward. Many senators were shun-
ning its sessions, and while their absence meant fewer opposition
voices, Caesar fretted over the scant turnout. One day he asked a
very old senator why his colleagues were staying away. The man
replied that the senators were afraid of Caesar's armed soldiers.

"Then why aren't you just as afraid? Why don't you stay at
home?"

"Because old age has deprived me of fear," the senator
said.

Caesar used the remainder of his term to reform laws for
the provinces and to provide for strict conduct of trials for officials
who abused their power. Making those revisions, he deferred
enough to the senate that even Cato didn't oppose him. As both
consul and governor of Gaul, Caesar extended Roman citizenship
there, the cause he had championed when he returned from Spain
eight years earlier. He also directed Vatinius to propose a law to
settle new colonists on farms in the Latin town of Comum. The
5,000 people who flocked there were not officially citizens, but
Caesar treated them as Romans—even the 500 who were Greek—
and they repaid him with unusual devotion.

Although he valued loyalty, Caesar was prepared to welcome opponents back into his favor. Growing up amid the blood-
thirsty excesses of Marius and Sulla, he understood that Romans
craved leadership that was firm but merciful. Pompey's humane

treatment of the pirates had been widely admired; Cicero's hasty executions were being increasingly criticized. But even though it was politically wise to be seen as kindhearted, there was a better explanation for Caesar's behavior. After two decades of converting his lovers into friends, Caesar had become convinced of his own appeal. He was sure that sooner or later any target of his attentions must succumb. Cicero, for example, had an erudition and acerbic wit that caused Caesar to indulge him, and he may have regretted unleashing Clodius. Certainly, he didn't want to alienate forever a politician of Cicero's reputation. When Caesar offered him a seat on the new agricultural commission, Cicero knew he should accept, although he went on stewing over what Rome's best people would think.

Bibulus had succeeded in delaying the consular elections until mid-October, but when they were held, Caesar approved the results. Gabinius and Piso, Caesar's father-in-law, were the winning candidates. Clodius was elected tribune. Taking office on December 10, Clodius immediately launched his own populist program by offering wheat free rather than at a subsidized low cost. He also called for an end to a hundred-year tradition that high-ranking officials could overrule a tribune's law by claiming to find ill omens on land or in the sky. Bibulus' frequent use of those omens—and the way Caesar ignored them—had already undercut their authority.

Clodius knew Cicero would resist several aspects of his program and proposed a deal: if Cicero did not speak against his legislation, Clodius would spare him punishment for the Catiline affair. Cicero agreed and dissuaded his allies from vetoing Clodius' laws. But the day they passed in early January, Cicero watched Clodius begin to turn the Temple of Castor into an armory. When Clodius had the steps torn down, Cicero was sure the temple was being turned into a fortress, ready to withstand a patrician siege.

Pompey hoped to avoid this possible unpleasantness by retreating to his villa in the Alban Hills to enjoy its gardens with his new bride. From time to time, he offered Cicero tepid assurances that Clodius meant him no harm.

Cicero was skeptical about Pompey's political acumen, but the reception he got in the Forum convinced him that Romans blamed Caesar and his cronies for the desperation and rage that had engulfed the city. "I myself—as I think, hope and imagine—am safeguarded by the staunchest support," Cicero assured Atticus. Caesar read the situation differently. He saw danger looming for Cicero and recommended that he protect himself by joining Caesar's staff in Gaul. Cicero declined.

The scope of Caesar's command was growing steadily. When the governor scheduled to go to Transalpine Gaul died unexpectedly, Pompey asked the senate to give Caesar that province as well. Pompey's secret alliance with Caesar and Crassus hadn't lessened his respect for the senate's authority, and he made the request to the senators rather than letting Vatinius present it directly to the people. Cato rose to protest that by giving Caesar so much power, the senate was hastening its own destruction. But the senators knew that if they didn't approve, the assembly would. They gave Caesar the rest of Gaul and another legion, extracting only the concession that this new governorship had to be approved every year.

Before Caesar could leave for Gaul, two newly elected praetors forced a debate over his behavior as consul by asking the senate to rule that all of his actions as consul had been unconstitutional. For a year, Caesar had joined with Vatinius in flouting the senate. Now he claimed piously that he would abide by its judgment on his term.

For three days, the debate allowed for the sort of give-and-take at which Caesar excelled. But despite his dexterity, the verdict could have gone against him, and he took the precaution of crossing the Pomoerium to assume the command that shielded him from prosecution.

Caesar camped near the city walls to learn the outcome of the intense political jockeying. As he waited, he circulated speeches against the two praetors who were his principal opponents. But Clodius was planning a far more ambitious attack against the patricians. First, he intended to silence Cicero, then Cato.

XXIII

CICERO

58 B.C.

When Clodius drafted legislation to exile any judge who executed a Roman citizen without a trial, it was a sham, a barely disguised attack against Cicero. There was no need for new legislation; the law already existed.

But then Cicero made a serious miscalculation. He could have ignored Clodius, or he could have cited the distinction between the law and what was permitted under the senate's ultimate decree. Instead, Cicero was so sure of his support that he challenged the issue. Wearing mourning clothes, he spoke publicly against Clodius' affront to his honor. At first, he found the backing he expected. Some aristocrats and businessmen turned out to defend the man who had served their interests, and crowds of young men also began appearing in mourning clothes.

A delegation called on Pompey to ask that he support Cicero, but Pompey dodged the request. None of this was really his

Portrait of a young man; perhaps a member of the Julio-Claudian family (perhaps Augustus). The Metropolitan Museum of Art, Rogers Fund, 1919.

157

business, he said. As a private citizen, he couldn't overrule a tribune. Let the delegation petition the consuls. He added that if the senate overruled Clodius and a riot broke out, his spear and shield would be on the senate's side.

Hearing of the rebuff, Cicero went to Pompey himself to appeal to their long friendship. But Pompey was too committed to Caesar to offer help, and he was too ashamed to tell Cicero so. As he slipped out a side door, Pompey's servants informed Cicero that the general was not at home.

Crassus and Caesar's handpicked consuls all declined to become involved. It appeared—and Clodius missed few opportunities to tell people—that his bill had been approved by all three members of the junta: Caesar, Pompey, Crassus.

Cicero found himself alone. During the past four years, he had reminded his countrymen that he was their most upright and selfless citizen, their savior, their father. But they had become deaf to his self-praise. Cicero could joke to Atticus that Romans were sick of him, because the idea was preposterous. But it turned out that they appreciated Cicero's accomplishments and still would welcome a respite from the sound of his voice.

Clodius called a meeting outside Rome's walls so that Caesar could attend. The consuls, Piso and Gabinius, reviewed Cicero's executions and stressed that they had dismayed men of compassion. Clodius asked Caesar to speak. With the surefootedness he had shown four years earlier in urging clemency, Caesar found a way to stand with both Clodius and Cicero. Yes, he had spoken out against executing the accused traitors. Yes, he had predicted this sort of reaction to the brutality. But no, he did not endorse a law that called for retroactive punishment.

Caesar's speech offered Cicero no comfort. Caesar had failed in his appeal for mercy four years ago, and he seemed content to fail again. As Cicero waited for the outcome, Clodius' gangs chased him through the city, mocking his funeral attire and throwing rocks and garbage at him. The senate now sided with Cicero, voting that the national emergency required all citizens to wear mourning. The consuls vetoed the idea. When Clodius surrounded the senate house with armed men, senators ran out, insulted and terrified, but the majority of Romans would not take up Cicero's defense. Piso, Caesar's father-in-law, spoke affably to Cicero: You saved the country once, he said. Now remove yourself until this row with Clodius has passed.

After Piso left, Cicero gathered his friends at his house. Only Lucullus thought he could prevail. The others saw an army of plebeians on the march against one unarmed former consul.

Since Cicero had no consuls among his ancestors, the statue in his hall that he most prized was a bust of Minerva. He carried it to the senate and left it with an inscription: "To Minerva, Guardian of Rome." That night, he stole away on foot from the city where his dreams had been fulfilled. Caesar stayed on a few days longer to watch Clodius' law take effect.

Cicero was pronounced an outlaw. He was to be denied both fire and water: no one within 500 miles of Italy was allowed to shelter him. Cicero's exile would be a vivid example for Caesar's other rivals. Now it was safe for him to leave for Gaul.

Clodius had driven Cicero from Rome just as Cicero had banished Catiline. Those who hated Cicero found it fitting and just. Cato, however, still sat in the senate, and for him Clodius devised another form of exile. Sending for him, Clodius praised him as the least corrupt man in Rome, and for that he was to be rewarded.

Ptolemy's extravagant bribes had enabled him to keep his throne in Alexandria, but his brother, another Ptolemy, was ruling over Cyprus. Clodius had private reasons to resent the Cypriots. Like Caesar, he had once been captured by pirates. He had appealed to the king of Cyprus for ransom, but the amount sent had been far less than the pirates demanded. In revenge, Clodius intended to annex Cyprus as a Roman province.

"Although many men have requested assignment to Cyprus to straighten out affairs with Ptolemy," Clodius told Cato, "I think you alone deserve it, and I desire to give you the favor of the appointment."

Cato sneered at the idea. That was no favor, he replied. That was an injury.

Clodius dropped his pretense. "If you will not take it as a kindness," he said, "you shall still go, however unwillingly."

Clodius persuaded the people to pass the necessary decree. They provided Cato with only two secretaries, one a known thief, the other Clodius' stooge. Although Cato was given neither a ship nor soldiers to accompany him, he was instructed not only to resolve the problem with the king of Cyprus but also to resettle any refugees that the war against Mithridates had displaced. Clodius thought those tasks should keep Cato far from Rome.

XXIV

CAESAR

58 B.C.

Caesar's victories in Spain had shown him to be a natural commander. He was now 43, more than twice Pompey's age when Pompey had first amazed Rome. But while Pompey had fought for Rome's glory and expected gratitude, Caesar's aim was to enhance his political power. In his lifetime, there had been five revolts against Rome in Transalpine Gaul, and reports from the north indicated new turmoil. But even if Gaul's tribes had been tranquil, Caesar would have found a way to provoke a confrontation.

The territory was inhabited by three distinct peoples. The Aquitani, of Spanish descent, occupied the land between the Pyrenees and the Garonne River. The Belgae controlled territory from the mouth of the Seine to the mouth of the Rhine and inland to the Marne and the Moselle. Caesar speculated that the Belgae, a tall and fair-haired tribe, had originally come west from Germany. The rest of the land—the interior plains to the Atlantic seaboard—was claimed by descendants of the Celts, whom the Romans called Gauls. Romans estimated Gaul's total population at

12 million, with 6 or 7 million in Transalpine Gaul, the rugged province northwest of Italy. They were split into 45 large tribes and perhaps 250 lesser ones.

Caesar got word that the Helvetians, a large Celtic tribe, had outgrown their land north of Lake Geneva and were heading west with a three-month grain supply, intending to settle near the Alps. Before they left, their leaders had burned every village to stop families from deserting and going back.

Romans in Transalpine Gaul estimated that at least 150,000 Helvetians were swarming toward them. By March 24, they would be assembling opposite Geneva, ready to cross the Rhône on the 28th. The only barrier was the Allobroges tribe, which seemed unlikely to interfere.

Rome would have to depend on its legions of infantry to repel the invaders. Each legion was divided into 10 cohorts of six units, called centuries because each was composed of 100 men. But legions seldom mustered their full strength of 6,000 men.

The army was always recruiting. To enlist, a potential legionary brought a letter of recommendation from a veteran in his family and, if accepted, was sworn in. The oath had scarcely changed from the Republic's earliest days: the first recruit in line promised to follow the consuls to whatever war Rome might be fighting, neither breaking the law nor deserting. The other men simply said, *"Idem in me"*—the same for me.

Basic training was arduous—days of running, jumping and, if the camp was near a river, swimming. A trainee learned that marching in step and rapidly was essential to his survival since enemy snipers picked off stragglers. He was expected to cover about three miles in an hour, with full gear. In earlier days, each man had provided his own armor, and only rich soldiers could afford a thick shield. Marius had started to provide legionaries with a helmet and shield, a sleeveless wool shirt, a leather tunic reinforced front and back with bands of metal, cloth strips to wind around legs and thighs, hobnailed shoes and a wool cloak for cold or rainy weather. Each man carried a javelin and short sword.

Soldiers wrapped their grain and hardtack, cooking pot, hatchet, saw and spade in a bundle to carry on a pole over their left shoulders. They joked that they were *muli Mariani*—Marius' mules—because of the 70 pounds of equipment they had to carry on their backs.

To build up their shoulders and arms, recruits drilled with a wicker shield twice as heavy as the one they would be issued. In place of a sword, they were given a massive wooden stave to flay against a six-foot stake in the ground. Sometimes they were told to aim for the height of a man's eyes, sometimes for his knees. Veterans considered those long hours at the stake the backbone of their instruction.

Young soldiers next moved to the *pilum,* much like a hunting spear, which they practiced throwing with force and accuracy. Marius had devised an ingenious way of fastening the head of the spear to its shaft so that it broke off and couldn't be hurled back. Caesar improved on the device until the *pilum* lodged in the enemy's shield so securely that he had to throw the shield down.

When the recruits had mastered those skills, they learned to vault onto a horse, although they usually had only wooden horses to practice on. Training was often lax since the cavalry by this time was a colorful but minor component of a commander's force. During a siege, he would dislodge an enemy with artillery, including the catapults that rained heavy stones against a hostile town.

The senate had voted Caesar four legions, but only the Tenth, Legio X, was available to halt the Helvetians. With auxiliaries, that gave him at most 4,000 soldiers. Forty thousand armed Gauls were moving toward Roman territory.

Their enemies usually underestimated the speed at which the Roman army could move, and Caesar was an energetic commander. Getting out to the countryside was proving a tonic. Military life was gradually transforming this tall, middle-aged man, who had never been robust. His pale skin was tan and tough, and exercise had burned off the rounded flesh from his cheekbones. Veins stood out on his forehead, and the bridge of his nose grew sharper. Above his severe jaw, Caesar's thin lips were framed by light lines of amusement.

Headaches had plagued him in the city. Now they lifted or became easier to ignore. In Córdoba, Caesar had once fallen to the ground in a seizure that seemed to be epilepsy. But in Gaul, the tremors did not recur despite the relentless pressures. As a boy, Caesar had learned to gallop his horse with his hands clasped behind his back. In Gaul, he no longer showed off, but he dictated letters to one secretary, sometimes two, as they raced beside him on horseback. Borne by litter or chariot, Caesar could catch snatches of sleep on the road as he pressed forward at speeds that became legendary. A good day's march was 50 miles. In the present crisis, Caesar covered 90. Within a single week, he had dashed from Rome to the banks of the Rhône.

Three days after he arrived in Geneva, Caesar ordered the bridge over the Rhône destroyed. The Romans' superior engineering gave them an enormous tactical advantage; commanders could demolish a bridge and then have it rebuilt almost immediately. On April 5, the Helvetians found their passage blocked and sent a delegation to Caesar.

The chieftains said they didn't want war, only safe passage to the western lands far beyond Rome's control. But they weren't aware of how they would serve Caesar's ambition. He stalled, claiming he needed time for consultation. He would issue his decision in eight days.

Caesar had already made up his mind: the Helvetians couldn't be trusted. In his father's time, they had defeated a Roman consul, killing and taking his soldiers prisoner. Caesar thought that now they would plunder every village they passed through. Or they might decide to settle as squatters on his province's fertile land. As the Helvetians waited, Caesar brought up new forces and put them to work. The Roman army had developed a formula for building forts. During a march, they built a complete temporary camp at the end of each day, throwing up walls and digging trenches, protecting the installation with heavy wooden stakes. One admiring Roman said that it was "as though they carried around with them a fortified city wherever they go."

Caesar wanted even greater security—a wall 16 feet high and a trench 17 miles long from Lake Geneva to the Jura mountain range that separated the Helvetians from a tribe called the Sequani. When the chiefs returned on April 13, Caesar gave them an ultimatum he couldn't have issued a week earlier. Roman custom made it impossible to permit them to march through the province, Caesar said. If they tried to force their way past, he would stop them.

The Helvetians withdrew to consider Caesar's threat. The only other passage to their destination was narrow and difficult and cut through Sequani territory, and their permission to pass might be harder to get than Caesar's. The Helvetians decided to defy him. Tying boats together to make rafts, some attempted to break through the Roman line by night as others waded across the Rhône at its shallow points. Caesar's men proved alert and drove them all back.

The chiefs' first appeals to the Sequani were refused, as they had feared. They sought out a friendly third party: Dumnorix, a prince of the Aedui. Although the Aedui and the Sequani had warred for years over which tribe should collect tolls from the river traffic on the Saône, Dumnorix was hearty and popular and was married to a Helvetian. His negotiations succeeded. The Sequani would let them pass, and as proof of their good will, they would exchange hostages.

Their accommodation annoyed Caesar. He had come to Gaul to fight. Even if the Helvetians stayed off Roman soil, a new settlement of warriors along Rome's border would expose him to criticism at home.

Caesar put his most competent aide, Titus Labienus, in charge of the fortified line along the Jura Mountains and rushed back to Cisalpine Gaul. He ordered two new legions enrolled from towns he knew to be loyal and called up three more from their winter camp in Aquileia.

Caesar marched the five legions back to Transalpine Gaul, fighting off mountain tribes as he took the shortest route over the Alps. Despite the speed with which he returned, the Helvetians had already slipped past the Roman line and were marching through Sequani territory. As Caesar reported to Rome, that confirmed his worst fears. They weren't proceeding directly to uninhabited land but were pillaging the towns of the Aedui tribes. Caesar claimed the Aedui chiefs had appealed for help. They had always been loyal. Now Rome must defend them. Their crops were being burned, their children taken as slaves, and Roman soldiers were standing by, doing nothing.

That was the provocation Caesar needed. Three-fourths of the Helvetians had already crossed the Saône by the time he reached its east bank. He waited for midnight and then led a surprise attack on those waiting for morning to transport the tribe's baggage across the river. The Romans killed many of the Helvetians and chased the rest, including women and children, into a nearby woods.

Caesar told his engineers to throw up pontoon bridges, and caught the Helvetians off guard. It had taken them three weeks to cross the river; Caesar cut the time to a single day. The Helvetians knew they had to try again to negotiate, but they made the mistake of sending Divico, the ancient chieftain who had once defeated the Roman consul.

Divico's plea began reasonably, but then he reminded Caesar of his past victory. In this latest battle, Divico said, Caesar had beaten only a small part of the tribe because the rest couldn't come to their aid. That minor success should not cause Caesar to exaggerate his capacity or underrate theirs. He added a challenge: don't let this place where we stand go down in history as the site of another disaster for the Romans.

Caesar's response was predictably cool: He had not forgotten the consul's defeat. In fact, since the Romans had been innocent, he resented their deaths bitterly. But even if he had been willing to forget the past, he could not forgive Divico's insolence.

Writing about this incident later, Caesar would recall saying, "When the gods wish to take vengeance on humans for their crimes, they usually grant them, for a time, considerable success and quite a long period of immunity, so that when their fortunes are reversed they will feel it more bitterly."

That said, Caesar offered mild terms. He would make peace if Divico paid reparations for the damages to the Aedui and other tribes and provide hostages as a guarantee.

Divico's pride hardened. The Helvetian tradition was to take hostages, he said, not give them, as the Roman people should remember. With that, he left.

The next day, the Helvetians moved camp, and Caesar sent his entire cavalry of 4,000 men after them. But the Romans rode too close behind, and the Helvetian rear guard turned on them. That quick success encouraged the Helvetians, and they tried to draw more Romans into battle. Caesar succeeded in holding back his troops as the two armies marched west for 15 days, never more than five or six miles apart.

It was late spring in central Gaul, but the crops had not ripened and Caesar was short of feed for his horses. Each day, he sent messages ordering the Aedui to send the grain they had promised in exchange for his protection. Each day, the Aedui put him off with poor excuses—the grain was being collected, it was being shipped, it was probably already there. Caesar allowed himself to be lulled until he realized that soon his men would be expecting their ration of grain and there would be none to harvest or purchase. He halted the pursuit of the Helvetians and swung north to meet with the Aedui chieftains.

Caesar saw no reason to approach them delicately. I'm here at your earnest request, he told them, and I resent the way you have let me down.

One chief confessed the truth. Conspirators in their ranks were spreading the idea that it was better for Gaul if Rome lost. They were arguing that since both the Helvetians and the Romans would go on taxing the Aedui, they should prefer being ruled by other Gauls. Caesar suspected that the rebel was Dumnorix, who wanted to be king of his tribe, while the Romans had backed his brother, Diviciacus. If the Helvetians won now, they would reward Dumnorix and his Helvetian wife.

Caesar wasn't sure how to proceed. If he punished Dumnorix, he might offend his brother, who was not only a friend to Rome but personally loyal to Caesar. Sending away the usual interpreters, Caesar called on a Roman who lived in the province to convey his decision: he warned Diviciacus that either the Aedui government must hear the case against Dumnorix or he would.

At that ultimatum, Diviciacus embraced Caesar and burst into tears. The charges were true, he said. While he had been building a reputation throughout Gaul, his resentful younger brother had stayed at home, causing trouble. But he begged Caesar to be merciful.

"If you deal harshly with my brother," the king said, "everyone will think it was my idea, since I am such a friend of yours. If that happens, the whole of Gaul would turn against me."

Caesar took the king's right hand and told him to stop his weeping. He held Diviciacus in such esteem, Caesar said, that he would control his own anger and overlook the crimes against Rome. Asking Diviciacus to stay, Caesar sent for Dumnorix and gave him a stern lecture: he was forgiving him only for the sake of his brother; Dumnorix must not do anything in the future to make Caesar suspicious. Afterward Caesar assigned men to watch Dumnorix day and night and report on his meetings.

Now Caesar turned back to the Helvetians. His scouts reported that they had stopped eight miles from the Roman camp.

Caesar sent the same scouts back after midnight to guide two legions led by Labienus. He told them to march to the ridge of a nearby hill while Caesar led the rest of his men, with cavalry at the front, along the route the Helvetians had taken. By dawn, Labienus should control the hill, with Caesar about a mile and a half away from the enemy camp. But a messenger misinformed Caesar about Labienus' progress. By the time he received better intelligence, the Helvetians had moved. Caesar followed, pitching his camp three miles from their new site.

Food remained a pressing concern. The deadline for distributing grain was only two days away. Caesar decided to march north 18 miles and enter the prosperous Aedui capital. The Helvetians interpreted his shift as weakness and raced to attack the Roman rear guard. Caesar covered a nearby hillside with soldiers and sent his baggage there. At the top, he placed his greenest recruits. Midway down the hill, he posted his four veteran legions, three lines deep, and set the cavalry apart to counter any attack.

Caesar had the officers' horses led away, his own horse first. He wanted his lieutenants to be as much at risk as the legionaries. "After I have won the battle," Caesar said, "a horse will be useful for the pursuit. But now, let us get the enemy."

By lining up in close ranks, the Helvetian infantry was able to drive back the Roman cavalry. They moved toward the hill and the Roman front line.

Caesar led the charge on foot. His troops had two advantages: hurling a javelin down from the high ground gave it a punishing force, and Caesar's breakaway javelins—with a killing range of 100 feet—were far superior to Helvetian spears. The Helvetians had no choice but to drop their shields and fight on unprotected.

The battle wore on through the afternoon. When the Helvetians began to withdraw to a hill a mile away, the victory seemed to be Caesar's. But he had left his right flank exposed, and two enemy units combined to surround the Romans there. From their hillside, the other Helvetians observed that promising development and swarmed back to battle. Caesar threw his men into a double front, the first and second lines against foes they thought they had already defeated, the third to counter the fresh forces.

Caesar had to admire his enemy's persistence. Evening fell

and not one Helvetian soldier had bolted. Even wives and children joined the battle, barricading their wagons with baggage to create a fortress that let them throw spears at Caesar's men. Others lay between the wagon wheels and thrust their weapons upward. From that angle, they could inflict serious injuries.

It took until midnight for the Romans to break through and take the enemy camp. Only one-third of the Helvetians had survived. Many of them fled, marching through the rest of that night and then three more days until they reached the territory of another Gallic tribe. Caesar knew the Helvetians' strength had been sapped. He stayed behind to treat the wounded and bury the dead, but he sent word to other tribes that giving food or other aid to the Helvetians would make them his enemy.

After three days, Caesar gathered his forces and resumed the chase. The break in fighting had convinced the Helvetians that their situation was hopeless, and they sent envoys who threw themselves at Caesar's feet and begged for a truce. Caesar demanded hostages, their weapons and any slaves who had left their Roman masters to fight with the Helvetians.

About 6,000 Helvetians slipped from their camp at night, hoping to reach the Rhine and ask for German protection. But the runaways were rounded up and returned to Caesar. Having affronted his dignity meant that they couldn't expect kindness. Escapees were killed or sold as slaves to the traders who followed behind the Roman army looking for merchandise.

To the rest of the Helvetians, Caesar dictated the same terms he had offered before their leaders had sacrificed more than two-thirds of their countrymen. Because Rome needed the Helvetians as a buffer against the Germans, they were to return east and rebuild the villages they had burned. A treaty would restore their relations with Rome. Since they had no food, Caesar ordered the Allobroges to give them grain.

Caesar wanted to keep his men at war, and luckily for him, the Aedui were unhappy with his settlement. A group of chiefs, with Diviciacus as their spokesman, met with Caesar in a secret session. A German chief, Ariovistus of the Suebi tribes from across the Rhine, had brought his people into Gaul and made a pact with the Sequani. Now both tribes were harassing the Aedui. Ariovistus had respected a recent treaty with Rome and had stayed neutral in the war with the Helvetians. But the farmland of Gaul was more tempting than that of Germany. His men were pouring into Sequani territory. Romans had long feared the Germans, and Caesar predicted that if he didn't block this immigration, they would keep crossing the Rhine into Gaul. Since Rome's treaties with the Aedui recognized them as blood brothers, Diviciacus' latest appeal was no mere pretext for Caesar. Rome's honor demanded action.

Caesar's experiences with the Helvetians had given him a script. He called for a parley at a point midway between his troops and the Germans, but Ariovistus refused to enter that zone without his army. If this rebuff was not clear enough, he also sent a message: "I cannot imagine what business either Caesar or the Romans as a whole, for that matter, can have in the part of Gaul that is mine because I won it in war."

Caesar sent back specific demands that would protect the Aedui and forbid more Germans from crossing the Rhine. Ariovistus replied that he would not return the Aeduan hostages he had extorted, but if they kept paying tribute to him, they could live in peace. If not, they would find that their prized title as "brothers of the Roman people" would do them little good.

Hearing that other Suebi clans were on the move, Caesar marched his army within range of Ariovistus. But his troops began to hear stories from Gauls who had already seen the Germans, and those accounts were destroying the Roman will to fight. Although recruiters tried to find tall men for Rome's army, they usually had to settle for men of five feet five or six who were physically strong. The Gauls reported that the Germans were huge—six or more inches taller and far huskier than any Roman. Their training was known to be remarkable, their courage unbelievable. Many Gauls said that they couldn't bear to face a German, with his bristling mustache and the fierce glare in his eye.

Caesar cajoled his men and tried to shame them, but the Romans stayed in their tents bewailing their fate. Or they came to Caesar with transparent excuses, asking to return to Rome. His officers warned Caesar that when he gave the order to move forward, the men would not obey. Caesar called a meeting of centurions and reproached them for presuming that questions of strategy were any of their business or that they had the right to decide which of his orders they would obey.

He reminded them of Rome's past successes—Marius

against other German tribes, the Roman army putting down the slave revolt. Remember, Caesar said, that Ariovistus' troops are the same men the Helvetians had defeated regularly on German soil, and you have just proved that the Helvetians are no match for you.

Caesar said that soldiers sometimes refused to follow a commander because he had bungled an operation or was guilty of a crime, or because his luck had run out. "My own integrity has been evident all my life," Caesar said, "and the sort of luck I have was clear in my campaign against the Helvetians." He announced that he would test his troops now by striking camp just before dawn, somewhat earlier than he had planned. He wanted to see "as soon as possible whether your shame and sense of duty are stronger than your fear."

Caesar knew how to make his challenge irresistible: "If no one else follows me, I shall still march, with just the Tenth Legion. I have no doubts at all about the men of the Tenth, and I shall make them my bodyguard."

When he ended, the commanders of the Tenth Legion thanked him for his confidence. Throughout the ranks, eagerness was replacing pessimism. Officers flocked to him with reassurances that they had never doubted him.

At dawn, Rome's army marched within 20 miles of Ariovistus, who agreed to a conference but was less than conciliatory.

"I was in Gaul before your people were, Caesar," Ariovistus said. "This part of the country has always been my province, and you have no right to object." He claimed to have guessed Caesar's motives: "I can only suspect that the friendship with the Aedui is a sham and your reason for keeping an army in Gaul is to crush me."

Then Ariovistus revealed that he monitored Roman politics as closely as Caesar.

"If I killed you," he said, "my action would please many of the nobles and leading citizens of Rome. I am sure of it, because their agents have told me that killing you would gain me their friendship and gratitude. But if you agree to leave and cede Gaul to me, I will reward you well. Any wars you want fought, I'll fight for you."

Caesar was midway through a lengthy and reasoned rebuttal when some of his men rode up to say that the Germans had drawn near and were throwing javelins at them. Caesar ordered them not to respond, and the conference quickly broke up. But the arrogance of the assault, combined with Ariovistus' defiance, had aroused Caesar's men and for several days he marched them out in battle formation. Each time, Ariovistus refused the challenge, and at last Caesar learned the reason. Wives in the German camp depended on prophecies to decide when their men should go into battle, and they were saying that the Germans would lose if they fought any time before the new moon on September 8.

The next day, Caesar forced a battle by marching directly toward the enemy camp. When the Germans appeared, Caesar's men raced forward too fast to use their javelins. They fought with swords. The Romans drove the Germans east for 15 miles, to the banks of the Rhine. Ariovistus was among the few who was rowed to safety. Only the stronger swimmers were able to get across. Caesar's cavalry rode down the rest, including two of Ariovistus' wives and one daughter. A second daughter was taken prisoner. Across the river, the Suebi who had been massing to enter Gaul turned around and started home.

For Caesar, it had been a good summer's work. He sent his troops to their winter quarters earlier than usual and set off for Cisalpine Gaul. Throughout the months of warfare, Caesar's dispatches to the senate had been hasty justifications of his decision to fight, followed by reports of each success. Now, as he returned to untangling administrative snarls and settling disputes in the province, he had time for a more considered record, guaranteeing that future historians would see the battles through his eyes.

Caesar's temperament stopped him from speaking of himself as "I," the word *ego*. He was more at ease in the third person as "Caesar," and that approach gave his memoir a judicious tone. Caesar wanted his language to be so simple, his logic so straightforward, that the poorest Roman would grasp the scope of his achievements.

"*Gallia,*" Caesar began, "*est omnis divisa in partes tres . . .*"

XXV

CICERO AND POMPEY

58 B.C.

While Caesar was adding to his reputation in Gaul, Cicero was moving east, clutching his tarnished glories. After he left Rome, Clodius had confiscated his goods and forbidden the senate and assembly from reopening his case. On the day Clodius posted the last ban on the senate's door, his followers burned down Cicero's mansion on the Palatine, ransacked his villa in Tuscany and dug up his trees to carry off. Clodius ordered a shrine to Liberty built on the site of Cicero's destroyed house on the Palatine.

Cicero's family was safe with Terentia's sister in the house of the Vestal Virgins, but by April, a month after he had fled, Cicero was still undecided about where to go. He appealed to Atticus to join him in exile. "I know the trip is a nuisance," Cicero wrote, "but this whole miserable business is full of annoyances. I can't write any more, I am so wretched."

Two days later, Cicero left the estate of a friend, to spare him Clodius' retribution. He wrote to Atticus again: "My life is one long misery, and I am crushed by the weight of my sorrows.

I don't know what to write." He asked Atticus to come with him as he headed for Brundisium and perhaps Macedonia. Athens might be more congenial, but too many of Catiline's supporters were there. Atticus disappointed Cicero by not traveling to his side, but he was sufficiently alarmed at the despair in Cicero's letters that he tried to raise his spirits.

"Your pleas that I should not think of suicide have had one result," Cicero replied. "I refrain from doing any violence to myself. But you cannot make me cease to regret my existence. What is there to live for?"

Another two months passed before Cicero chose Thessalonica as his destination. His brother was to join him but hadn't arrived yet from Rome, and Cicero was desperate for news. When Atticus wrote about an encouraging meeting with Pompey, Cicero wondered whether his friend wasn't merely trying to comfort him.

In Thessalonica, Cicero kept to himself and sank further into depression. Going over and over the events that had ruined his life, he concluded that he should never have left Rome. His flight now seemed to him cowardly and a confession of guilt. Those who had advised him to flee had been false friends, particularly his old rival Hortensius. Shouldn't Atticus have seen the trap and saved him from it?

"From these rambling notes of mine," Cicero upbraided his oldest friend obliquely, "you can see the perturbed state of my wits. Yet, though I have been crushed by an incredible and unparalleled misfortune, it is not so much my misery as remembering my own mistake that affects me. For now surely you see whose treachery goaded and betrayed me. Would to heaven you had seen it before and had not let a mistake take over your mind as I did."

Quintus came to Thessalonica, but Cicero now decided that his brother could be of more use in Rome and sent him back. He had another motive as well—the pride of an older brother fallen on bad times. "I will confess the truth, and it will show you the depth of my misery," he wrote Atticus. "I could not bear in my great distress to look upon one so devoted to me and so tender-hearted, nor could I thrust upon him the misery of my affliction and my fallen fortune, or allow him to see me."

Atticus continued to urge Cicero to try to keep his spirits up. The election for next year's consuls was approaching; perhaps the winners would be better disposed toward him. At least, he should hope for that. But from other sources Cicero was hearing that the political dialogue in Rome had passed him by. Romans were wrangling over a number of issues, but his fate was not among them.

Cicero had lost weight. Most days, he wept and wrote letters. Recounting his virtues, the habit that had turned Romans against him, now plunged him deeper into despair.

He asked Atticus, "Did anyone ever fall from such a high estate in such a good cause, especially when he was so endowed with genius and good sense, so popular and so strongly supported by all honest men? Can I forget what I was? Can I help feeling what I am?"

Cicero worried that Clodius might be reelected tribune, and he was distressed to hear that a letter had been published in which Cicero attacked Curio, now one of his staunchest supporters. Publicly, Cicero had never said a word against the man; the harsh words had come in a moment of anger. In his present straits, Cicero was not above deceit, and he wrote to Atticus, "It appears to me more careless than my other writing. I should think it could be passed off as someone else's work."

He would not make the mistake of attacking the one man on whom his last hopes rested. Yes, Pompey had been ungenerous, but Cicero's letters no longer included mocking references to Pompey's inflated reputation. There was no more "our 'great' Pompey" or "the Pasha" or "my pet, Pompey." If he wanted to see Rome again, only Pompey could engineer his return.

Pompey, however, seemed to be letting his own prestige slip away. Many had predicted he would stand for the consulship with Crassus, but although he was willing to work with Crassus behind the scenes, Pompey wasn't prepared to share official honors with him again. Another reason for his absence from public life was his happy marriage. The gossips were claiming that either Pompey couldn't bear being separated from Julia or her incessant need was keeping him at home. This marriage of convenience had become a passionate romance.

Pompey had once mocked his rival Lucullus for claiming he was too old for politics and retiring to a private life of opulence. If one is too old for politics, Pompey had jeered, he is also too old to be living like a Sybarite. Yet here was Pompey, traveling through Italy, dallying with his bride at every pleasure spot.

Crassus' power had also waned. Before Caesar left Rome, he had thrust aside one of Crassus' allies in order to claim Transalpine Gaul for himself, and recently Caesar had hedged his support for Crassus' candidate for consul. Crassus' money once bought him a place among the triumvirs. But after five years in Gaul, Caesar would never need to apply to him for another loan. With Caesar and Pompey united by their love for Julia, Crassus had to scramble to shore up his position. Crassus' heavy bribes had helped Clodius escape punishment in the Bona Dea affair, and the two men seemed to be drawing closer. The alliance spared Crassus the slurs and insults that Clodius' roving band of young toughs shouted at Pompey.

In fact, with Pompey distracted and Caesar away from Rome, Clodius had become increasingly bold. In early May, he staged a peculiar kidnapping. Tigranes, the son of the king of Armenia, had been held hostage in Rome since Pompey's triumph to keep his father in line. Pompey had installed the prince in comfort at the home of Flavius, a friendly praetor. One night, Clodius dined with Flavius and, as their drinking progressed, asked casually if he might see the famous prisoner. Suspecting nothing, Flavius produced Tigranes, and Clodius suggested that the prince join their banquet. When Flavius agreed, Clodius claimed his immunity as a tribune and took the Armenian from the house.

The next day, Pompey heard Clodius was giving Tigranes the run of his villa. Pompey directed Clodius to return the prisoner to custody. Clodius answered by parading the prince through the Forum. That insolence stirred Pompey to act. Accompanied by his full train of attendants, as well as Gabinius, who was now consul, Pompey went to Clodius' house. His display of dignity should have awed Clodius into submission. Instead, Pompey ran into Clodius' band of demonstrators, who grabbed Gabinius' symbols of rank and drubbed his attendants with them.

Clodius knew he had pushed Pompey too far and tried to smuggle Tigranes from Italy. The scheme failed. Flavius' men and the prince's bodyguards clashed outside the city. The guards killed everyone in Flavius' party except the praetor himself.

In exile, Cicero heard of the bloodshed and hoped that the

breach between Pompey and Clodius might work to his advantage. But Pompey decided that any further display of anger would only increase his humiliation, and he retreated again into isolation. Clodius appeared unstoppable. In exchange for cash from foreign potentates, he began proposing legislation to undo the peace treaties Pompey had negotiated throughout the East. Clodius also pressed lawsuits against some of Pompey's allies, less to obtain convictions than to gauge Pompey's popularity. The tactic stung Pompey into coming to court for a rare public appearance. Clodius was ready for him with a well-rehearsed gang.

As the proceedings began, Clodius fired up his demonstrators with a series of scurrilous questions.

"What's the name of the lecherous commander?" he shouted, giving a dainty shake to his toga. Despite Pompey's notorious devotion to Julia, accusations of effeminacy went over well with this crowd.

"Pompey!" the gang roared back.

"What's the name of a man who is trying to find another man?" Another flounce of the toga.

"Pompey!"

"Who is it who scratches his head with one finger?" Again, the signal.

"Pompey!"

The jeers were upsetting enough. But Pompey saw that many patricians, senators he had tried to please, were enjoying the sight of him being mocked. At one point, Clodius' servant was discovered moving through the crowd with a concealed sword. Pompey had demonstrated his courage on many battlefields, but his skin was as thin as his heart was stout. He dreaded two things: ridicule and assassination.

With the apparent threat on his life as his excuse, Pompey spared himself more waves of coarse abuse by staying home through the rest of Clodius' term.

XXVI

CICERO

57 B.C.

The patricians tried to challenge Clodius without Pompey. They focused their attack on his adoption, claiming it had been carried out during a period of dire heavenly omens. Clodius had a pat answer: most of Caesar's program had been passed while Bibulus was making that same objection. If you will strike down Caesar's laws, Clodius told the senate, I will travel to Cicero and bring him back to Rome on my shoulders.

Cicero had moved to Dyrrachium on the Macedonian coast. Several tribunes called for an end to his exile, but Cicero knew that nothing would be done until Pompey backed the measure. Cicero's contentious spirit began to revive. Although he kept on reproaching Atticus—"You used none of your wisdom in saving me from ruin"—his complaints were only reflexive tics, and he was planning for his eventual return.

When a new consul took office in January and recommended that Cicero be brought home, Romans knew he couldn't have floated the idea without Pompey's approval. Then the second consul, Metellus Nepos, volunteered to put aside his hostility to Cicero, and other supporters found a legalistic way to restore Cicero without a popular vote. But Pompey wasn't ready to go against the people's will. He insisted that the matter go to the assembly, where the tribunes split over the issue. A public debate was scheduled.

The night before, Clodius brought gladiators to surround the rostra. As crowds filled the Forum, he provoked a riot. Long afterward, men recalled seeing bodies clog the city's sewers and dam up the Tiber. When the carnage was over, city workers with sponges had to scrub the Forum on their hands and knees to wipe away the blood.

Quintus Cicero was left for dead among the corpses, but he survived. By now, even some of the patricians who had sneered at Cicero thought his return from exile might embarrass and neutralize Clodius. The measure to bring Cicero home came up again, and 416 senators lined up across the chamber; Clodius' was the only nay. This time, the bill was taken before a special session of the assembly carefully weighted with wealthy men. Even so, Pompey packed the Campus Martius with veterans who had come for the vote from their new farms. When Cicero heard that Pompey was finally stirring himself, he sailed to Italy on the date the vote was scheduled, arriving at Brundisium the next day. Three days later, Quintus wrote to say that the nightmare had ended.

Cicero's homecoming exceeded his most extravagant daydreams. His daughter Tullia celebrated her twenty-first birthday by meeting Cicero's ship, and no face was dearer to him. Her brother Marcus was becoming a hearty young sportsman—in short, a disappointment. But in Tullia, Cicero saw his own features idealized—nose shorter, mouth less disdainful, slender neck free of his fleshy folds. Her mind sparked to his, and intelligence flashed in her eyes. Together, father and daughter set out on his return to Rome, accompanied by townspeople who had learned that cheering Cicero was safe again.

By the time he reached the city walls, 16 months after he slunk away, all of Rome seemed to have crowded around the Capenan Gate to cheer his return, and applause followed him to the Forum, which was packed with more admiring Romans. But the joy was not universal. Clodius had men circulating through the crowds blaming Cicero for the city's shortage of grain. Mobs formed outside the senate, and the celebration turned threatening enough for the senators to realize they had to take drastic action to increase the available supply.

The crisis gave Cicero a chance to repay Pompey for arranging his return. He proposed that Pompey be given an extraordinary command to manage the grain supply, much like his commission a decade ago to crush the pirates. The Cicero of past years would have resisted the sweep of powers he was recommending for Pompey, but now he found it gratifying to hear men applauding him again. The day after that proposal, Pompey again accepted the role of Rome's savior and named a 15-member committee to assist him, with Cicero as chairman. Pompey added that Cicero was authorized to speak for him in all matters.

Next came a hearing to discuss repaying Cicero for damage to his property. Clodius spoke against reparations for nearly three hours, until the senate hooted him down and voted 2 million sesterces for Cicero's house in town, and a total of 750,000 sesterces for two outlying estates. Cicero considered the settlement stingy, but even as he began rebuilding, Clodius' thugs tore up his restored porch and smashed and burned his brother's house.

Cicero hoped that the constant violence was costing Clodius support; he complained that by setting gangs to menace him in the street, Clodius was making "Catiline look ultraconservative." But on the patrician side, a tribune named Annius Milo had hired his own raucous bands to fight for control of the open spaces between the Capitol and the Campus Martius.

Cicero deplored the breakdown of law even as he contributed to it. When Clodius was out of town, Cicero led his own supporters to the Capitol and tore down the tablets that listed Clodius' acts during his year as tribune. Cicero claimed that Clodius' fraudulent adoption made his bills invalid.

But Cicero ran into unexpected opposition from Cato, who had returned from his enforced absence and didn't want to see his own adroit achievements in Cyprus erased on a technicality. When the senate decided against rewriting history, the distance between Cato and Cicero widened.

Amid the turmoil, there were just enough moments of normalcy for Rome's political life to go on.

Administering the grain supply occupied Pompey's energies, and he sailed to granaries in Sicily, Sardinia and Africa to oversee the transactions and sent aides to every market where wheat was sold. In December, a storm broke as Pompey prepared to travel home. The commander warned him that it wouldn't be safe to sail.

Boarding the first ship, Pompey insisted the sailors weigh anchor. "To sail is necessary!" he shouted, launching the successful voyage. "To live is not!"

That same winter, lightning struck the statue of Jupiter on Alban Hill. Frightened citizens insisted that the senate consult the Greek hexameters of the Sibylline prophecies. The original books had been brought to Rome in the age of the Tarquin kings but destroyed in a fire. Priests had patched together a new collection, and when the verses were deciphered, their message was timely and explicit: if the king of Egypt comes requesting aid, you will face danger if you either refuse him entirely or send any great force to assist him.

Since Pompey had shown interest in going to Egypt to put Ptolemy the Flute Player back on his throne—and enrich himself along the way—Cicero believed the prophecy was a fake, designed to deny Pompey the Egyptian command. Cato forced the priests to reveal the message before the senate had authorized its release, and by the time the senate took up the issue, Roman opinion was set against intervening in Egypt's affairs. Only after three days of debate in the assembly did the people's mood begin to swing in Pompey's favor.

Again Clodius staged a disruption. He had protected himself against prosecution as tribune by getting himself elected aedile. Yet the minute that Milo's tribuneship ended, Clodius took him to court on charges of disturbing the peace with hired gladiators. Pompey and Cicero backed Milo, and Clodius knew that his prosecution would not succeed except in giving him another chance to insult Pompey. But Pompey kept his temper and spoke for hours on Milo's behalf, until even the paid jeering died away.

Clodius couldn't match Pompey's calm, especially with the opposition hurling vile insults against him and his sister Clodia. Furious, Clodius broke off his prepared remarks and returned to a reliable attack.

"Who is the man," he demanded of his gang, "who is trying to starve you with famine?"

"Pompey!" they shouted.

"Who wants to be sent to Egypt?"

"Pompey!"

"But who do we want to send?"

With rehearsed precision, they yelled, "Crassus!"

Crassus had been present throughout the performance, standing with Pompey in support of Milo. But Pompey had suspected that Crassus was underwriting the cost of Clodius' hoodlums, and now he had proof. Shouts gave way to spitting, then to shoving and blows, before Clodius was driven off the rostra. Cicero found it prudent to head home.

XXVII

ANTONY

57–55 B.C.

Mark Antony had never forgiven Cicero for putting his stepfather Lentulus to death in the Catiline affair. He had turned away from politics and was living a life that even young Romans considered wild. Besides his drinking and gambling, he was notoriously extravagant. But high spending was a tradition in Antony's family. His father's estate had been sunk so far in debt that Antony had refused to accept it, and Lentulus had once been expelled from the senate for unpaid bills.

Antony's closest companion was Scribonius Curio, who was somewhat older. Cicero still saw Curio as a protégé but, when irritated with him, would write the young man off as a mere "slip of a girl." Curio's family had money; Antony was extremely handsome but broke. When Curio's father learned that his son had been underwriting Antony's massive debts, he had servants bar the young man from his house. To visit, Antony had to climb to the roof and lower himself into Curio's room.

Portrait head, perhaps Mark Antony. The Metropolitan Museum of Art, Rogers Fund, 1924.

Then Antony left his teens and outgrew adolescent friend-
ships. He raised a beard and built his body to imposing propor-
tions. Dropping his fashionable, languid poses, he began an affair
with an older woman and boasted that he had fathered two of her
three children. For a while, Antony drifted at the edges of Clodius'
circle and enjoyed the spectacle of Cicero driven into exile. But as
Rome's politics grew ever more volatile and menacing, he followed the example of Caesar and Cicero in the previous generation and went abroad to study.

In Greece, Antony joined in military exercises but concentrated on rhetoric. Molon had cured Cicero of his tendency to be
overblown; Antony held on to his vivid, emotional language. Caesar reminded Romans that he was descended from Venus; Antony's family claimed Hercules, and he began affecting a military
swagger and carrying a heavy sword. Antony's nature was forth-
right and his generosity greater than his finances should have
permitted. He liked to laugh, and men and women liked to laugh
with him.

Antony might have continued his indolent life in Greece if
Gabinius had not passed through on his way to his new post as
governor of Syria. In the 10 years since Gabinius had Pompey
awarded the command against the pirates, he had continued to
tend Pompey's interests. He had won the consulship and developed his own following among the people. He had also remained
friendly with Clodius, who had managed to get for him the province of Syria and the authority to go to war without further approval from the senate. Gabinius offered to make Antony
commander of a mixed cavalry of Gauls, and the two left for Judaea, where new fighting had broken out.

The fraternal dispute Pompey tried to resolve six years earlier had broken out again. Aristobulus and his son had escaped
and led an army of dissidents on Judaea to seize Jerusalem and
other fortresses from Hyrcanus.

Antony was a reckless and daring soldier, the first to climb
the walls of the city where Aristobulus was hiding. Aristobulus
and his son got away again, but Antony chased them south for a
day, wiped out their army and took them back into custody.

To ensure better control in the future, Gabinius broke up
the Jewish state into five areas overseen by Jewish councils and
also reinforced the authority of Antipater, governor of a desert
wasteland south of Judaea. The Jews resented Antipater's influ-

ence but with Rome's support he and Herod, his teenage son, were emerging as powerful figures throughout the region.

Antipater used his influence to help Ptolemy, who had an array of influential backers but no throne. Buying the support of Pompey and Caesar two years earlier had required such high taxes that his subjects had rebelled. The Egyptians also resented the way he had let Cato annex Cyprus; rather than step down as king, Ptolemy's brother had swallowed poison. When Alexandrians drove the Flute Player out of the city, he had expected his friends in Rome to make good on past promises. But with Caesar occupied in Gaul and Pompey remote in Rome, he had been forced to appeal instead to Cato at Rhodes.

Their interview began badly. Cato's heavy drinking had upset his digestion, and he refused to pay a call on the king, sending word that he was midway through a regimen of laxatives. Ptolemy would have to come to him. When the king arrived at the governor's residence, he found Cato anchored firmly to his seat. He made no show of rising for the traditional courtesies. Nor was Cato helpful about Ptolemy's complaints. Don't bother to go on to Rome, he said. Go home and win over your subjects.

Hearing Cato's stern, self-assured voice woke Ptolemy from his fever of indecision. But his Egyptian advisers persuaded him to go to Rome after all. That was when the bolt of lightning warned Romans not to commit troops to his cause.

Now Gabinius had both troops and permission to use them. When Ptolemy offered a bribe of 10,000 talents to restore him to Egypt's throne, most of Gabinius' officers opposed the idea. But when Antony argued for it, Gabinius decided to invade on the pretext that Egypt somehow posed a threat to Rome.

In Ptolemy's absence, his eldest daughters had competed for his crown, and Berenice IV won. Since Egypt's queens could not reign without a male consort, Berenice married a royal lout, then had him strangled three days after the wedding. Next she took a man rumored to be an illegitimate son of Mithridates. That was provocation enough for Gabinius, who marched on Egypt—Antony at the front of Rome's troops—and made the Flute Player king again.

Ptolemy had Berenice killed, leaving another daughter as his heir. Cleopatra VII was now 14, a dozen years younger than

Antony. She was a plain child, but her father had seen to her education, and she could be clever and vivacious. With Rome guaranteeing Ptolemy's crown, Cleopatra could expect suitors to overlook her prominent nose and jutting chin and concentrate instead on her inner beauty and the immense wealth she would one day inherit.

When Gabinius and Antony went on to Palestine to put down another revolt, they left behind large numbers of Gauls and Germans in Alexandria to keep Ptolemy propped up. Those mercenaries quickly forgot their allegiance to Rome and adopted the sweet life of Alexandria. To make sure Ptolemy would pay what he had promised, Gabinius installed a prominent Roman moneylender to collect Egypt's taxes.

At home, the senators had become jealous of Gabinius' successes and envious of his new wealth. They refused to give him a festival of thanksgiving for his Eastern victories, and in fact only Pompey's intervention prevented a vote of censure. Word of Caesar's victories in Gaul had reached Antony, who wrote to Caesar asking for a commission with him. For the time being, Caesar did not respond.

Waiting in northern Italy for the next summer campaign, Caesar stayed in close contact with Rome. The news he was getting did not displease him. Clodius had never been a dependable protégé. If a showdown came, Pompey would be the more formidable ally. As he was balancing that political equation, Caesar got reports of a new military threat that didn't require any exaggeration by him.

Caesar's legate Labienus warned him that the Belgae were conspiring against Rome. United, the Belgic tribes could field an army of 300,000 men. Their chiefs suspected that Caesar meant to conquer their land up to the channel that separated them from Britain, but in his dispatches to Rome he was playing down their fears. Other tribes had been agitating among the Belgae, Caesar said. The Gauls were notoriously fickle and pleased with change for its own sake.

Without consulting the senate or the assembly, Caesar recruited two new legions in Cisalpine Gaul at his own expense. That doubled the strength Rome had authorized him. As summer began, he led 40,000 men into Champagne, an area controlled by a friendly tribe, the Remi. He crossed the Aisne River and began to break up the Belgae's fragile coalition. He sent Remi leaders and his friend Diviciacus to assure individual tribes that Rome would treat them well if they signed peace terms.

Many chieftains were not so easily persuaded. The Nervii launched a surprise attack from a wood, rushing at Caesar's troops with a speed he found incredible. It was a near-disaster, but afterward Caesar decided that what had saved the day were his commanders, who were so resourceful that each Roman unit could function on its own initiative. At a low point, Caesar had snatched a shield from a rearguard soldier and had ridden through the ranks, shouting to his officers by name. The legionaries hadn't waited to find their usual positions. They were clustering around any raised standard.

The Nervii's tenacity earned Caesar's admiration. When they surrendered, they claimed that only 500 of their 60,000 troops had survived. Caesar extended his clemency, which was becoming legendary—and seductive—throughout Gaul. Caesar's rules were explicit. If a town surrendered before his battering rams struck its walls, he would spare the citizens, but they had to hand over their weapons to him. If a tribe only pretended to accept his terms and then attacked, Caesar stormed the town and took the entire population as slaves. Merchants reported that the number sold at auction after the Belgic campaign had reached 53,000.

By autumn, Caesar considered Gaul subdued. When he reported the extent of his victories to the senate, the news set off rejoicing in Rome that even the patricians couldn't deflate. A normal thanksgiving of sacrifices and public feasting ran five days. Pompey had been honored with 10. Now Pompey asked Cicero to propose a thanksgiving of 15 days for Caesar, and Cicero did as he was told.

Although Pompey sponsored the decree, his informal agreement with Caesar and Crassus was fraying badly. From Gaul, Caesar had to decide whether the pact still served his interests, or whether his victories in Gaul had made him strong enough to risk standing alone.

XXVIII

CICERO

56–55 B.C.

After six months back in Rome, Cicero's popularity was astonishing, or so he persuaded himself. Pompey was now a regular caller, sharing his fears—that Crassus was financing Clodius, that the senate remained hostile to him, that Romans were gullible and young people hopelessly depraved. After Cicero won several court cases without depending on a mob, he began edging back toward the conservative patricians, the men who worried that Caesar's successes in Gaul might somehow make Pompey a dictator.

Cicero had been delighted when Pompey was denied the Egyptian command, but he knew that Pompey expected either support or silence, and he obliged. When the chance came to attack Caesar in court, however, Cicero couldn't resist it. The most discerning of other men's flaws, Cicero remained innocent of his own. He truly believed, as he ignored Pompey's wishes and insulted Caesar, that he was honoring his vow to stay out of politics.

Soon afterward, Cicero persuaded the senate to schedule a debate on the distribution of public land in Campania. No issue

had more bitterly divided the people from the conservative senators, but Cicero calculated that with Pompey's veterans already
settled on farms, he could defy Caesar. He argued that Rome's
treasury required the income from the land. And, indeed, Pompey
didn't give any sign of objecting. He would soon be leaving for
Sardinia, and Cicero rode by litter to his house to say goodbye and
make a request: he wanted his brother Quintus sent back from
Sardinia, where he had been overseeing the grain supply. As
usual, Pompey was gracious and obliging. "Immediately!" he
promised. He told Cicero that he would be sailing to Sardinia from
Labro or Pisae.

Cicero left pleased, but Pompey was annoyed with him
over the land measure and was already scheming to repair the
damage he had done.

Pompey had private reasons for going north of Rome to sail for
Sardinia, an island in the south. Caesar was waiting for him in
Luca, a town in Cisalpine Gaul close to the Italian border. Pompey
and Crassus had agreed to join Caesar there for a meeting to mend
their unraveling alliance. Each man realized that he still needed
the others. Pompey alone couldn't control the popular movement,
Crassus lacked a solid political base, and Caesar needed more time
to consolidate his conquests in Gaul without harassment from
Rome. They were all worried that Cato's brother-in-law, Lucius
Domitius Ahenobarbus, who was closely allied with the most ungiving patricians, might be elected consul.

Domitius' family had a following in south Gaul and was
certain to want to replace Caesar there at the end of his term.
Caesar knew the only way to guarantee his position would be to
reunite the uncongenial but potent political ticket of 15 years ago.
Crassus and Pompey must end their fruitless rivalry, stand together for consul and extend Caesar's term in Gaul for another five
years.

Caesar had also been meeting with senators. Some 200
flocked to Luca with pledges of support. In return, they came back
to Rome laden with Caesar's money. He also pledged to give his
troops leave time so they could travel to Rome for the vote.

Aware that envy could poison an alliance, Caesar agreed
that when Pompey and Crassus ended their year as co-consuls
they should reward themselves with provinces as rich as his own.

They should also hold those provinces for a full five years, and Caesar's proconsulship should be extended to expire on the same day as theirs; that would give him a total of 10 years in Gaul. Caesar could remain in control of his provinces—safe from lawsuits—until he was ready to return for his own second term as consul.

Caesar was assuming powers that Roman law had never entrusted to one man. The secret agreement at Luca was another reminder that for many of Rome's powerful men, the Republican system had become a nuisance to be outwitted.

Cicero was one of the first to feel the chill of the new political climate. When Pompey moved on to Sardinia, he ran into Quintus Cicero almost at once. During the months of Cicero's exile, Quintus had assured Pompey that his brother had learned tact and obedience during his absence from Rome.

"Just the man I wanted to see!" Pompey began. "Nothing could have been more opportune! Unless you lecture to your brother, you will have to pay me what you guaranteed for his good behavior."

At the same time, Pompey sent Cicero a message: drop the agitation over distributing the Campanian land. When the measure came up again, Cicero wasn't in the senate for the vote.

More indignities were to come. Cicero wrote a letter pledging himself to Rome's three leaders, but he was too embarrassed to let Atticus see it before he posted it to Caesar. Later, he explained that he wanted to tie himself to the alliance so firmly that he could not go back on his word.

"Enough!" Cicero concluded, sounding like the patricians' spurned suitor. "Since those who have no power will not love me, let us see that those who have it do. I know this is what you have wished for a long time, but I was a complete ass."

Knowing he would not be refused this time, Caesar shrewdly offered Cicero membership in the secret cabal. Caesar's other partners might have money and prestige, but no one else had Cicero's voice. When the patricians wanted to strip away one of Caesar's proconsulships in Gaul, Cicero stood up in his defense: since Caesar was winning Gaul for Rome, he was clearly the man to finish the job. Cicero also supported a measure that forced Rome's treasury to repay Caesar for the four legions he had raised

at his own expense. It was not the money Caesar needed—the
riches he was extracting from Gaul easily covered the costs—but
the senate's approval. By passing the resolution, the senate acknowledged that Caesar's actions in Gaul during the past three
years had been legal.

Romans mocked Cicero for capitulating to Caesar, but he
justified his actions by saying that he had always appealed for
conciliation; he simply wanted Pompey—and Caesar, he implied—to work smoothly with the senate. To shore up his reputation, Cicero tried to inveigle a writer to publish a book about
him. Cicero outlined the chapters—first Catiline's treachery, then
Cicero's exile, which was bound to touch the reader's heart since
"reading an account of the suffering that others have experienced
casts a most agreeable melancholy over the mind."

Cicero would have written his own account, he added, but
then he would have to be more reserved in his self-congratulation.
Praise was more persuasive coming from someone else. "I am
ambitious to be known to the present generation by your writing,"
Cicero said, "and to enjoy, in my lifetime, a foretaste of that little
share of glory that I may expect from future ages."

Cicero was reduced to dwelling on his past glories because
he no longer heard the small voice of approval from within his
own breast. He wrote Atticus, "What is more shameful than our
lives, especially mine?"

Even successes in his private life couldn't lift his spirits. He
rebuilt his three magnificent houses; writing inventories of their
furnishings had once lightened Cicero's mood. Not now. Atticus
married that spring, and Cicero bought an aristocratic new husband for his daughter, Tullia, who had been widowed for about a
year. But the happiness of those occasions quickly evaporated.
Cicero felt exiled again, not from the city but from power and
respect. He turned to writing.

The result was De Republica, a meditation on the state and society.
Cicero argued against the Epicurean philosophy that a wise man
held himself aloof from public life. He wrote that the desire to
serve others through politics was basic to man's nature. Duty to
country outweighed even duty to parents. Public affairs were not
an extraneous activity but central to men's lives.

Cicero analyzed the three systems of government as the

Greeks had defined them—kingship, aristocracy and democracy. Each had a weakness that led inevitably to demands for reform, and Cicero compared government to a ball being tossed from one faction to the next. Aristocrats expelled a tyrant. Then a people's revolution overthrew that elite. And inevitably a dictator emerged to quell the mob.

To ensure stability, Cicero argued for a mixture of all three systems. He found it in the government of his grandfather's day—before Rome's latest conquests, before the agitation for land reform, before warlords competed for power. The Republic had rested securely on harmony between the people and the few aristocrats of the senate.

The essay ended with a dream set in heaven. Cicero's vision of an afterlife was vague; he endorsed religion more for its good influence on the national character than because of any deeply held belief. Now he had a Roman looking down on Earth, realizing how small it was and how short man's time upon it.

The scene consoled Cicero. Although his own glory had been fleeting, Caesar's conquests in Gaul would count for no more.

XXIX

POMPEY

55 B.C.

As reports of the meeting at Luca reached Rome, other candidates for consul demanded to know what plan Crassus and Pompey had hatched. Marcellinus, the current consul, rose before the assembly and asked the two men whether or not they were going to stand as candidates.

The people shouted for a reply. Taken aback, Pompey said weakly that the answer was maybe yes, maybe no. And Crassus, equally evasive, said his decision would depend on what was best for the Republic.

When Marcellinus began to denounce them, Pompey recovered his wits and cut him short. "Marcellinus," he said, "should be grateful to me for giving him something to say when he has always been so tongue-tied. He used to be starved for words and now he is positively choking over them."

Crassus' answer, once decoded, discouraged the other pa-

A Roman coin with a portrait of Pompey. The New York Public Library Picture Collection.

trician candidates except for Domitius. Cato, endorsing his brother-in-law's candidacy, said sternly, "We are not fighting merely for office but for liberty against an oppressor."

Less than 24 days before the election, Pompey and Crassus dropped their show of support for other candidates and announced that they would seek the post. When Marcellinus pointed out that their announcements came past the period specified by law, he did them an inadvertent favor. The elections were delayed until January, which allowed Caesar to release enough legionaries from winter quarters to guarantee the outcome.

The delay outraged the patricians backing Domitius, and they put on robes of mourning, trying to arouse the people against Pompey and Crassus. But the senate had stopped functioning, and after Luca, Clodius had swung back into the camp of the three dominant men, putting him and Cicero reluctantly on the same side.

When the vote was held, Caesar sent troops commanded by Crassus' son, Publius, and although Domitius went off before dawn to the polling site on the Campus Martius, it was too late. His enemies were already out in force, and they wounded Cato and killed the man carrying Domitius' torch. Crassus and Pompey were elected unopposed.

No one could thwart them now, though Cato kept trying. He proposed legislation that would have exposed the winners in a campaign—not just the losers—to prosecution for electoral violations. The consuls rejected that amendment, and the patricians could only respond with a loud moan of dismay. Pompey and Crassus, Cicero wrote, "have everything in their power, and they want everyone to know it."

The new consuls observed the outward forms of the law, despite the underhanded and transparent stratagems that Romans had come to expect. As Cato led in the early voting for praetor, Pompey claimed to hear thunder and got the election postponed. When polling resumed, Vatinius was the winner.

It wasn't Pompey's only hypocrisy. He and Crassus proposed a law against *luxuria* to curtail private spending on public entertainments, an expenditure that swayed elections almost as effectively as direct bribery. The timing of the resolution was particularly frivolous because Pompey was ready to open his great open-air theater, the first in Rome to be built of stone. He had planned it since his return from Mytilene, and 13 years later, the monument on the Campus Martius would be dedicated during his term as consul.

Rising up three stories, with columns of red granite and arches cut from quarries of peperino left by Mount Alba's volcano, the amphitheater could hold 40,000. A semicircular auditorium extended 170 yards in diameter, with a stage 100 yards wide. Within the arches around the entrance were statues of Rome's gods and heroes, chosen by Atticus and stretching out in a panorama that dazzled, and finally overwhelmed, the eye. Pompey's freedman Demetrius had overseen the project and hadn't stopped with the theater. The complex also included a garden and portico 200 yards long and nearly as wide where Romans could stroll on a spring evening. The columns were hung with gold-embroidered curtains. Carefully clipped plants and trees lined the walk, and small streams splashed from the many fountains. The portico's final grace note was the jewel of Pompey's art collection: a 400-year-old painting by Polygnotus, an artist from Delphi famed for his delicate female figures.

The theater and the ambles had been designed for the people. For the senators, Pompey built a second meetinghouse, the Curia Pompeii, which adjoined his handsome new residence. Because all of Pompey's buildings lay outside the Forum, a general would not have to sacrifice his command to cross into the senate. The chamber was dominated by a large statue of Pompey, a reminder to the patricians of whose generosity had made their comfort possible. The grandeur stirred even greater envy among Pompey's rivals, and he tried to defuse it by claiming that his theater was actually a temple to Venus, which happened to include seats for gladiator shows.

For the dedication, Pompey intended to outdo any spectacle Rome had ever seen. He imported three times as many female leopards as in previous games and six times as many lions. He commissioned the staging of farces and dramas until he had at least one critic groaning; Cicero felt compelled to attend the performances and praise them publicly. But to a discreet friend—not Atticus, who had shared in the preparations—Cicero unburdened himself.

"What pleasure could it afford a judicious spectator," Cicero demanded, "to see a thousand mules prancing about the stage in the tragedy of 'Clytaemnestra'? Or whole regiments clad in foreign armor for 'The Trojan Horse'? In a word, what man of sense could be entertained with viewing a mock army drawn up on the stage in battle array?"

Cicero granted that the spectacles had been extremely well done "to captivate vulgar eyes." But the farces were tedious, and the animal attractions repellent. The one exception was a beast called the rhinoceros, which Pompey was displaying for the first time to enthusiastic Romans. Otherwise, Cicero found no pleasure in watching a lion or any other noble beast struck to the heart by a merciless hunter, or seeing "one of our own weak species cruelly mangled by an animal of much superior strength."

Cicero thought only the other "elegant and humanized" minds among the audience shared his revulsion. But at the end of the games, an entire day was given to contests between 18 elephants and men in heavy armor. Pompey had expected the exotic beasts to inspire terror, but when wounded, some of the elephants refused to charge their assailants. They lumbered about the arena, trunks trumpeting their pain. Cicero said the elephants aroused not only compassion but a feeling of kinship, and people rose in the stands to demand that they be spared.

Despite the inevitable criticism, Pompey had staged the greatest show in Roman history. With his popularity soaring, he risked his hard-won prestige on an unprecedented lunge for power.

The plan devised at Luca was to make the three rulers more nearly equal. In Rome, a friendly tribune introduced the legislation: Crassus would control Syria for five years, and Pompey would hold Libya and Spain's two provinces for the same term. Caesar's term in Gaul would run for another five years, and he would be given two more legions.

Draining money from a province was the traditional way for aristocrats to retire their debts. In one stroke, Pompey had closed off future revenue to dozens of candidates for high office. Even Romans who wouldn't suffer from the legislation began to protest when they learned that Pompey had no intention of going. to Spain. He was turning its provinces over to legates so he could stay at home in his new villa, controlling the senate and enjoying the company of his wife.

Their romance had not cooled. Once during an election-day riot Pompey had been splattered with blood. He changed into a fresh toga and sent the soiled one home. Julia was pregnant, and when she saw servants coming with the bloody garment she was sure Pompey had been killed. She fell into a faint and miscarried.

Romans were disappointed in Pompey for ignoring his province, but they were outraged by Crassus, who intended to leave for Syria when his consulship ended and go to war against Parthia. Crassus' victory over Spartacus had faded from the popular memory, and he seemed driven to attempt a new military conquest even though he was deaf and well past 60. Age hadn't been kind to him: he had begun to seem childish, rambling on to strangers about defeating Parthia, although Rome had no quarrel with that country. After Parthia, Crassus boasted, he would push on for India and the world's last sea that lay beyond it. Friends tried to discourage him, but Caesar was happy to get him out of Rome and sent encouragement from Gaul.

Ateius, a tribune, objected to the prospect of fighting Parthia and marshaled a gang to stop Crassus. At first, Pompey's presence at Crassus' side calmed the crowd, but Ateius persisted and ordered an aide to arrest Crassus. Other tribunes overruled him.

Racing ahead to the city gate, Ateius poured fuel into a metal container. As Crassus approached, Ateius set the vessel on fire and added incense and potions. As he stirred the brew, he shouted curses that chilled the blood, appeals to dark, half-forgotten gods who would strike down Crassus for his stubbornness. The curses were considered so terrible that they endangered even the man who uttered them. Crassus turned a deaf ear and left for Syria, but Romans berated Ateius for the way he had jeopardized—such was the potency of the curses—the survival of Rome itself.

From the start, the spell seemed to work. Crassus insisted on sailing from Brundisium despite the winter storms, and lost many ships. He marched with the survivors to Galatia, where he was met by its extremely old king, who was building a new city. Crassus mocked him for it: "Your majesty, I see that you are starting your project at the twelfth hour."

Smiling, the old king inspected Crassus' bald head and wrinkled face. "But you yourself, Imperator, are not early in marching against the Parthians."

XXX

CRASSUS

55–53 B.C.

At Luca, Caesar had relied on family loyalties to bolster the alliance. He had given important posts in Gaul to Crassus' son and counted on Julia to maintain the strong bond with Pompey. But Caesar knew they were his partners only by necessity; by inclination, they were rivals and alert to any sign of weakness. He had worked to convince them that Gaul was pacified.

That made the reports from his provinces especially alarming. An officer, Servius Galba, had been attacked by tribes Caesar thought he had already conquered. As soon as Galba put down that insurrection, more rebels had come from northwestern Gaul and, according to some reports, even from the mysterious island across the channel.

The Veneti were skilled at sailing that turbulent channel, and they had been seizing Roman officials, a crime that Caesar felt compelled to avenge. If he didn't make an example of the Veneti, all of Gaul could erupt again.

The Veneti's ships were better constructed for the open

seas than his, with prows and sterns high enough to stand up to
the buffeting waves. Their hulls were made entirely of oak, and
their crossbeams were a foot thick, fastened with iron bolts as
thick as a sailor's thumb. Their sails, made of hides and soft
leather, were better at steering the heavy ships than Caesar's cloth
sails.

But Caesar's fleet had one advantage, the speed of its oars-
men. Even so, when Caesar's ships sailed up the Loire River into
enemy territory, they seemed outmanned by the 220 ships that
sailed out of the harbor and took up positions across from them.
Since their taller ships loomed over the Romans, the Gauls' lances
would be devastating. Caesar had prepared a secret weapon: The
Romans had fastened sharp hooks to long poles, to snare the
ropes on the yardarm of an enemy mast. A quick spasm of rowing
caused the hooks to snap the ropes and bring down the yardarm.
Becalmed, a ship was a sitting target. The Romans then surrounded it and leaped aboard.

When the Gauls understood the strategy, they tried to sail
away, but the wind abruptly died. They were stuck. The engagement started at 10 A.M. By sunset, only a few of the Veneti's ships
had escaped back to their harbor. The tribes along the Atlantic
coast had staked everything on their impregnable ships. Now they
were disabled and overrun.

Caesar had cultivated a reputation for forgiveness. But this
time he decided on measures of "particular severity." In his la-
conic account of the engagement, he wrote, "Caesar put all the
elders to death and sold the rest into slavery."

Like Caesar in Gaul, Crassus had come to Syria eager to fight and
turned at once toward Parthia. That land, north of Hyrcania, was
a kingdom controlled by seven Pahlavi families. Parthians had
been a nomadic people, excellent on horseback, superb as hunt-
ers. Settling down, they had drawn heavily on Greek culture, but
they still sent only cavalry into battle, their noblemen fighting in
heavy armor.

The Parthians were hardly warlike and posed no threat to
Rome. But they were rich, and that was provocation enough. Crassus had owed his *auctoritas*, his political authority, to his wealth.
With Pompey and Caesar piling up huge fortunes, Crassus
thought he might soon be the poorest. It was a matter of degree;
he was immensely rich, but he wanted more.

The political situation in Parthia was tangled. Phraates III had pledged allegiance to Pompey to protect his country from the Armenians, but Pompey had been won over by Tigranes, the Armenian king, and reneged on the bargain. While relations remained strained, Pompey had decided that war with Parthia represented too great a sacrifice of men and effort. Then Phraates had been murdered by his two sons. The older brother had taken the throne, and the younger brother had appealed to Gabinius. If restoring Ptolemy in Egypt hadn't been more lucrative, Gabinius might have attacked Parthia with the same excuse Crassus was using now.

Caesar had contributed 1,000 Gauls from his cavalry led by Publius Crassus, whom Caesar had decorated often for courage. With his son at his side, Crassus expected little challenge. He crossed the Euphrates River, pillaging a swath far into Mesopotamia. Except for losses at one treacherous town, Crassus was advancing at a quick and rather painless pace.

But much as he wanted military honors, Crassus wanted money more. Instead of hurrying to carry the battle to the unprepared Parthians, he dawdled wherever there was profit to be made. At the temple in Hierapolis, he squandered many days hauling out gold and weighing it for his treasury. In Jerusalem, he carried away the treasure Pompey had left untouched.

But inevitably the Romans had setbacks, and Ateius' curse was fresh enough to Crassus' men that those mishaps seemed ominous. Leaving the temple at Hierapolis, Publius Crassus stumbled and his father fell on top of him. Next, one of Crassus' beautifully caparisoned horses was pulled into a turbulent river and its groom drowned. Frightened men swore that the eagle's head on their leading standard had twisted around so that it would face away from battle. When lentils and salt were offered as rations, the men were upset: those were normally funeral foods.

And when a priest handed Crassus the entrails from a sacrifice and they slipped from his hand, Crassus laughed, hoping to sound reassuring. "See what it is to be an old man," he said. "But I shall grip my sword fast enough."

Crassus led his army to seek the enemy he had created, but scouts reported no sign of them. Crassus' senior officer, Gaius Cassius, wanted him to pause at nearby towns until they got more reliable intelligence. The legionaries, homesick for Italy's summer lushness, were appalled by the desert.

A friendly Arab chieftain rode into the encampment and taunted them: "What's this? Did you imagine you would be marching through Campania? Did you expect to find springs and shade trees? Baths? Inns for your relaxation?"

The grumbling persisted. Among themselves, the Romans asked what evil spirit had brought this chieftain to them, urging Crassus to make an immediate assault. Don't wait, the chief said. A Parthian general was nearby with only a few men. Strike at once and you will have victory. Crassus believed him.

But it was a trap. The Parthians had hidden their cavalry behind one meager rank of soldiers, cloaking the horsemen with skins so their armor wouldn't glint in the sun. Beating enormous drums, which struck dread in the Romans, the Parthians leaped into view, swarmed over Publius Crassus and killed him.

As the Romans struggled with the enemy facing them, the Arab chief drew up his men and charged from the rear. The Romans spun around helplessly to fend off each lunge, while Parthian horses' hooves sent up stinging sand. Roman corpses piled up until the survivors couldn't keep their footing on top of them. Slipping and sliding, some Romans chose to fall on their swords; others killed their wounded friends to spare them more misery.

Because the Parthians relied on their horses, they fought only by day. As the sun set, they galloped off for the night, leaving Crassus and the remnants of his army to creep to the city of Carrhae, with its population of loyal Romans. Crassus had to leave behind his dying and wounded.

The terrible defeat, combined with the loss of his son, left Crassus shaken and fearful. The men despised him for his blunders and his greed. They called on Cassius to assume command, but Cassius refused to mutiny.

Crassus intended to escape from Carrhae by night. Under the bright desert moon, however, he and a band of troops got only as far as the nearby mountains. The Parthian general sent a message offering Crassus a truce if Rome would give up its claim to all land east of the Euphrates. Crassus was ready to accept the terms gratefully, but the Parthian said the truce could only be negotiated between him and Crassus. Deceived once, Crassus was wary and tried to convince his men that if they waited one more night, they could slip farther into the mountains and be safe from pursuit.

His men no longer listened to him. They forced Crassus to go in person and ask for peace. As he left, Crassus turned to his lieutenants with a grim request. When you escape, he said, tell all of Rome that Crassus chose to die at the hands of his lying enemies rather than at those of his disobedient countrymen.

Crassus set off for neutral land between the two armies. Coming down from the hillside, he found a horse waiting for him. The groom said it was a gift from the Parthians to speed him to the conference, but the gesture added to Crassus' suspicions. As he weighed his options, the Parthians grabbed him and forced him onto the horse. Crassus' troops were marooned too far up the slope to save him.

Crassus was killed. The Romans who escaped said that his reputation for avarice had followed him to the desert. The Parthians had mocked his greed by pouring molten gold down the throat of his corpse. Whether that story was true or not, Crassus was dead, and Rome's expansion had been stopped at the banks of the Euphrates.

XXXI

CAESAR

55–53 B.C.

While Crassus marched to Syria, Caesar had scored easy victories over two renowned German tribes, killing or scattering as many as 400,000 Germans. He made a show of Roman expertise by building a bridge over the Rhine in 10 days. He led his men across it, reconnoitered for two and a half weeks, then returned to the river's western bank and ordered the bridge demolished.

That scouting expedition had impressed the Germans, but Caesar had a more provocative expedition in mind. He intended to cross the channel and invade Britain. No one knew the size of the island across the channel; a few scholars had speculated that Britain was merely a name and didn't exist at all. But Caesar had seen its white cliffs.

Caesar had outlined modest goals. He planned to visit the island, gather information on its terrain and natural harbors and see for himself what sort of people lived there. And, in fact, that was all he accomplished. Setting sail at midnight late in August with two legions in 100 transports and warships, Caesar took only limited supplies. He reached the coast of Britain at 9 A.M. and found the Britons armed and waiting along the cliffs. Caesar moved east on the coast and had his warship rowed in for a late-afternoon landing.

Caesar's men hesitated to leave their boats until the Tenth Legion's standard-bearer went over the side, calling, "Come on, men! Jump!" By sunset, the Romans had beaten back the Britons in harsh fighting. But a summer storm and high tides battered Caesar's ships, and after a few more skirmishes he had to return to the continent, less than three weeks from the night he left. Brief as it was, however, the expedition had whetted Caesar's appetite.

In Rome, the senate voted Caesar another thanksgiving. For pressing past the channel, senators rated Caesar's adventure in Britain worth 20 days of festivities.

Caesar returned to Britain the next July. This time he brought a fleet 10 times the size of his last flotilla, and when the Britons saw the forest of masts they disappeared inland. Caesar pitched camp but did not want to take the time to drag his boats onto the shore. It was already after midnight when he led his cavalry and cohorts over unknown terrain to find the Britons. In the morning, they reached the natives, who had traveled by chariot to the safety of a wood. The Romans were victorious, but there was no defense against British weather, and Caesar lost his gamble. A gale damaged almost the entire fleet. Forty ships were lost altogether, and the rest required massive repair. Caesar sent orders to Labienus across the channel to build as many ships as possible. Meanwhile, he had the damaged vessels dragged over greased logs into his camp. The men dug for 10 exhausting days to build an earthen wall to protect the repair work against attack.

When Caesar was ready to march north again, he found that tribes had gathered from all over the island. Cassivellaunus, a chief whose territory was some 80 miles from the sea, had persuaded his rivals to unite behind him as their commander-in-chief.

Caesar led his army to a point where the Thames River could be forded. The tribes had hidden sharp stakes below the water's surface to impale attackers, but Caesar sent his men into the river, and they moved cautiously but swiftly in water up to their necks. The cavalry and infantry emerged together, and that panoply of strength routed the Britons.

The local tribes had put on their own spectacle, coloring their bodies blue with dye from the woad plant. Although they shaved every other part of their bodies, they let the hair on their heads grow wild and long. Caesar learned from prisoners that Britons took wives and acknowledged their children but also shared their women with their brothers and sons. Caesar recorded his findings with few judgments.

Caesar quickly learned that stories of Britain's great riches were Roman fables. Britons had limited iron, and they imported bronze. From interviewing traders, Caesar calculated that the island was a triangle, its eastern side pointing to Germany. There was more ocean to its north. Britons kept herds of cattle for food but considered it wrong to eat rabbits, geese or chickens; they kept those as pets. The interior peoples seemed to have been born there, but along the coast were Europeans who had crossed the channel as soldiers and stayed on as farmers.

Caesar's men could not let down their guard. When they did, the Britons attacked again. From the experience of his first expedition, Caesar anticipated their tactics: They used cavalry to break through the Roman lines and then rammed in their chariots. When the chariots drew close enough, soldiers jumped to the ground and fought on foot while the chariot drivers retreated to safety, ready to gallop back and pick up their men for a strategic retreat. But knowing what to expect had not taught Caesar how to counter it. When the Romans saw the chariots pulling away from battle, they were reluctant to break ranks and follow. The Britons didn't fight in a tight order; they spread out in clusters, charging, withdrawing and letting fresh reserves take up the battle.

Caesar was frustrated, and the following noon, while the Romans were foraging for food, the Britons struck again. The terrain favored conventional tactics, and Caesar's legionaries stood their ground. When the Romans prevailed, the Britons didn't risk another pitched battle. Envoys called on Caesar, pledging loyalty to Rome and pleading the cause of one chieftain over another. As he did in Gaul, Caesar listened to their arguments, weighed the political nuances and issued instant rulings.

Still on the loose, Cassivellaunus hoped to catch Caesar's men unprepared at their beached ships, but the Romans were ready for his attack. Cassivellaunus had watched his country being destroyed while lesser kings sued for peace. Now he too asked for terms. He didn't know that Caesar had already decided that Gaul was a far richer prize than this remote island and was as anxious to cross the channel again as Cassivellaunus was to see him gone. By the time Caesar accepted the peace offer and took hostages, many of the Roman ships had been repaired, and Labienus had sent another 60. But they were not enough. Caesar had taken many prisoners. He decided to pack the men tightly and sail before the September winds struck again. Even at that, he would have to make two trips.

Caesar had the luck that eluded Crassus. As he prepared for the crossing, the sea fell calm, and Caesar's two night voyages took his troops and his British slaves safely back to Gaul.

Once there, Caesar received news that soured his achievement. Some weeks earlier, his daughter had died in childbirth, and the infant survived her by only a few days. Although Pompey had loved Julia no less for coming late to his life, she had been his fourth wife. But she had been Caesar's only child, and he felt her loss profoundly.

Crowds of Romans shared their leaders' grief and wanted to honor Julia in their own way. Ignoring official objections, they carried her body to a somber burial on the Campus Martius, the people's field. From Gaul, Caesar broke precedent, as he had done 15 years earlier for Julia's mother, and ordered his gladiators to present games, followed by a banquet dedicated to his daughter. For every Roman who knew Julia, hundreds more realized that she had been the fragile link between two powerful and dangerous camps. Her elaborate funeral was the chance to express their hope that Rome was not on the verge of more violence.

Caesar's mourning had not ended when news reached him that his mother, Aurelia, had died. In less than a year, Caesar had lost the two women he loved best.

XXXII

CICERO AND CAESAR

53–52 B.C.

For Cicero, the months of Caesar's bereavement brought one embarrassment after another. Gabinius had returned to Rome demanding a triumph, but when he reached the city gates he learned how unpopular he had become for flouting the Sibyl's prophecies and putting Ptolemy back on Egypt's throne. Instead of leading a parade, Gabinius had to slip into the city at night to avoid being insulted on the street. When he was summoned before the senate to report on his term abroad, Cicero attacked him. Gabinius responded with only one word: "Exile!"

The insult was too raw for the other senators, and they left their seats in protest.

When Gabinius was put on trial for leaving Syria to restore Ptolemy, Quintus Cicero advised his brother to say nothing at all, but this time Cicero's pride wouldn't let him completely duck a showdown. He gave a bit of tepid testimony for the prosecution and then reported the outcome to his brother: "Gabinius is acquitted." The prosecution had been stupid, Cicero complained, and

Pompey had taken "incredible pains"—which meant massive bribes—to ensure the not-guilty verdict.

The verdict coincided with the heaviest rains in memory. They swelled the Tiber and launched a flood that swept away shops and houses. Cicero quoted to his brother a passage from Homer about Jove opening the floodgates of the sky upon guilty mortals and corrupt judges. Rome's magistrates may have agreed, because they decided to try Gabinius again, this time for looting his province.

Pompey knew who should defend Gabinius. "Pompey has not yet made a dent in me," Cicero assured Quintus. "And as long as I retain a speck of liberty, he never shall." But by late summer Caesar was making the same request, and Cicero could not stand up to both men.

The trial was designed to compel Gabinius to repay the 60 million denarii that Ptolemy had allegedly paid him—that was about 20 times more than it took to bribe an entire bloc of electors in the voting for consul. With Cato presiding and Cicero giving a half-hearted performance, the result was predictable: Gabinius was ordered to repay the bribe. Since he could not, he now became the exile.

Gabinius' fate sent a direct challenge to Caesar. If he returned from Gaul as a private citizen, the patricians would do the same to him. And if Pompey couldn't save his chief lieutenant, how well would he protect Caesar? Even if the tribunes agreed to let him run for consul before he surrendered his command, he wouldn't be eligible for another four years. That meant he must hold on to Gaul at least until the summer before the election. The timing would be tricky, but with Pompey's support perhaps Caesar could manage it.

With Julia gone, however, Pompey was drifting back toward the patricians, and for months Caesar had been working through Quintus to win over Cicero. When he sent Balbus with another approach for a closer alliance, Cicero's written reply arrived unreadable; it had fallen into a river on the way to Gaul. Caesar complained to Balbus that, from the scraps he could decipher, "it was something to be wished for, rather than hoped for."

Hearing of the mishap, Cicero sent Caesar a letter that he considered to be friendly without being undignified. Caesar pressed the advantage by sending beguiling notes, by piling honors on Quintus and by doing favors for Cicero's young protégés. Cicero basked in his brother's successes, although he assured Quintus that he had no great faith in Caesar's promises. But to Atticus he joked about Caesar: "If one does not fall in love with such a man, which of the others could one fall in love with?"

Caesar's next request to Cicero was a more pleasant one. With his riches from Gaul, Caesar wanted to build a new Forum. He had a budget of 60 million sesterces and was prepared to pay the owners of private land near the Campus Martius large sums for their property. He proposed to partition the voting grounds of the field itself and roof them with marble. The circumference of the portico would extend one mile, with a vast public building attached. When Caesar asked Cicero to oversee the construction of his vision, Cicero saw none of Pompey's vulgarity in the plan. He called it a glorious undertaking.

For months, Pompey's friends had been muttering that conditions were so bad—with bribery, mob violence and interest rates at 10 percent—that Rome required a dictator. Pompey had shrugged off the suggestion, but Cicero knew his pattern of open denials and backstage manipulation.

When the current consuls' term was about to expire, one of Pompey's cousins began calling for him to assume the dictatorship. Elections were delayed. Then Pompey's allies blocked a temporary interregnum, and Cato accused Pompey of "promoting anarchy to achieve monarchy." The year opened without consuls in place, but elections were scheduled to fill the last six months of the term.

Caesar monitored the disarray and suggested from Gaul that he and Pompey refresh their alliance with a new round of marriages. His great-niece would divorce her husband and marry Pompey, and Caesar would leave Calpurnia and wed Pompey's daughter as soon as she could break her current engagement. The patricians were cheered when Pompey turned down that quadrille to remain a widower.

Even by the following January, no consuls had been installed. Milo thought Pompey had reneged on a promise of support and withdrew in disgust to his native town of Lanuvium. As he was traveling along the Appian Way with his friends and bodyguards, Milo ran into Clodius, 12 miles south of Rome. Clodius was heading back to the capital after a trip to Africa. Their years of hatred boiled over into a brawl. As their slaves fought, Clodius was wounded in the back with a dagger. Friends carried him to a nearby tavern.

Milo faced a crucial choice. He could continue on his way. But if Clodius recovered, he was sure to seek revenge. To protect himself, Milo sent his entourage into the tavern to drag Clodius outside and kill him. When that was done, Milo paid for the loyalty of his slaves by setting them free. As freedmen, they couldn't be tortured into testifying against him.

A senator on his way to Rome found Clodius' body in the road and sent it ahead to the city in his litter. When the body reached Clodius' house on Palatine Hill, his widow's screams roused his allies. The city was convulsed. Throughout the night, men ran to the Forum to protest the murder, and the next day Clodius' body, naked except for his senatorial red shoes, was laid out on the rostra. Pompey joined the tribunes as they praised Clodius. But the people, enraged at the death of another of their leaders, stormed the senate and broke up its benches as kindling for a pyre. They burned the corpse a few steps from the rostra, but the fire could not be contained. It grew until it consumed the senate building.

While Clodius' mourners laid out a funeral banquet in the Forum, the senate met on the Palatine and finally elected Marcus Lepidus as a temporary consul called the *interrex*. But the mob had their own choices and their own plans. They attacked Lepidus' house and smashed the statues of ancestors in his hallway. Refusing to be intimidated, Lepidus cited the binding legal restrictions that stopped him from resigning. Inflamed and growing larger, the mob moved on to other politicians, until they came at last to Pompey. They had forgotten past disagreements and seemed to remember only that he and Clodius had recently united to bring grain to Rome's hungry. Sometimes they hailed Pompey as "Consul!" Other times they shouted, "Dictator!"

Pompey, though, could not ignore the lessons of Sulla's dictatorship. Among the people, Sulla's memory had always been hated, and now Sulla was deplored even by the patricians he had championed. Public opinion was fickle, and the burning of the senate seemed to be causing a shift of sentiment.

A month passed. Milo, who had fled the city, was back—in

hiding but ready to face the inevitable murder charge. Rome still had no consuls and no peace. Under the pretext of searching for Milo, Clodius' gangs were bursting into wealthy houses and carrying off anything valuable. At the senate's request, Pompey went to outlying areas to round up his veterans to keep order in Rome. They followed him loyally to his estate just outside the city, where he installed them as an armed guard in his gardens. Pompey's lifelong fear of assassination was inflamed, and he had heard that Milo planned to kill him too.

The political solution to the turmoil, when it finally emerged, was clever. With Cato's support, Bibulus proposed that Pompey be named consul, not dictator, but without a second consul. Pompey would rule alone; it was the first time in Rome's history that one man would hold the post.

If the patricians hoped that the singular honor would draw Pompey away from Caesar, their plan seemed to work. Within three days of taking office, Pompey proposed new laws, including a retroactive anticorruption measure. It threatened many politicians, including Caesar. Pompey soon exempted him and claimed it had simply been a hasty oversight.

Pompey also tried to make the courts more honest and efficient. He limited the number of lawyers on each side and restricted the time for taking evidence. Jurors would only be drawn from a list of 360 Romans whom Pompey considered incorruptible. To prevent anyone from knowing whom to bribe, all 360 would have to sit through the presentation of evidence. Then a smaller number, drawn by lot, would hand down the verdict. Pompey also did away with character witnesses. Men would be convicted on the evidence, not acquitted because of a parade of distinguished citizens vouching for them.

But Pompey's elaborate precautions couldn't erase a generation of political intrigue. One tribune, who had broken off a messy liaison with Clodia, now supported Milo and claimed that the new rules had been imposed only to hamper his defense. Pompey replied that he would support his reforms with force if necessary.

Cicero's loyalty to Milo never wavered. Milo had led the movement to call him back from exile, and killing Clodius, the man who had banished Cicero, was but another mark in his favor.

All of Rome seemed to have gathered in the Forum for the

opening of Milo's trial. Shops were closed. Pompey was on hand with many bodyguards. His new rules called for brisk presentations—two hours for the accusers, three for the defense. Cicero had written out his speech, a wise precaution since the jeering of Clodius' friends was already unnerving him.

Cicero claimed that on the night of the killing Clodius had deliberately gone to the Appian Way to fight. He produced a witness to testify that Clodius had boasted a few days before the mêlée that Milo would soon be dead. Cicero chose not to bring up the way Milo's men had abandoned Clodius' body on the Via Appia but focused instead on the cremation of his corpse, reducing the people's expression of their grief to a tasteless barbecue.

"You took the bloody corpse of Publius Clodius and hurled it out of doors," Cicero began. "You flung it into the open street and left it there, denuded of funeral portraits and mourners, deprived of its procession and farewell speech, charred on a pile of unlucky timber, cast away to be torn to pieces by those dogs that prowl in the night. This was, indeed, such a shameful thing to do that I can find no words to defend it."

Cicero ended with a reminder that Clodius had hardly been a model citizen, dredging up the charge that Clodius had "committed disgusting acts of incest with his own sister." And Cicero couldn't pass up the chance to remind the court that Clodius had forced into exile "the citizen who had been pronounced by the senate and the people of Rome and all nations of the world to be the savior of the city and all of its citizens." His modesty did not permit him to name the savior.

In a Roman court, the defendant was supposed to be so moved by his own innocence and by his lawyer's eloquence that his tears flowed freely. Milo was not weeping. Cicero knew the jury could see that his client had sat unemotionally through his gales of oratory. Cicero had thundered, had lowered his voice insinuatingly, had summoned up past Roman massacres. His passion had wrung tears from many jurors but not from Milo. Cicero tried to overcome that bad impression.

"If, while we all weep," he said, "you have seen no tears from Milo, if you have noted that his expression is unchanged, and his voice and speech remain steady and unfaltering, you should by no means on that account feel less willing to acquit him."

He compared the killing of Clodius to combat between gladiators. Audiences dislike those whimpering losers who beg for their lives, Cicero said. Instead, they want to spare only the spirited fighters who ask no sympathy. If that's our reaction to a slave's life, the jury's attitude "should be the same, even more so, when it is the life of a valiant Roman citizen that is at stake."

Cicero sensed the coming verdict but hoped to forestall it: "If Milo went into exile, he would be welcomed by every other city in the world. How, then, could anyone venture to vote for the banishment of such a man as that? Blessed is the land that shall give sanctuary to this hero! Ungrateful Rome, if it shall cast him out! Unhappy Rome, if it shall lose him! But enough. Tears choke my voice, and my client does not want a tearful defense."

Cicero called on the jury to be brave enough to vote its convictions and redeem the trust that Pompey had placed in them. The bow to Pompey was politic; he had assigned bodyguards to Cicero for the trial and made it clear that Cicero's personal loyalty to Milo wouldn't compromise their own friendship.

Cicero had not argued a cause so entwined with his own pride and reputation since the Catiline affair. But Clodius' murder had shaken Rome to its unstable foundation, and the evidence outweighed Cicero's inspired flights of language.

Most of the 51 jurors had marked their secret ballots before Cato announced loudly that he was voting to acquit. Spectators agreed afterward that if had spoken earlier, he might have swayed some of the jurors.

But when the vote was tallied, it was 38 for conviction, 13 for acquittal. A day or two later, Milo left for exile in Marseilles, and his estate was sold at auction to satisfy his creditors. An ally was charged with committing the actual murder. It took two trials, but Cicero got that man acquitted by a clear margin.

In exile, Milo recovered a measure of his good humor. Cicero sent him a copy of his defense, which he had vastly improved with arguments he wished he had made in court. Milo responded with a pointed joke. It was just as well that Cicero hadn't actually spoken those persuasive phrases, Milo wrote, because if he had been found not guilty, he'd have missed the red mullet dinners he was enjoying in Marseilles.

XXXIII

POMPEY

52 B.C.

Admirers saw Pompey as a dedicated reformer. Detractors pointed out that Pompey could conveniently close his eye to corruption and unbecoming behavior.

Much as Pompey had adored Julia, no one expected him to mourn her for the rest of his life. When the death of Crassus' son in Parthia made a widow of Metellus Scipio's daughter, she was just the sort of woman Pompey preferred. Cornelia was young, lovely and well educated. She played the lute and almost certainly understood geometry and the intricacies of philosophy better than her new husband. Some Romans felt those accomplishments made a woman pretentious or argumentative, but even they acquitted Cornelia on both counts. Still, she might have been a more appropriate bride for Pompey's son, and the wedding provoked criticism when Pompey, 53 years old, cavorted about with a crown of garlands, oblivious, it seemed, to the dangerous times Rome was experiencing.

Cubiculum (bedroom) from the Villa near Boscoreale, ca. 40–30 B.C. The Metropolitan Museum of Art, Rogers Fund, 1903; Gift of J. Pierpont Morgan, 1917; anonymous gift, 1945.

When his new father-in-law went on trial for corruption, Pompey summoned the 360 jurors to his house and appealed for mercy. Scipio's accuser saw the defendant entering court surrounded by the same Romans who would be judging him and withdrew his charge.

Pompey ruled by fiat. He stopped future consuls and praetors from going out to govern a province until five years had passed from the time they left office. The restriction was designed to prevent another Caesar from plunging into debt to buy an election and then rushing to a province to bail himself out. But again, there was a prominent exception: Pompey had his own governorship of Spain extended for five more years and had himself voted a thousand talents from Rome's treasury to pay for his standing army.

Despite those lapses from his own rules, Pompey seemed to be giving aristocratic Rome a respite from violence, a sense of regeneration. Cicero joined in prosecuting the tribunes involved in burning down the senate, and even though Pompey spoke for the defense in another case, Cicero managed to get a conviction. The return to the rule of law gratified him. To a friend, Cicero wrote that he'd rather have his enemies banished than killed. "For in the first place, I love to pursue by a trial rather than by the sword." And Cicero found that the sight of a jury rejecting Pompey—"the most eminent and powerful"—gave him great pleasure.

Caesar's agents saw how Pompey was rewarding himself and demanded that Caesar receive new favors in return. There was a crisis in Gaul, but Caesar delayed resolving it, holding out to stay in Ravenna to negotiate terms with Pompey. With Crassus dead and most patricians intimidated by the size of the popular crowds, Pompey should have been able to deal with Rome's politics as neatly as he had reformed its laws. But he had never resolved his own conflict. He wanted to be his country's most powerful man, but only within the legal framework of old Rome. Senators had long thought of him as a potential Sulla, and now he seemed unable to convince them he was not.

And although he had rejected Caesar's offer of new marriage bonds and had taken a Metella as his bride, Pompey wanted to placate Caesar in other ways. He broke his own rules to support a move that would let Caesar stand for the consulship in three years without coming to Rome to campaign. Caesar would be safe from prosecution as proconsul in Gaul and could return to Rome wrapped in the protection of his second consulship. When Cicero visited Ravenna, Caesar asked him to stop a young tribune from vetoing the measure, and Cicero was so persuasive that in the end all of the tribunes supported it. When a later bill required candidates to come to Rome, Caesar was specifically exempted.

With Caesar mollified, Pompey turned to the patricians. He named his father-in-law as co-consul for the last five months of his term and set elections for the coming year. Despite the past corruption charges against Scipio, no one demonstrated against him as Pompey's interim choice. For the election, Cato offered himself as consul but ran a predictably stiff-necked campaign and refused to mingle with the voters. They responded to his disdain by electing two other men.

XXXIV

VERCINGETORIX

52 B.C.

The crisis that forced Caesar to leave Ravenna for Gaul had been been building since Clodius was murdered. One tribe, hearing the news, concluded that Caesar would certainly return to Rome. They murdered his commissary officer and some local Roman grain traders and raided Roman supply lines.

Elders of the Arverni tribe opposed joining the insurrection, but a towering young noble named Vercingetorix overruled them and led his people to war, along with a dozen neighboring tribes. Caesar had treated Vercingetorix as a friend, but the young man was aiming higher than Roman patronage. He hoped to unify the Gauls and become their king. Vercingetorix led his troops vigorously but harshly. Those found guilty of major crimes were tortured to death, and lesser infractions were punishable with an ear cut off or an eye gouged out.

Vercingetorix dispatched a lieutenant at the head of his

Coin with a head of Vercingetorix. The New York Public Library Picture Collection.

growing army in the direction of a Roman settlement at Narbo. Caesar moved up from the south with reinforcements to block him, then traveled without sleeping across the snowy countryside to round up recruits. When he rushed the Gauls with those forces, Vercingetorix declined the challenge and chose instead to fall back and attack a tribe still loyal to Rome.

Caesar faced a quandary. If the Gauls saw that he couldn't protect an ally, they might all join the revolt. But releasing his legionaries from winter quarters this early would expose them to starvation when the grain ran out. For Caesar, a choice between losing prestige or taking a great risk was no choice at all. Leaving behind two legions, he marched to the rescue. When Vercingetorix heard that Caesar was on the way, he lifted the siege and set out to confront the Romans in a cavalry battle. But Caesar had hired 400 professional horsemen from Germany, and they routed the Gauls.

Vercingetorix called on his war council for a change in tactics. From now on, their energies should go into cutting off the Romans from their supplies. To prove their determination, Vercingetorix urged them to set fire to any town that couldn't be made impregnable. That would deprive the Romans of grain and discourage fainthearted Gauls from hiding at home to avoid fighting.

Vercingetorix wanted the Gauls to understand that losing their towns was far less wrenching than seeing their wives and children dragged off as Roman slaves. The townspeople of Avaricum—where the meeting was being held—fell to their knees and begged Vercingetorix not to set fire to their houses. Not only was Avaricum considered the loveliest town in Gaul, but its residents also insisted that its river and the surrounding marshland made them secure. Only a narrow strip of land led to the town gates, and they could defend that. Vercingetorix considered their arguments and relented.

He selected a campsite 16 miles from Avaricum and waited for the Roman troops to starve. To punctuate his strategy, he picked off any Roman squad that left camp to forage. Caesar varied the times and routes of those expeditions, but Vercingetorix succeeded in killing large numbers of his men.

The Romans began to construct a siege platform against Avaricum. But Caesar was again disappointed when the friendly tribes didn't send the grain they had promised. Although the Romans had seized cattle from a few distant villages, their supplies were almost exhausted, and for several days they went without grain at all. Caesar rode from legion to legion, offering to lift the siege and retreat if their hunger became unbearable. After six years, the loyalty of his men was legendary. He had shared their hardships, promoted them for merit rather than birth and shared the plunder. Now they begged him not to give up. If he did, they said, they would be disgraced.

Caesar learned that Vercingetorix planned to set an ambush at the next place he expected the Romans to be scavenging, and at midnight he slipped away to ambush the ambushers. But despite his precautions, the Gauls heard the Romans approach and moved to a slight hill surrounded by marsh. If the Romans attacked, they would be easy targets, bogged down in mud.

To goad the legionaries on, Vercingetorix's men stood up in plain view. Caesar's men wanted to ignore their tactical disadvantage and fight, but Caesar refused. The victory would cost too much in Roman life, he said. Afterward, Caesar assured readers of his commentaries that the soldiers had been eager to add to his glory. Those readers wouldn't know that Caesar's men had been near starvation and Avaricum's larder was full.

When Vercingetorix returned to camp, he was met by angry critics who charged that by taking away the cavalry, he had left the camp poorly defended with no capable lieutenant in charge. Was he betraying his people? Did he prefer to receive the kingship from Caesar's hand rather than to fight for it? Vercingetorix answered each of the charges. He said he hadn't left a subordinate in charge because that man might have been stampeded into fighting a pitched battle with the Romans, and this was not the time.

"As for supreme power," Vercingetorix said, "I have no need to get that from Caesar as a reward for treachery. I can get it through the victory that I—and all of the Gauls—have already nearly won. To understand that I am telling the truth," he added, "listen to what Roman soldiers have to say."

With that, he brought out Roman prisoners in chains and told them to describe conditions in their camp. Caesar had rehearsed all of his men with the same story, and they repeated it dutifully: Hunger among the Romans was so intense that men had no strength for their daily jobs. If the siege didn't succeed within the next three days, Caesar intended to withdraw.

For Vercingetorix, their testimony confirmed the wisdom of

his tactics. "Thanks to me, without spilling a drop of our blood, you see this great and victorious army dying from hunger." When Caesar's men slunk away in defeat, he added, no tribe in Gaul would allow them in its territory. At that, his soldiers gave him a Gallic ovation—cheering and banging their lances and shields together.

The Romans' siege platform faced Avaricum and supported towers that rose above the town walls. Vercingetorix was camping north of the platform. As the siege went on, Roman soldiers tried in vain to penetrate the walls. Caesar was forced to admire the Gauls' adaptability. "They are a most ingenious race," he noted, "very good at imitating and making use of any ideas suggested to them by others."

The Gauls had learned from the grappling hooks that the Romans used to disable ships. They threw nooses over the siege hooks and pulled them inside their walls. Protected in their own towers by thick curtains made of hides, they darted out only to throw fire down on the Romans' wooden framework.

The Gauls had an ally in their perpetually cold and rainy weather. But after working unceasingly for 25 days, the Romans finally raised a platform that almost touched the town walls. All through that time, Caesar hadn't left his men's side. The result was a structure 330 feet wide and rising 80 feet into the air.

One midnight as Caesar was exhorting his workers not to relax, smoke wafted up from beneath his feet. He discovered that the Gauls, who once mined the iron ore beneath their land, had tunneled under the Roman platform and lighted a fire there. With the smoke as their cover, soldiers swarmed out from two town gates. Other Gauls hurled down torches and burning wood to spread the blaze. Amid the smoke and flame, Caesar had to decide whether to fight the fire or the enemy. He had been holding back two legions from work on the towers, and now he sent them to rush the Gauls coming out of their gates. Roman soldiers from camp hurried to beat out the fire while others shifted Caesar's towers so they wouldn't burn with the platform.

Fighting raged through the night. To Caesar, the Gauls seemed to be fighting as though their country's fate depended on this single moment. He would never forget the way one Gaul stood in front of the town gate and threw chunks of tallow and tar onto the fire that was threatening to engulf the Roman towers. When the man was killed by an arrow, another Gaul stepped over his body, took his place and hurled more tar at the Romans. An arrow struck him, and his replacement, and the next, but Gauls kept stepping up to the fatal line until the Romans had beaten out the fires and the battle was over.

With the Gauls pushed back behind the walls, Vercingetorix urged the local troops to evacuate the town quietly the next night and march to his camp. When the moment came, however, the women pleaded with their men not to abandon them and their children. Caesar understood why the appeal was ignored. "People facing extreme danger themselves," he noted, "are too afraid to feel pity, and the men remained unmoved."

When the women saw that they were being deserted, they cried out to the Romans on a nearby tower, alerting them to the proposed escape. The uproar convinced the Gauls to give up their scheme.

If few generals excelled Caesar in tactics, there were none who could match his timing. The next day brought a heavy downpour, and Caesar noticed that guards along the enemy's wall seemed less alert than usual. He told his men to move more languidly themselves and edged one siege tower closer to the wall. Partially hidden by the rain, Caesar readied his legions. You have wanted action, he told them. Today you can enjoy the rewards of all your work. There will be prizes for the first men to scale the wall.

He gave the order to attack. From every spot, Romans sprang out and wrested command of the wall from its panicky sentries. The Gauls rallied long enough to form ranks in the marketplace, but instead of lowering his men into their midst, Caesar marched the Romans along the top of the wall until they controlled it entirely. Terrified, the Gauls threw down their weapons and rushed for the gates, where Caesar's cavalry waited to cut them down.

Once inside, the Roman legionaries weren't content with looting. Enraged and exhausted from the prolonged siege, they tore through the town. Caesar observed later that they had not spared the old, or the women, or the children. With no apparent regret, he recorded that barely 800 of 40,000 Gauls within the town escaped to Vercingetorix's camp.

It was still dark when those refugees reached camp. Vercingetorix ordered them to enter quietly. He was afraid of his men's reaction when they learned of the mass slaughter. But at dawn, he couldn't delay any longer and called a council of war. The Romans hadn't won because of their courage, Vercingetorix assured his fellow chieftains, but only because they were more skilled than the Gauls in conducting a siege. He could legitimately absolve himself of blame since he had recommended against defending Avaricum. Now he would enlist those tribes that hadn't already joined. Once united, no force on earth could stop the Gauls.

His confidence buoyed the others. After a humiliating defeat, Gallic generals often went into hiding to avoid being seen by their troops. But as Caesar soon learned from informants, this debacle had somehow increased Vercingetorix's stature.

Storming the town had given the Romans grain and supplies, and spring was near. Caesar intended to move against Vercingetorix's camp but was called away to put down disloyal stirrings among the Aedui. The distraction irritated him, since he felt that he had always treated the Aedui especially well. Both Caesar and Vercingetorix took their armies to Gergovia, where Caesar discovered the reason for the trouble: the Aedui had heard that Caesar had insulted their leaders. Caesar convinced them that the rumors were slanders, and they threw down their weapons in apology. Caesar took the episode as more proof of Gallic impetuousness, but he didn't punish them for it.

Through a series of well-timed feints and ruses, Caesar provoked a battle with Vercingetorix at Gergovia. At first, the Romans had the advantage. Women inside the town thought their men had lost and threw down silver coins for the Romans. Pleading with Caesar's men not to kill civilians as they had done at Avaricum, the women leaned forward, stretched out their hands, bared their breasts.

But then Gallic reinforcements showed up in vast numbers. Those same women called out encouragement and held up their children to inspire them. Caesar's officers lost control of their men, who had expected a quick victory. The Romans panicked when still another force of Gauls arrived. They saw only their Gallic clothing and didn't notice that the Aedui had their right shoulders bared in the customary sign of friendship. Before Vercingetorix broke contact, 700 Roman legionaries and 46 centurions had been killed.

Caesar called his battered troops together. He assured them

that they were victims of their bad position, not of superior forces. But he also chided them for being overeager when the battle began. "I look for self-control and discipline in a soldier just as much as valor and bravery," Caesar said.

The Aedui had fought at the Romans' side, but now they were defecting. When their leaders sent envoys to sign a peace treaty with Vercingetorix, Gauls across the countryside also began swarming to him.

Caesar had left some troops with Labienus and started with the rest back to the Aedui base at Gergovia. Now he found his army divided and Gauls rampaging along the Loire River. They intimidated neutral tribes and were trying to force Caesar back into the Roman provinces. There were strong tactical reasons to retreat, but "it was out of the question," Caesar explained, "because of the disgrace and humiliation involved."

Labienus heard exaggerated reports of Caesar's setbacks, which convinced him to move his army to Caesar's side. When he succeeded, a decisive battle was assured. Either Caesar would win, or Gaul would be rid of foreigners. As Caesar's political enemies saw it, either way Rome would be the loser.

Caesar moved his troops down toward the province's border, hoping to keep his supply lines open. The Gauls saw his retreat and thought they had won, but Vercingetorix knew Caesar better. If the Romans left briefly for their province, they would come back again in greater numbers. Instead of celebrating, the Gauls must attack.

Vercingetorix hit the Roman column while its men were loaded down with baggage. To terrify them, he drew his immense army in front of their camp, hoping the Romans would flee—leaving behind their weapons, their supplies, their reputations. But Caesar formed his men into a hollow square with their baggage inside. The German cavalry he had brought repaid his faith by forcing the Gauls off a ridge and back into their camp. Caesar had the satisfaction of seeing three Aeduan generals among his prisoners. When Vercingetorix marched to an armed town called Alesia, Caesar chased after him, killing 3,000 rearguard troops.

Vercingetorix had sought refuge in a well-protected community high on a hill, with a river running on both sides. On top, the town of Alesia faced onto a level stretch of land some three miles long. But the siege was a technique the Roman army had perfected and Caesar had raised to an art. He surrounded the town with eight heavily fortified camps and 23 redoubts, all connected by a ring of siege platforms. The circle had a perimeter of 11 miles.

Vercingetorix risked one hard skirmish at the three-mile field outside the walls. Again, Caesar's German cavalry drove them back. In panic, the Gauls jammed the town gates, and many were slaughtered before they could get inside.

The rout convinced Vercingetorix that he needed even more reinforcements to stop Caesar from sealing him in. Just before midnight, he sent his entire cavalry through a gap in the tightening Roman blockade. He told them not to fight but to ride to their tribes and recruit every man of fighting age. They must stress that Vercingetorix had already done so much for Gaul's independence that it would be terrible to fail him now.

Some 80,000 troops were barricaded in Alesia with rations for only 30 days. But by rationing and parceling out a large herd of cattle they had amassed, the provisions should last long enough for the reinforcements to arrive and attack Caesar's ring of troops.

When informers gave Caesar the details of Vercingetorix's plan, he increased the fortifications. He instructed his men to dig a new trench 20 feet wide and to move the siege platforms back from that trench by 40 paces. He had two more trenches dug and diverted water from the nearest river to fill the inner trench. Behind the two trenches, Caesar added a new platform and tower, and a breastwork with forked branches to ward off any Gauls who tried to scale it.

A circle so enormous was difficult to patrol adequately. To stop the Gauls from bursting out at a weak point, Caesar had more trenches dug with sticks embedded in the bottom so that only the sharp points projected above ground. Anyone who tried to cross risked being run through; Roman soldiers called the sticks "gravestones." Wood blocks were hammered into the ground of the other pits, with only an iron hook exposed to stab and maim. The men called them "stings."

But the job was only half done when Caesar called on his exhausted men to repeat their intense efforts, to protect their backs against the reinforcements that the Gallic cavalry were recruiting.

The outer circle of trenches was to be three miles longer than the inner line. It billowed out and nipped in, following contours of the hillside where the ground wasn't level. North of Alesia, one hill was too massive to include within the defense perimeter. Caesar built a camp on its slope and left officers there with two legions. Caesar now had two perimeters to defend, a total of 25 miles. He warned his men to stock up with a month's provisions since they would not be leaving this double ring of safety.

Caesar was prepared, but Vercingetorix's cavalry was having trouble raising reinforcements. Tribal elders were worried about their ability to control so many warriors at one spot. Instead, the tribes imposed quotas—35,000 men or 10,000; smaller tribes were sending 2,000. Even at that, the massing became impressive. Finally 240,000 infantrymen and 8,000 cavalry were assembled. Marching toward Alesia, they were exhilarated by their sheer numbers. The Romans would surely be demoralized by the sight of them. When the other Gauls charged out from inside the town, the two forces would grind the Romans to dust.

Inside Alesia, however, spirits were sinking. The relief force was late, and the grain was gone. When Vercingetorix met with his council, some voices urged immediate surrender. Others thought they should try to break free while they still had the strength to fight. Critognatus, an Arvenian nobleman, suggested another way out. He reminded them of what an earlier generation of Gauls facing starvation had done: "Instead of surrendering to the enemy, they stayed alive by eating the flesh of those they considered too old or too young for battle."

His listeners found the idea shocking but not unthinkable. They reached a compromise: anyone unfit to fight would be expelled from the town. They would resort to Critognatus' option only after all else had failed.

They drove out the women from Alesia, along with the old men and the children. Pushed out from the gates, they ran to the edge of Caesar's fortifications and begged the Roman soldiers to take them as slaves; they would do anything for food. Caesar wouldn't permit another drain on his own rations or the presence of the enemy inside his lines. He posted guards to keep the refugees out.

Starving and without water, the men and women who had

built the town of Alesia died in agony on the plain outside its gates.

The Gallic relief forces arrived at last. They took over a hill a mile from the outer Roman circle. The next day, the soldiers spread themselves across the three-mile plain, to let themselves be seen by Vercingetorix and his beleaguered troops behind their walls. When the Gauls inside Alesia realized that deliverance had arrived, they set off a clamor of congratulation and readied themselves for battle.

In the first two days of battle, the Gauls challenged Caesar's fortifications, but each time Caesar prevailed. Back at camp, the Gauls reviewed their situation. For all of their overwhelming numbers, they had been defeated twice. Caesar had prepared his defenses brilliantly, but every defense had a weakness. They dispatched local scouts to find it.

Caesar had known his vulnerable point from the beginning: the camp north of the town. When the Gauls saw that breach in the Roman line, they picked 60,000 soldiers from their most ferocious tribes and mapped an attack for noon the next day. To lead the charge, they chose one of Vercingetorix's kinsmen, who took his huge army to a hiding place behind the hill. At sunrise, he told the soldiers to rest throughout the morning.

From his higher vantage point inside Alesia, Vercingetorix watched the cavalry of his fellow Gauls heading toward Rome's sparsely guarded outer circle. Caesar had ridden to his own high ground to survey the scene. If the Roman line held, Vercingetorix and his thousands of men locked inside Alesia could not survive. But if Gallic troops breached the Roman defenses, Caesar would be ruined or dead.

The Romans' hillside camp was as open to assault as Caesar had feared, and the tens of thousands of Gauls could do many jobs at once—forming a moving wall with their shields, hurling spears, building up earthen ramps against the fortress walls, boosting themselves up to the ramparts. The Romans were tiring, and their ammunition was exhausted. They could not hold out much longer.

From his command post, Caesar saw the danger and sent Labienus and six cohorts to their aid. He gave the camp's officers permission to withdraw if they absolutely could not hold on. As

Labienus rode off, Caesar moved along the line, urging on his troops. He called to them: The rewards of all the other battles depend on how you fight today! On how you fight this very hour!

Behind their walls, Vercingetorix's troops fired enough arrows to drive the Romans from the guard towers, and they filled in Caesar's deep trenches with wattles and dirt. As they got close enough, they began tearing down the fortifications with grappling hooks. The Romans facing the town were alarmed by the din from the battle behind them.

Hurrying to the vulnerable points, Caesar brought fresh troops to relieve his exhausted men. When he had satisfied himself that they could beat back the Gauls on his inner ring, he rushed farther up the slope with his cavalry to where Labienus' men were buckling under pressure. They recognized Caesar by the scarlet cloak he always wore in battle.

The Gauls made one last push to overrun the camp. The Romans threw aside their javelins and waded into the enemy with swords. Under that unrelenting pressure, the Gauls broke, and Caesar's cavalry cut them off as they ran. Even after seven bloody years, Caesar considered the slaughter that followed to be enormous. From each crushed unit, his legionaries brought him a fresh Gallic standard. By the end, 74 were heaped at Caesar's feet.

From the high vantage point of the town walls, the scenes of devastation were unmistakable. The Gauls could see handfuls of the reinforcements straggling back to their camp. More wrenching still was the sight in the far distance of Romans carrying off Gallic breastplates dripping with fresh blood. Gaul's officers lay dead among their men, and Vercingetorix's kinsman, head of the relief army, was captured and taken to Caesar. Alesia's forces withdrew again inside their barren town.

When the survivors reached the Gauls' relief camp, those who had been left behind got ready to flee, but it was too late. Caesar sent his cavalry after them, and by midnight he had captured or killed great numbers. If the legionaries had not been worn out, the Romans could have destroyed the entire horde. As it was, Caesar's proconsulship had wiped out an entire generation of young Gauls—farmers and workers, husbands and fathers.

The next morning, Vercingetorix called his last council meeting. He asked his officers to remember that he had not taken on this crusade for personal glory but for an independent Gaul.

He had failed. Now he was putting his life in their hands. They could appease Caesar by killing him outright. Or they could hand him over alive to the Romans.

The chieftains sent a delegation to ask Caesar what he would prefer. Caesar had his curule's chair carried to the front of the fortifications and called for Gaul's soldiers to be marched out with their weapons and lined up by tribes. He parceled out prisoners to his men, one slave for each legionary. He sent other troops to protect the tribes that had honored their treaties with Rome. Hoping to win back the loyalty of the Aedui and the Arverni, Caesar announced plans to travel to Aeduan territory to accept their surrender in person and release their prisoners of war, about 20,000 in all.

Vercingetorix was sent to Rome for Caesar's triumph. He could live until Romans had cheered his humiliation, and then he would go down into the dungeon to die.

XXXV

CICERO

51–50 B.C.

While Caesar was planning his return to Rome, Cicero was preparing to leave. Pompey's reforms had created a shortage of governors, and eligible men from past years were being pressed into service, including a reluctant Cicero. The assignments were made by lot, and he drew Cilicia. He felt as though he were being exiled again and called his new duties a colossal bore.

In the six years since Cicero returned to Rome, he had suffered embarrassments but had also received rewards. Pompey and Hortensius had nominated him to replace Crassus' son as one of Rome's 15 augurs, a lifetime appointment. Augurs were supposed to read the signs for proof that the gods approved a proposed action. The methods were said to date from Romulus' time, but the augurs could play a useful political role in keeping Rome's citizens docile. Cicero was elected easily.

He was adding to his philosophical writings and enjoying conversations with his brother and friends as they strolled along Pompey's new portico or around Cicero's own promenades in

Arpinum. A noted Greek scholar was helping to catalog Cicero's growing library, and Tiro, a well-educated young slave acting as his secretary, became like a son. Cicero's prudent life was uneventful in comparison to what had gone before, but it suited the sedentary, 56-year-old man he had become. Even before he left Italy, Cicero implored friends to keep the senate from extending his service abroad. He wrote to Atticus, "Do not imagine that I have any consolation in this great trouble except the hope that it will not be continued past the year."

Quintus had left Caesar to go to Cilicia as Cicero's lieutenant; each took his son. For some time, Atticus had been distressed by the way Quintus was treating his sister, and he urged Cicero to be sure that the couple at least parted amicably. Cicero reported that when they reached Quintus' villa for a farewell dinner, his brother had asked Pomponia in the most civil way, "Please invite the women for dinner, and I will ask the men."

Pomponia resented the way Quintus had sent a servant ahead to order the food. She replied, "I am only a stranger here myself."

"See," Quintus said to Cicero, "what I am forced to endure every day."

Pomponia declined to dine with them. Quintus sent courses to her; she returned the plates untouched. On the night of their parting, she refused to sleep with him. Atticus believed his sister's complaint that Quintus was a peevish husband, but Cicero assured his friend that "no one could be more good-natured than my brother or ruder than your sister."

Cicero didn't hurry to his new post. It took 16 days to reach Tarentum. There, he stayed with Pompey, who was recuperating in the town's mild air. Pompey was often indisposed. He had never thrived in Rome's rough-and-tumble and looked for reasons to retire to his quiet villa. He invited Cicero to spend three days, and Cicero was eager to hear his assessment of the political scene. Cicero's friends wanted him to write immediately after his visit to reveal Pompey's intentions. "He says one thing and means another," one complained, "but he is not really clever enough to hide his true desires."

Cicero had to disappoint them. Pompey wasn't ready to bare his heart to a man who had proved unreliable under stress.

Writing home, Cicero put a good face on his disappointment. He and Pompey had talked nothing but politics, he said, "but our conversation could not and should not be repeated in writing."

Cicero saw Cilicia as a prison, though the province was a plum for most ambitious Romans. It lay far east on the Mediterranean, separated by mountain passes from Anatolia on one side and Syria and Mesopotamia on the other. Before his murder, Clodius had added the island of Cyprus and swatches of rough Asian coastline. The people of the province's cities spoke Greek. They expected a Roman governor to keep the peace, settle disputes and collect taxes.

Cicero, a thorough civilian, had recruited men with military experience in case any soldiering was required. Besides his brother, he had enlisted Pomptinus, a commander during the Catiline uprising. But Pomptinus, conducting a romance in Rome, was as reluctant as his chief to sail. His delay allowed Cicero to fritter away more days in Brundisium and also to clear up the mild stomach upset he seemed to have developed at Pompey's.

When Pomptinus still didn't arrive, Cicero set sail without him. In Ephesus, Cicero found that crowds had come from the countryside to see the famous writer and orator. He allowed himself to bask in their adulation for three days before starting out for Laodicea, the first city that was actually within his province. The moment he arrived, he notified Atticus so that the onerous year abroad could officially be calculated from that hour.

Despite his reluctance, Cicero burst upon his province with his usual energy and integrity. Other Roman governors had passed on the expenses of their entourage to the towns they visited. Wherever Cicero went, he heard his new subjects complaining about their poverty and their taxes and announced that no funds, public or private, should be spent on him.

"All the people are, as you might imagine, tired of life," Cicero wrote to Atticus. He forbade his officers to accept even the food and firewood normally due them, and he moved them from commandeered houses into field tents. His officers responded to Cicero's code by curtailing their past abuses. When Appius Claudius, the former governor, heard about the reforms, he wrote chiding Cicero for rescinding his harsh taxes and extortions; Cicero replied diplomatically. To Atticus, he complained that during his tenure Appius had not been "a human being but some kind of wild beast."

The people cheered Cicero's honesty, but less than a month after his arrival he was alarmed to hear that the Parthians who had killed Crassus two years earlier had crossed the Euphrates and planned to invade Roman territory. Suddenly, Cicero faced a crisis. He led a force of 12,000 infantry and 2,600 horsemen to a safe campsite in Cappadocia with an ample supply of grain and trusted to the approaching winter to be his best defense. He didn't intend to fight if he could avoid it.

To ease his isolation, Cicero wrote to Atticus more often than ever, but a letter from Rome took 47 days to reach him. "Ah," Cicero wrote, "what a long way it is!"

He soon learned that he couldn't wait passively in camp after all. The Parthians had shifted course and were heading for Cilicia. Cicero marched his troops to Tarsus and then to the mountain range that divided Cilicia from Syria. He was thankful that Pomptinus had arrived to lead an assault against the enemy in mid-October. Cicero followed it up the next day with an attack of his own. Together, they cut up the Parthian forces and burned their forts. "I was hailed as 'Imperator,' " Cicero wrote incredulously to Atticus, and for a few days he had even occupied territory once used as a campsite by Alexander the Great. Although, Cicero added quickly, "he was rather a better general than you or I."

The victory encouraged other Roman commanders, and the Parthians were turned back. Cicero's adventure had convinced him that he might be able to cope with his distasteful military responsibilities. He laid a siege against a rebellious town called Pindenissum. "With my toil and preparation I settled the business without loss of life," he boasted to Atticus, "though many were wounded."

Cicero declared a holiday and allowed his troops to take what they wanted from the town, except for the horses, which would become Roman property. Selling the Pindenissians as slaves brought another 12 million sesterces. Cicero knew that his victory was unlikely to echo through the Forum. " 'The Pindenissians!' you will be exclaiming," he wrote to Atticus. " 'Who the plague are they? I never heard the name.' " That was hardly his fault, he added. He couldn't turn his small army into the stuff of military legend, and that suited him fine.

But not every problem could be neatly resolved. Cato's nephew, Marcus Brutus, who had served as quaestor in Cilicia the previous year, asked Cicero to protect the interests of two Roman moneylenders. Cicero discovered that the men were charging 48 percent interest—four times the limit Cicero had recently imposed and the senate had approved. And Cicero objected to the tone of Brutus' letters. "Even when he asks a favor," he complained to Atticus, "he writes in a way that is brusque, arrogant and ungracious." Looking further into the matter, Cicero found that the actual creditor was Brutus himself, who had circumvented the law that forbade such loans. With that, Cicero refused to intervene.

Atticus didn't applaud Cicero's righteousness. He saw Brutus, now in his mid-thirties, emerging as one of his generation's leading patricians. In fact, Atticus had warned Cicero that the most important treasure he could bring back from his province would be Brutus' good will.

"Well, I shall be sorry that he is angry with me," Cicero wrote, "but I shall be far sorrier at discovering he is not the man I imagined he was."

During his absence from Italy, Cicero had asked friends to look after his daughter. Widowed at 18, Tullia was trying to get out of an unhappy second marriage. Cicero wanted a suitable third husband for her. Before leaving Rome, he had heard rumors of troubles in the marriage of Cornelius Dolabella and asked a friend to promote a match for Tullia with him. The girl had other suitors, but Dolabella was gratifyingly aristocratic. He was dashing, temperamental and committed to Caesar, which Cicero knew. He was also deeply in debt, which Cicero did not know until after the couple had married.

Cicero began a letter-writing campaign to win a *supplicatio*, days of thanksgiving such as had been voted to Caesar after his victories in Gaul. When the senate took up the request, Cato argued without success that the honors had become cheap and should be abolished.

After the thanksgiving had been approved, Cato wrote to assure Cicero that his vote had not been personal. But, he added, the honor would not guarantee a triumph: "And much more honorable than any triumph is a senate decree that a general preserved a province for Rome by his mildness and good character than by force of arms and luck from the gods."

He concluded, "Farewell, and still esteem me"—which might have been easier for Cicero if he hadn't found out that Cato had voted a *supplicatio* of 20 days for his son-in-law, a man who had not stirred from his province capital, while Cicero had marched out to meet the enemy.

"Forgive me, I cannot and will not bear it," Cicero complained to Atticus. But when he received a flattering and consoling letter from Gaul, he also understood that Caesar was promoting a rift between him and the aristocrats, and Cicero was not prepared to let that happen.

XXXVI

CURIO

51–49 B.C.

In Rome, the issue had become one of trust. Caesar was sure the senate aristocrats were trying to trick him into giving up his command in Gaul before he could assume the legal protection of a second consulship, and they suspected that Caesar did not intend to give up his military command at all.

Pompey, caught in the middle, was distrusted by both sides. He tried to reach a compromise by delaying the decision over Caesar's provinces until March 1. But after that, Pompey said, he would not hesitate to act.

The patricians pushed him for a stronger commitment. What if the senate told Caesar to give up Gaul but a tribune vetoed the order? Pompey said he would consider it the same as Caesar himself defying the senate. A senator raised another possibility: "But suppose that Caesar tried to become consul and keep his military command at the same time?"

Wall painting of a lady playing the cithara, from the Villa at Boscoreale. The Metropolitan Museum of Art, Rogers Fund, 1903.

Pompey lost his temper and demanded, "Suppose my own son should attack me violently?"

That ended the debate but didn't resolve it. Pompey thought he had done enough for Caesar by tabling the discussion until March. It would take at least until the following July for Caesar's replacement to reach Gaul. By that time, Caesar would have been elected consul for the coming year. By waiting outside the city walls until January, he could combine his military triumph with his inaugural parade.

Even if Pompey was acting in good faith, Caesar couldn't take the chance. He might surrender his command only to find that his enemies had delayed the consular elections. That would leave him stranded outside Rome and vulnerable to any number of lawsuits. He wanted to be elected consul in absentia and hold on to his troops until the day he took office.

Looking for a dependable tribune to protect him, Caesar picked Curio, once Cicero's protégé and Mark Antony's intimate friend. Curio was no longer a dependable patrician voice. He had married Clodius' widow and seemed to take on Clodius' politics.

As tribune, Curio revived the explosive issue of land reform. He also began to promote Caesar's interests, which convinced the patricians that he had been bribed. Curio had become rich when his father died, but he was no less spendthrift than in the days he and Antony had run up enormous gambling debts. To court public favor, he had built two theaters in a startling half-shell design that could accommodate two different plays in the morning and then be swung around and united into an oval in the afternoon as a gladiators' amphitheater.

Many senators believed that his lavish display had made Curio receptive to receiving a regular allowance from Gaul.

Caesar directed Curio to make a proposal that sounded fair but would probably be unacceptable to Pompey: if Caesar was forced to give up his provinces, Pompey should do the same. Once all of the extraordinary commands were ended, Curio said, Rome could enjoy lasting peace.

Pompey's faction struck back angrily, pointing out that since Pompey's term had not expired yet, the issues were entirely different. But in the streets, Curio's bold challenge won him respect, and Pompey offered to bend the rules again: Caesar could keep his provinces until the Ides of November. Caesar would have to leave Gaul by mid-November anyway, if he planned to take office the following January, after winning in absentia.

The concession didn't relieve Caesar's suspicions. Any fixed date for turning over his command had become unacceptable; and since Pompey was making the rules, there had to be a trick to them.

The intrigue broke off abruptly when Pompey fell ill while visiting Naples. He had suffered from bouts of sickness before, possibly the same malarial fever that Caesar had in his youth. But this attack looked alarming. The entire city of Naples made sacrifices to the gods, imploring them not to let Pompey die.

After weeks of hovering near death, Pompey recovered. Feasts of thanksgiving spread throughout Italy. Pompey had always craved respect more than power, and now the affection of his countrymen overwhelmed him. Men, women and children lined his route back to Rome, wearing garlands and tossing flowers in his path. As the sun set, they brought torches to light his path. The display left Pompey exalted, a mood that had seldom served him well. Before leaving Rome, he had been nervous about Caesar's military might. But now the gods must have spared him for a reason. No army could withstand this outpouring of love.

Home again, Pompey praised Caesar extravagantly, offered to lay down his own command and predicted that his friend and former father-in-law would volunteer to do the same. Caesar had been fighting ferocious tribes in Gaul for eight years. Surely he would welcome the chance to come home to well-earned honors and repose.

Caesar's supporters found Pompey's compliments only another attempt to win the propaganda war. They derided Pompey's protests that his own vast powers had been forced on him and, not satisfied with his promise to resign from office, they challenged him to do it now.

A recent transfer of troops also called into question Pompey's sincerity. He had once sent Caesar a legion to fight in Gaul. Now reports from the East indicated that the Parthians were finally making the assault Cicero had expected. The senate voted to send two legions to Syria as reinforcements, and Pompey suggested that he and Caesar each supply one—his own contribution the legion he had lent to Gaul. The result weakened Caesar by two legions, not one. And when the transfer was finished, Pompey didn't send the troops to Syria after all. He kept both legions near Rome.

Since Caesar wouldn't be running for consul until the next year, he released Mark Antony from active duty to stand for tribune and tend to his interests, as Curio had been doing. But Caesar's candidate for consul was defeated, and his deputy Labienus seemed ready to desert Caesar for the senate patricians. Those developments—and reports of low morale among Caesar's troops—bolstered Pompey's confidence. When senators asked again where he would find the forces to defend Rome if Caesar challenged the senate, Pompey answered, "Wherever I stamp my foot in Italy, there will spring up enough troops in an instant—both cavalry and infantry."

In Cilicia, Cicero was getting letters that predicted a military clash between Caesar and Pompey. One friend, not sure which side to support, assumed that Cicero faced the same dilemma.

"On the one hand," the man noted, "I have an interest and connection with Pompey's party. And on the other, it is only Caesar's cause I dislike, not his friends." He added a reminder that Cicero scarcely needed: "You are aware, I'm sure, that so long as the rifts in our country are confined to talking, we should always join the more righteous side. But as soon as the sword is drawn, the strongest party is always the best."

Pompey's November 13 deadline passed with Caesar still entrenched in Gaul. On December 1, Marcellus, a consul and one of Caesar's rabid foes, called for a vote on the issue of sending commanders to replace Caesar. A majority of senators withdrew to one side of the chamber to show they endorsed the idea.

Curio read the senators' mood accurately. Most of them had seen too much violence and bloodshed in their lifetime. They wanted peace, and Curio was ready with a proposal to ensure it. He asked for a vote on his suggestion that Pompey and Caesar leave their commands at the same time.

Three hundred and seventy senators voted yes, only 22 voted no. Elated, Curio bounded past the senate door to join Caesar's supporters outside. Convinced that a civil war had been averted, they showered Curio with flowers.

Marcellus disagreed. He told his fellow senators sourly, "Enjoy your victory. You have won Caesar as your master."

The next day, Marcellus assured the senate that Caesar had already crossed the Alps with his army and was marching on Rome. Curio denounced the rumor as false and promised to veto any attempt to label Caesar a public enemy. Marcellus responded that he would take steps on his own authority as consul.

With his entourage and crowds of curious townspeople, Marcellus strode to Pompey's house just outside the city walls. He had brought along a sword and pressed it into Pompey's hand. "My colleague and I hereby order you to march on your country's behalf against Caesar." He assigned to Pompey the two legions intended for Syria but held at Capua and authorized him to raise whatever additional forces he needed.

Without a senate decree, those orders were illegal. Caesar's demands may have stretched the existing precedents, but he had been careful not to defy the senate. And in their latest vote, the senators had returned his wary respect. Now a small group of patricians—Marcellus, Cato and their most ungiving allies—were the ones undermining the senate's authority. Pompey genuinely wanted to preserve Rome's rule of law, but he faced a handful of aristocrats demanding that he defy history and tradition.

After he had heard Marcellus out, Pompey replied evasively, "If there is no better way."

A few days later, Pompey left to inspect the two legions stationed at Capua. On his way, he crossed paths with Cicero, who had finally been relieved of his command in Cilicia and was passing through Campania on his way back to Rome. They spent two hours together. Although Pompey had other matters on his mind, Cicero wrung from him a promise to support his triumph at some later date.

Pompey warned Cicero against getting caught up in the current debate or antagonizing Caesar's tribunes. If Pompey had gone south to round up more troops, he didn't announce it to Cicero. But he did let him know that the situation was bleak.

On December 25, Cicero and Pompey met again outside Rome. By then Cicero had concluded that most Romans would rather yield to Caesar's demands than risk war. Back on Italian soil, he found the patricians divided and most merchants and bankers opposed to Pompey's policies. As for Caesar, Cicero had decided that "it is late to resist him when, for ten years, we have nurtured this viper in our bosom."

But it seemed Pompey no longer wanted to avoid a show-down. He had become convinced that no matter how peaceable Caesar's return to Italy might appear, his goal would be to over-throw the Republic. He was confident that his forces could repel Caesar's challenge "if he should go mad" and launch an attack.

Cicero began to talk himself into a convenient hostility to-ward Caesar, even though Caesar was still trying to charm him with friendly letters.

Atticus asked him, "What will happen when the question is put, 'Your vote, Marcus Tullius?' "

"Briefly," Cicero answered, "I vote with Pompey."

Before the senate debate resumed on January 1, Curio presented a proposal, a thinly veiled ultimatum that Caesar had conveyed to him three days earlier in Ravenna. Caesar would lay down his arms at the same time Pompey laid down his. But the threat was clear: if Pompey didn't agree, Caesar would march quickly to avenge the wrongs being done to him and to the country. It was largely propaganda. But the new consuls considered his message so potent that they refused to let its terms be read to the senate.

Pompey had returned from Capua with a contingent of veterans and recruits, and those soldiers were camped outside the city; Caesar's army was far away in the north. Either the senators were reassured by Pompey's circle of protection or intimidated by it, but they voted overwhelmingly for a measure that amounted to a declaration of war. Despite their earlier concessions, the senators now said that Caesar must not keep a single soldier past what they termed "a certain date." The phrase was vague but meant some-time within the next two months. After that, he would be consid-ered an enemy of the state. The law allowing him to run for consul in absentia was repealed; Caesar would be forced to sacrifice his immunity and enter Rome to seek the office. And even if he won, he would be exposed to prosecution for six months.

Mark Antony and another tribune vetoed that measure.

When the debate resumed four days later, Cicero came to the senate with a compromise: let Caesar keep one legion past the senate's deadline. Pompey agreed. But before Caesar had the chance to accept it, Cato and his circle announced they would not.

Nor would the senate defer its decision for six days while an official rode to Caesar's camp in Ravenna to tell him that the compromise had been rejected. Instead, with a vehement shout, the senate voted to approve Domitius as Caesar's successor in Gaul and send him there with 4,000 men. Once again, the tribunes exercised their veto.

By now, enough senators believed that Caesar threatened their lives that they passed the ultimate decree, calling on the ranking officials to protect the Republic. A consul urged the tribunes to leave the chamber immediately or expect violence. Antony jumped from his chair and called on gods and Romans to witness this indignity to the office of tribune. Shouting predictions of war and slaughter, he ran out of the senate. Curio and Gaius Cassius followed.

Disguising themselves, they rented a carriage and hurried to tell Caesar that the senate had passed the decree against him. Cicero's weapon against Catiline had now been turned against Caesar. To his troops, Caesar pointed out that after years of devoted service to their nation, they were being termed Rome's enemies.

Many veterans in the ranks knew how far back the struggle went. Some 80 years later, this was the senate versus Tiberius and Gaius Gracchus all over again. But this time the people's tribunes could not be clubbed down. This time, they spoke for a vast army and for a man who would settle for nothing less than Rome's most sweeping powers.

XXXVII

CAESAR

49 B.C.

After reporting the senate's decree to Caesar, Antony, Curio and Cassius stayed on in Ravenna, along with one legion stationed in Cisalpine Gaul. Caesar had given secret orders for three other legions to move close enough to the Spanish border to bottle up the troops loyal to Pompey. He had also alerted two legions in Transalpine Gaul and another 22 cohorts to be ready to march on Italy. He was ready to use the speed that had confounded the Gauls against his own countrymen.

He left at once with five cohorts of soldiers for the Italian town of Ariminum, which lay beyond the small river that divided Gaul from Italy. Its riverbed was made up of *rubri*—red stones— and Italians called the stream the Rubicon. The senate already considered Caesar an outlaw; crossing the Rubicon with 5,000 armed men and 300 cavalry would give them proof.

Once Caesar crossed into Italy, he knew the odds would turn against him. Despite his superbly trained army, Rome's provinces were filled with citizens who had no reason to prefer Caesar to Pompey. Caesar had no navy, no reliable supply of grain. If he seized Rome itself through a lightning assault, the war would have only begun. If he lost the first battle, Caesar's war would be over.

Caesar was not given to self-doubt, but it was said later that he lapsed into a thoughtful silence as he reached the Rubicon and prepared for his fateful step. Some claimed that he mused aloud: "My friends, not to cross this stream would cause me great distress, but to cross it, for all mankind."

Historians had Caesar quoting a fragment from Menander, a Greek poet he was known to admire. In the Latin translation, it would have been *"Alea iacta est."* The die is cast.

In his own account, Caesar said only that he took a legion and set out for Ariminum. But in any language, Caesar had embarked on the gamble of his life.

Caesar had sent soldiers ahead wearing civilian clothes. The people of Ariminum knew what they faced and made no attempt to resist. By the morning of January 11, Caesar had taken the town without bloodshed. He received a delegation from Pompey and sent them back to Capua with a high-minded statement about the way the senate had impugned his dignity, which he placed above his life. Again, he proposed that everyone lay down arms but made it clear that he would not be the only one to do it, or the first.

Ariminum had been painless. Caesar still had to convince his troops to take up arms against Rome. In an emotional speech to the 13th Legion, he recited the history of the wrongs against him and threw open his tunic to show how vulnerable he was to his soldiers' wishes. He also had to change their opinion of Pompey. Years ago, when many of these legionaries had left for Gaul, Pompey had been a hero, conqueror of the world. But since then, Caesar explained, Pompey had been led astray, had become jealous of him for the military successes that he owed to these troops standing in front of him. He had always respected and championed Pompey's dignity, but now Pompey wanted to undercut Caesar's.

As Caesar spoke, the roar was great, with men shouting their oaths of loyalty. Soldiers at the back and along the sidelines could see Caesar better than they could hear him. When he pointed to the seal ring on his thumb and said he would gladly reward his followers with that seal, his men saw only a flash of gold and concluded that Caesar was promising to make them all knights. That was an offer beyond even Caesar's ability; it cost a merchant 4,000 gold pieces to wear the gold ring.

When he began to speak, Caesar had little reason to doubt his men's loyalty. When he finished, he had none.

By January 14, his army had occupied two more towns. It took three days for news of Caesar's inexorable march south to reach Rome. Until then, senators had been busy parceling out Caesar's provinces as though they were still the senate's to bestow. They confirmed Cato's brother-in-law Domitius for Transalpine Gaul and named a praetor for Cisalpine. But with Caesar storming toward them, the senate was forced to acknowledge the coming battle. They called on Pompey to divulge his strategy. When he did, the patricians were stunned and furious.

XXXVIII

POMPEY

49 B.C.

On paper, Pompey's forces and Caesar's were evenly matched; on the ground, they were not. Caesar's legions were close at hand in Gaul, while most of Pompey's were in Spain. Of Pompey's three legions in Italy, two were the disputed units that had served with Caesar, and their loyalties were unclear. The recruits and veterans in Pompey's third Italian legion had never fought together.

Pompey's plan resembled the organization of his campaign against the pirates. He divided Italy in grids and assigned senate leaders to each region. They were to spread over Italy, stamp their feet in Pompey's name and watch the troops rise up—130,000 men who would put down the insurrection with ease.

Cicero was beginning to understand that this might not be the right time for his triumph. Joining Pompey's council of war, he agreed to take military responsibility for Capua. He told a friend that rebels had never been led by a better-prepared general than

Statuette of a slave boy with a lantern, fallen asleep while waiting to light his master home. The Metropolitan Museum of Art, Rogers Fund 1923.

Caesar but that Rome had little to fear, given Pompey's authority, energy and the fact that he was "starting to be afraid of Caesar."

The senators expected Pompey's lieutenants to take control of Italy's leading towns and outposts, cut off Caesar's supplies and keep him well away from Rome. Soldiers loyal to the Republic might harass Caesar occasionally to keep him off guard, but they'd be waging a defensive campaign and protecting Rome until Pompey's legions could get there from Spain.

If that was the patricians' understanding, Pompey had seen no reason to disillusion them—until Caesar swept past Ariminum and the next three towns on the Flaminian Way. At the same time, Mark Antony's capture of Arretium gave him control over a second route into the capital. Rome's unease turned to hysteria. Not only would there be war, it might be fought inside the city walls. The senators went to Pompey, demanding to know what had become of his defenses and exactly how many men stood ready to protect Rome.

Pompey was obviously reluctant to answer. He finally replied that, counting the legions Caesar had sent home from Gaul, he might be able to field 30,000 men.

One senator spoke for all: "Oh, Pompey, you have deceived us!" He recommended they send a delegation to Caesar at once to ask for peace. Another senator challenged Pompey to stamp on the ground and make his forces appear. Cato reminded him that during the years that the patricians were warning against Caesar, Pompey had been his partner. He concluded his harangue by recommending that Pompey be elected commander-in-chief, but only because those who had created great crises should be the ones to end them.

Pompey was learning how superficial his alliance with the patricians had been. Even in this desperate hour, they would never accept him. He would always be Sulla's brutal tool, Crassus' ally in restoring the tribunal powers, Caesar's son-in-law. At different times, Pompey and Cicero had reached Rome's pinnacle, but each was destined to remain an outsider, while Caesar, the one true aristocrat, was marching south to crush them in the name of the people.

Rome's senators had made serious political errors in recent weeks; now they made a tactical one. They voted down giving Pompey supreme command and insisted on dividing the provinces among themselves. But much as the patricians disparaged him, Pompey was their best strategist, and they had to listen when he told them bluntly what they must do. If Caesar was rushing down to Rome, the only response for the legitimate government was to evacuate the city. The senators loathed the idea.

On his own authority, Pompey issued a statement of imminent danger called a *tumultus*. All senators were to leave the city at once. Anyone who stayed would be considered Caesar's ally.

On the morning of January 18, Cicero paused in flight outside Rome to send a hurried note to Atticus: "I have suddenly decided to leave town before daybreak so I may escape sightseers and gossips, especially with my bay-decked lictors. For the rest, what to do now or later, I am sure I do not know. I am so upset by our rash and lunatic policy."

Cicero still hoped that Pompey would make his stand in Italy. The second-best option would be for Pompey to head for Spain and gather his combat forces there.

Pompey had a different plan. When he conquered the East, he had left behind kings and chieftains loyal to his name. Spain was already secure; with the ships he commanded, Africa was also safe. Pompey intended to sail for Greece and raise a huge army there. Let Caesar and his troops be sucked into the vacuum in Rome, be boxed in on three sides, starved and defeated. Then Pompey would return.

In Cicero's civilian eyes, Pompey's flight meant abandonment and surrender. But Caesar was a soldier and thought like Pompey. He anticipated the trap for him if Pompey's legions got away now. Like Pompey, he remembered Sulla fighting in the East while his enemies held Rome. But when Sulla was ready to march home, no power on earth could have stopped him.

Even if he had understood Pompey's thinking, Cicero would not have endorsed it. For him, Rome represented civilization. Caesar was a "wretched madman" who was fighting merely to defend his honor, Cicero wrote to Atticus. But how honorable was it to hold on to an army after you've been ordered to give up its command? To seize cities in one's own country? And what of Pompey's deserting Rome? "Leave the city? Would you have done the same if the Gauls were coming? He may object that the state does not consist of earth and plaster. But it does consist of hearths and altars."

In Rome, the news of Caesar's approach exposed the citizens' deepest superstitions. Men swore that in some parts of the city it had rained blood and that a mule had foaled. The roads were awash with rural families streaming toward Rome, sure they would be safer behind its walls than in the country. They jostled with the patrician senators heading out.

Caesar's army included both Gauls and Germans, the northern barbarians Romans had feared for centuries. Who could expect them to be more merciful than the Roman troops of Marius or Sulla? And for Caesar's supporters, who waited in the city with more foreboding than they would admit, the flight of the senate had ended all semblance of law.

The consuls had left in such a hurry that they hadn't offered the usual sacrifices to the gods for Rome's safety, and the consul in charge of Rome's treasury left without it. The senators who stayed behind were either Caesar's allies or some who thought they could remain neutral. Caesar played to them with open letters daring Pompey to face him in a court of law, rather than on the battlefield. To Romans who hadn't left the city, Caesar promised favors and no reprisals.

Pompey and his allies had camped at Teanum Sidicinum, a little northwest of Capua. When Titus Labienus rode up to join them, it was their first bit of good news. Winning over Caesar's senior legate was sure to encourage Romans who remembered his courage. But most people didn't know that over the years his pride had been wounded when Caesar kept for himself the chief role in nearly every Gallic battle.

Labienus spoke sincerely, but he confused his own disaffection with widespread unhappiness in the ranks. Pompey was so encouraged by his accounts of low morale that he briefly considered changing his strategy and fighting on Italian soil after all. Meantime, he sent Caesar a message promising peace if Caesar would withdraw from the towns he had already taken and allow the government to return to Rome. But it was little more than posturing on both sides since Caesar hadn't admitted coming any farther south than Ariminum.

Atticus had stayed in Rome shut up in his house, and Cicero asked him for a reading of the public mood. "Is Pompey missed? Does Caesar seem disliked? What do you think about Terentia and Tullia? Should they remain in Rome, or join me, or seek some refuge?"

His daughter's safety seemed assured by the fact that her new husband served with Caesar, but Cicero thought that all the women in his household should leave Rome to avoid compromising his position with Pompey's faction. Cicero welcomed Labienus' defection: "If he has done nothing else, he has at least hurt Caesar's feelings." But he ridiculed Pompey's military skill the way he had once denounced his shortcomings as a politician.

"Pass over other faults of the last ten years," Cicero wrote to Atticus. "What compromise would not have been better than this flight? I do not know what he is thinking of doing now, though I inquire by constant letter. It is agreed that his alarm and confusion have reached their limit."

And finally, Cicero offered his most withering summation of his lifelong military idol: "I already knew him to be the most incompetent of statesmen. Now I know that he is also the most incompetent of generals."

At moments, even Pompey might have agreed. The attempt to recruit troops in Apulia and Campania was going badly, even though most of the farmers there were veterans of Pompey's campaigns in the East. They seemed more grateful to Caesar for passing the laws that got them their farms. By early February, the recruiters were admitting that they didn't dare to show their faces in some neighborhoods.

Desperate, the consuls contemplated impressing the 5,000 slaves from the gladiators' school in Capua, which Caesar had bought years earlier. They soon realized that they couldn't count on those men, and the idea was dropped. Instead, Pompey sent gladiators by pairs to trustworthy families around Italy.

Cicero was making quiet attempts to ensure his own safety. A friend wrote on January 22 to relay Caesar's request that Cicero stay near Rome. Cicero was annoyed that Caesar had not written to him directly but decided again that he couldn't afford to be offended. His dignity would not permit him to respond to Caesar himself, but he instructed his friend to inform Caesar that he was living on his country estate, taking no part in recruiting for Pompey's army, or any other senate business.

XXXIX

CAESAR

49 B.C.

Pompey had lost Rome, but Caesar feared he himself had lost his moral justification. His months of positioning himself as the injured party would be compromised if he marched against an undefended capital. He heard that some Romans were cursing him for putting his ambition ahead of their lives.

Once Caesar understood that winning Rome's good will might be difficult, he accelerated his attempt to control the territory around the city. His reception among the farmers of northern Italy was friendly; they were saying that Caesar had done great deeds for Rome and shouldn't be punished for them. By early February, he had reached central Italy and taken command of Picenum along the Adriatic, once a stronghold for Pompey's father.

Caesar's march was beginning to look like a victorious homecoming. With some trepidation, he passed through a town that Labienus had founded in the days he was still loyal to Caesar. Even there, delegates came out to greet him and agreed to lend him their soldiers. When another legion joined him from Gaul, Caesar marched to the town of Corfinium to confront the 20 cohorts led by Domitius, the senate's choice to replace him in Cisalpine Gaul.

Domitius had believed Pompey's public assurances that he intended to fight Caesar on Italian soil and had fortified Corfinium to stop Caesar there. Pompey had tried to warn Domitius that his true plan was far different, discreetly reminding him that much of his strength consisted of the two legions recalled from Caesar. Pompey hinted that if Domitius were in trouble, he shouldn't be surprised when Pompey didn't come to his rescue. Domitius missed the warning. Until the day he was besieged, he was sending Pompey urgent instructions on how to combine their two armies to crush Caesar.

Cicero was sure that Romans were gossiping about the way he had left his post at Capua after just three days and retired to his more congenial country estate, but he assured Pompey, "I do not trouble myself about criticism of inactivity from anyone but yourself." Still, he couldn't disguise his reluctance to join in the fighting about to engulf the country.

Pompey replied tactfully, "I was glad to read your letter, for once again I recognized your proven courage in the interests of public safety." But he disregarded Cicero's hesitation. "I believe that you should travel by the Appian road and come with speed to Brundisium."

Caesar's victory over Domitius was more political than military. Boxed up in Corfinium, Domitius at last admitted to himself that Pompey wasn't coming to save him. To his men and the townspeople, he continued to give assurances that they should not lose heart, that Pompey was on his way. Meanwhile, he and a few friends prepared to escape. Domitius spoke bravely, but he looked flustered and nervous. People saw him whispering with his confidants and grew suspicious. The troops concluded that he was ready to abandon them. A few soldiers wanted to fight without him; the rest realized that Caesar could overrun their defenses. Stationing guards around Domitius, they sent envoys to Caesar, promising to open the gates and deliver their general.

Caesar hesitated. By now, it was night. He could occupy the town, but he might have trouble stopping his men from looting. This would be the first true victory of a civil war, and Caesar wanted its lessons to be clean and reassuring. He encircled the town, stationed men close enough together so that they could touch hands and warned them against attempts by the Roman aristocrats to slip away. No one slept that night.

During the fourth watch, Lentulus Spinther called to the guards from inside the wall and asked for a meeting with their commander. Brought before Caesar, he recounted his many services, including his help in Caesar's campaign for consul and for the College of Pontiffs.

Caesar interrupted him. This was his moment to establish, in person, on Italian soil, that he had come only to protect himself against the small oppressive faction of patricians. Lentulus asked permission to return to the town; he said Caesar's promise of safe conduct would reassure the others. Caesar sent him on his way.

At dawn, Caesar called for the Roman nobles within the town to be brought out. With Lentulus, Domitius and his son were two senators, a quaestor and some young merchants whom Domitius had ordered to accompany him. After complaining briefly about their ingratitude for his service in Gaul, Caesar released them all unharmed. He returned 6 million sesterces that Domitius had brought to Corfinium—state money that Pompey had allotted for military pay. Caesar wanted to make it clear that he was as generous with his opponents' property as their lives. Given the relief and gratitude of those he spared, Caesar felt he could bring Domitius' men into his own ranks. He had them take an oath to him.

Caesar's actions that morning became known as "the clemency of Corfinium." When Cicero praised his mildness, Caesar wrote back promptly: "You are right to presume—for you know me well—that my nature is not cruel."

Either Caesar had total confidence in his own persuasiveness or he doubted Pompey's resolve. He sent a message asking for a face-to-face meeting in Brundisium. Pompey questioned Caesar's sincerity. This stalling smacked of the tactics he boasted of using against the Gauls. Caesar's commentaries on his campaigns had raised his prestige in Rome but had also exposed his methods. Cicero was genuinely shocked when he came upon a letter from Caesar to Balbus making it clear that the overture to Pompey had been cynical. "Could anything be more cold-blooded," he asked Atticus, "or more ruthless?"

In any event, Pompey wasn't interested. He was already

preparing a second evacuation; first he had surrendered Rome, now he would give Caesar all of Italy. By March 4, he had sent the consuls and much of his army on troop ships from Brundisium across the Adriatic to Dyrrachium. When Caesar arrived at Brundisium, he found that Pompey had secured most of the available ships. To keep Pompey on Italian soil, Caesar had his men build piers and dams to block the harbor. Because the current might snap a breakwater, Caesar completed his line with two rafts 30 feet square and fitted with defensive towers.

Pompey built higher towers on the several large trading ships he had commandeered and broke up Caesar's rafts. When the troop ships returned from Dyrrachium, Pompey and the remaining men slipped away at nightfall. Caesar's piers snagged two ships. The others, with Pompey safely aboard, cleared Brundisium and headed for Greece.

XL

CICERO

49 B.C.

Frustrated on the shore, Caesar pondered his next move. Rounding up ships to give chase could take months. Meantime, he had to guarantee that grain from Sicily and Sardinia continued to reach Italy, and he knew he should eliminate the threat of Pompey's legions in Spain. First, however, he needed to establish his authority in Rome. Mark Antony would endorse his legitimacy, as would other tribunes and praetors, but Caesar needed former consuls as well.

Caesar requested Cicero's presence, but the invitation sounded more like a command. "Be sure that I have thanked you often," Caesar wrote, "and I expect to have occasion to do so still more often in the future, so great are your services to me. First, I beg you, since I trust that I shall quickly reach Rome, to let me see you there and rely upon your advice, favor, position and help of all kinds."

The request threw Cicero into a fever of indecision. He wrote relentlessly to Atticus, pointing out that if Atticus hadn't recommended caution, Cicero would now be with Pompey on the high seas and spared this dilemma. He preferred to forget how he had grasped at every excuse to stay in Italy.

After a second summons from Caesar, Cicero told Atticus that he would go to Rome, sense Caesar's mood and decide his next step from that. He was hoping to be allowed to go to Arpinum to celebrate his son's sixteenth birthday. He was also anxious about the failing health of Tiro, his former secretary. "Arpinum, I think, will be the place," Cicero concluded. "Please consider what I should do next, for my troubles have made me stupid."

Cicero met with Caesar at Formiae, near one of Cicero's country houses. The interview did not go well. From Caesar's ingratiating tone, Cicero had assumed that he would be setting the agenda for their discussion. But all Caesar wanted from Cicero was obedience.

"We were mistaken in thinking he would be easy to manage," Cicero wrote immediately afterward. "I have never seen anyone less easy."

Cicero told Caesar he would not be going to Rome for the mandatory senate meeting Caesar had called.

Caesar replied that his absence would be more than a personal slight. Other senators who had remained in the city would be less likely to come if Cicero stayed away.

Cicero repeated his position. Caesar hammered away. At last Caesar said, "Well, come and discuss peace."

"On my own terms?" Cicero asked.

Over the years, Caesar had come to appreciate the quickness of Cicero's mind, even when he was thwarted by it. This day, he retained a glint of humor and tried to suggest that two civilized men were merely bantering. "Need I dictate to you?"

"Well," Cicero replied, "I shall argue that the senate cannot sanction your invasion of Spain or your taking an army to Greece."

Cicero was being forced to make that fateful commitment without an admiring throng to cheer his words and remember them. His only audience was the man driving him into a corner, but Cicero spoke as though later generations would hear his every word; and, because Atticus saved his letter, they would.

Cicero said finally, "I shall lament Pompey's fate."

"That is not what I want."

"So I gathered," Cicero said. "But I do not want to be in Rome because I must say that—and much else about which I cannot keep silent—if I am there. Or else I cannot come."

The conversation was reaching its end. Caesar asked Cicero to think the matter over. Cicero couldn't refuse to consider it further, especially when Caesar made his last appeal without his usual obliqueness.

"If I may not use your advice," Caesar told him, "I shall use what advice I can, and I shall go to any length."

Cicero ignored the threat. He was feeling, for once, the exhilaration of not needing to apologize.

"So we parted," he told Atticus. "I am sure, then, that he has no liking for me. But I like myself, as I have not done for a long time."

On April 1, those senators who had stayed in Rome obeyed Caesar's order to meet outside the Pomoerium. Caesar repeated to them Pompey's recent remark that anyone who sought peace was acting from fear. On the contrary, Caesar said, it was that sort of thinking that betrayed weakness and low morale. The senate—or the remnants of it—then approved sending peace envoys. But no one wanted to go; each senator assumed that by staying in Rome, he had already angered Pompey.

After that, Caesar addressed the assembly. He promised allotments of grain and a gift of 300 sesterces to every man who remained loyal to him. For the moment, the grain supply from Sicily seemed secure. When Caesar's lieutenant arrived to take command of the province, Cato had demanded to know by whose authority.

"The master of Italy has sent me on this business," said Caesar's man.

Cato withdrew and joined Pompey.

But the Roman people were less easily won over. Too many remembered Marius and Sulla or had heard stories from their fathers. The promise of money was enticing, but the gifts were not being distributed immediately even though Caesar was helping himself to the public funds the senators had left behind. When a tribune tried to protect the money by standing guard over it, Caesar threatened to have him killed. But that wasn't necessary. Caesar's men split the treasury door's bolt with axes and carried off

15,000 bars of gold, twice as many bars of silver and 30 million sesterces in coin.

In every other respect, however, Caesar's return to Rome had proved a disappointment. Once he had seized the state monies, Caesar broke off his talks with the senate, left Mark Antony in charge of Rome and headed for Spain.

As he had hoped, Cicero was able celebrate his son's birthday at Arpinum, but then he would prepare to join Pompey at last. Pompey "will be more gratified by our arrival," Cicero predicted nervously, "than if we had been with him all along."

En route, Cicero stopped at his brother's house in Arcanum. Caesar's frustrations with the senate had left him all the more determined to keep Cicero neutral, and he sent a last appeal, excusing him for not coming to Rome and saying he took Cicero's refusal in good spirit. The note was little comfort. Cicero seemed on the edge of the kind of depression he had suffered in exile. His ceaseless inner arguments cast Caesar as the villain, but Pompey wasn't much better. His offenses went back more than a decade, to the night that Clodius hounded Cicero from Rome and Pompey "would not even give me a helping hand when I threw myself at his feet."

With Atticus, Cicero wasn't embarrassed to measure the civil war chiefly by how it would affect his own reputation. "These are our great men, but I do not hold their achievements one whit superior to mine, nor even their fortune, though they may seem to have basked in fortune's smiles while I have met her frowns."

Cicero's eclipse was underscored when his nephew made overtures to Caesar's camp. Young Quintus, Cicero lamented, "has turned out the bitterest disappointment of my life"—spoiled, disrespectful toward his father, he had even passed along to Caesar Cicero's plan to leave Italy.

At that, Cicero broke off his woeful account to Atticus because Curio, who was prominent these days in Caesar's camp, had come to see him. By the end of their talk, Cicero hadn't wavered in his intention to join Pompey. "Still, I do not fancy that I shall be found in the line of battle," he wrote Atticus, "but instead at Malta or some similar place." He would have preferred to wait in Italy and hope that Caesar would be driven from Spain. But if that happened, how much would Pompey value Cicero's loyalty?

Even Curio would probably defect to Pompey then. In hindsight, Cicero could see that he should have left with Pompey nearly three months before. He had stayed behind, he confessed, because "I thought that peace might be made and, if it should be, I did not want Caesar to be angry with me when by then he would be friendly again with Pompey. For I realized how exactly alike they were."

As Cicero fretted, Caesar's camp intensified the pressure to keep him from sailing away. Mark Antony made the unlikely claim that Caesar's allies cared more for Cicero's dignity and position than Cicero himself. He called Tullia "that queen among women" and asked how Cicero could ignore her husband Dolabella's loyalty to Caesar. He said that he wouldn't pretend Caesar loved Cicero—that was out of the question—but that Caesar would always wish Cicero to be safe and respected.

Caesar himself weighed in again, greeting Cicero as "Imperator to Imperator" and asking him not to leave Italy. To join Pompey would be the greatest harm Cicero could do him, Caesar wrote, short of publicly condemning his actions. "Finally," he concluded, "what better role for a good and peaceful man and a loyal citizen than to keep out of civil disturbances?" He signed the note, "April 16, on the march."

Cicero read into Caesar's letter a permission to go to Malta if he stayed aloof from Pompey's camp. He soon found out differently. Antony, in charge of Rome in Caesar's absence, was not permitting anyone to leave Italy and would not make an exception for Cicero. As immobilized now by regulations as he had been by his own indecision, Cicero could only pray for a victory by Pompey's forces in Spain.

XLI

CAESAR

48 B.C.

In Spain, Caesar made quick work of Pompey's best lieutenants. Breaking the back of their forces took 40 days. When they asked for a truce, Caesar convened both armies to explain yet again that his only aim was to make peace with Pompey's legions and spare the lives of soldiers who might be on opposing sides but were after all Romans. "If there is any gratitude among you for these favors," Caesar said, "tell about them to all of Pompey's soldiers." He disbanded the legions, promised Roman citizenship to the people of Gades and announced that no one would be forced to take an oath of allegiance against his will.

As Caesar marched back to Italy, the port of Marseilles resisted him. After a long successful siege, he appropriated the treasury but left the ancient Greek settlement unharmed. He put down a mutiny among his troops—they were finding his policies toward the enemy too merciful—by announcing that he would

Votive relief, probably offered by a wine merchant. The Metropolitan Museum of Art, Fletcher Fund, 1925.

execute the troublemakers in one legion and discharge the rest as
not worthy of serving him. When they begged for another chance,
Caesar did execute a dozen of the 120 ringleaders and then granted
the legion's request to go on fighting.

As Caesar was leaving the port, he learned that a friendly
praetor in Rome had nominated him as dictator by order of the
people. That title would allow Caesar to call consular elections and
begin to establish an alternative government to the senators with
Pompey at Dyrrachium. Caesar's troops, swelled now to 12 legions, went to Brundisium, set to chase after Pompey in Greece.
But first Caesar went to Rome for 11 hectic days.

Caesar had himself and a friendly colleague elected as consuls for
the coming year. His first act was to confront the economic upheaval that the war was causing. Debtors hoped he would cancel
all obligations, but Caesar's compromise required creditors to take
tracts of land appraised at their prewar value as payment. He also
adjusted the interest rates and limited men to holding no more
than 60,000 sesterces in cash. The measures did not favor lenders
or borrowers but did stabilize the city's finances. As a further
reward to Romans who had stayed in Rome, Caesar sponsored the
festival of Jupiter Latiaris, a celebration that the former consuls
had postponed when war broke out.

His political base repaired, Caesar joined his troops in Brundisium, determined to confront Pompey in Dyrrachium. During
his year in exile, Pompey had collected forces and a large fleet
from Asia, Pontus, Bithynia, Syria, Egypt—all places where his
name was still identified with Rome's grandeur. Pompey seemed
intent on invading Italy in the spring, and Caesar wanted to challenge his nine legions before they were ready.

Caesar began marching the same day his troops landed on
the Greek coast. Along the route, citizens opened their town gates
to him. Pompey heard of his reception and worried about the
loyalty of Dyrrachium. He took his men there on a forced march so
strenuous that many new recruits slipped away at night to hide in
ravines until they could escape home. Caesar's march was as frenzied. "If we can reach Dyrrachium before him," he told his commanders, "we will possess his military arsenal and everything his
troops worked last summer to collect."

Pompey ordered trees cut down and laid across the road to

slow down Caesar's men. He destroyed every bridge after he had crossed it and set fire to crops and supplies as he passed. When dust arose on the road or smoke filled the sky, each army thought it was coming from the other camp and redoubled its efforts. Both armies believed the gap was narrowing.

Pompey pushed his exhausted men into camp near Dyrrachium, while Caesar staked out a base across the Apsus River. Their cavalries crossed back and forth for a few skirmishes, but neither commander was ready for battle. Pompey was still recruiting men from around the province, and Caesar, severely outnumbered, waited anxiously for the troops he had left behind at Brundisium. He thought their best chance of eluding Pompey's patrol boats was to sail immediately, in the winter, and sent orders for them to hurry.

Marcus Bibulus, Caesar's antagonist from their days as co-consul, had effectively bottled up the port. But Caesar's men were equally adroit at keeping Bibulus' troops away from the shore. Confined to his ship for many days, Bibulus fell ill and died. Command of Pompey's fleet passed to each of the ship captains.

Convinced that Gabinius and Antony were missing their chance to make the crossing, Caesar decided that only he could rouse the troops at Brundisium to break free and sail to Greece. Telling no one of his plan, Caesar sent servants to the river to hire a fast boat with an experienced pilot. They were to say it was for Caesar's messenger.

That night, Caesar left early from supper, telling his lieutenants that he was tired. Changing from his uniform, he boarded a carriage, along with servants to relay his orders so his voice wouldn't be recognized. Muffled in his cloak, he drove through the darkness to the waiting boat. A hard night wind was blowing, but his servants urged Caesar to cast off at once before Pompey's sentinels could spot them. The pilot and his men rowed to the river's mouth but found the ocean surf high and rough. The pilot recommended turning back. Caesar threw off his cloak and ordered him, "Fight the storm bravely! You carry Caesar and Caesar's fortunes!"

Astonished, the men fell on their oars, but the storm overwhelmed the small boat. As dawn approached, and with it the risk of discovery, Caesar gave the command to return to shore.

Back at camp, Caesar's aides were impressed by his courage, but they told him bluntly that it had been a foolhardy stunt, one that might do honor to a soldier, not a general. Since he couldn't risk a second attempt, Caesar sent Postumius to Brundisium with instructions to cross over at once. If Gabinius refused, the orders were to go to Antony and finally to the third in command. In case all three hesitated, Caesar had sent along a second letter to be read to all troops, saying that every willing hand should board ships with Postumius and sail wherever the winds took them along the Greek coast. They weren't to worry about the ships being wrecked upon landing. I don't want ships, Caesar exhorted them. I want men.

If Caesar was too rash, Pompey was too cautious. He had intended to attack before Caesar's reinforcements arrived. But when two scouts were killed searching for the best place to cross the river, Pompey took it as an omen. He drew back his troops, much to the disgust of his Eastern allies, who saw an opportunity lost.

Caesar learned that Gabinius had ignored his order to sail and had led a contingent of volunteers overland by way of Illyria. They were wiped out on the march. But Antony's ships, filled with reinforcements, managed to reach the Greek coastline. As the ships appeared on the horizon, one of Pompey's allies sailed out with a fleet from Rhodes, trying to catch them as the wind dropped, when they would be most vulnerable. But the wind abruptly shifted and shattered all 16 of Pompey's ships. Caesar pardoned the survivors and sent them home. Caesar had come to expect good fortune, but even he found it "an incredible piece of luck."

Pompey hoped to ambush Mark Antony's men before they could join Caesar, but Greek informers warned Antony, who got a message through to Caesar. While Antony waited in camp, Caesar led his men to the scene. To avoid being caught between the two armies, Pompey retired quickly and pitched his camp in the town of Asparagium, but his prospects remained favorable. Caesar's combined forces totaled 34,000 infantry and 1,400 cavalry; Pompey's men outnumbered them by at least 8,000.

The two armies spread out their camps on facing hillsides. Caesar's situation was perilous. Pompey's blockade on the seas had stopped him from importing supplies. He dispatched 12,000 men to protect his rear position and to gather food in Macedonia and Thessaly, but his troops grew hungry, then famished. When they began to dig up roots to bake into a tough bread, deserters carried a sample to Pompey, sure that the proof of desperation would please him. But Pompey read another message into the coarse loaves. "What wild beasts we are fighting," he said.

Caesar couldn't wait any longer. He brought his army to cut Pompey off from the supplies at Dyrrachium. It was another reckless gamble, but it seemed to work. Caught off guard, Pompey moved to a plateau—not his first choice, but it did put Dyrrachium's bay behind him, and that allowed him reinforcements. Adapting one of his bold strategies from the campaign in Gaul, Caesar planned to surround Pompey's larger army with trenches and redoubts. Win or lose, the ambitious project would guarantee Caesar respect from future historians. Pompey built his own line of defense in a semicircle extending more than 14 miles, which pushed Caesar's perimeter out to 17 miles, a length almost impossible to construct for men less experienced than Caesar's.

Pompey's troops could still harvest food within their protected line of forts, and they could charge out on unexpected raids, wounding Caesar's troops with their arrows and slings. But Pompey didn't press his advantages.

In a minor engagement, one of Caesar's centurions, Scaeva, was struck in the eye by a dart. He lurched to the front of his men, holding up his hand for silence. Scaeva had known one of Pompey's centurions from the days they fought together. Now he called across the field to him that he was ready to defect. "I am wounded," Scaeva shouted. "Send someone to lead me by the hand."

Two of Pompey's men came forward to take him behind their lines. Scaeva ran one through with his blade and hacked off the arm of the other. At that, Caesar's forces, ashamed, charged again and saved their redoubt.

The stalemate continued, but Caesar tried to create the impression that his victory was inevitable. He asked Pompey's ally Metellus Scipio to intervene to end the war. Caesar's message flattered Scipio, as if only he had the stature to cut through Pompey's delusions and become Italy's peacemaker. But a friend of Cato's overheard and interrupted the messenger, and the war went on.

In June, Caesar told Dolabella to write to Cicero. Dolabella laid out Caesar's insinuating line to his father-in-law: Dolabella hadn't urged Cicero to join him at Caesar's side before. But now that the end was in sight, it was impossible for him to be silent. Dolabella assured Cicero that he had already done everything for Pompey that friendship could expect. Without irony, he urged Cicero to consider for once what was best for him. Come over to Caesar's side, he urged. Their past friendship, combined with Caesar's natural generosity, would guarantee that Cicero could obtain any honorable conditions he might demand.

But Caesar's fortunes were not so glowing as he was painting them. Four days after Caesar's fifty-second birthday, Pompey broke through his line at its southern point and threw up a camp that undid Caesar's strategy of containing him. It was a devastating defeat. Caesar tried to recover the initiative by going after an isolated enemy unit. But when Caesar's men saw Pompey's reinforcements in the distance, they broke and ran. Even Caesar's veterans were panicked, and for once he couldn't control them. As he raced among his troops, men threw down their standards, and one turned his standard's blunt end toward Caesar, threatening to strike him with it. Caesar's bodyguard cut off the man's arm before he could swing. That was not the only standard-bearer to disgrace himself. Caesar lost 32 standards that day, and 1,000 men.

Pompey's brilliant success ought to have ended the war. Caesar's camp had been left undefended, and Pompey could have stormed in and clinched his victory. Instead, Labienus had persuaded him to chase after the soldiers who were fleeing in every direction. The advice couldn't have been worse if Labienus had been a double agent on Pompey's staff, but Pompey listened and turned away from Caesar's camp. Pompey may have suspected a trap. Or he may have believed that the war was won and he had only to capture and kill the cowards who were bolting. In a second engagement, Pompey did inflict terrible casualties on Caesar's army, but Caesar's base remained secure.

"The enemy would have won the war today," Caesar told his lieutenants, "if they had a commander who knew how to use a victory."

XLII

CICERO

48 B.C.

Cicero watched the tragedy unfolding, disenchanted with his allies. Cato had given up Sicily without a struggle, and Cicero thought he should have held out; Pompey's fleet had been close enough to protect him. Cicero wrote to Atticus that he hoped the governor of Sardinia would resist: "If so, how low Cato's action will appear!"

But it was easier to find fault with others than to live up to his own standards. Cicero himself had retired to his villa south of Naples so that if he were to decide to join Pompey he could sail away quietly. There he was visited by officers from the three cohorts stationed at Pompeii, who asked him to assume control of the city and their troops. The command of a small unit of men in potentially hostile territory held no appeal for Cicero, and he rose early the next day and slipped away before they could ask him again.

Then, after all the indecision, Cicero had resisted Caesar's appeals and he followed his heart to Pompey. Now his ardor for his former friend cooled, and he was saying merely that he would support Pompey because, of the two rivals, he was the more modest, honest and upright king. But king, all the same. Cicero thought that if Pompey were to lose, the very name of the Roman people would be extinguished. And if he won, "his cruel and bloody reign would follow the manner and example of Sulla."

After Dolabella's last letter, Cicero sailed to Dyrrachium. Leaving his wife and daughter behind, he took his teenage son, his brother and his nephew, Quintus, despite the young man's dubious loyalties. Caesar had blocked all the land routes, but they could reach Pompey's camp by sea. Since Cicero knew how belatedly he was in joining Pompey, he tried to compensate by bringing money for the camp's expenses. He considered the payment a loan, with self-interest the only dividend. "I have lent Pompey a large sum of money," he wrote, "thinking that, when things settle down, it will bring me honor as well as profit."

Cicero continued to hope for a negotiated settlement, but when he arrived, he was alarmed by the mood in the camp. Pompey's victory in July had made him seem invincible—to himself and to his less experienced lieutenants. Now that he seemed destined to win, the Eastern princes were sending well-equipped troops. Cicero cautioned Pompey's advisers that Caesar's men were more hardened and experienced, but they called him timid, even cowardly. Cato struck back at Cicero for his criticism by informing him that he would have been of more use if he had stayed in Italy.

Ignoring the derision, Cicero continued to press unwanted advice on Pompey but refused any specific role in the war. Instead, he moved through the camp expressing himself as frankly as though each listener were Atticus. He lamented that he had come, he denounced each strategy he overheard. The sight of the foreign troops provoked his ridicule. As Cicero went from campfire to campfire, making jokes with a pained expression, Pompey's troops laughed in spite of themselves. When a commander promoted an indifferent officer, saying that at least the fellow was prudent and gentle, Cicero snapped, "Then why don't you keep him to look after your children?"

Since Pompey angrily rebuffed any suggestion that he negotiate with Caesar, Cicero tried another approach. Don't yield to the temptation to follow up your recent victory with more fighting, he told Pompey. He advised him to extend this period of informal truce. Both sides were suffering as a result of the blockades and the resulting shortages. Perhaps Caesar's men, tough as they were, would give in first.

But Pompey's inner circle was nudging him to battle. To his face, patrician senators were accusing him of prolonging the war in order to remain the ranking general. Behind his back, Pompey's men were calling him "king of kings" because of all the Eastern noblemen he presided over. Some senators were so sure that the enemy had been crushed that they were already squabbling over who should take Caesar's seat as Rome's high priest. One patrician proposed that in the future those senators who had supported Pompey by coming to Greece should have three votes instead of one.

As he watched Pompey being pushed by the desires of his supporters rather than asserting his own strategy, Cicero remarked, "From then on, this great man ceased to be a general."

Unexpectedly, Marcus Brutus arrived in Pompey's camp, although it meant joining the man who had put his father to death. Since he was also the son of Servilia, widely regarded as Caesar's favorite mistress, his decision was doubly surprising. But Brutus was also Cato's nephew and shared his veneration of the Republic. Having decided that Pompey's victory would be better for the nation, Brutus had sailed on his own to Macedonia.

When Caesar learned of Brutus' presence in the enemy camp, he told his lieutenants that they should capture him alive in the next battle. Caesar did not want Servilia's child killed. If Brutus wouldn't allow himself to be taken prisoner, they must let him escape.

Caesar would not admit that the recent defeat had been his fault, but he had absorbed its lessons. He observed that the survivors were deeply ashamed of their conduct. Caesar's men weren't supposed to break ranks, much less lose. When he didn't punish them harshly, their chagrin increased. They demanded that a tenth of their number be put to death in the old Roman way. Caesar refused. His legionaries argued that Caesar at least should put to death the standard-bearers who had thrown away their emblems. They argued that they would not have broken and fled if they had seen the standards in front of them. With a show of reluctance, Caesar agreed to punish the most flagrant offenders.

Next, his men urged Caesar to let them erase their shame by engaging the enemy right away. This time, they swore, they would leave the battlefield only as winners. His lieutenants advised Caesar to take advantage of his men's eagerness, but he declined, saying that the soldiers should remember this moment so they could draw on their zeal when the time was right. To his confidants, Caesar explained that his men needed longer to forget the terror of the last battle. He also wanted more time to pass for Pompey's troops to lose their confidence.

Caesar did acknowledge one mistake. He should not have bottled up Pompey at Dyrrachium, near his store of supplies. Next time, they would fight at a spot where both armies would suffer from the same shortages.

With that last determination in mind, Caesar marched by night to Thessaly. Along the route, the small town of Gomphi refused to open its gates. A few months earlier, when Caesar had passed through on his way to Epirus, the same citizens had sent men out to greet him and offer supplies. Now, having news of Pompey's victory at Dyrrachium, they wanted nothing to do with him.

Gomphi's resistance gave Caesar a pretext to smash past its walls and throw open its houses. His hungry soldiers gorged on food and drained the vats of wine. The German mercenaries became loud and drunken, and in a pharmacist's shop 20 veteran legionaries were found dead, not from wounds but from poison slipped into their goblets.

Pompey could have caught Caesar's men reeling around their campsite, but instead he called another strategy meeting.

XLIII

POMPEY

48 B.C.

At Pompey's council of war, two strategies emerged. The first was to fight a slow war of attrition, relying on the naval force that gave them mastery of the sea. Ships should put into port long enough to attack Caesar and pin him in the East while Pompey sailed to Italy to take Rome. From that stronghold, he could subdue Spain, then Gaul, and with the power of those united forces finish Caesar off.

Pompey's more ardent advisers saw no reason to postpone victory. If they pursued Caesar now, to the plains at Pharsalus seven days away, his men, hungry and outnumbered, were bound to begin deserting. They appealed to Pompey's pride: He had won at Dyrrachium. Why should he retreat from the battlefield?

Not wanting to lose face in front of his Eastern allies, and concerned about his Italian troops elsewhere in Macedonia, Pompey agreed to fight. With his supply lines secure by land and sea, Pompey marched confidently after his enemy and halted on the vast green fields some distance from Caesar's new camp.

From intelligence reports, Pompey had a clear picture of the enemy's morale. Caesar's veterans were superior to Pompey's raw recruits from the Eastern kingdoms, but 10 years of constant warfare had taken a toll. Caesar's legionaries had less strength for the routine of digging ditches every day, building fortress walls and scouring the countryside for food. They were muttering that it would be better to fight one great battle than to waste away in camp. But that desperation gave Pompey pause, and his mood shifted from day to day. When his advisers urged him to accept Caesar's invitation to battle, he agreed but halfheartedly.

Pompey's strategy was predicated on a victory won cheaply. His cavalry would attack Caesar's open right flank and surround his column from the rear. Caesar's men would be stampeded before they could hurl their lances. Pompey promised his officers that they would finish the war almost without a wound. Labienus endorsed his optimism.

"Do not suppose," Labienus said, "that this is the army that conquered Gaul and Germany. I was there for all those battles and I don't speak rashly on matters of which I am ignorant. A very small part of that army survives. Most of it has perished—the autumn epidemics killed many in Italy, and others have deserted or been left behind."

Caesar was resigned to the prospect that Pompey would not fight but try to starve him out. When he heard that Pompey might be forced into a battle the next day, he was certain his luck had returned. At midnight, Caesar offered a sacrifice: if Venus bestowed victory on him tomorrow, he promised to build a new temple for her in Rome.

When a comet flared across the night sky from the direction of Caesar's camp toward Pompey's, the men in each army interpreted its meaning. Caesar told his troops that it illustrated the way he would fall upon Pompey's camp and extinguish it. Pompey's soldiers took the light that had come their way as a good omen. But later that night, Pompey's sacrifice was ruined when a swarm of bees settled on his altar, and he had to make the rounds to assure his troops that they hadn't been cursed. When he returned to his tent, Pompey fell into a deep sleep. Friends said later that he awakened to say he had dreamed of dedicating a temple in Rome to Venus Victrix, Bringer of Victory. Whatever the war's outcome, Venus was assured of her temple.

Pompey's men were in boundless good spirits as they prepared for the last battle. They draped their tents with the laurel branches of victory and told their slaves to prepare a sumptuous banquet to celebrate a quick victory. Pompey was disapproving but too distracted to stop them. Echoing Cicero, he told his troops that whichever army won, the day would mark the beginning of great evils for all future Romans. He remembered the aftermath of Sulla's civil war.

At daylight, Caesar rode close enough to Pompey's camp to see for himself the enemy's deployment. At the left wing were the two legions that had been extracted from his army in Gaul. Pompey was with them. From the way Pompey had positioned them, Caesar concluded that he considered them his best-trained force. In the middle were the legions from Syria, to the right a legion from Cilicia, along with cohorts brought from Spain. Pompey's right flank was well protected by a stream with steep banks, which allowed him to station all of his cavalry, archers and slingers with him in the left wing.

It was a polyglot crew. Pompey's past exploits had brought to his side men of almost every nation in the Levant—Bithynians, Phrygians, Phoenicians; soldiers from Thrace, Ionia and the Hellespont; Jews and Arabs; Cypriots and slingers from Crete. In addition, Pompey had the naval force to blockade Caesar into submission. The rulers of Egypt, the young woman named Cleopatra and her brother, had sent 60 ships to support Pompey; they lay at anchor in port.

Caesar calculated that 45,000 fighting men were arrayed against him. Another 2,000, who owed their rank to politics, had been salted throughout each formation, and to protect his camp Pompey had left behind seven cohorts. Cicero was among those left behind. He was feeling ill and would not be taking part in the battle.

Caesar laid out his forces in his traditional pattern, his prized Tenth Legion on the right, the Eighth and the Ninth on the left, even though the Ninth had been sharply reduced at Dyrrachium; Antony was commanding them. Caesar had about 22,000 soldiers, half the number confronting him. He stationed himself directly opposite Pompey.

Caesar began the exhortation that an army expected before

a battle. He told his men that they had already overcome the more formidable enemies of hunger and deprivation and now were facing mere men.

"This day will decide everything," he said, though not a soldier within the sound of his voice needed that reminder. "Remember what you promised me at Dyrrachium. Remember how you swore to each other in my presence that you would never leave the field except as conquerors."

Their enemies, Caesar told them, were the same men who tried to disband their army without a triumph or reward, even though in 10 hard years together they had brought 400 tribes of Spain, Gaul and Britain under Rome's control. Caesar said he had learned that Pompey had been fearful and reluctant to come to this battle. "His star has already passed its zenith," Caesar said, of a man six years older than he. "He has become slow and hesitating in all his actions, and he no longer commands but obeys the orders of others."

He instructed his troops to concentrate only on defeating the legions from Italy and not the Syrians or other foreigners, who were slaves ready to flee the battlefield, or be taken into custody by new masters. Once they had put the enemy to flight, however, "let us spare the Italians as being our own kinfolk but slaughter their allies in order to strike terror in the others."

Taking his cue from the Helvetians, Caesar told his men that they could prove their determination by tearing down the walls of their camp before they marched to battle, "so that we may have no place of refuge if we do not conquer, and so that the enemy may see that we have no camp and know that we are compelled to use theirs."

He turned for a response to Crastinus, a former centurion from the Tenth Legion who had left retirement to come fight with him. The answer came back: "Today, General, I will give you reason to thank me, living or dead."

With the Italians in each army dressed alike, their commanders had to issue a password that would prevent one Roman from striking a friend in the confusion of battle. Caesar chose "Venus Victorious."

As they filed out in silence, Caesar's soldiers dismantled their camp as they had been told, pulling down its walls and filling in its trenches. Those left behind to guard the baggage were 2,000 of Caesar's oldest troops. Across the misty stretch of plain, Pompey's lieutenants saw that the enemy was breaking camp and sent up a cheer: They're running from us! But Pompey recognized the wager of a born gambler who trusted to fate and his own wits.

On opposite sides of the field were relatives and friends, men joined by heritage and tradition who knew that they might die this day for nothing more than the prestige of their generals.

Pompey reminded his men that he had preferred to wear Caesar down and that they had insisted on this battle. "We are contending for liberty and country," he said, "against one pirate who is seizing supreme power." Remember Dyrrachium, "and the great number of their standards that we captured in one day." Pompey's watchword was "Hercules the Invincible."

Pompey planned to let Caesar's men charge and then fall upon them as their ranks broke up. Caesar knew what Pompey was thinking: if Pompey's men held their unbroken line, Caesar's troops would have to run twice the distance and would arrive breathless and disheveled. But though he understood the strategy, he didn't care. Men needed to be stimulated to fight, not sedated. Running, whooping, feeling their coursing blood raised their martial spirit.

Pompey's men were nervous from all the waiting. Some were in tears. The Eastern allies were especially edgy. Pompey was first to sound the signal, and Caesar ordered an answer. Trumpets blasted through the silence and gave men heart.

Caesar expected Pompey to try to outflank and isolate his Tenth Legion, and he had prepared a surprise. As Pompey's cavalry charged, six cohorts that Caesar had concealed as a fourth line rose up. His instructions to them were fierce: When you attack the enemy's cavalry, aim your spears at their faces. They can endure body wounds or the goring of their horses, but they will turn and run if you threaten to rip open their mouths or gouge out their eyes.

He had guessed right. Pompey's legionaries held their line bravely, but the fury of the assault finally scattered them.

Pompey's Eastern allies looked on as Roman fought Roman, amazed by the discipline in both lines. The Eastern forces were dazed. When Pompey's left wing was forced to give way, his men withdrew in a textbook retreat. But the Easterners ran past them, shouting, "We are beaten!"

And Pompey, for one, believed them. The soldiers near

him watched in dismay as he seemed to lose his will and headed back slowly to his camp. Caesar claimed afterward that Pompey had stopped at a guardhouse to call out, "Protect the camp and defend it well if anything goes wrong. I am going to the other side to encourage the guards there."

But even if Pompey's character would have permitted that deceit, he was now beyond dissembling. When he reached his tent, he slumped into his chair and said not a word.

Caesar rode among his troops, exhorting them to keep fighting until they had captured Pompey's camp. Unless you do that, he warned, you'll be victors for this one day only. Press on, and the war is over. Stretching out his hand to them, Caesar led the charge himself and his men, exhausted from the summer sun, were buoyed. Rushing with their javelins, they drove Pompey's guards into the hills.

Inside the camp, Caesar's troops found the laurel leaves of victory hanging from the officers' tents and banquets laid out on silver plates. As they tore through the camp, word of their approach was brought to Pompey, who stirred himself to ask, "What? In our very camp?"

Assured that his defeat was total and his capture imminent, Pompey changed out of his uniform and left camp on horseback with four friends for the town of Larissa to the north.

Caesar entered Pompey's tent and made it his own. His lieutenants estimated the enemy losses at 6,000 men, including 40 wealthy merchants and 10 patrician senators. They reported that Caesar had lost 30 centurions and 200 legionaries, although actual casualties may have been substantially higher. Among the dead was Crastinus; he had fulfilled his prophecy, fighting as though Mars had taken over his body. When Caesar located his corpse, he rewarded his centurion with a private tomb built next to the common grave.

Casualty figures from the slaughter at Pharsalus reflected only the Italian dead. Losses among Pompey's various Eastern allies were never recorded, either because they were too numerous or because the Romans felt nothing but contempt for them.

Caesar's notable trait as a general was insisting that his troops force a battle to victory rather than pause to congratulate themselves on a job half-done. He warned his troops not to relax amid

Pompey's luxuries but to finish the job. Caesar could see Pompey's survivors moving toward Larissa across the mountaintops. He set off with four legions by a faster lowland route. When he caught up with Pompey's men, they were still in the hills but they could see a river and were desperately thirsty.

Although it was nearly dark and his men had been fighting and marching since dawn, Caesar put them to work building an earthen wall to keep Pompey's soldiers from the water. That show of determination broke his enemies' spirit. Tired and leaderless, Pompey's legionaries sent down delegates to negotiate their surrender. A few senators slipped away at night, but by dawn Caesar had Pompey's men streaming toward him in tears and begging for his mercy, which he immediately extended. They were Italians.

By Caesar's estimate, 24,000 had surrendered, and he had regained the standards lost at Dyrrachium, with interest—180 of them, and nine eagles. Sending back for the forces he had left at the camps, Caesar pushed on for Larissa, reaching the city late in the day. He had to make sure Pompey wasn't able to raise a new army.

But Pompey was staying ahead of him. He went to Mytilene on the isle of Lesbos, where his wife Cornelia was waiting to welcome him. When a sobbing courier told her to come down to the harbor to see Pompey, reduced to one borrowed ship, Cornelia fainted. When she revived and ran to the port, Pompey caught her up in a sad embrace.

Cornelia reproached herself for bringing bad luck upon two husbands. Weeping, she said it would have been better if she had died before the news had come from Parthia of young Crassus' death.

Pompey hushed her. It was as possible to rise again, he said, as it had been to fall.

The citizens of Mytilene were willing to risk Caesar's reprisals and invite Pompey inside their city. But he declined and encouraged them to trust in Caesar's mercy.

As Cornelia sent for their son and servants, Pompey prepared to set sail. He cursed himself again for fighting so far inland, away from the navy that had been his best weapon. Cato had crossed to Africa with a sizable retinue, but the officers who thought Pompey should follow him were overruled by others who persuaded him to head for Egypt by way of Cyprus.

Pompey collected 2,000 men, borrowed quantities of brass

coin and sailed for Pelusium, where he would have to beg for his life from the king of Egypt. The timing couldn't have been worse. Ptolemy was already locked in his own civil war against his sister, Cleopatra.

Cleopatra had occupied the throne for three years that hadn't been serene for her or her countrymen. At 19, she had been chosen by Auletes to govern at his side. When he died soon afterward, Cleopatra decreed that a 10-year-old half brother share her throne as Ptolemy XIII. Egyptians saw their royalty as the embodiment of gods; Cleopatra now had an Osiris to rule with her Isis—brother and sister but also husband and wife.

Ptolemy was a boy, but surrounded by a council of regents headed by a eunuch named Pothinus. He detested Cleopatra, who was old enough to rule without advisers. She was remarkably shrewd and determined to maintain strong ties to Rome.

When Pompey fled Italy, his son, Gnaeus, had come to Egypt to solicit military support. He found Cleopatra and the regents receptive. They loaned the 60 ships and also a contingent of raffish soldiers. Eight years before, when Gabinius and Mark Antony had restored Cleopatra's father, they had left behind a detachment of soldiers to keep him on the throne. Those troops married Alexandrian women and quickly adapted to the languor of Egyptian life. Caesar complained that they had "ceased to think of themselves as Romans"; they had "forgotten the standards of discipline of the Roman people."

Cleopatra sent 500 of those lapsed warriors to fight Caesar. Now Pompey hoped to lure the rest of them away from Alexandria to form the spine of his new army. But by the time he sent an envoy to consult with the boy-king's regents, Cleopatra and her brother had broken into warring camps, and Ptolemy had taken his troops to a nearby mountain to fight the soldiers who remained loyal to Cleopatra.

When Pothinus heard of Pompey's approach, he consulted the young king's other advisers about how they should receive the defeated Roman general. They sent a message to Pompey at sea, telling him to delay his landing until they had reached a decision. Once Pompey could have crushed Egypt. Now he did as he was told. He spent his fifty-eighth birthday awaiting permission from a child.

Ptolemy's advisers were split. Theodotus, a teacher of rhetoric, summed up the unappealing choices: They could receive Pompey and enrage Caesar. Or they could refuse Pompey and make him their enemy. Or, Theodotus said, there was a third possibility.

The advisers listened and agreed to that third way. To carry it out, they appointed a group of men that included Septimius, one of Pompey's former officers. Seeing Septimius heading toward them in a fisherman's boat made Pompey's men wary. They told their general that something was wrong and urged him to sail at once.

But Septimius, standing in the small craft, hailed Pompey in Latin as Imperator. Another member of the Egyptian party called to him in Greek that he should not be offended: they had taken this crude boat only because the water was shallow. They would row Pompey ashore.

The Romans now saw Egyptian soldiers boarding their galleys. Even if Pompey had been inclined to flee, he no longer had that option. Sensing a trap, Cornelia began to weep. But Pompey, who had worried much of his life about treachery, had moved beyond fear. He asked two centurions, a freedman and a slave, to accompany him. As men from the fishing smack stretched out hands to help him aboard, Pompey recited a couplet from Sophocles:

> He that goes once through a tyrant's door
> Becomes a slave, however free before.

Aboard the fishing boat, Pompey found the mood sullen. No one spoke to him, and when he tried to make conversation, he was rebuffed. He asked Septimius, "I'm sure I am not mistaken that you have been my comrade in arms?"

Septimius nodded curtly. At that, Pompey took out a small book and began to study the appeal to the boy-king he had written out in Greek.

Left behind on Pompey's ship, Cornelia pressed forward to see his reception as the boat docked. The sight reassured her. Notables from the Egyptian court were coming forward, apparently to give her husband the welcome he deserved. Pompey extended his hand to his freedman in order to rise from his seat.

As Pompey got to his feet, Septimius drew his sword and

stabbed him in the back. The other two Egyptian escorts also flashed their weapons. It was a moment Pompey had seemed to foresee, and he met it nobly. He made no protest or plea but pulled up his robe with both hands and covered his head so that his face would not reveal his terror. A few groans escaped him as the murderers shredded his tunic with their knives.

When Theodotus had devised the plot, he had offered its rationale with a smile: "Dead men don't bite."

Cornelia screamed. A merciful wind carried her galley out to sea before the Egyptians could pursue it. She was spared seeing the final outrage. The Egyptians aboard the fishing boat cut off Pompey's head as a trophy and threw his body overboard.

Pompey's freedman stood guard over the naked torso where it had washed up on the sand. He wanted the world to witness what had befallen a great man.

He bathed Pompey's body in salt water and stripped off his own shirt for a shroud. He gathered enough rotted planks from a beached skiff to make a funeral pyre. As he was preparing the kindling, an old Roman who had once served with Pompey came to help him. The man said that he had spent much of his life in this strange land. Now he wanted to atone by touching Pompey's corpse and joining in final rites for Rome's greatest general.

When Caesar reached Egypt four days later, Ptolemy's advisers thought they knew how to ingratiate themselves. As proof of their loyalty, they sent an Egyptian bearing Pompey's head. But Caesar shrank back from it, appalled. Trying to make amends, the man presented Caesar with Pompey's seal—a lion holding a sword. That token, even more than the grizzled head, recalled the years of kinship with Pompey and their wayward affection. Julius Caesar burst into tears.

XLIV

CLEOPATRA

48–47 B.C.

Caesar arrived in Alexandria as a Roman consul, behind 12 attendants carrying his *fasces* of power. The Roman soldiers who were serving as Ptolemy's guard rushed to greet him, and the Alexandrians took that show of respect as a slight to their king. They roamed the streets in mobs, killing soldiers. But the murder of Pompey had convinced Caesar that Ptolemy's advisers would accept him. Moving into the royal palace, Caesar sent Pompey's ring back to Rome as proof he was dead and ordered that Pompey's head be buried decently.

Egypt had initially supported Pompey, and Caesar intended to tax the nation harshly for its bad judgment. He set a figure that included the 17.5-million-denarii debt that Auletes had incurred 11 years earlier. Pothinus balked at the payment and fanned the city's resentment against Caesar.

Caesar continued to stay at the palace but sat up all night to

A gold aurei minted by Mark Antony.

avoid the kind of sneak attack from Pothinus that had killed Pompey. Perhaps the Egyptian queen, still exiled outside Alexandria, would be more pliant than her brother and his eunuch. He sent an invitation for Cleopatra to join him.

The queen chose a Sicilian named Apollodorus to help her, and together they sailed at dusk from Pelusium in a small skiff. They reached the palace to find her brother's troops standing guard. Slipping past cordons of enemy soldiers might have daunted another woman. But Cleopatra was a queen, with a lineage that made the Romans look only slightly more civilized than the woad-painted Britons.

She instructed Apollodorus to lay out a sack of bedding. She stretched out full length as he tied up its ends with cord. Hoisting the bedroll to his shoulder, he carried his queen inside the palace and untied the sack at Caesar's feet. Out sprang a 21-year-old creature unlike any woman Caesar had ever known.

The next morning, Caesar invited Ptolemy to call on him. The young king arrived to find that his half sister had not only slipped into the palace but in a single night had converted Caesar to her cause. Tearing the crown from his head, Ptolemy ran outside to a crowd of protesters, wailing that he had been betrayed. Caesar's men seized the king and returned him to the palace, but they lacked the numbers to put down the insurrection that was spreading among the city's half-million people. Caesar turned instead to diplomacy. Displaying a copy of the Flute Player's will, Caesar promised that Ptolemy and Cleopatra would rule together as Auletes had intended. He gave the two younger royal children the sop of a joint command in Cyprus, which Rome had annexed under Cato a decade earlier.

To celebrate the royal reconciliation, Cleopatra ordered a feast that not even a Lucullus could stage in Rome. In a paneled hall, its beams covered with gold, its walls and floor laid with agate, onyx and marble, the queen reclined between Caesar and her brother, eating from gold dishes on ivory tables. Their slaves had been imported from across the world. Most were dark, but Caesar also saw servants blonder than the Germans of the Rhine.

Caesar flattered his hosts by asking about the origins of their sacred river. He said that in his language, "to seek the source of the Nile" meant to search for the impossible. Cleopatra's priest answered that the source remained hidden from foreigners, but that he could assure Caesar the river was older than the oldest race of men.

Caesar's tact had for the time stilled the unrest, but then Pothinus ordered the Egyptian army back to Alexandria from Pelusium. Caesar knew those 20,000 men could swamp the Romans, so he had Pothinus executed as a traitor. The royal army, caught up in nationalistic fury, ignored Ptolemy's call to lay down its weapons. To control the crowds, Caesar's men had to set fires around the city, and one blaze destroyed Alexandria's library, the greatest of its time. No one could say how many scrolls were lost—at least 400,000, possibly twice that number.

The ships that had gone out in support of Pompey were burned as they returned to Alexandria's harbor. At great cost in lives, Caesar seized the island of Pharos in the harbor to give his reinforcements a place to dock.

Cleopatra's younger sister, dissatisfied with the bribe of Cyprus, escaped to join the Egyptian army. But the street fighting had begun to subside. Caesar drew a cordon around the city's center and settled down to wait for his relief forces. He had Cleopatra with him to pass the time.

Cleopatra's first plan had been to arouse Caesar's pity. The night they met, she had wept and raged at the indignity of a queen of heaven being humiliated by a boy and a eunuch. But she soon saw that she could draw on emotions more powerful than Caesar's sympathy, even though hers was no ordinary beauty. Her nose was long and thin, her mouth fleshy, her hair coarse. But Egyptian women knew arts of makeup that aristocratic Roman women shunned—ways of enhancing the eyes, causing the hair to shine, beguiling the senses with subtle perfumes. Lampblack could make the eyelids dramatic and darken the eyebrows to contrast with the pallor of powdered skin. Mulberry juice served as rouge and lipstick. Should Caesar request it, Cleopatra even knew a treatment for baldness—burnt mouse and horse's teeth, bear grease and deer marrow, mixed with honey and rubbed into the scalp until hair sprouted again.

Caesar was 52. Whatever the depth of his romances at home, they had almost always involved women who could advance him politically. But Caesar was not in Rome. And Cleopatra, who had been surrounded by brothers and eunuchs, may have come to Caesar a virgin but wise in the arts of seduction. She had already proved her daring and verve on the throne, and those qualities appealed to a gambler like Caesar. Her voice was thrilling as she fixed her bright eyes on him. For more than a decade in Gaul, Caesar had been living a rough soldier's life. His youth was gone, middle age was riding him hard, and now he had found an incomparable woman who could make the liaison between Rome and Egypt something more than a crass political deal. Caesar may not have loved a woman since his daughter Julia died, and he may have been too worldly to succumb to Cleopatra now. But he couldn't resist playing at love with this spirited young queen.

The siege of Alexandria dragged on. Caesar went out to his troops each day and returned at night to the palace and Cleopatra. But by December two very different events were giving Caesar great satisfaction: a legion from Asia arrived by sea, and Cleopatra was pregnant. The queen had every incentive to have a child by the most powerful man in the world. And if for any reason he hadn't been able to oblige her, she would have been clever enough to find a substitute. Actual paternity mattered less than whom her nation believed the father to be.

The Alexandrians told Caesar that if Ptolemy was allowed to leave the palace, he could negotiate peace. Under Caesar's eye, the boy had been docile, and Caesar let him leave to join his younger sister with the Egyptian army. But as soon as he was on his own, Ptolemy swore he would drive Caesar from Egypt. Cleopatra divorced him; in time, she would marry a younger half brother.

By March, Caesar's reinforcements had reached Egypt's eastern border. Among the Syrian and Arab troops were Jews led by Antipater, who had been placed in power by Pompey and had taken his side. He was making amends now, leading troops to relieve Caesar in Alexandria.

Caesar stationed enough guards at the palace to protect Cleopatra, then slipped past the Egyptian lookouts and joined the reinforcements. On March 27, he routed the Egyptian army. That night, he came back to Cleopatra as the master of her capital.

Ptolemy XIII had drowned during an attempt to escape. Caesar ordered the Nile dredged until his body in its gold armor was recovered. He did not want Egyptians believing stories that the river had made the boy-king immortal.

Cleopatra's younger sister had been captured in the battle and shipped to Rome to await Caesar's triumph. Cleopatra's latest consort, the 12-year-old Ptolemy XIV, would be less troublesome in Cyprus, and Caesar sent him there. To reward the Jews, Caesar returned the territories that Rome had stripped away, including the port of Joppa. He also had the senate remove synagogues in Rome from the restrictions that outlawed the city's other guilds and congregations.

Caesar controlled the capital, but in the rest of the country Cleopatra's subjects distrusted the city and felt estranged from it. Caesar assembled an armada of 400 ships to sail down the Nile to demonstrate that the queen could depend on Caesar to protect her. It was a show of force, and a belated honeymoon of sorts. Caesar put aside his laurel wreath for a headdress made of flowers, and the couple sailed on a pleasure barge decorated as an arbor.

Caesar's troops, now many months in Egypt, were growing restless and were pressuring him to take up his duties in Rome. By summer, Caesar had returned to Alexandria, and arranged to station three legions of troops there to protect Cleopatra. In gratitude, the queen began building a vast monument in the harbor; it would be called the Caesareum.

And when she gave birth soon after Caesar left Egypt, her subjects accepted her son as another prize from Caesar's stay among them. She called the infant Caesarion.

XLV

CICERO

47–45 B.C.

Although Cicero had stayed behind in Pompey's camp at Dyrrachium, he barely escaped the catastrophe at Pharsalus. When Labienus raced in with the unthinkable news of Caesar's victory,
Pompey's eldest son heard Cicero refusing to take command of
the 15 cohorts his father had left to guard the camp. As the senior
Roman official, it was Cicero's duty, but he had concocted an
excuse. At that, young Pompey's frustration and grief overflowed.
He drew his sword and threatened to run Cicero through. Only
Cato's intervention had stopped him.

While Cato and other survivors sailed to Africa to carry on
the fight, Cicero urged an end to the war. He had been halfheartedly committed to Pompey for 18 months. Now, late in the year,
he decided to sail to Brundisium and see what terms he could
strike with Caesar.

But as soon as Cicero was back on Italian soil, he had another
change of heart. Perhaps he should have waited overseas for an

invitation to return. There was also the question of his lictors, still marching in front of him with their *fasces*. To give them up would diminish his prestige. But a rude populist spirit was sweeping the country, and a display of pomp might expose him to even greater indignities.

When Cicero received word of Pompey's grisly end, his response was tepid. He wrote to Atticus that Pompey's defeat had made the murder predictable, and added, "I cannot help feeling sad about his fate, for I knew him to be a man of honor and high integrity."

Cicero tried the backstairs maneuvering that usually had gone badly for him. Mark Antony, ruling Rome in Caesar's absence, contacted him to say that Caesar had forbidden any of Pompey's followers to return to Italy without an order from Caesar himself. Cicero claimed that he had permission, forwarded by his son-in-law. Antony then issued an edict that named Cicero as a specific exception to Caesar's decree. For a man who had hoped to retain the respect of the patricians, that publicity was highly unwelcome. Cicero complained to Atticus that Antony might have exempted him without mentioning his name. Tell me, Cicero begged, "that I have not entirely lost the good opinion of the loyalty party." But Atticus should also take care "that nothing is done under the present circumstances to offend the great man."

Certainly Caesar would not be pleased to learn that Cicero's son, who had led one of Pompey's cavalry units at Pharsalus, had distinguished himself with the javelin. But other members of Cicero's family were compromising his future more directly. His brother and nephew were traveling east, hoping to receive Caesar's pardon in person. Quintus' situation was delicate, given the kindnesses Caesar had shown him in Gaul. Quintus blamed his disloyalty squarely on Cicero. Young Quintus had written a denunciation of his uncle that he planned to read aloud to Caesar if he received an audience.

In June, when Caesar was still in Egypt, Cicero's daughter Tullia came to visit him in Brundisium, bringing troubles of her own. Dolabella had been adopted by a plebeian family in order to become a people's tribune and now, short of money, he was neglecting her. Cicero was also finding it hard to offer her support. He accused his wife of being spendthrift and sinking him into debt. And the money that Cicero had invested in Pompey's campaign was lost as well. Throughout his life, Cicero had been equally protective of his reputation and his estate. As he approached 60, both were slipping away.

The troops massing in Africa against Caesar might have delighted Cicero once; now they only added to his woes. Before Pharsalus, Curio had tried to overrun Pompey's African allies and had lost his own life and most of four legions. Cato, Labienus and Scipio were currently collecting troop remnants from Greece and Spain, and the number of soldiers opposing Caesar would soon outnumber his own. If they succeeded in retaking Italy before Caesar came back from Egypt, they might regard Cicero as a traitor. Against his every inclination, Cicero had to pray for Caesar's victory.

Caesar was still showing an amused tolerance for Cicero's transparent self-interest. He sent Quintus' letters to him, apparently to show his contempt for such groveling and betrayal within a family. But Cicero took the opposite message. He thought Caesar was toying with him, demonstrating the evidence against him, merely delaying a punishment that would be unforgiving.

In a welter of indecision, pondering whether to send his son to intercede with Caesar, Cicero learned in September that Caesar was back in Italy and went at once to Tarentum to greet him and relieve his mind. As Caesar's entourage drew near, Cicero approached on foot. The moment Caesar saw him, he alighted from his carriage, walked the distance between them and clasped Cicero in an embrace. He chatted as though nothing but geography had ever separated them. Crassus was dead, Pompey was dead. Caesar's towering rivals were dying away, but Cicero could remember the young Caesar and understand, if not applaud, how far he had come.

When Cicero finally returned to Rome in late October, he discovered that Caesar had no intention of restoring the Republic's ancient, inefficient system. Pliable senators, no longer checked by the patricians, were competing to shower him with new honors and powers. One law gave Caesar complete authority to decide the punishment for Pompey's supporters. Other legislation allowed him to hold the consulship for five consecutive years without a vote, and exempted him from consulting the senate before he declared war.

If the civilians had not handed those prerogatives to Caesar, he would have taken them. He had once remarked that only two things were needed to rule—soldiers and the money to pay them. Now that Cleopatra was making good on Egypt's debt and the Roman provinces were sending hundreds of gold wreaths to honor his victories, Caesar had both. With that kind of absolute power, he had less need for diplomacy or tact. But he did need economic stability. As tribune, Dolabella was provoking riots with his proposal to cancel all debts and rents. Caesar struck a compromise—rents would be suspended for a year and interest forgiven from the time he went to war against Pompey. In governing Rome, Antony had been despotic and ineffectual. Caesar withdrew his support for him as consul and appointed two other men. Caesar himself had to leave the capital soon again to confront the resistance in Africa.

Shut up in his house, Cicero waited for news from that African campaign. In a letter, he said that he had "made my peace again with my old friends, my books, which have been annoyed with me for not obeying their precepts to live quietly with them." But Cicero's marital problems were increasingly difficult. In the thirty years he and Terentia had been married, he had never become accustomed to her imperious manner or the way she regarded his political power as her own. Cicero saw enemies everywhere these days and was convinced that Terentia and her servant were in league against him. Pressed for money, wounded by the reversals in his career, Cicero resolved to divorce her. But if he did, he would be required to repay her large dowry. The solution was to marry again, promptly and well.

He found Pompey's daughter attractive, but such an alliance would be too dangerous. His friends proposed another woman; Cicero took their suggestion as an affront. "I never saw anyone more hideous," he wrote. He selected instead a pretty girl named Publica, who had been made his ward. She was rich, and her family was esteemed by Caesar. She was also very young. At first, Terentia had written off the affair as the infatuation of an old fool.

Cicero went ahead with the marriage, knowing that most Romans agreed with Terentia that an age difference of nearly 40 years was unbecoming. When a man at the wedding commented on the propriety of marrying a girl so young, Cicero responded, "She will be a woman tomorrow."

Like Caesar, Cicero had reserved his deepest love for his daughter, and his bride had to understand that she would take second place behind Tullia. Now in her early thirties, Tullia had announced that she was divorcing Dolabella. Their marriage had been unhappy from the start, but her father had discouraged her from leaving Caesar's ally while he was still uncertain about his own status.

Dolabella was away in Spain when they divorced, and Tullia was pregnant. She stayed on in his house for the delivery and gave birth to a son. But she never recovered from a difficult labor. Weeks later, she died at Cicero's house in Tusculum. Friends came from Rome to console him, but Cicero was convinced that Publica was pleased to have her rival eliminated. He told her coldly that he wanted to be alone, and she went back to her mother. Seven months after the wedding they were divorced.

Cicero took refuge in Atticus' library, reading those Greek philosophers who might help him to endure his grief. But Atticus received too many visitors to suit him, and Cicero moved to his farm in Astura. He slid into the same depression that had clouded his exile, hiding away in the woods, taking no consolation in his books. He spent many days weeping uncontrollably.

Tullia had died in January. In March, Atticus warned Cicero that excessive mourning could undermine his stature. People's sympathy was giving way to impatience, and his grief was beginning to look self-indulgent. Cicero was indignant, but he couldn't risk further damage to his reputation.

"When I come to Rome," he wrote in May from Astura, "they will have nothing to find fault with in my look or conversation." That hardly meant his sorrow was lifting. For all his past exaggerations, his boundless enthusiasms and crushing despair, Cicero assessed his future somberly: "That cheerfulness with which I used to temper the sadness of the times—that I have lost forever."

XLVI

CAESAR

47–45 B.C.

Caesar had rounded up six legions to fight in Africa, mostly fresh recruits. At one point, his veterans revolted, tired of war and eager for their rewards. Caesar had promised each man an extra 1,000 denarii, but that wasn't enough, and even the Tenth Legion joined the uprising. When the disgruntled soldiers marched on Rome, Caesar went unannounced to Campus Martius.

He opened his speech with the salutation "Citizens," rather than the usual "Fellow soldiers." He guaranteed them estates carved from public land or from his own holdings, and offered to buy them the farming tools they needed. But he warned them that anyone who continued in the demonstrations against Rome would sacrifice one-third of his bonus. The troops were appeased.

In his attack on Africa, Caesar trusted to the combination of will and daring that he called luck. He couldn't tell his ship captains where to land because he didn't know which harbors would be hospitable. But he sailed from Lilybaeum on December 25,

A coin with a portrait of the older Caesar wearing his laurel wreath. The New York Public Library Picture Collection.

hoping to launch an attack before his opponents expected it. He landed south of Cato's forces at Utica, but he tripped and fell as he got off the ship. Knowing his men would take his stumble as a bad omen, Caesar reached out from the ground, grasped a handful of earth and shouted, "I hold you, Africa!"

The early engagements went badly, but Pompey's successors were no more inclined to push success to victory. Caesar had to shame his reluctant troops once again, seizing a man who had fallen back with the eagle standard and hauling him to the front line. *"That,"* Caesar said, pointing, "is where your enemies are!"

Juba, the African king supporting Cato, was distracted when a rival tribe seized his capital. In the next engagement, Caesar killed and scattered a force of 80,000 men. Their general, Pompey's father-in-law Metellus Scipio, escaped by sea.

When Cato heard that Caesar was marching on the city of Utica, he responded with rigid correctness, providing ships for any patricians who wished to abandon him. Utica's residents volunteered to intercede on his behalf with Caesar, but Cato smiled thinly and said that it would not be necessary. He spent the day attending to city business, putting his seal on financial accounts and records of public property.

As evening approached, he bathed and went to dinner. Since Pompey's death, Cato had stopped reclining for meals and ate seated upright. He was gracious to his guests, asking the names of those who had already sailed and whether the winds would carry them to safety. His guests noticed that as Cato was about to retire, he embraced his son more warmly than usual.

His servants had been troubled by his manner at dinner and had removed his dagger from its place by his bed. When Cato found it missing, he called for its return. He told them he needed a weapon to protect his life, not to end it. Besides, Cato assured them, he didn't need a knife to kill himself. "Couldn't I strangle myself with my clothes if I wished to? Or knock my brains out against the wall? Or end my life by holding my breath?"

Reluctantly, his servants gave Cato his weapon, as well as a book he had requested—Plato's essay on man's soul. Cato began to read and when he was certain the guards outside his door had fallen asleep, he stabbed himself in the belly.

As much as Cato prided himself on his self-discipline, he couldn't hold back a groan.

His son burst in with the servants. The gash had laid open

Cato's intestines but left them undamaged. The doctors sewed Cato up and bandaged his wound.

Cato revived and thanked the doctors. He assured them that he needed only rest and seemed to fall asleep. Again, the servants withdrew but took the dagger with them. Once the door had closed, Cato swore his body to silence and began to rip away the bandages. He gouged his fingernails into the stitches until he had opened the wound, then tore out his organs.

When Caesar arrived the next day, he found his implacable enemy safe from the reach of his mercy.

In Africa, the fighting was over but not the bloodshed. To avoid being captured, King Juba and a Roman general held a banquet and killed each other with swords. Caesar claimed Juba's kingdom for Rome and took his four-year-old son into custody. Overtaken by Caesar's ships, Metellus Scipio stabbed himself and threw himself into the sea. Three hundred patricians who had declared themselves a senate in exile were taken prisoner, and at least three were put to death, although it was unclear afterward who had given the order. Caesar pardoned the people of Utica but levied a fine to be paid over three years. In keeping with his policy of reconciliation, Caesar forgave Cato's son and Pompey's daughter. He sent the young woman back to her brothers; Gnaeus and Sextus Pompey had left for Spain with Labienus to carry on their father's struggle.

Several of Pompey's lieutenants did not live to reach Spain. They were killed in skirmishes with Caesar's men or captured and put to death at his command. As resistance continued, Caesar's clemency was flagging. When he found that Lucius Caesar, from his own clan, had committed war crimes, Caesar had him put to death, but secretly, so he could later claim that it had been done without his permission.

Caesar sailed on to Sardinia, levying taxes and fines on those who had supported Pompey. Concerned that his older troops might mutiny again if they went home, he sent them to Spain to fight Pompey's holdouts and then headed to Rome, where he planned a homecoming that would be unequaled in the history of the Republic. But did the Republic still exist? Cicero hoped Caesar's conciliatory attitude meant that he would limit his dictatorship and restore the Republic's political system.

Caesar was signaling something quite different. As he arrived in Italy, the senate ordered a thanksgiving of 40 days and made him dictator for 10 years. Caesar had once called Sulla a fool for resigning his dictatorship, and now he was heard ridiculing the Republic as a name with no substance. Caesar had lived away from Rome for almost all of the last dozen years, traveling to his nation's farthest borders, from Spain to the north coast of Gaul, to Egypt and Africa. He had begun to reject the idea that a few men in a single city should direct Rome's far-flung enterprises. And still he believed that one man, himself, with a breadth of vision and the courage to enforce it, was equipped to rule that world.

But as Caesar consolidated his power, he had to rely on the trappings of the Republic. He might no longer respect tradition, but many Romans did, and those included his soldiers. His authority must seem to be based on rules and traditions that dated back 600 years. When Caesar made it clear that he would retain the senate, senators hastened to shower more honors on him. They gave him control over public morals for three years, power normally wielded by Rome's censors, and assigned him a permanent chair between the consuls in the senate. Caesar would speak first on every question.

Caesar had the name of Catullus erased in the Capitoline temple and his own inscribed, and he erected a statue of himself with the world at his feet. Some men tried to ingratiate themselves by adding to the statue a description of him as a demigod. Though Caesar had often claimed to be descended from Venus, he knew how to read the public mood and had the reference deleted.

Caesar declined other honors approved by the senate, but he did accept four triumphs to be staged over 12 days at the height of the summer. The ancient prohibition against a general appearing inside the walls before his triumph—a rule Caesar had once been forced to honor—was now forgotten. The moment the senate made him dictator, Caesar entered Rome. His first aim was to be reassuring, and he began his address to the senators by using Rome's hallowed title for them: "Let none of you, Conscript Fathers, suppose that I shall make any harsh proclamations or do any cruel deed merely because I have conquered and can say or do whatever I please."

Caesar recalled that Sulla, and even Marius, had spoken gently at first and then had acted ruthlessly. He would be different. He had not "become so elated or puffed up by my great good fortune to want to play the tyrant over you."

Caesar supervised his four triumphs for victories in Gaul and Egypt, and over Juba in Africa and Pharnaces, whose army he had destroyed after the Egyptian campaign. He estimated that his campaigns had killed 1,192,000 of Rome's enemies.

Caesar's festivals drew on his instinct for showmanship. He gave each of the triumphs a different theme, and men, women and children poured into Rome for the galas, raising tents and sleeping on rooftops. Some spectators, including two senators, were crushed to death as crowds surged from one extravagant display to the next. Caesar brought princes from Asia to perform a sword dance. He produced plays in different languages to accommodate Rome's multitude of foreigners. He offered chariot races, gladiators who fought to the death, an epic naval battle staged on an artificial lake hollowed out on the Campus Martius. His wild-beast hunt lasted five days and ended with a showpiece battle of 500 infantry, 30 cavalry and 20 elephants.

For his African triumph, Caesar marched to the Capitol with two lines of the elephants carrying torches to light his way. The Gallic triumph suffered a minor hitch when an axle broke and Caesar was nearly pitched from his chariot. To offset the bad omen, Caesar climbed the steps of the Capitol on his knees.

Because the victory over Pharnaces had come so quickly— the battle had lasted only four hours—Caesar was offhand about the success. He remarked that since he had seen the poor caliber of Eastern soldiers, he could understand why Pompey had been called "Great." Writing to a friend in Rome, Caesar had summed up the campaign against Pharnaces even more laconically: "I came. I saw. I conquered." That was his theme for the triumph. The wagon that normally would have been decorated with scenes from the war displayed only his boast: *Veni, vidi, vici.*

Caesar's veterans were paid off at last. Each infantryman received 240 gold coins, in addition to the 20 that Caesar had promised them for going to war against Pompey. They also received a farm, two and a half bushels of grain, 10 pounds of oil and a ration of meat. In one stroke, men who had joined the army with nothing but their nerve became landowners. Caesar had promised another three gold pieces as a bonus; he raised it to four and called the extra coin their interest.

Caesar's largess raised his standing still higher, and for the triumphs his men outdid themselves in ribald marching songs. During the Gallic triumph, for example, they sang:

> Home we bring our bald whoremonger.
> Romans, lock your wives away!
> All the bags of gold you lent him,
> Went his Gallic tarts to pay.

The words were pleasing to a man who had cultivated a reputation as an irresistible lover. But the soldiers also sang a verse that reminded Romans of an episode Caesar preferred they forget:

> Gaul was brought to shame by Caesar,
> By King Nicomedes, he.
> Here comes Caesar, wreathed in triumph
> For his Gallic victory!
> Nicomedes wears no laurels,
> Though the greatest of the three.

More than three decades had passed, but the accusation still stung. Caesar bore every other insult without complaint and smiled at gibes about Cleopatra. He didn't even object when his men had shouted their variation of a Roman nursery rhyme: *"Si bene faxis vapulabis, si male faxis rex eris."* If you do right, you will be flogged; but if you do wrong, you will be king.

Only the jokes about Nicomedes, and the knowing laughter they set off, caused Caesar to lose his composure. When the triumphs ended, he denied the accusations and swore an oath that nothing of the sort had ever happened in Bithynia. The laughter grew louder.

Caesar's parades were wildly popular, except among a few naysayers. The senate voted him 72 lictors for the triumphs, a number that scandalized the traditionalists. Others resented the African tableaux that glorified Caesar's defeat of Cato and Scipio. Though Cato had lost the war, few men doubted his devotion to the Republic. But he was the one rival Caesar held in scorn, even in death, for being a man who had mistaken rigidity for backbone.

When Cleopatra's sister, Arsinoë, was marched down the

Via Sacra, the sight of a young princess in chains provoked pity. But she was not executed, and Juba's little boy was also put on display and then spared. Vercingetorix, who had been languishing for years in order that he could be exhibited, went to his death unlamented.

Gaius Octavius, now 16, had come to Rome to join in the honors to his great-uncle. On the night of the last festival, the entire population of Italy seemed to be streaming behind Caesar and the boy, reluctant to see the glorious days come to an end.

Caesar plunged into his civic reforms with the same zeal he had shown in war. In a letter two years earlier, he had set out his blueprint for government: *quietem Italiae, pacem provinciarium, salutem imperii.* Tranquility for Italy. Peace for the provinces. Harmony for the empire.

Despite his impatience with the legislative process, he was scrupulous about informing the senate of his decisions. He restored control over the courts to senators and merchants and limited a retired consul's term abroad to two consecutive years. Caesar wanted no more five-year generalships in Gaul.

He forbade large expenditures by the wealthy on litters, pearls and funerals. He also cut back the number of Romans receiving free grain from 320,000 to 150,000. Because years of warfare had depleted the population, he offered prizes for large families.

When Caesar turned to reforming the calendar, he drew on what he had learned in Alexandria. Romans had measured their months by the revolutions of the moon, which led to a shortfall of at least 22 days. That error had kept increasing until the calendar year was running far ahead of the solar year. The Egyptians divided the year into 12 months of 30 days each, with an extra five days added at year's end. Caesar began by increasing his new calendar by 67 days, a one-time change to bring the annual total to 365. He subtracted two days from the second month and parceled those days and the five added days from the Egyptian calendar among seven months. He was still left with a spare day every four years. And despite his efforts, Caesar's year ran about 11 minutes too long, which would add still another day every 128 years. But compared to its predecessor, the Julian calendar was a model of precision.

Such a variety of changes was sure to provoke complaints, especially since Caesar had not limited debate and all were free to criticize him. Pompey had put through reforms designed to cleanse Rome of his opposition. Caesar seemed more concerned with healing discord. Still, Romans noticed that he was enrolling new senators less for their distinction than for their past loyalty. But he touched off the greatest furor with his welcome for a royal guest.

Cleopatra had given birth only two weeks before Caesar's triumphs began. Now that he was installed as dictator, she came to Rome with her infant son, her 13-year-old husband and a massive court. Cleopatra came as queen to negotiate a new treaty to protect Egypt against annexation, but she stayed on to be at Caesar's side. She didn't need to hear bawdy soldiers' songs to learn that Caesar had been courting other women, including the queen of Mauritania. Nor did she pretend to herself that marriage to Caesar was possible, even if she could overcome the impediment of her marriage to her brother. A Roman could not marry a foreigner or have two wives, and Caesar was married to Calpurnia.

All the same, Caesar was a considerate host. He installed Cleopatra in his own villa across the Tiber from the Forum and provided her with the company of clever Romans. When Cicero met the queen, he felt Cleopatra had treated him with insolence, promising him a rare book and then not remembering to give it to him. "I hate the queen," he told Atticus. Caesar, however, was still charmed by her and ordered her bronze statue placed beside his own in the new Temple of Venus.

Cleopatra's influence on Caesar was significant. Besides inspiring the revised calendar, Egypt was filling Caesar's head with ideas for ambitious construction projects. Almost 200 years earlier, the Egyptians had built a canal connecting the Mediterranean with the Red Sea. Now Caesar announced a plan to drain the Pontine Marshes and link the Tiber to the town of Terracina. He also proposed a canal at Corinth in Greece to connect the Aegean and Ionian seas. At Alexandria, Caesar had witnessed— may have inadvertently caused—the destruction of a great library. With Cleopatra at his side, he intended to build a replacement in Rome.

∎

But Caesar couldn't linger to enjoy another extended holiday with the queen. Pompey's sons had reached Spain, where they were encouraging rebellion; Gnaeus Pompey had already raised 12 legions and was acting as Imperator in Farther Spain. Caesar didn't intend to let the revolt simmer until Pompey's sons became as troublesome as Sertorius had been to Sulla. At the end of the year of his triumphs, he left Cleopatra and went to Spain to crush that last holdout of resistance.

Caesar traveled at his usual breakneck pace—50 to 60 miles a day by carriage. The return to an outdoor life invigorated him. In Italy, he had been suffering from headaches and fainting fits that suggested recurring epilepsy. But on his way to his base, Caesar was robust enough to write a poem called *Iter*, "The Journey," chronicling his 24-day trip from Rome. He also kept in contact with his friends by letters written in code; he simply took the 22 letters of the Roman alphabet and moved each down four places, so that D stood for A.

Because he had already dismissed most of his troops, Caesar traveled with only two legions—the Fifth from Transalpine Gaul, and the Tenth, no longer his trusted instrument but filled with new recruits. Once in Spain, Caesar canvassed for more volunteers, then went to relieve a siege at Córdoba. The city had been loyal to him but seemed about to fall soon to Gnaeus Pompey. Labienus persuaded Pompey's sons to drop their siege and cause Caesar to spend the winter in a region with little food or shelter. Instead, Caesar forced a battle and won a victory that diminished the Pompey brothers' manpower and morale. By early March, their only option was to challenge Caesar at the town of Munda.

With his undivided authority now confirmed by the senate, Caesar's policy toward the Italian troops fighting against him had changed. The rebels had become traitors, and Caesar began to execute prisoners. Fear drove the Pompeys' men to acts of desperate courage, but Caesar bucked up his troops by demanding to know if they were going to turn him over to boys like Gnaeus and Sextus. When the battle ended, so did this last, anticlimactic chapter of the civil war.

Labienus was among the dead, and Caesar arranged a proper burial for him. Both Gnaeus and Sextus Pompey fled, but Gnaeus was caught and his severed head shown in Hispalis as proof that the rebellion was over. Caesar went on to Gades, where he spent the next three months designing an improved administration for Spain. He created new colonies, extended citizenship to reward the faithful and approved constitutions that were generous toward freedmen. He taxed all settlements, the hostile ones more severely. He went on to Gaul for a few weeks, implementing similar policies there, settling his veterans on farms and granting full Roman citizenship to the higher-ranking officials. While he was in Narbo, Caesar put an end to a quarrel that had been troubling him.

Since the battle of Pharsalus, Mark Antony had exercised immense power in Caesar's name, taking both his soldiers and prisoners back to Rome while Caesar pursued Pompey to Egypt. When Caesar lingered with Cleopatra in Alexandria, Antony had acted as his *magister equitum*, Master of the Horse, which brought Rome under his control. The honor was a sign of Caesar's affection for the brash soldier, now in his late thirties, more than an acknowledgment of Antony's administrative abilities. As a tribune, he had been too lazy and impatient to hear grievances and had spent his time carousing and seducing other men's wives.

Antony had always been bold in battle, and his men loved him. But as Master of the Horse, Antony fell out with Dolabella; he suspected that Cicero's son-in-law was having an affair with his own wife. Antony invoked Caesar's double standard and left her. Next, Antony opposed Dolabella's bill to cancel all debts and lost favor within the popular movement. He had already outraged the aristocrats, who reminded each other of the occasion when Antony had gone to a morning wedding with a hangover and had vomited in front of the bride.

Antony badly wanted Pompey's house and considered it an appropriate payment for past services. Caesar refused to let him acquire it at the bargain price of Sulla's time, and Antony was visibly disappointed. When Caesar passed over Antony as consul, the rift between the two deepened.

Bad feelings had increased until, when an assassin was discovered at Caesar's house, he was assumed to be in Antony's employ. Caesar denounced his protégé in the senate and stripped him of his powers. And without Caesar, Antony knew he was just another wastrel. He took steps to reform himself by marrying Clodius' widow, Fulvia, who had no intention of throwing herself away on a man with no political future. She oversaw his reform, and before long he was thinking of pranks to coax a smile from her.

By the time Caesar left Spain, he was prepared to give Antony a second chance. Octavius, his niece's son, had been among those who had made the journey to Gaul to escort Caesar back to Rome. When Antony also appeared, he was given a warm welcome and invited to share Caesar's carriage. Octavius rode behind. During the journey, they repaired their friendship, and when Caesar named him as his next year's co-consul, Antony seemed established as Caesar's heir.

It was a time of reconciliations. Marcus Brutus had written to Caesar from Larissa saying he had escaped the battle unhurt. Caesar had missed him. He had always enjoyed arguing with Brutus and had once remarked, "I don't know what that young man means, but whatever he means, he means it vehemently." Now Caesar replied immediately, telling Brutus that he should come at once, with full pardon, and retake his place as one of Caesar's dearest friends. Brutus then intervened successfully for his friend Cassius.

In Rome, Brutus sounded more like his late uncle Cato than like Caesar. He believed that laws were meant to be enforced and bridled at Caesar's easy pardons of others. When Caesar put him in charge of Cisalpine Gaul, however, Brutus turned out to be more compassionate than his harsh language had promised, and his honesty and efficiency won him new friends.

Brutus and Cassius both campaigned to be first praetor, the traditional post for overseeing Rome. Cassius claimed the longer military record, having served with Crassus against Parthia. Caesar listened to their arguments and ruled, "Cassius makes the stronger case, but we must make Brutus first praetor."

It was an arbitrary decision, one of many. Caesar saw that putting down the new threat from Parthia might require him to be away from Rome for as long as three years, and he proposed making Dolabella co-consul to serve with Antony in his absence. Antony's protest was loud and abusive, and Dolabella returned it in kind. Weary of all the arguing, Caesar yielded and named Dolabella as deputy consul. To ensure that no further wrangling broke out while he was away, Caesar named in advance trusted allies to serve for the two years after Antony's consulship. He was observing the outward forms of the Republic. But as the intimidated senators heaped ever more honors on him, their resentment began to outweigh their fear.

Assassination was a constant specter, although Caesar treated the prospect with more equanimity than Pompey had shown. At the height of the dispute between Antony and Dolabella, an informant had come to warn him that one or the other might be plotting to kill him. Contrasting the florid self-indulgence of Antony and Dolabella with Brutus' white intensity and Cassius' gaunt appearance, Caesar remarked, "It is not those well-fed, long-haired men that I fear, but the pale and hungry-looking ones."

XLVII

BRUTUS

44 B.C.

As the new year opened, Caesar entered upon his fifth consulship, with Antony as his partner. Caesar could afford to share the honor. The senate had heaped tributes on him until his powers overlapped and fed on themselves. "Imperator" now preceded Caesar's name and "Father of His Country" followed it. In February, he was voted dictator for life.

Caesar's honors fell into two categories, those with real power behind them, and those that merely indulged his vanity and outraged his opponents. He seemed to wish to hoard every title to keep it away from younger challengers. But he might have turned down the gilded chair reserved for him on the rostra, and he could certainly have discouraged Antony's new chapter of an ancient priesthood—"Repellers of Wolves"—that Antony formed to celebrate Caesar's divinity.

In mid-February, Antony's fraternity took part in the feast of the Lupercalia, which involved racing through Rome's streets naked except for a loincloth made of goatskin. As the spectacle was about to begin, Antony stepped forward with a royal diadem to place on Caesar's head. Romans had been cheering for months as Caesar accepted titles and powers, but the idea of kingship itself remained unacceptable, and groans alerted Caesar to the people's mood. He brushed aside the crown to a resounding cheer.

In the past, Caesar's habit of wearing a wreath of laurel leaves to disguise his baldness had drawn complaints, but he had laughed them off, and most Romans had forgiven his vanity the same way they accepted the loose, somewhat royal, robes that Caesar was wearing these days. His choice in footwear, though, was more troubling—tall red boots like those worn by the early kings.

At Caesar's side, Antony proffered the crown again, and then once more. "Through me," he shouted, "the people offer this to you."

Caesar answered, "Jupiter alone is king of the Romans." He ordered that the crown be carried to the Capitoline and dedicated to Jupiter there.

Despite Caesar's rejection of the title, two tribunes were particularly alarmed by the drift toward kingship. They discovered private citizens placing a laurel wreath on Caesar's statue and threw them in jail. The tribunes said they were only obeying Caesar's wishes and began sending to prison anyone who greeted Caesar as "Rex."

Caesar thought the tribunes were harping on the question of kingship in order to keep the fear alive. Angered, he brought them before the senate on charges of sedition. He could have won a death sentence but settled for stripping them of their office. Still, people wondered whether the affair didn't, in some way, reveal Caesar's true desires. When men shouted, "Long live the king!" he was quick to answer, "No, I am Caesar, not king." But for how much longer, some wondered. Rumors were spreading that before Caesar left for the East, priests would announce that according to their book of prophecy only a king could conquer Parthia.

And Romans worried about what role Cleopatra was playing. In Egypt, she had been a tantalizing figure for gossip. Now, living in Caesar's house, she added to the speculation that he planned to move the capital from Rome to Alexandria, taking with him every man of military age and leaving Romans to govern the city as best they could.

Graffiti began to appear on Roman walls and statuary. On the pedestal of Caesar's statue, someone wrote a verse about the ancient day when a Roman named Lucius Brutus had deposed the Tarquins:

> Brutus was elected consul
>> When he sent the kings away.
> Caesar sent the consuls packing,
>> Caesar is our king today.

Inscriptions on statues of Lucius Brutus were even more inflammatory: "Your descendants are not worthy of you" and "You should be living at this hour." And on the walls of Marcus Brutus' house: "Brutus, are you bribed?" "Brutus, are you dead?"

The appeals to Marcus Brutus involved a bit of playacting. There was no real family connection from Marcus to Lucius, who had put his only two sons to death and left no descendants. As the unrest spread, Caesar's friends recommended that he have a bodyguard. Caesar rejected the idea. Better to die once, he said, than to live expecting death.

The fact was Caesar seemed bored these days, and no amount of either danger or tributes could change that. He was getting ready to fight the Parthians, but he had already conquered more challenging enemies. After his certain victory, he might march around the Caspian Sea and through the Caucasus to invade Scythia. Possibly he would take over Germany and then return to Italy by way of Gaul, showing Romans he had given them a domain protected on every border by oceans.

After that, some thought, peacetime building might revive his interest. The Corinth channel, redirecting the Tiber, grading the marshes around Pomentinum and Setia until thousands of farmers could settle on new acreage—those were projects that would illuminate Caesar's name through the ages. Yet none of it seemed enough.

Marcus Brutus had just turned 40. He had grown up in Caesar's shadow, and when he had come of age he attached himself to the political faction that opposed his mother's lover. After Pharsalus, Servilia had persuaded him to abandon Pompey's cause, but he had returned to Italy determined to stay aloof from Caesar and his friends. When Cato died, Brutus had turned to Cicero. They had patched over the lingering awkwardness that dated back to Cicero's term as proconsul in Cilicia, and now they shared a disgust for the way the Republic was being abused. In *De Republica*, which Cicero had published seven years earlier, he had set out a Greek definition of absolute rulers: a king might possibly be good, a tyrant was always corrupt and dangerous. Cicero had identified Tiberius Gracchus as an example of the wicked man whose death had to be cause for celebration.

Cassius shared Cicero's outrage, perhaps more than Brutus did. One of Cassius' ancestors had killed his son, whom he suspected of preparing to seize power illegally. There was a story that as a child Cassius had hit Sulla's son for bragging about the dictator's power. Cassius had confessed and said that if the other boy repeated his boast, he'd hit him again.

Cassius had planned to back Pompey in the civil war by sailing against Caesar, but Caesar had caught him off guard and he had surrendered. He kept his hot temper in check with his stoical approach to life, eating moderately, drinking only water. Cassius had returned to Rome a disappointed man whom Caesar had fully pardoned but had never again trusted. When Cassius married Brutus' sister, the two men became inseparable.

Caesar wanted badly to overlook Brutus' politics, and even as reports of a plot spread, he dismissed the notion of Brutus as a conspirator. No, Brutus would never seek his death; "Brutus will wait for this shriveled skin."

Cassius began to sound out senators about getting rid of Caesar before he left for Parthia. No one was quick to join the conspiracy, and they all wanted to know where Brutus stood. If Brutus led the way, the people would see that this was no patrician cabal but a patriotic band dedicated to saving the country.

Cassius caught up with Brutus outside Pompey's temple, where the senate was meeting temporarily while the Forum building was being repaired.

"What shall we do," Cassius asked Brutus, "if Caesar's toadies in the senate propose a decree at the next meeting that would make him king?"

Brutus said he didn't intend to be there.

"But what if we are summoned to the senate as praetors?" Cassius persisted. "What shall we do then, my good Brutus?"

"Then I will not remain silent," Brutus replied. "I will stand up and die for the liberty of my country."

The reply was general but it was spirited enough to make Cassius think that Brutus was ready to join a conspiracy. "Do you think it is weavers and shopkeepers who have written those messages secretly on your wall? Or is it instead the most powerful men of Rome? From the other praetors, they ask for games, horse races and combat between wild beasts. But from you they ask liberty, a gift worthy of Brutus."

With that, Brutus embraced him, and Cassius considered the deal struck. He had said aloud what had been in Brutus' mind. But they had to proceed delicately. Cicero had driven Catiline out of Rome for much less than what Cassius was proposing.

Cassius and Brutus spoke to trusted friends, then to those men they knew were ready to challenge the direction that Caesar's ambitions seemed to be heading. Brutus rejected several recruits after testing them. One man eliminated himself when he said that the worst monarchy was better than civil war.

Cassius was increasingly certain that Brutus' participation was essential. A wealthy owner of gladiators had given him a noncommittal response. But when the man consulted with Brutus and found that he was involved, he had enlisted at once.

Cicero was not told of any of this. Brutus and Cassius knew that he wouldn't betray their secret, but at 62 Cicero had developed a reputation for vacillation. He had once confided to a friend, "If any man in the world is a coward in important matters that involve any risk and always inclined to predict an unfavorable rather than a favorable result, I am that man." Brutus and Cassius did not want him to dull their spirit.

Cicero was of use to the plotters in other ways, however. He mocked any man whose power was greater than his own, and Caesar was again a target. Cicero's gibes were clever enough to circulate widely. When one of Caesar's puppets died at eight o'clock in the morning of the last day of his term as consul, Caesar immediately appointed a successor to fill in the hours until midnight. To Cicero, that adherence to the letter of the law was one more example of Caesar making the law itself ridiculous.

As Cicero joined the friends who were accompanying the interim consul to the senate, he said, "Let us go quickly so that the gentleman won't be out of office before we get there." Afterward,

Cicero pretended to praise the diligence of Caesar's nominee, noting that no crimes had been committed during his term of office because the man had not closed an eye.

Cicero could mock, but he was unamused. After joking about the consul's brief term, he wrote, "If you were an eyewitness, you could not keep back your tears."

Yet Caesar still hoped to harness Cicero's talents. Cicero had sought a pardon for one of Pompey's backers named Ligarius when the case looked hopeless. Caesar had gone to the proceedings even though he considered Ligarius a wicked man who deserved punishment. "But why," he had asked his courtiers, "shouldn't we hear a speech from Cicero?" Even now, Cicero's language in court could thrill Caesar, and when Cicero invoked the battle of Pharsalus, Caesar's hand trembled and papers slipped from his grasp. When he finished, Caesar acquitted his client.

But the trial had only soured Ligarius and left him bitter that he should need a pardon for trying to preserve the Republic. Brutus heard that he had become ill and went to call on his old comrade. Standing by his bed, Brutus said, "Oh, Ligarius, what a time you have found to be sick."

Ligarius raised himself on an elbow. "But, Brutus, if you have any plan that is worthy of you, I am well."

Caesar extended another mark of favor to Cicero by inviting himself to Cicero's country estate for the third day of Saturnalia, a holiday usually spent with friends and family. Caesar's visit was intended to be a great honor, but Cicero let Atticus know he considered it only an expense and a chore.

Caesar arrived with 2,000 soldiers, who camped in a field behind Cicero's house. He walked along the seashore, bathed in the early afternoon and then listened to reports of what Romans were saying about him. Cicero knew that Caesar always wanted to hear the latest gossip about himself, even when it was unflattering. Before his death at 30, Catullus had circulated scathing verses about Caesar and one of his officers: "How well these two bad fairies fit together, this queenly couple, Caesar and Mamurra." Now, as he watched Caesar's face during the recital, Cicero noted that his control was total, his expression never changed.

When the reading was over, Caesar went off to be massaged and perfumed. Before he sat down to dinner, he made himself vomit in order to show his confidence in Cicero's hospitality. He was ready to eat and drink what was offered.

Caesar and Cicero did not discuss politics, only literature. Caesar hadn't been trying to charm Cicero when he wrote that extending the boundaries of the mind was better than expanding a nation's frontiers.

After Caesar left, Cicero felt that the visit had gone well. The food had been good, and Caesar had been cheerful. "Yet," he wrote to Atticus, "he is not a guest to whom one would say on parting, 'Please call upon me again when you return.' "

Rather than hammering out agreements through senate debates, Caesar was drafting his proposals at Balbus' house and sending them to the senators as decrees. When it suited him, he had Cicero's name added as a witness to the drafting, which meant that Cicero sometimes heard by way of Syria or Armenia what he was supposed to have signed. "Don't think this is merely a joke on my part," Cicero wrote to a friend. "I would have you know that I have received letters from rulers in the furthest reaches of the world, thanking me for my vote in giving them the title of king. I remain not only ignorant of the fact that they got that title but of their ever having been born."

Brutus' wife, Portia, realized that something was worrying him. As Cato's daughter, she had grown up in political life and had been hardly more than a girl when she wed Brutus, although she had already been married before and had given birth to a son. Her love and concern for Brutus were well known, and now she watched him sleeping fitfully and starting up in bed from his dreams. Yet Brutus didn't confide in her, and Portia couldn't bear his secrecy. Her response was as premeditated as her father's suicide, although she had only a small knife that she used to pare her nails. She plunged the blade into her thigh and twisted until she struck a vein. The wound produced a dangerous fever that brought Brutus to her bedside.

She spoke to him angrily. "I was given to you in marriage, not like a concubine to share only your bed and board but to share all your good fortunes and all of the bad."

Portia was offended that he would consider her in the category of women too weak to be trusted with a secret. Didn't he appreciate her heritage and the education that had shaped her character? She could bear any pain, and as proof she pulled aside the bandage and showed him her wound.

Shaken, Brutus told her about the plot and prayed aloud at her bedside that his plot's success would make him worthy of such a wife.

Time was running out. It was reported that Caesar was planning to leave on his campaign in four days. From then on, he would be surrounded by an impenetrable bodyguard. Brutus and Cassius had reached their decision late in February and had been recruiting for two weeks. The old dividing line between the patricians and the popular movement had all but disappeared. Now men were either for Caesar or against him. The conspirators concluded that he had disillusioned many of the people's leaders by treating the tribunes as an annoyance, and they believed that the popular faction was now as hostile to Caesar as the aristocrats had always been. Of the 60 senators who had joined the plot, most had once been Caesar's supporters.

The leaders had considered and rejected several places for their attack. The Via Sacra? During the gladiatorial games? The senate's meeting place seemed the most appropriate site. They chose a date: the Ides of March, when most of Caesar's partisans would be celebrating a festival outside the city's walls.

The conspirators hoped that accosting Caesar in a public place would revive the memory of Romulus being killed by senators for his regal manners. It would show that their act was not motivated by jealousy or revenge, and the people would rise up and hail them for restoring Rome's liberty. Some plotters argued that Antony should also be killed; his popularity with the army made him dangerous. Brutus vetoed the idea. Only Caesar was trying to make himself king. To attain the pure honor of tyrannicide, they must kill that man alone.

The conspirators had kept their secret well, but they were edgy. Casca, a tribune who had agreed to join the plot, was astonished when an acquaintance walked up to say, "You concealed the secret from us, but Brutus has told me everything."

Before the flabbergasted Casca could answer, the man chuckled and explained that he had just learned that Casca intended to stand for an aedileship.

All the same, death was in the air. A meeting of the senate

was scheduled for March 15. The night before, Caesar went to dine with Lepidus, his latest Master of the Horse. Caesar took along a man he regarded as a friend but who was one of the conspirators. Was Caesar merely sensitive to the mood around him, or was he having macabre sport with the other guests when he asked over wine, "What is the best kind of death?"

Around the table, men offered their opinions until it came to Caesar's turn. "A sudden one," he said.

Caesar woke during the night feeling faint. His wife, Calpurnia, also spent a restless night; in a dream, she had seen Caesar streaming with blood. At the morning sacrifice, the omens were also bad. Caesar presided over the killing of an ox. The animal's heart was so small that the priests first thought he didn't have one.

Caesar told Calpurnia that a fortune-teller had warned him lately to beware the Ides of March. She pleaded with him to put off the senate meeting. Calpurnia was not normally superstitious, but further sacrifices yielded more unfavorable signs for the day. Caesar decided to give in to his wife's entreaties. He would stay home.

When the conspirators heard of Caesar's intention, they panicked. Evidence of their plot might reach him at any moment. Caesar had to die that day. They sent one of his most trusted friends—a man Caesar had named as an heir in his latest will—to chide him for staying home. It was an odd performance. Julius Caesar, who had risked death and disgrace dozens of times in his life, was being told that the senate would ridicule him if he gave in to womanish fears.

What made Caesar listen? Any accusations of weakness may have still rankled him. Or since he had always scoffed at portents, he may have been ashamed of momentarily yielding to them. Perhaps he believed that the senators were ready to bestow a new title on him. One suggestion going around the Forum had been to make Caesar king of all the provinces but not of Italy itself. If that was the compromise the senate had negotiated, Caesar would hold power constitutionally in Italy as dictator, consul and censor. But he would march against Parthia bearing the East's most esteemed title, and in Egypt he could be king to Cleopatra's queen. If that was why the senate had assembled, Caesar would be foolish to let the moment slip away.

The senate's messenger kept up his urging. At least, he said, come to the senate in person to order the postponement. That way, people wouldn't say they had to stand by until Calpurnia had better dreams. Taking Caesar by the hand, the man was leading him outside when a slave slipped through the open door and rushed to find Calpurnia. Keep me safe until Caesar returns, the slave begged her. I have important news to report.

As Caesar moved among the throng in front of his house, a Greek teacher who had overheard the plot brought him a small scroll outlining the conspiracy. But Caesar was treating every parchment handed to him as another petition and turning it over to an attendant. The teacher pressed forward, slipped his scroll into Caesar's hand and shouted above the din, "Read this, Caesar, for yourself, and quickly. It contains important matters that concern you."

Caesar was about to pause right there and read the message, but too many people were clamoring for his attention. He did keep the scroll apart from the others and several times tried to concentrate on it. The jostling and confusion were too great. Caesar arrived at the senate still holding the warning in his hand.

The senators were gathered around the statue of himself that Pompey had installed in his lavish hall. Brutus and Cassius, as praetors, had stayed at their desks all morning until they heard that Caesar was on his way. When Caesar appeared at the door, Cassius turned to Pompey's statue. He would normally have rejected anything superhuman, but today he seemed to be asking for Pompey's blessing. Antony had been following close behind Caesar, but he was stopped by one of the conspirators and engaged in conversation.

By the time Caesar reached the session, he had shrugged off his apprehensions. He saw the soothsayer who had warned against the Ides of March and called out to him jovially: "What about your prophecies now? Don't you see that the day you feared has come and I am alive?"

"Yes," said the prophet, "it has come but it has not gone."

The glum answer could not shake Caesar's confidence. He paused for a senator who came running up to speak to him. Brutus and Cassius couldn't overhear what the man was saying, but a few minutes earlier he had approached them to say that he was praying for them and that they should hurry. Terrified by what he seemed to know, they hadn't answered. Now he might be warning Caesar. The conspirators had agreed that if their plot failed, they would kill themselves rather than be taken prisoner.

Caesar broke off the conversation. Apparently from the way the senator was thanking him, he had merely asked a favor. Caesar paused to let a priest offer a sacrifice before he entered. Once again, the animal's innards were deformed; the priest called it a mark of impending death. Caesar laughed and told him about another ill omen that had come before one of his most successful military campaigns.

Gently, the priest reproached Caesar for his disbelief. However that campaign may have turned out, he said, Caesar had been in great danger then, and this omen was even more deadly. When Caesar asked for a new sacrifice, the omens were again unlucky. By that time, conspirators were at his elbow urging him not to keep the senate waiting any longer.

Caesar entered the chamber. The senators rose in respect, and Caesar took his gilded chair. When one senator, Tillius Cimber, approached to ask that his exiled brother be allowed to return to Rome, Caesar said that the matter must be held over. He had not come to conduct routine business. But Cimber was part of the plot and was only playing a role. As though to give urgency to his petition, he took Caesar's purple robe in his hands, a gesture that exposed Caesar's neck, and shouted, "Friends, what are you waiting for?"

Casca had been listening for that signal and struck at Caesar's neck with his dagger from behind. He was too nervous, and the blade only grazed Caesar's chest. Caesar pulled his toga from Cimber's hands and turned around to grasp the knife. Holding the blade tight, Caesar cried, "Damned Casca! What are you doing?"

Casca called, "Help!"

Some senators, unaware of the plot, stood frozen and helpless as their colleagues swarmed around Caesar for the kill. The conspirators had agreed that each of them must deliver at least one blow. Cassius and Brutus had been hiding daggers beneath their togas all morning. To meet his obligation, one senator plunged his dagger into Caesar's side while he was still wrestling with Casca.

As Caesar twisted and ducked to avoid the blades, Cassius

opened a wound in his face and others struck at his back and chest. Before the battle of Pharsalus, Caesar had told his troops to aim for the faces of the enemy cavalry. Now instinctively he pulled up his toga to protect his eyes from the blows. Writhing and turning, he was still fighting back when he caught sight of Brutus approaching for his turn. When Brutus raised his dagger, Caesar stopped resisting.

Brutus drove the blade deep into Caesar's thigh, near his groin, and Caesar gave a cry, stumbled forward and fell at the foot of Pompey's statue. That didn't stop the blows. Senators laid into the corpse with their knives, slashing into Caesar's robe and wounding each other in the melee.

Some witnesses said Caesar's last words had been unintelligible, no more than a grunt of pain and exhaustion. Others said that when he recognized Brutus, Caesar had lost his will to live. They couldn't agree whether he had spoken in Latin or Greek, but they said that as he watched Brutus—Servilia's child—lift his dagger, Caesar had asked, "You, too, my son?"

Most of the senators didn't know that the conspirators had agreed to stop with one murder. In panic, they rushed screaming past Caesar's bloody corpse to escape from the hall. "Run!" they shouted. "Bolt the doors!"

Outside the building, men took up their cry and soon the city was filled with warnings that assassinations on an epic scale were sweeping Rome. At Brutus' house, Portia's nerves had frayed, then snapped. She had been sending a flurry of messages to the senate, but by the time of the killing she had collapsed.

Senators hid in houses and shops while the assassins hurried to the Forum to assure the people they needn't be afraid, not an obvious message since their swords glinted with blood. They wrapped their togas around their left arms to parry blows from Caesar's loyalists. One senator carried a spear with the cap that was given to freedmen as proof of their release from slavery. The conspirators hoped that Romans would see it as a symbol for the liberation they had brought them.

Aristocrats like Lentulus Spinther and Dolabella, who had taken no part in the murder, joined the conspirators in the street, all of whom were expecting praise for their daring act. Instead, they were met by sullen resentment from the crowds and from

Caesar's veterans. Some men cried, "Down with tyranny!" But that was not the prevailing mood. Gladiators who had been given weapons for the day's games came running into the streets, and families climbed to their roofs to protect themselves. A riot erupted that left several senators wounded. Stores throughout the Forum were plundered. As Master of the Horse, Lepidus brought a legion of troops to the Campus Martius to provide Antony with the armed force to respond. Lepidus' first instinct was for revenge, but he couldn't be sure about Rome's reaction. After he located Antony, they took refuge in a house across the Tiber.

The conspirators hoped to increase their respectability by calling for Cicero to join them, but his name was not impressing the crowd, nor did he appear. By the time the assassins reached the Forum, the hysteria seemed to be dying down. Apparently, Romans were curious to know what had happened and were willing to give Brutus a hearing. He called for silence and invited various distinguished persons in the crowd to join him on the rostra. Caesar had promised Dolabella the consulship when he departed for the East. At the rostra, Dolabella claimed the office and at the same time denounced Caesar with stinging invective. Ignoring his hypocrisy, the assassins embraced him as a convert to their plot. He offered himself as their consul, to offset whatever Antony might do.

But the conspirators' key figure was still Brutus. With his hand bleeding from the blows to Caesar's body, Brutus spoke proudly of his actions and those of his allies. Brutus was considered a serious man, neither ambitious nor impetuous, and he was heard out. With measured words, careful not to threaten any political faction, Brutus gradually eased the uproar in the Forum. Romans seemed to be grieving for Caesar, but calmly now.

The mood remained tense, however. The conspirators withdrew to the Capitol for protection and announced they would spend the rest of the day and night in earnest prayer.

At daybreak, how Rome would react was still unclear. Although people were mourning Caesar and resisting any endorsement of his assassination, they didn't seem inclined to attack the men who killed him. What they wanted was civic peace with no more bloodshed. Yet when a praetor described Caesar as a tyrant, the crowd stoned him and burned down his house. Lepidus had to intervene to save him.

The conspirators were ready with bribes for those of Caesar's friends whose forgiveness and neutrality could be bought, and messages went back and forth to Antony. Forget any private grievances, they urged. For the public good, give up your animosity.

Antony could count on Lepidus' legion, but even so his military position was insecure. Caesar had previously named one of the assassins as governor of Cisalpine Gaul, which gave him control of a large army only a few days' march from Rome. After weighing his options, Antony began his reply belligerently but trailed off in conciliation. He said that his solemn oath to protect or avenge Caesar committed him to punishing the guilty parties. But he added that he and Lepidus would discuss the matter with the neutral senators and abide by their decision.

Cicero had gone to the Capitol to meet with Brutus and urge him to make the murder legitimate by calling the senate together and passing a public declaration that Caesar had been a tyrant. With Antony in seclusion, Brutus had the authority as urban praetor to convene the session. Meantime, the assassins were referring to themselves as the "liberators."

Lepidus marched his troops into the Forum, and under their protection Antony called on Calpurnia to gather up Caesar's documents and his personal fortune of 700 million sesterces from the state treasury. The Vestal Virgins also turned over to him the will Caesar had left with them for safekeeping. Antony preempted Cicero's recommendation to Brutus by scheduling his own senate meeting for the next day, March 17, at the Temple of Tellus.

The senators arrived to find the temple ringed by Antony's veterans. The assassins remained in the Capitol until they could learn what Antony had to propose. His terms turned out to be mild. Uphold all of Caesar's laws, Antony told the senate, and I will agree to spare the murderers.

"Those who are asking for a vote on Caesar's character," Antony said, "must first know that if he was an elected ruler of the state, all his acts and decrees will remain in full force. But if it is decided that he usurped the government by violence, his body should be cast out unburied and all his acts annulled."

Antony's challenge altered the equation. It was a difficult and revealing test: Would the men who had joined in the assassination now resign the positions that Caesar had assigned to them?

Cicero was also confronted with a hard choice. To accept

Antony's terms would guarantee that Caesar's changes in the fabric of the Republic would outlive them all. But if he resisted Caesar in death, might Antony turn menacing? Not for the first time, Cicero rejected martyrdom. He told the senate that mistakes had been made, but this was no time to investigate them or to punish anyone. He pointed out that there was much to criticize about Caesar and, for that matter, about those who killed him. Instead of placing blame, Cicero called upon Romans to "regard what has happened as if it were a hailstorm or a flood and consign it to oblivion."

Cicero went home and apologized by letter to Atticus for accepting Antony's terms. He had no real choice, he said.

With the agreement struck, Antony and Lepidus sent their sons as hostages to the Capitoline, and the assassins came down the hill to shake hands with Caesar's closest friends. Cassius agreed to dine that night with Antony, but first he demanded and received a pledge of safe conduct. At the table, Antony asked him, "By any chance, do you have a dagger under your arm even now?"

By that time, Cassius was feeling secure enough to answer, "Yes, and a large one, too, if you also should want to make yourself a tyrant."

Antony emerged from the negotiations with a reputation as a statesman. He had averted another civil war, but he began to wonder if he had forgiven too quickly and cheaply. Caesar's corpse, not yet buried, was a reminder of how weakly Antony had honored his oath of loyalty and revenge.

Immediately following the murder, those who stayed behind in the hall had been afraid to approach Caesar's body, until at last three slave boys rolled the corpse into a litter and carried it home to Calpurnia. Along the way, Romans could see Caesar's lifeless arm exposed and dangling. A physician who conducted the postmortem concluded that only one blow—to the chest—had been mortal. Caesar could have survived the others.

The assassins had intended to show their contempt by dumping Caesar's body into the Tiber. But now that Antony had negotiated posthumous acceptance of Caesar's regime, his corpse had to be honored. On March 18, Piso convinced the senate that his late son-in-law was entitled to a full consular funeral two days later. Since none of Caesar's male relatives were in Rome, Brutus agreed that Mark Antony should deliver the funeral address.

On March 20, Caesar's body was carried to the Forum amid wailing and scenes of grief that showed the depth of the people's feeling. In front of the rostra, Antony had placed a large model of Caesar's new temple to Venus. Inside, Caesar's body was displayed on a funeral couch, along with the torn and bloody robe he had been wearing when he was stabbed. Antony arranged for actors to recall Caesar's life through dialogue from plays that seemed appropriate, and a line from a play by Pacuvius echoed through the Forum: "What, did I save these men that they might murder me?"

Before he began his formal oration, Antony instructed a herald to read two senate decrees. The first bestowed on Caesar all human honors, the other made him a god, Divine Julius. Because Caesar had no Roman children, Antony might have hoped for a substantial inheritance. But Piso, as the will's executor, had already read the document aloud at Antony's house, and Caesar had remembered him only as an alternative heir. Three-fourths of Caesar's estate went to his sister's grandson Octavian, the other quarter to Octavian's younger brother. Caesar also formally adopted Octavian in his will, giving him the name of Caesar. Antony told the multitudes about those terms before he read another surprising clause: Caesar had left his elaborate gardens to Rome, and to every Roman citizen he had bequeathed 300 sesterces, a workingman's wage for two and a half months.

At that proof of Caesar's generosity, the laments and angry cries rose higher. Antony shouted above the clamor to apologize in advance for the length of his tribute. A man as celebrated and accomplished as Caesar, Antony said, deserved to have his lineage and life, his career and character, reviewed in language that this audience would choose if they could speak with one voice. They should remember that Aeneas once ruled as king of Rome, but Caesar had proved himself superior to Aeneas by refusing the kingship.

In his eulogy, Antony endeavored to redefine Caesar's most distinctive qualities. He praised the rash commander as a sober military analyst and called the spendthrift politician a prudent manager of his resources. Antony's exaggerations might be outrageous, but they were beguiling: "So strong was his natural bent toward virtue that he not only had no vice himself but would not believe that it existed in anybody else."

In Antony's version of the Civil War, Caesar had fought a rapacious Pompey on behalf of all the decent Romans who were mourning today. "Indeed, if you wished to recite the whole story in detail," Antony said, he could "show the renowned Pompey to have been a mere child, so completely was he out-generaled at every point."

Antony had designed his apologia to confront each of the prevalent rumors and lay them to rest. Had Cleopatra sapped Caesar's resolve? Antony recalled the brevity of the campaign against Pharnaces after Caesar left Egypt. "This better than anything else showed that he had not become weaker in Alexandria and had not delayed his departure from there because of voluptuousness."

Antony extolled Caesar's mercy to his defeated rivals and reminded his audience that it was the Romans themselves who had insisted on bestowing Caesar's many titles. "Therefore, for the gods he was appointed high priest. For us citizens he was consul. For the soldiers, Imperator and, for the enemy, dictator. But why do I list all these details when—in one phrase—you called him the father of his country."

Under Antony's pact with the assassins, he should have ended his eulogy there. Instead, he left his place to stand in front of the corpse and turned from praising Caesar as hero to pitying him as victim. As he listed Caesar's achievements, Antony's speech had grown more impassioned until his voice had risen to an inspired frenzy. Now he spoke in sad and measured tones.

"Of what use, O Caesar, was your humanity?" Antony asked, speaking to the body laid out before him. "Though you enacted many laws to prevent men from being killed by their personal enemies, yet how mercilessly you yourself were slain by your friends!

"And now—" Antony took up a spear and pulled away Caesar's robe on its point. He lifted the torn fabric to show Caesar's dried blood. "And now, the victim of assassination, you lie dead in the Forum through which you often led a triumph. Stabbed to death, you have been cast down upon the rostra from which you often addressed the people. Woe for blood-spattered locks of gray, alas for the torn robe, which you seem to have put on only so you could be slain in it."

On its ivory funeral couch, Caesar's body was too low for the crowd to see, but now loyalists raised a wax image of him and spun it slowly to show the 23 wounds across his body. It was the final goad to mourners already stricken. Weeping with anger and regret, the crowd cried out against Caesar's murderers, and those senators who had stood by and not saved him.

Preparations for the cremation had been made in the Campus Martius, but leaders of the throng seized Caesar's body from its place in front of the rostra and debated whether to carry the corpse back to the chamber where he had been struck down, as further reproach to the criminals, or carry it up to the Capitol. At either spot, they could show their veneration by burning it as they had once burned Clodius' body.

Caesar's former officers feared that a fire might spread and thwarted that plan. They clashed with the demonstrators and succeeded in keeping them penned up. But men began tearing up court benches, tables and railings, dry branches from the ground. Despite the troops, they stacked the wood in a pyre. Caesar's body would be burned in the Forum.

Musicians and actors had walked in the funeral procession wearing the same robes Caesar had worn during his triumphs. As the wood was ignited, they stripped them off, tore them to shreds and hurled them into the fire. Women pulled off their jewelry and their children's clothes to add to the blaze. Foreigners throughout the city had considered Caesar their reliable protector. Now Romans looked on curiously as those strangers came out from their neighborhoods to grieve. Caesar had singled out the Jews for honors during his brief rule, and they gathered around the pyre and expressed their pain and loss.

Throughout the night, thousands of mourners stayed in the Forum. Long after Caesar's body had been consumed, they went on feeding the flames.

XLVIII

OCTAVIAN

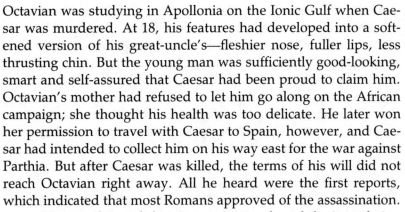

44–30 B.C.

Octavian was studying in Apollonia on the Ionic Gulf when Caesar was murdered. At 18, his features had developed into a softened version of his great-uncle's—fleshier nose, fuller lips, less thrusting chin. But the young man was sufficiently good-looking, smart and self-assured that Caesar had been proud to claim him. Octavian's mother had refused to let him go along on the African campaign; she thought his health was too delicate. He later won her permission to travel with Caesar to Spain, however, and Caesar had intended to collect him on his way east for the war against Parthia. But after Caesar was killed, the terms of his will did not reach Octavian right away. All he heard were the first reports, which indicated that most Romans approved of the assassination.

He soon learned that Antony's speech and the immolation of Caesar's body had led to a public outrage that had forced Brutus and Cassius to leave Rome. Caesar's faction now saw Antony as

Portrait on a coin of Octavian as Augustus. The New York Public Library Picture Collection.

his political heir. He was letting his beard grow long as a symbol of mourning and taking personal charge of settling Caesar's veterans on farmland in Campania. Since Antony also controlled Caesar's papers, he could make any appointment he chose and claim to be following Caesar's wishes. No one dared challenge him. Antony could never be Caesar, but his power was beginning to seem as absolute.

By the time Octavian landed at Brundisium in April, he knew of his inheritance and went to pay Antony a friendly visit. He soon realized, however, that Antony did not take him seriously. When Octavian reminded him of the money Caesar had left for every Roman citizen, Antony laughed at the boy and warned him that trying to act as Caesar's executor would place too great a burden on his young shoulders. Antony seemed to think he was dealing with a youth as irresponsible and pleasure-bent as he had been at the same age, not a prickly young man alert to snubs and sneers.

Octavian began to court friends among the Romans, men who feared or disliked their new leader. Cicero was certainly in that number. Although he had been in the chamber when Caesar was murdered and had applauded the act, Cicero didn't feel that Octavian reproached him for it. Their first conversations went well enough. "He is completely devoted to me," Cicero assured Atticus after meeting the young man. But he didn't accept the impression of Octavian as harmless and impressionable. Octavian's servants were already calling him Caesar, and Cicero suspected that one day he might seek revenge against the conspirators.

And from the start, Octavian's actions confirmed that judgment. He arranged to stage the plays and shows that Caesar had scheduled, and he placed Caesar's empty gold chair at every public spectacle. His intention was to suggest that Caesar had ascended to the heavens, but unsympathetic tribunes removed the chair.

Meanwhile, through his diligent correspondence, Cicero was keeping his lines open to the conspirators. "I have always loved Marcus Brutus for his great ability, his most agreeable manners, his extraordinary uprightness and constancy," he wrote, knowing his words would reach their subject. "However, on the Ides of March my affection was so enhanced that I was surprised there was any room for an increase in what I had long thought had reached its culmination."

To Atticus, however, Cicero complained that the assassination had not restored the Republic: "For though the tyrant is dead, I see that the tyranny persists."

Cicero had reconciled with Dolabella. His former son-in-law had arrested worshipers at a makeshift altar dedicated to Caesar and had them executed without a trial. But with Antony consolidating his hold over Rome, Cicero found it prudent to behave courteously to him as well.

Brutus and Cassius were living quietly on their estates south of Rome, near Lanuvium. They waited in self-imposed exile to see how Romans would finally judge the murder and issued assurances that their intentions were peaceful. Even though they were praetors, they said, they would remain away from Rome for the rest of their lives rather than provoke another civil war.

Cicero was respected as a senior statesman, but he was not one of the four Romans who now had real followings. Antony's travels throughout Italy had rallied the troops loyal to Caesar. A former comrade-in-arms spoke for many legionaries when he wrote, "It was not Caesar I followed in the Civil War but a friend. I did not like his acts, but I would not desert him."

In speeches from the rostra, Octavian played to the civilians who believed Caesar was divine. In midsummer, a comet flashed through the sky, and Octavian's friends announced that it was Caesar taking his place in the heavens.

Brutus retained support among the aristocrats, despite Cicero's scathing remarks about his inertia: "Is all our Brutus has done come to this, that he might live at last at Lanuvium?" And Lepidus commanded legions in Narbonese Gaul and Nearer Spain and had negotiated a truce with Pompey's son in Spain. Throughout the provinces, the cities and tribes were uncertain about the future, but they were not revolting against Rome.

Antony wanted to be seen both as Caesar's true heir and as the defender of the Republic. He made several symbolic moves to cut into Octavian's growing support. He changed the month called "Quintilis" to "Julius," and announced that games honoring Apollo would begin on July 9. He also made a gesture of reconciliation to Brutus and Cassius by assigning them the small provinces of Crete and Cyrene; neither command included military troops.

Insulted but stymied, both men consulted with their friends

at a meeting organized by Brutus' mother, Servilia. Cicero counseled them to accept the provinces; at least, they would be safe there. Reluctantly, Brutus and Cassius left Rome, determined to raise armies large enough to take over Macedonia and Syria.

But the clouds were gathering, and Antony attacked Cicero for refusing to attend a senate memorial for Caesar. When Cicero did at last appear in public, it was to deliver a denunciation of Antony, the first of many attacks on him. Cicero called the orations his Philippics, hoping that the Romans would compare them with Demosthenes' speeches against the father of Alexander the Great.

Antony struck back furiously. He accused Cicero of being the agent behind Caesar's murder, and read with contempt from Cicero's recent ingratiating letters to him. Antony had expected Cicero to be in the audience for his speech, but as usual Cicero stayed away. He had gone south to his estate near Naples, where he was writing a second Philippic. Bragging that he had scorned the daggers of Catiline and would not tremble before Antony's, Cicero listed every allegation that had ever been leveled against Antony: drunkenness, homosexual affairs, corruption, cowardice. Antony persuaded an ally to assail Cicero with the same kind of invective, but there were no direct confrontations between the two men. By the time Antony saw Cicero again, the debate would be over.

While Antony was away from Rome recruiting soldiers, Octavian felt he had sufficient backing to seize the government, but he had misjudged. The coup failed.

Antony also had a setback when the proconsul of Cisalpine Gaul refused to turn the province over to him. He responded by launching a new siege against the town of Mutina. He couldn't batter Mutina into submission, however, and wound up losing most of his army. Cicero exulted and called for 50 days of thanksgiving.

Initially, Octavian joined the effort to drive Antony and his band of survivors into Transalpine Gaul. But Octavian's men were torn. How could they fight Caesar's friend Antony, when their efforts would benefit his murderers? Octavian, realizing that their doubts were weakening his position as Caesar's heir, gave up the effort.

■

Brutus had peacefully assumed control of Macedonia from its governor, and quaestors from Asia and Syria recognized him as Rome's legitimate representative and gave him the funds they had planned to send home. But Antony had allotted Macedonia to his brother, Gaius, and when Gaius arrived in Illyria, Brutus moved quickly to take him prisoner. Back in Rome, Cicero persuaded the senate to transfer legal authority over Macedonia to Brutus and over Syria to Cassius. Only such a staunch defender of the Republic as Cicero would have dared the maneuver. Invoking a higher power than senate decrees, Cicero claimed that Brutus and Cassius were obeying the law of Jupiter, which held that what served the Republic was legal and moral.

Once again, Cicero had yielded to reality. He urged Brutus to put Gaius to death as a criminal, but Brutus preferred to let him live. He also spared Lepidus' captive sons; their mother was Brutus' half sister. When Cicero realized that Brutus was determined to protect his nephews, he changed course and argued for their lives before the senate.

In Macedonia, Brutus heard that Cicero was praising Octavian, and he wrote to Atticus saying he was sure that Cicero was motivated always by patriotism, "but in some respects he seems to me to have acted—how shall I put it—amateurishly for a man of his political wisdom." Brutus thought it presumptuous of Cicero to think he could save the Republic by alienating someone so powerful as Antony to promote Octavian as the more trustworthy leader. "There is only one thing I think I can say to you," Brutus concluded. "Cicero has stimulated rather than checked the boy's greed and ambition."

After he saw a cringing letter that Cicero had sent Octavian, Brutus addressed his barbs directly to Cicero. "Look at your words again," he wrote, "and dare to deny that your appeals are those of a subject to a king." Brutus reminded Cicero of his mortality: "You set a very high value on the years that remain to you at your age if, for the sake of them, you can beg from that boy."

But Brutus was calling on Cicero to change the habits of a lifetime, and since he could not, Brutus struck at his vanity. "I shall keep away from those who are willing to die slaves," he wrote, "and shall imagine my Rome to be wherever I can live free." He pitied Cicero for continuing to cling to life at any price.

He got no reply.

■

After his defeat at Mutina, Antony had rebuilt his forces. First, he struck a deal with Lepidus, who commanded seven legions in Narbonese Gaul, and then he made overtures to Octavian. A number of senators were highhanded toward Octavian as they once had been toward Pompey, using him when their enemies threatened but ready to drop him when the danger passed. Octavian's resentment made him receptive to Antony's blandishments, especially since he had cause to wonder whether Cicero was the stalwart older friend he had first seemed. Lately, he had heard that Cicero had remarked that Octavian was "to be praised and lifted up." But the verb for "lifted up" not only meant "extolled" but also "removed." Could Cicero be so two-faced? The play on words was very like him.

Octavian now told the senate that he expected to be made consul for his achievements. The senate refused him. And so a second Caesar, with eight of Gaul's legions behind him, would cross the Rubicon, storm Rome and take by force what the senate had denied him.

After the months of feints and false starts, Caesar's true legacy was beginning to emerge. Antony and Lepidus had the stronger armies, Octavian the illustrious name. The authorities had finally approved his adoption, along with a legal change that made his name Gaius Julius Caesar Octavianus. A year and a half after Caesar's murder, Antony, Octavian and Lepidus openly formed their version of the clandestine triumvirate of Caesar, Pompey and Crassus. They found an obliging tribune to make their arrangement legal for the next five years.

Antony had outlawed dictatorships during his term as consul, and now he demanded that Octavian relinquish the consulship he had seized. It was of little importance. The three men would be sharing powers that made the title of dictator or consul irrelevant. Acts by the triumvirs would not require senate approval. The senators were relegated to the management of Rome's day-to-day affairs.

Working out the details of their agreement took two days of intense negotiation, after which they reinforced their ties in the traditional Roman way. Octavian became engaged to Antony's stepdaughter, Claudia.

The triumvirs thought they had identified Caesar's fatal

failure. It was the way he had forgiven his enemies, and they would not make his mistakes. Brutus and Cassius had blocked the payments to Rome from their Eastern provinces, sharply reducing Rome's money supply. To fill the treasury, Antony, Octavian and Lepidus ordered proscriptions even harsher than Sulla's. They drew up lists of wealthy men, then sent soldiers to kill them and confiscate their property. Each member of the triumvirate could add names to the list. It began with 130 senators' names and quickly grew until 300 senators and 2,000 businessmen were proscribed.

Antony had moved into Pompey's mansion, where he was behaving more like Sulla, filling his house with actors and jugglers, drunkards and flatterers, and turning away the worthy but dull officials who came on business. Killing their enemies had made the triumvirate rich, but nothing seemed to satisfy Antony. Some were claiming that he had looted the treasury of the Vestal Virgins.

Now only Brutus and Cassius represented a threat. Octavian persuaded Antony that they should divide the army between them, leave Lepidus in charge of Rome and set out together for Macedonia to secure their future.

With troops from Asia forced into service, Brutus and Cassius were tightening their grip over the East and preparing to take Italy back. But the two commanders couldn't work together without friction, and each attempt to resolve a quarrel led to another. Cassius was the better soldier. Brutus was the more upright and meted out his harshest punishments for friends he caught embezzling; those were the men Cassius was inclined to forgive. Yet they were bound by the blood they had spilled two years earlier. When Octavian got a law passed that described Caesar's assassins as enemies of Rome, Brutus and Cassius knew they must resolve their differences and fight together for Italy and for their lives.

Brutus saw the end in a vision. With his men, he had marched with Cassius' army to the Hellespont and was about to cross over on the way to Italy. He sat up late one night, reading by lantern in his tent. As his eyes grew tired, a strange form appeared before him.

"Who are you?" Brutus demanded. "Man or god? And why have you come here?"

"I am your evil genius, Brutus," the apparition answered. "And you will see me at Philippi."

In his trance, Brutus was unafraid. He said, "I shall see you."

But when he awoke, he was shaken and demanded of his slaves whether they had seen the figure. Cassius made light of the incident; Brutus had merely been overwrought, he said.

Brutus and Cassius marched their armies into Macedonia and pitched camp west of the town of Philippi. Antony and Octavian sailed across the Adriatic to stop them there. The day of the battle, Octavian fell ill, but he insisted on being carried by litter from Dyrrachium to make the rounds of his troops and bestow a Caesar's blessing.

Before the battle, Brutus told Cassius that he no longer thought less of Cato for taking his own life. He said that he had been living on borrowed time and that he would leave the world praising his good fortune. "On the Ides of March, I gave my life to my country," Brutus said, "and since then I have lived another life for the sake of freedom and glory."

Cassius smiled. "In that spirit, let us go against the enemy. Either we shall conquer or we shall not fear the conquerors."

Once the fighting began, however, communication between the two failed. Brutus won the first battle against Octavian's troops and thought Cassius had defeated Antony's. In fact, Cassius' men had broken and run. Cassius survived long enough to order his shield-bearer to slay him.

In late October, three weeks after that first engagement, Brutus' men compelled him to fight, although a delay would have drained Antony and Octavian's supplies. Recalling Pharsalus, Brutus said, "I seem to be fighting the battle like Pompey, less as leader than as led."

He was overwhelmed and escaped from the field only when an aide disguised himself as Brutus and distracted the cavalrymen who were hunting him down. After sunset, Brutus came to a riverbank, where he rested and recited lines of Greek poetry. As he spoke the names of the men who had died fighting for him, a lieutenant interrupted him to say that they must plan their escape.

"Yes, indeed," Brutus agreed. "We must escape. But with our hands, not our feet."

Calm and smiling, he shook hands with each of his senior officers and urged them to save themselves. He could say without irony that he was glad none of his friends had been false to him. He was more blessed than the victors, Brutus added. He was leaving behind a reputation for virtue.

Withdrawing with a few friends, Brutus drew his sword, grasped it by the hilt with both hands and fell forward. The blade went through his breast.

His aides dispatched his body to Rome, but during the voyage a storm blew up. The sailors thought the presence of Brutus' corpse was bad luck, and they pitched his body overboard.

Octavian, who had just turned 21, was like Pompey at that age. He was too unsure to show mercy. His leadership in the recent battles had been unimpressive, and he treated his prisoners harshly. When one man asked for a decent burial, Octavian replied that he would leave that decision to the carrion birds. He pitted a father and son against each other, calling on them to play a game to decide who would live. The father refused and gave up his life for his son; the boy committed suicide. The prisoners detested Octavian and hailed Antony as Imperator to rile this new Caesar.

Antony planned to subdue the Eastern provinces while Octavian returned to Rome and settled veterans from 34 legions on government land. Lepidus had become irrelevant. His troops were merged with the regular army and he was allotted no province. Power was again split between two men, neither of whom upheld the Republic's cause. Rome faced two Caesars—one in name, one in nerve.

Antony moved as a majesty through the East, taxing methodically, spending lavishly. Although Egypt remained independent, he ordered the Egyptian queen to sail across the Mediterranean to Tarsus in Cilicia to explain why she had done so little to help Caesar's heirs. Cleopatra had no choice but to go.

She had planned to leave Rome with Caesar when he went to Parthia. After his murder, she could not count on support from any quarter and knew she must get away. Caesar's will had not provided for either her or Caesarion—it would have been in violation of Roman law—and Cleopatra expected Octavian to deny that the boy was Caesar's son. She had returned to Egypt with her teenage half brother, but he died before the year was out; her enemies said that he had been poisoned at Cleopatra's command. She put Caesarion on the throne by her side as Ptolemy XV Caesar, Lover of His Father.

In the scrambling after the assassination, Cleopatra had sent her Roman guards to fight for Dolabella against Cassius. But Dolabella was defeated and killed himself, and those troops went over to Cassius. Meeting with Antony, Cleopatra could only assure him that she had stayed true to Caesar's memory.

She remembered Antony from the day when she was a young princess and he arrived in Alexandria, and her stay in Rome had given them the opportunity to see each other again. Caesar's lust, however calculating and intermittent, was shaping the next generation of Romans. Brutus had slain his mother's lover, and now Antony, although slighted in Caesar's will, could inherit his mistress. For Cleopatra, a liaison with Antony was nearly as advantageous as her affair with Caesar had been.

To greet Caesar, Cleopatra had sprung from a roll of bedding. For Antony, she chose to sail up the Cydnus River in a barge overlaid with gold and propelled by silver oars and purple sails. If Antony fancied himself a descendant of Hercules, she would be Venus. She lay beneath a golden canopy, fanned by small boys dressed as Cupid. Crowds had waited for hours along the harbor to watch her step off the barge and present herself to Antony on the dock. But at dusk Cleopatra, the queen, summoned him to join her instead.

Antony was content to humor her. Boarding her barge, he found hundreds of lamps and lanterns in patterns so dazzling that he felt apologetic about his own rustic hospitality. But this queen was also a military commander, and she responded to the rough soldier in Antony much as his troops did. She wanted her people to understand that their coupling was between two divinities. But it was only Antony, a susceptible man past 40, who went to bed that night with a sly woman of 32.

Antony was endlessly indulgent. He had already assured the senate that Caesar had acknowledged the paternity of Caesarion, although many months had passed when Caesar could have made that declaration for himself. Perhaps Antony only wanted to undercut Octavian, but all three members of the triumvirate had agreed to put the boy on Egypt's throne. On his way to Cleopatra, Antony had visited Ephesus without disturbing Arsinoë, Cleopatra's half sister, who had taken refuge in the Temple of Artemis. Now, in the grip of his infatuation with Cleopatra, Antony sent orders that Arsinoë be dragged from her sanctuary and killed. The murder ensured that Cleopatra's power would be unchallenged for the first time in her life.

Cleopatra returned home, and Antony followed her the next winter. Cleopatra arranged an ongoing party to amuse him, a group of revelers who called themselves the "Inimitable Living" club. After Antony left, Cleopatra gave birth to twins, a boy and a girl. With Rome's civil war still raging, Antony and Cleopatra would not meet again for four years.

In Rome, Octavian was finding that administering the peace was harder than waging war. Civil strife had depleted Italy's resources, and the people were on the edge of rebellion. Crime was spreading through the city. The Vestal Virgins could travel only with bodyguards. Farmers had been thrown off their land to accommodate promises to the troops, and crop yields had fallen.

Octavian had mastered one of Caesar's keenest abilities. He knew how to shape the public perception of his actions. The prisoners' hatred and contempt after Philippi had taught him that cruelty only tarnished a commander's reputation. As he rewarded tens of thousands of veterans, Octavian reminded them that the largess came from him, not from Antony, who had been gone now from Rome for two years and had never built a civilian following there.

In the capital, Antony's family tried to protect his interests. His wife, Fulvia, was a skillful political manipulator. She bribed two of Octavian's legions to mutiny against him and raised three legions in her own right. Antony's younger brother, Lucius, commanded three more. But from the East, Antony gave them no signal to take decisive action. He seemed willing to go on cooperating with Octavian, who quickly put down Fulvia's challenge.

Octavian practiced his new forgiveness and took no reprisals against Antony's family except for divorcing Fulvia's daughter, Claudia. In a startling act of clemency, he made Lucius governor of Nearer Spain. Antony's mother preferred to join Sextus Pompey, even though the triumvirs had branded him an outlaw. Besides Farther Spain, Sextus held Sardinia, Sicily and portions of the African coast.

Fulvia took a few thousand troops to Greece. In time, she and Antony quarreled over her adamant opposition to Octavian. When Fulvia died, Romans said it was from disappointment: her husband had not risen to her ambition.

Octavian had been winning over the immense army in Gaul at a time when Antony had given up his planned campaign against the Parthians and was prepared to negotiate an alliance with Sextus Pompey. While Fulvia was alive, Antony had resisted her call to challenge Octavian, but after her death he seemed prepared to oblige her. At Brundisium, however, soldiers in both armies refused to fight another civil war and demanded a reconciliation. Antony's mother was among the negotiators; it helped that she was also related to Octavian. With the pact concluded, Octavian offered his beautiful sister to Antony as his next bride. Widowed only a few months, Octavia would bring peace, as Caesar's daughter had once subdued Pompey.

Romans hailed a new era of domestic tranquility, while Antony renewed preparations for war with Parthia. Inevitable frictions arose between him and Octavian, but Octavia proved capable of preventing an open rupture. Seven years after Caesar's murder, the triumvirate still held firm, and Antony and Octavian—with Lepidus as a formality—extended their rule for five more years. After a meeting at Tarentum, Antony and Octavian agreed to serve as co-consuls the following year, and they tightened their bonds of kinship by engaging Antony's young son to Octavian's baby daughter Julia. And Octavia gave birth to a daughter.

Octavian's military performance continued to be inept, but a talented ally, Marcus Agrippa, devised a naval strategy to challenge Sextus Pompey's control of Sicily. Years of intermittent warfare destroyed more than half of Sextus' 300 ships and allowed the triumvirate to retake Sicily. Sextus went to Lesbos to beg Antony's protection, but he learned there that Antony had suffered his own setbacks. In Parthia, Antony's forces had defeated and killed Labienus, but after betrayals and travail, Antony had been driven into Syria. Sextus decided to use his surviving ships and soldiers to take over sections of Asia and Bithynia. When their governors resisted him, Sextus was killed by men loyal to Antony, and the saga of the Pompeys at last was over.

Lepidus, who had observed Octavian's military blunders, demanded Sicily as his command. He had forgotten that most Roman soldiers remained devoted to the memory of the greatest commander of their lifetime. Octavian had only to beckon to them as Caesar, and the men deserted Lepidus. He was struck from the triumvirate but allowed to live on, protected by his title of Pontifex Maximus.

During his separation from Cleopatra, Antony had not forgotten his queen. Caesar had already bestowed Cyprus on her; Antony added a portion of Cilicia, another section of land that included the Dead Sea, and all of Phoenicia, except its two main ports. In return, Cleopatra went to Syria to ease Antony's distress with food and supplies for his soldiers. As a shrewd judge of odds, however, she found reasons not to invest her gold in his future campaigns.

Antony was indeed finished. His army of 100,000 men was cut by one-third by Phraates of Parthia, but the true victor was Octavian. After the defeat of Sextus Pompey, Octavian sent his sister to Athens, along with a scant one-tenth of the troops he had promised Antony for his Eastern campaigns. Antony mortified Octavia by telling her to send along the men and supplies to Alexandria and return to her brother. Octavian made certain that all of Rome heard of Antony's insult. They were outraged at this latest evidence that Egypt's queen had seduced another of their generals.

In Caesar's last months, some senators had believed that Rome would benefit from making his union with Cleopatra legitimate and were said to be preparing a bill to authorize him to take more than one wife. Antony did not wait for senate approval. Although Octavia was still waiting at home, he married Cleopatra in Egypt.

Caesarion was 13 and the twins already six when Cleopatra gave Antony a third child. She named her new son Ptolemy Philadelphus, after a remote ancestor, and turned over to the infant much of the land Antony had given her. Antony had now been away from Italy for five years. At home, it was easy to believe that he had put Egypt's interests above Rome's.

Octavian attacked Antony publicly for his licentiousness, and Antony responded crudely: Why was marrying Cleopatra worse than fucking all the women Octavian was known to have had? But since Octavian's women were Roman matrons, not the harlot of the Nile, the outcome of their exchange favored Octavian.

The second triumvirate ran out, and Octavian pronounced the alliance dead. He held no formal title, but that was a minor technicality. Men had once pledged their allegiance to the state. Now they swore it to Octavian. His sister had accepted her humiliation in Athens, and her forbearance with Antony seemed inexhaustible. But as another round of warfare loomed, Antony was the one to seek a divorce.

The climactic battle came at Actium, 13 years after Caesar's murder. Octavian sailed into a harbor at the southern entrance of the Gulf of Ambracia, with Agrippa commanding his 400 warships. Agrippa cut off Antony from his supply line to Egypt and put his troops under siege. Many of Antony's men defected to Octavian. Those who stayed loyal urged Antony to break away and go overland to Macedonia. Cleopatra had come with her fleet, but she desired to sail to Egypt to keep Alexandria as a secure base for future operations. Antony agreed to wage a sea battle that would provide a distraction. Antony was not a naval commander, and his combined fleet totaled only 230 ships.

On a clear morning in early September, Antony sailed from the harbor to confront Agrippa. Soldiers from both armies watched from the shore. Antony hoped Cleopatra's 60 ships could slip through the blockade and carry the queen and her treasury to safety in Alexandria. In that alone, Antony's strategy succeeded: Cleopatra sailed home. But 12 of his ships were captured, and Antony escaped only by leaving his flagship for a lighter craft. His land forces, who had witnessed the rout, refused to march back to Macedonia and went over instead to Octavian.

Cleopatra reached Alexandria determined to salvage her own position by negotiating with Octavian. Antony withdrew to quarters near the Alexandria lighthouse. Desperation was in the air. The "Inimitable Living" members began calling themselves the "Dying Together" club. When Caesarion, 16 years old, was declared a man in the Roman fashion, so was Antony's Roman son, although he was only 14.

In the spring, Octavian marched against Alexandria, stopping in Judaea to pick up supplies from Herod. Fourteen years after Caesar's murder, on the last day of the seventh month, which was now named for him, Antony launched his attack. Octavian's men had already reached the outskirts of Alexandria. The skirmish started well for Antony, but everybody, both the soldiers and civilians, knew that Octavian would prevail. Antony, although he was 20 years older, proposed to fight Octavian man-to-man. Or he would kill himself if Octavian would let Cleopatra live. From her palace, Cleopatra sent Octavian offers of large cash bribes. He rejected all conditions.

On the morning of the first day of the eighth month—it was later named for Octavian—Antony sent out what was left of his fleet to do battle. But his sailors shouted their loyalty to Octavian and added their ships to his fleet.

Cleopatra's schemes to keep her children on the throne seemed to Antony proof of her disloyalty. She had sent Octavian her crown and scepter with the request that if he wouldn't let her keep the throne, one of her sons be installed as king. Now that she was approaching 40, Cleopatra regarded her wealth as her greatest appeal. She hid away her gold, jewels, ivory and ebony, walling them into an unfinished stone tomb, and planned to receive Octavian in its upper room, attended by two handmaidens, Iras and Charmion, and surrounded by her treasure. She also stored flammable materials. Octavian, she knew, needed her fortune to pay his veterans, but if her wealth could not buy her life or her throne, she would make it worthless to him.

Cleopatra's retreat to the mausoleum may have led Antony to believe the rumors that she was dead. Perhaps he wanted to think that she could not bear to live if they could not be together. He ordered his servant, Eros, to kill him, but Eros killed himself rather than do it. Antony drove his own sword into his bowels.

Octavian's response to Cleopatra's overtures was stiff and correct. When he received her crown, he sent a private message that she need not fear him, but he made no further promises. As Cleopatra waited for him, she sent word to Antony to join her in her tomb full of treasure.

But Antony was already dying when he learned that Cleopatra was still alive. His servants carried him to the mausoleum's locked door, and Cleopatra's women let down ropes and somehow pulled him up to a window. His face contorted with pain and thirst, Antony asked for wine. While Cleopatra clawed her breasts in grief, he drank the wine and died in her arms.

Octavian entered Alexandria later that same day. His men tricked their way into the tomb and seized Cleopatra before she could stab herself. They carried her back to the palace, where she was held in custody. She assumed that Octavian wanted her alive as a spectacle for his triumph. On the third day, she was allowed to leave the palace long enough to bury Antony with full honors. Five days later, Octavian called on her. Again, he rejected her offers. Cleopatra's fortune could not secure Egypt's crown for her son. Octavian listened unmoved as Cleopatra spoke of her love for his great-uncle.

But Octavian didn't wish to see Cleopatra dragged through the Forum. Even those Romans who hated and feared the queen would remember that Julius Caesar had honored her. Octavian wanted Cleopatra dead, and here in Egypt. But he could not kill her.

He gave her permission to go to Antony's grave. Cleopatra was behaving as if this would be her last visit, and she told Iras and Charmion that she wanted to be buried beside Antony. Octavian later denied that he had any hint of what Cleopatra might intend. One of her maids brought into the palace a nest of brown-and-yellow Egyptian cobras concealed in a basket of figs. Egyptians considered the bite of a poisonous snake the quickest, kindest means of execution, and according to legend, the bite made its victim immortal.

Cleopatra died seated on her golden throne. Iras and Charmion took poison. When Octavian's guards arrived, Charmion was using her last breath to straighten Cleopatra's crown.

"Charmion, was this right?" a guard asked.

"It is entirely right, and fitting for a queen descended from so many kings," she replied.

Octavian circulated a report that Cleopatra had chosen to kill herself, and he had her buried next to Antony in the royal tomb. He executed a handful of Romans living in Egypt, among them two of Caesar's assassins. He put Caesarion to death, as well as Antyllus,

Antony's Roman son. From this day, there was to be one Caesar only.

Octavian sent Egypt's treasury to Rome. The huge infusion of money lowered the interest rate from 12 percent to 4 percent. Before the month was out, Octavian had proclaimed himself ruler of Egypt, ending the dynasty that went back to the death of Alexander the Great. Rome's system of government, which had survived nearly five centuries, had also ended, although another three years would pass before Octavian took the name Augustus and the Roman Empire would arise from the ruins of the Republic.

By the time Antony committed suicide in Egypt, he had already revenged himself on Marcus Cicero. When the triumvirate began sentencing men to death, there had been no method for one member to spare a victim selected by the others. Lepidus' brother and Antony's uncle had been among the enemies marked for execution, and then Antony had named Cicero. When Octavian had objected, Antony had agreed to keep his uncle on the list if his partners would add Cicero. The Philippics had doomed him.

Cicero's son was also named, but he was safely away, studying in Athens. Cicero's brother Quintus and his nephew, who had swung from Antony to Brutus, went on the list. Atticus had lent money to Antony and so was spared.

The triumvirs had hoped to keep the identity of their victims secret until the executions had taken place. But friends managed to alert Cicero at his Tusculan villa. It was early December, less than four weeks before he turned 64. Cicero hurried to his seaside estate at Astura, where he hired a boat and was launched toward safety until winds blew up and forced the captain to dock several miles down the coast. Cicero spent a feverish night at Circaeum, reviewing his alternatives and pouring out his fears to his servants. In his raving, Cicero vowed to go back to Rome and damn Julius Caesar for eternity by killing himself on his doorstep.

At dawn, the servants persuaded him to sail to another villa at Formiae. He went ashore exhausted but defiant. He would not go abroad after all, he said. He would die in this land he had so often saved.

Cicero reached his house, where he slept for several hours. When his servants learned that soldiers had been seen nearby, they awakened him and convinced him to go to the sea through the back lanes of his estate. He had scarcely left when the soldiers burst in, learned his route and gave chase through the woods.

The captain was a man Cicero had once successfully defended in a murder case. But that wouldn't be enough to save him. Rome's age of honor was long past. And yet Cicero's servants were ready to fight for him. Instead, he commanded them to put down his chair and offer no resistance. Cicero's hair was disheveled, his eyes tired and red, but he seemed calm. As the soldiers raced up, he thrust his neck forward and told them to take what they wanted.

They cut off his head. Then they cut off his hands. Shouting with joy, they rode back to Rome. Antony had been in the Forum when his soldiers drew up. Surrounded by the crowd, he hadn't seen Cicero's severed head until the captain held it high. Antony had been jubilant and had given the captain a large reward. He ordered that Cicero's head be mounted on the rostra and, on either side, his hands.

Romans of every faction came to the Forum to grieve at the sight. They recalled Cicero's weakness and vanity, but they honored him for the very crime that had cost him his life: Cicero had died for embracing the Roman republic more ardently than he could endorse the flawed men who schemed and battled to possess it.

ACKNOWLEDGMENTS

For 2,000 years, readers have sifted through the collapse of the Roman republic for clues about their own political condition. As they measured their leaders against the Romans, their judgments reflected the age in which the comparisons were made. Admiration for Caesar's dictatorship has risen and fallen with the world's opinion of men like Napoleon and Hitler. In evaluating Cicero, John Adams said that "all the ages of the world have not produced a greater statesman and philosopher." And yet Cicero was described recently by a Harvard professor as an "intellectually pretentious and thoroughly heartless slumlord."

Present-day readers in the United States will find their own parallels and draw their own conclusions. We aren't likely to be surprised by the Republic's widespread bribery and corruption. The slanders of a Roman election campaign produce in us only a weary recognition. We are aware that a filibuster can block legislation. We understand that subsidizing grain may win votes. And we surely can't feel superior as we read about the assassinations that cut down Rome's foremost politicians.

But this book wasn't written to offer warnings, or as one more history of the Republic. Instead, I wanted to draw on the known facts to tell again a timeless story. For me, the difference between story and history was captured by an essay in the *Cambridge Ancient History* in which the writer dismissed any consideration of Sulla as a man: "His private life and character are of slight concern to the historian."

337

In a story, even one that holds to the facts, character does matter. Evaluating human traits and quirks isn't easy, however, especially after 2,000 years. One problem is the unfair way the degree of available information may color our opinion. Caesar offered his austere *Commentaries* in the third person. But Cicero, in his letters to Atticus, exposed every vanity and naked fear. John Adams, a man who kept his own unbuttoned diaries, could appreciate Cicero's candor and not think less of him. I've been very grateful for Cicero's letters and have tried to resist the temptation to mock their vulnerability.

I have also sought to respect the rules Cicero established for writing about the past: Tell the truth, he said. Hold to the sequence in which events happened, and sometimes add a description of the place. Show to what degree fate or rashness or prudence shaped an action. Describe "all the great persons who bear any considerable part in the story," and "dress up the whole in a clear and balanced style, without affecting any ornamentation or seeking any praise except for perspicuity."

Being perspicuous was the challenge. The last decades of the Republic are better documented than most eras of antiquity, and still we can't even be sure in which year Caesar was born. Later generations have depended on the same sources—Plutarch and Suetonius, Dio and Appian, Livy and Sallust. But most of them were writing long after the events they described, and their emphasis and sympathies reflected the political mood of their time. Whenever faced with ambiguity among the ancient sources, I have based my choice on modern scholarship. The writings of Matthias Gelzer, Elizabeth Rawson, Peter Greenhalgh, J. P. V. D. Balsdon, Michael Grant, Eleanor Goltz Huzar and Ronald Syme have been particularly valuable.

Although Professor Syme calls several men by their Latin names— Pompeius Magnus, Marcus Antonius, Octavianus—I have followed the practice of referring to them as Pompey the Great, Mark Antony and Octavian. With cities and provinces, I have kept the Roman names except in those cases where a contemporary name makes the geography much clearer—Marseilles, for example, rather than Massilia.

Professor Meyer Reinhold not only has edited, with Naphtali Lewis, two important volumes on Roman civilization, but has graciously answered the occasional questions I have put to him. Professor Thomas Habinek of the University of Southern California read the manuscript, as did Ronald Replogle of Hopkins, Minnesota. Mr. Replogle became a classic scholar after he and I were mesmerized in Minneapolis years ago by Mrs. Blanche Savage's high school Latin class. He and Professor Habinek have spared me embarrassment by helping me to correct my errors and refine the translations. Any mistakes in the completed book were inserted after their readings.

For their support and assistance, I would also like to thank the staffs at these institutions: the American Academy in Rome, the Library of Congress, the British Library, and the Doheny Library of the University of Southern California. I also appreciated the sabbatical leave that USC granted me during the writing of this book.

My university colleagues Norman Corwin, Joe Saltzman, Sue Horton, Ed Cray and Clancy Sigal offered suggestions and encouragement; so did Rennie Airth, Sarah Bingham, Marshall and Sue Blumenfeld, Marcia Brandwynne, Marilyn Burns, Carl Byker, Joan Dew, Joe and Judy Domanick, Dani and Ben Donnenberg, Charles and Julie Fleming, Karl and Anne Taylor Fleming, Donald and Patty Freed, Betty Friedan, Albert B. Friedman, Jean, Julia and David Halberstam, Laurette Hayden and Miles Beller, Richard and Peggy

Houdek, Gene Lichtenstein and Jocelyn Gibbs, Patt Morrison and Jim Blair, Lynn O'Leary-Archer, Frances Ring, Barbara Saltzman, Robert J. Schoenberg, William Tuohy and Frank Woodson. Sebastião Santos made valuable contributions to my research.

My gratitude to Lynn Nesbit of Janklow and Nesbit Associates began 29 years ago when she first agreed to represent me. It grows with every year.

This is my third book for Alice Mayhew at Simon & Schuster. Although the subjects have varied, the loving care she takes with every manuscript continues to be a revelation. In addition to her own superb taste and talent, she recruits the very best associates; in this instance, Eric Steel has been a model of intelligence and dedication. Marcia Peterson oversaw the copy editing with great patience and ability. I also want to thank Honi Werner for the book's handsome jacket.

NOTES

For the writings of Dio, Plutarch, Suetonius, Caesar and Cicero, the numbers refer to the sections and, in some cases, paragraphs of their works. Otherwise, the numbers are the pages in editions cited in the Bibliography. Except in the few instances where the Dryden translation is indicated, all citations from Plutarch's Lives refer to the Perrin translation.

I: CAESAR AND CICERO

page

17. 19-year-old Caesar: Scholars debate the date of Julius Caesar's birth. This book follows Suetonius and Appian, who have him born in 100 B.C. Caesar was assassinated in 44 B.C., and Plutarch says Caesar died at the age of 56. Mommsen, among others, sets Caesar's birthdate as 102 B.C.
17. Sulla demands divorce: Plutarch, *Lives*: Caesar, 1.
17. Caesar's clothes, grooming: Grant, *Julius Caesar*, 24.
18. Sulla executes slave: Plutarch, *Lives*: Sulla, 1.
18. Sulla's appearance: Ibid., 2.
18. *gravitas, levitas*: Barrow, *Romans*, 22.
18. Metrobius: Plutarch, *Lives*: Sulla, 2.
18. Caesar's first engagement: Suetonius, Julius, 1.
18. Caesar's parents' ceremony: Balsdon, *Julius Caesar*, 27–28.
19. quartan fever: Suetonius, Julius, 1.

19. size of bribe: Balsdon, *Julius Caesar*, preface.
19. "You are stupid": Suetonius, Julius, 1.
19. two-year-old Julia: Most scholars give her birthdate as 83 B.C. Gelzer, 21n, prefers about 76 B.C. since the earlier date would make her 24 when she first married.
20. Cicero's grandfather: Taylor, *Party Politics*, 38.
20. chickpea: Plutarch, *Lives:* Cicero, 1.
20. Cicero's mother: Cicero, *Letters to His Friends*, III, XVI, 26.
20. Cicero impresses classmates: Plutarch, *Lives:* Cicero, 2.
20. Roman homes: Cowell, 20.
21. Cicero's military service: Plutarch, *Lives:* Cicero, 3.
21. Zeno's oratory: Middleton, 8.

II: POMPEY

24. *patres*: Abbott, *Roman Political Institutions*, 6.
24. praetors, or leaders: Ibid., 25.
25. 31,000 pounds of gold: Marsh, *History*, 2.
25. death sentences: Barrow, *Romans*, 48.
26. Twelve Tables: Lewis and Reinhold, 107–16.
26. mundane provisions: Crook, *Law and Life*, 259.
26. Oppian Law: Lefkowitz and Fant, 176–79; Livy, *Rome and the Mediterranean*, XXXIV, 1–7.
27. Roman land policy: Marsh, *History*, 34; *Abbott, Roman Political Institutions*, 30.
27. small farmers driven off land: Kildahl, 19–21.
27. patricians resist voting rights: Ibid., 22.
28. Tiberius runs: Appian, I, 16; Velleius, II, 3.
28. grain prices: Fowler, *Social Life*, 37.
28. Gaius' skull: Plutarch, *Lives:* Gaius Gracchus, 17.
28. Marius first sees city: Baker, 88.
29. Marius married to Julia: Plutarch, *Lives:* (Dryden): Marius, 496.
29. Marius stopped conscription: Marsh, *Founding*, 41.
30. first "ultimate decree" passed against G. Gracchus: Taylor, *Party Politics*, 18.
31. Marius ignores friend: Plutarch, *Lives:* Marius, 43; ibid., Pompey, 4.
31. "Imperator": Ibid., Pompey, 8.
31. Pompey slaughtered animals: Ibid., 12.
31. Pompey's men threaten mutiny: Ibid., 13.
32. Pompey the Great: Ibid.
33. "Let him have his triumph!": Ibid., 14.
33. Pompey's appearance: Ibid., 2
33. Flora the courtesan: Ibid.
33. Sulla's atrocities: Cronin, 34.
34. rich man killed by mansion: Plutarch, *Lives;* Sulla, 31.
34. dictatorship unused in 120 years: Velleius, II, 28.
34. dinner parties: Cowell, 77–78.
35. Sulla's twins: Plutarch, *Lives:* Sulla, 34.
35. "There's no reason": Ibid., 35.

III: AURELIA

37. Caesar's name: Balsdon, *Julius Caesar*, 1–3.
38. vestals: Cowell, 38.
38. Antonius Gnipho: Gelzer, 23; Bradford, *Julius Caesar*, 21.

38. morning ritual: Cowell, 40.
39. tribes within city electorate: Marsh, *History*, 20.
39. Fabia: Taylor, *Roman Voting Assemblies*, 283.
39. "Among the candidates": Kahn, 18.
40. priestly restrictions: Gelzer, 21, 69.
40. amusing company: Bradford, *Julius Caesar*, 31.
41. Caesar and Nicomedes: Plutarch, *Lives:* Caesar, 1; Suetonius, Julius, 2.
41. Roman sexual attitudes: Veyne, 24, 204.
42. Lucullus at Mitylene: Plutarch, *Lives:* (Dryden): Lucullus, 595–96.
42. Caesar's oak leaves: Suetonius, Julius, 2.

IV: CICERO

44. Forum history: Romanelli, 6, 8–9.
44. Roscius: Plutarch, *Lives:* Cicero, 3.
44. value of Roscius' land: The price of a victim's land depended on the coins used to pay for it. An Attic talent from Greece represented 57 pounds of silver; gold was valued at nine times more. A talent also equaled 6,000 Greek drachmas, and Rome's silver denarius was exchanged at the same rate as the drachma and further divided into fourths, called sesterces: *Oxford Classical Dictionary*, 2nd ed., 698; conversion rates are also given in Grant (*Cleopatra*, 281).
45. *parricidium:* Cicero, *Murder Trials*, 25–26.
45. *"Cui bono?":* Ibid. 74.
46. "Take a glance": Ibid., 99.
46. "How do we explain": Ibid., 80.
46. "You murdered my father": Ibid., 47.
46. Solon: Ibid., 65.
47. "And so, they ordained": Ibid.
47. "And at the end": Ibid., 66.
47. Cicero's health, voice: Plutarch, *Lives:* Cicero, 3.
47. Terentia and daughter: Elizabeth Rawson, *Cicero*, 25, has Cicero married in 79 B.C., before his travels to Greece; other authorities put the marriage in 77 B.C., after his return.

V: CAESAR

48. "I have lifted": Cobban, 4.
48. Sulla has judge strangled: Plutarch, *Lives:* Sulla, 37.
48. Postuma: Ibid.
49. "No friend has ever": Ibid., 38.
49. Sulla's funeral: Ibid.
49. Roman women to wear black: Kahn, 73.
49. Caesar and Lepidus: Suetonius, Julius, 3.
50. Pompey kills Brutus: Plutarch, *Lives:* Pompey, 16.
51. Lepidus dies: Ibid.
51. Caesar prosecutes Dolabella: Suetonius, Julius, 4.
51. "the female rival": Ibid., 49.
51. "every woman's husband": Attributed to Curio the Elder. Ibid.
51. Caesar and pirates: Ibid., 4; Plutarch, *Lives:* Caesar, 2.
52. "How pleased you will be": Plutarch, *Lives:* Crassus, 7.
52. Caesar increases ransom: Ibid., Caesar, 2.
53. Caesar crucifies pirates: Ibid.; Suetonius, Julius, 4.

54. Caesar raises troops: Ibid.
54. Antonius and pirates: Huzar, 14–15.
55. Caesar made pontiff: Gelzer, 25.
55. Caesar fears pirates: Bradford (*Julius Caesar*, 44) cites Velleius.
55. Caesar as military tribune: Plutarch, *Lives: Caesar*, 5.
55. command of 1,000 men: Ferrero, 84.

VI: SPARTACUS

56. Batiatus and gladiators: Plutarch, *Lives: Crassus*, 8.
56. 17,000 Roman soldiers: Grant, *From Alexander*, 133.
57. Spartacus: Plutarch, *Lives: Crassus*, 8.
58. Lucullus disobeys order: Duggan, 52.
58. Crassus' background: Plutarch, *Lives: Crassus*, 2–3.
59. Crassus' troops run away: Ward, 6.
59. soldiers beaten to death: "Decimation" involved taking 500 men from the unit that had most disgraced itself, dividing that group into 10 and, by lot, beating to death soldiers from each squad. Plutarch, *Lives: Crassus*, 10.
60. Crassus builds ditch: Ward, 89–90n.

VII: POMPEY

61. "A general must" and Sertorius' trap: Spann, 96–97.
62. "Having exposed me": Greenhalgh, I, 51.
63. Perperna's betrayal: Plutarch, *Lives: Sertorius*, 25–26.
63. "876 towns": Lewis and Reinhold, I, 305.
63. Spartacus' body never found: Appian, III, 223.
64. Pompey's boast: Plutarch, *Lives: Crassus*, 11.
64. Via Appia: Hamblin and Greuensfeld, 7.
64. crucifixion: *Oxford Classical Dict.*, 2d ed., 300.
64. 6,000 slaves crucified: Perowne, 129.

VIII: CICERO

65. Cicero's self-appraisal: Elizabeth Rawson, *Cicero*, 28.
66. "the Greek," "the scholar": Plutarch, *Lives: Cicero*, 5.
66. competitors shouted: Ibid.
66. Africa, Sardinia, Sicily as granaries: Cobban, 57.
66. Romans expected three pounds each day: Fowler (*Social Life*, 35n) calculated Rome's total at 1 ½ million pounds a day, with each adult getting 4½ pecks of grain each month. (A *modius* contained about 20 pounds of wheat.)
67. Cicero at Puteoli: Plutarch, *Lives: Cicero*, 6; Forsyth, 53.
67. politicians prompted by a slave: Middleton, 22.
67. "They withhold their interest": Cicero, *Verrine Orations*, V, 49, 129.
69. Heraclea procession: Ibid., 129.
69. "With this election": Ibid., I, 7, 19.
70. climbed onto colonnades: Petersson, 64n.
70. "We say that Caius Verres": Cicero, *Verrine Orations*, I, 18, 56.
70. Verres chooses exile: Elizabeth Rawson, *Cicero*, 42.
70. "O tempora, o mores!": Cicero, *Verrine Orations*, IV, 25, 56. O the times, O the morals. In his version of *The Verrine Orations*, L. H. G. Greenwood translates the phrase as "What an age we live in."
71. Cicero disposes of gifts: Plutarch, *Lives: Cicero*, 8.

IX: CAESAR

73. Roman male grooming: Carcopino, *Daily Life*, 159.
73. "When I notice": Plutarch, *Lives:* Caesar, 4.
74. "The family of my aunt Julia": Suetonius, Julius, 6.
74. "That means our stock can claim": Ibid.

X: CLEOPATRA

75. "Everything fears time": Bradford, *Cleopatra*, 21.
78. Alexandrians were furious: Bevan, 342.

XI: CAESAR AND CICERO

79. Rome's harsh policies: Castro, 26.
80. bust of Alexander: Suetonius, Julius, 7.
80. Cicero moves to Palatine: Plutarch, *Lives:* Cicero, 8.
81. Caesar's dream: Suetonius, Julius, 7.
81. Caesar pauses in Cisalpine Gaul: Ibid., 8.
82. Caesar as curator of the Appian Way: Plutarch, *Lives:* Caesar, 5.
82. Caesar marries Pompeia: Ibid.

XII: POMPEY

83. pirates' excesses: Plutarch, *Lives:* Pompey, 24.
84. pirates' treatment of Romans: Ibid.
84. Gabinius: Ibid., 25.
84. Caesar supports Gabinius: Leach, 66.
85. "Surely, I am not": Dio, XXXVI, 26.
85. "If you lost Pompey": Plutarch, *Lives:* Pompey, 25.
85. "You!": Ibid.; Dio, XXXVI, 36.
86. size of Pompey's fleet: Plutarch, *Lives:* Pompey, 26.
87. Pompey's terms for pirates: Ibid., 28.

XIII: CICERO

89. "I was too young": Cicero, *Selected Political Speeches*, 35.
89. "A speech on such a subject": Ibid.
89. Asian investments: Balsdon, "Roman History, 65–50 B.C.," 137.
89. "He has waged more wars": Cicero, *Selected Political Speeches*, 48.

XIV: POMPEY

90. "How sad it makes me": Plutarch, *Lives:* Pompey, 30.
90. Pompey and Lucullus: Ibid., 31.
91. Mithridates' troop strength: Ibid., 32.
92. bronze vessels: Anderson, 105.
92. Tigranes and Pompey: Plutarch, *Lives:* Pompey, 33; Dio, XXXVI, 53.
93. Pompey marches on Palestine: Dio and some modern scholars put this campaign after the news of Mithridates' death; Plutarch and other modern writers put it before.

93. Jews regarded as Syrians: Radin, 217.
94. Pompey in temple: Leach, 233, cites Flavius Josephus, *Jewish Antiquities,* XIV, 57–73.
94. Mithridates and poison: Dio, XXXVII, 13.
95. Pompey's return to Rome: Plutarch, *Lives: Pompey,* 41.

XV: CICERO

96. 15 new men to be elected consul: Middleton, 41.
96. Cicero's tributes to Aristotle, Plato, Demosthenes: Plutarch, *Lives: Cicero,* 24.
97. "Then how can you be": Ibid., 26.
97. "That's odd": Ibid.
97. "I'd rather have that": Ibid.
97. "lay on a golden couch": Suetonius, *Julius,* 49.
97. "Enough of that": Ibid.
97. "since you have never": Cicero, *Handbook,* 20.
98. "You must also make sure": Ibid., 51.
98. "the sun does not shine": Cicero, *Letters to Atticus,* I, 1.
99. "At the moment, I am thinking": Ibid., 2.
99. "I hope he will be": Ibid.

XVI: CAESAR AND CICERO

100. "Make Caesar aedile": Stearns, 53.
101. "In the Forum": Suetonius, *Julius,* 10.
102. "You are no longer operating": Plutarch, *Lives: Caesar,* 6.
102. "Every day, as you go": Cicero, *Handbook,* 2.
103. Cicero's appearance: Statue in Capitoline Museum, Alinari photo 27119 in Carpenter, "Observations on Familiar Statuary."
105. Campanian properties: Hardy, *Some Problems,* 83; Gelzer, 43.
105. Sulla's veterans: Petersson, 225.
105. "Pompey rejects": Cicero, *Contra Rullum,* II, 12.
106. "Meet me at Sinope": Petersson, 231.
107. "And never use your votes": Cicero, *Murder Trials,* 289.

XVII: CATILINE

109. "Today, Mother": Plutarch, *Lives: Caesar,* 7.
109. birth of Octavian: Velleius, II, 59.
109. Sempronia: Petersson, 242.
109. Catiline's clean slate: Kaplan, 59.
110. "What is the meaning": Haskell, 176.
110. "by the auctioneer": Ibid.
111. Cicero delays voting: Hardy, *Catilinarian,* 44, argues that the elections were not, as Mommsen had suggested, delayed until October.
111. "I see two bodies": Plutarch, *Lives: Cicero,* 14.
112. Crassus and three scrolls: Ibid., 15.
112. "I have been informed": Cicero, *Letters to Atticus,* I, 14.
114. "How long, Catiline": Cicero, *In Catilinam,* I, 1.
115. "In these circumstances": Ibid., 10.
115. "Cleanse the city": Ibid.
115. "What sort of life": Ibid., 16.

115. "Put the proposal": Elizabeth Rawson, *Cicero*, 75.
115. Catiline's letter to Catulus: Haskell, 185.
116. "At long last, citizens": Cicero, *In Catilinam*, II, 1.
116. "I saw that": Ibid., 4.
116. "But the men": Ibid.
116. Cato's character: Plutarch, *Lives:* Cato the Younger, 1–2.
117. "the destruction of the entire": Kahn, 164.
117. "a paragon of every virtue": Cicero, *Pro Murena*, 61.
117. "My friends, what a droll fellow": Plutarch, *Lives:* Cato the Younger, 21.
117. "Servius soldiered with me": Cicero, *Pro Murena*, 19.
118. "Your profession, as I have": Ibid., 28.
118. "It is vital, gentlemen": Ibid., 79.
118. "Plans have been laid": Ibid., 80.
118. 12,000 men joining rebels: Haskell, 186.
118. Allobroges: Plutarch, *Lives:* Cicero, 18.
120. "Surely this seal": Cicero, *In Catilinam*, III, 10.
120. "You know who I am": Ibid., 13.
122. Bona Dea: Plutarch, *Lives:* Cicero, 19.
122. bright flame: Ibid., 20.
123. "Men who deliberate": Plutarch, *Lives:* Caesar, 7; Dio, XXXVII, 36; Haskell, 191; *Sallust's Bellum Catilinae*, sec. 51.
123. "All bad precedents": Haskell, 192.
124. "even hope": Cicero, *In Catilinam*, IV, 8.
124. "There passes before my eyes": Ibid., 11.
125. "Take it, you drunkard!": Plutarch, *Lives:* Cato the Younger, 24.
125. "You have always valued": *Sallust's Bellum Catilinae*, 52, 5.
125. "How cold, Romans": Forsyth, 149.
126. *"Vixere!"*: Elizabeth Rawson, *Cicero*, 85; other writers give *"Vixerunt."*

XVIII: Cato

128. "I swear in the very truth": Plutarch, *Lives:* Cicero, 23.
128. "Who is *your* father?": Ibid., 26.
129. "My achievements were such": Cicero, *Letters to His Friends*, V, 7.
130. "Look at that flagrant coward!"; Plutarch, *Lives:* Cato the Younger, 27.
131. Catiline's death: *Sallust's Bellum Catilinae*, 59.
132. Pompey's return: Plutarch, *Lives:* Pompey, 42–43.
133. "Go and tell Pompey": Ibid., Cato the Younger, 30.

XIX: Pompei

134. sacrifice of pregnant sow: Kraemer, 54.
135. "Pretty Boy": Cicero, *Letters to Atticus*, I, 16.
135. Quadrantaria: Forsyth, 177.
135. *"Odi et amo"*: Catullus, Poem 85, Sesar trans.
136. events at ceremony: Plutarch, *Lives:* Caesar, 9–10.
136. "The affair is causing": Cicero, *Letters to Atticus*, I, 12.
136. Vestals performed the rites again: Ward, 205.
136. "I do not sleep": Petersson, 501.
137. "I have discovered": Cicero, *Letters to Atticus*, I, 14.
137. Caesar's wife: Plutarch, *Lives:* Caesar, 10.

XX: Caesar

138. Caesar needed 25 million: Appian, II, 8.
139. "No doubt, even these": Plutarch, *Lives: Caesar*, 11.
139. "As far as I am concerned": Ibid.
139. Pompey's third triumph: Ibid., Pompey, 45.
140. "Your friend—you know": Cicero, *Letters to Atticus*, I, 13.
140. "Gnaeus Cicero": Ibid., 16.
140. "Twenty-five of them": Ibid.
141. "As you know, the strength": Ibid., 19.
141. persistent resistance in Spain: Mommsen, 65.
142. "Imperator!": Stearns, 83.
143. "a better citizen": Cicero, *Letters to Atticus*, II, 1.
143. Cato defends corruption: Suetonius, Julius, 19.
144. "Balbus assured me": Cicero, *Letters to Atticus*, II, 3.
145. "I prefer to be with Cato": Dio, XXXVIII, 3.
146. "You can have this law": Ibid., 4.
146. "You shall not": Ibid.
146. "But, at present, since Rome": Ibid., 5.
146. "If anyone dares to raise": Ibid.
147. "During the consulship of Julius": Suetonius, Julius, 20.

XXI: Cicero

149. "Vatinius did nothing gratis": Gelzer, 69.
149. Caesar cut debts one-third: Balsdon, "Roman History, 65–50 B.C.," 137.
149. "And also to get away": Cicero, *Letters to Atticus*, II, 5.
149. Cicero's speech: Suetonius, Julius, 20.
150. "If the senate's power": Cicero, *Letters to Atticus*, II, 9.
150. "the Pasha": Ibid., 23.
150. "Pompey is the king of Rome": Bradford, *Julius Caesar*, 85.
150. "Caesar was once in love": Ibid., 88.
150. Julia marries Pompey: Plutarch, *Lives: Caesar*, 14.
151. a year's rent for 3,000 Romans: Cowell, 21.

XXII: Caesar

152. "the friend and ally": Grant, *Cleopatra*, 13.
153. "stomp on their heads": Suetonius, Julius, 22.
153. "Why not?": Ibid.
153. Vettius affair: Cicero, *Letters to Atticus*, II, 24.
154. "Victius, always full of shit": Catullus, Poem 98, Sesar trans.
154. "I am sick of life": Cicero, *Letters to Atticus*, II, 24.
154. "Then why aren't you": Plutarch, *Lives: Caesar*, 14.
156. "I myself—as I think": Cicero, *Letters to Atticus*, II, 25.

XXIII: Cicero

157. Pompey evades supporting Cicero: Plutarch, *Lives: Cicero*, 31.
159. "To Minerva": Ibid.; Dio, XXXVIII, 17.
159. "Although many men": Plutarch, *Lives: Cato the Younger*, 34.
159. "If you will not take it": Ibid.

XXIV: CAESAR

160. Celts: Holmes, *Caesar's Conquest*, 314.
161. 150,000 Helvetians: Stearns, 103n; Holmes (*Caesar's Conquest*, 46) uses figure closer to Caesar's own 386,000.
161. *"Idem in me"*: Watson, 44. Watson notes that variations in ancient sources have sometimes led historians to estimate that a Roman soldier carried as much as 100 pounds, which would include provisions for a 17-day march. More often, men took food for three days.
162. Caesar's appearance: Carpenter, "Observations on Familiar Statuary," Alinari photo 30603.
162. Caesar's seizure in Córdoba: Plutarch, *Lives: Caesar*, 17.
163. reaches Rhône in a week: Ibid.
163. Caesar delays eight days: Caesar, *Battle for Gaul*, I, 8.
163. "as though they carried around": Watson, 66.
164. war over river tolls: Brogan, 12.
164. Helvetians get past Roman line: Caesar, *Battle for Gaul*, I, 12.
165. Divico's challenge: Ibid., 13.
165. "When the gods wish": Ibid., 14.
166. Caesar admonishes Aedui: Ibid., 16.
166. "If you deal harshly": Ibid., 20.
167. "After I have won": Plutarch, *Lives: Caesar*, 18.
168. escapees killed or sold: Bradford, *Julius Caesar*, 106.
169. "I cannot imagine": Caesar, *Battle for Gaul*, I, 34.
169. recruits' height: Watson, 39.
170. "My own integrity": Caesar, *Battle for Gaul*, I, 40.
170. "If no one else follows": Ibid.
170. "I was in Gaul": Ibid., 44.
170. "If I killed you": Ibid.
171. *"Gallia est omnis divisa"*: Ibid., 1.

XXV: CICERO AND POMPEY

172. "I know the trip": Cicero, *Letters to Atticus*, III, 2.
172. "My life is one long misery": Ibid., 5.
173. "Your pleas that": Ibid., 7.
173. "From these rambling notes": Ibid., 8.
173. "I will confess the truth": Ibid., 9.
174. "Did anyone ever fall": Ibid., 10.
174. "It appears": Ibid., 12.
174. Pompey once mocked Lucullus: Plutarch, *Lives: Pompey*, 48.
175. Tigranes freed: Dio, XXXVIII, 30.
176. "What's the name": Plutarch, *Lives: Pompey*, 48.

XXVI: CICERO

177. "You used none": Cicero, *Letters to Atticus*, III, 15.
178. workers scrub Forum: Greenhalgh, II, 19.
178. Cicero's homecoming: Cicero, *Letters to Atticus*, IV, 1.
179. "Catiline look ultra-conservative": Ibid., 3.
180. "To sail is necessary!": Plutarch, *Lives: Pompey*, 50.
180. "Who is the man": Middleton, 121.

XXVII: ANTONY

182. Antony's background: Plutarch, *Lives: Antony*, 1–2.
184. Cato's interview with Ptolemy: Ibid., *Cato the Younger*, 35.
184. Berenice's marriage: Grant, *Cleopatra*, 17.
185. Caesar recruits legions: Suetonius, *Julius*, 24.
186. 53,000 slaves sold: Caesar, *Battle for Gaul*, II, 33.

XXVIII: CICERO

188. "Immediately!": Cicero, *Letters to His Brother Quintus*, II, 5.
188. Domitius was closely allied: Elizabeth Rawson, *Cicero*, 129.
188. 200 senators visit Caesar: Plutarch, *Lives: Pompey*, 51.
189. "Just the man": Greenhalgh, II, 39.
189. "Enough!": Cicero, *Letters to Atticus*, IV, 5.
190. "reading an account": Cicero, *Letters to His Friends*, V, 12.
190. "What is more shameful": Cicero, *Letters to Atticus*, IV, 6.

XXIX: POMPEY

192. "Marcellinus should be grateful": Plutarch, *Lives: Pompey*, 52.
193. "We are not fighting": Ibid.
193. "have everything in their power": Greenhalgh, II, 49.
193. Pompey's theater: Dio, XXXIX, 38.
194. "What pleasure": Cicero, *Letters to His Friends*, VII, 1.
195. "elegant and humanized": Ibid.
196. Julia's miscarriage: Plutarch, *Lives: Pompey*, 53.
196. Crassus seemed childish: Ibid., *Crassus*, 16.
196. "Your majesty": Ibid., 17.

XXX: CRASSUS

198. sea battle with Veneti: Caesar, *Battle for Gaul*, III, 1–15.
198. "Caesar put all the elders": Ibid., 16.
198. Parthians: Dio, XL, 12.
199. Crassus in Jerusalem: Grant, *Jews*, 57–58.
199. "See what it is": Plutarch, *Lives: Crassus*, 19.
200. "What's this?": Ibid., 22.
200. Cassius refuses command: Dio, XL, 28.
201. Crassus' request to lieutenants: Plutarch, *Lives: Crassus*, 30.

XXXI: CAESAR

202. Britain didn't exist: Plutarch, *Lives: Caesar*, 23.
202. white cliffs: Caesar had been campaigning near modern Flanders.
202. 100 ships: Caesar sailed to Dover from modern Boulogne.
203. "Come on, men!": Caesar, *Battle for Gaul*, IV, 25.
203. Forty ships lost: Ibid., V, 11.
205. Julia's funeral: Plutarch, *Lives: Caesar*, 23.
205. Aurelia dies: Suetonius, *Julius*, 26.

XXXII: Cicero and Caesar

206. Gabinius returns: Middleton, 141.
206. "Exile!": Cicero, *Letters to His Brother Quintus*, III, 2.
206. "Gabinius is acquitted": Ibid., 4.
207. "incredible pains": Ibid.
207. "Pompey has not yet": Ibid., 1.
207. "it was something": Ibid., II, 12.
208. "If one does not fall": Cicero, *Letters to Atticus*, IV, 19.
208. a glorious undertaking: Ibid., 17.
208. "promoting anarchy": Elizabeth Rawson, *Cicero*, 137.
209. Clodius' murder: Dio, XL, 48.
209. body sent to Rome: Middleton, 149.
210. Clodius' gangs: Appian, II, 22.
210. one man as consul: Dio, XL, 50.
210. mechanics of jury: Greenhalgh, II, 82; Dio, XL, 52.
210. Pompey would use force: Middleton, 149.
211. "You took the bloody": Cicero, *Pro T. Annio Milone*, Sec. 13, 34.
211. "committed disgusting acts": Ibid., Sec. 27, 72.
211. "If, while we all": Ibid., Sec. 34, 92.
212. "If Milo went": Ibid., Sec. 38, 104–5.
212. Pompey assigns guards: Cicero, *Letters to His Friends*, III, 10.
212. Milo's response from Marseilles (Massilia): Dio, XL, 54.

XXIII: Pompey

213. Cornelia: Plutarch, *Lives:* Pompey, 55.
214. Pompey appeals for Scipio: Ibid., 55.
214. "For in the first place": Cicero, *Letters to His Friends*, VII, 2.
215. Caesar prevails upon Cicero: Gelzer, 151.

XXXIV: Vercingetorix

216. Arverni: The Arverni's territory, west of the Rhône River, is now called Auvergne.
216. Caesar had treated Vercingetorix as friend: Dio, XL, 41.
216. Narbo is now Narbonne.
217. exposing army to famine: Caesar, *Battle for Gaul*, VII, 10.
217. burning villages proposed: Ibid., 14.
217. Avaricum is the modern Bourges.
218. Caesar's men begged him: Caesar, *Battle for Gaul*, VII, 17.
218. "As for supreme power": Ibid., 20.
218. "Thanks to me": Ibid.
219. "They are a most ingenious": Ibid., 22.
220. "People facing extreme danger": Ibid., 26.
221. rumors were slanders: Gelzer, 159.
222. Alesia was near the modern village of Alise-Ste.-Reine.
223. Gallic provisions: Caesar, *Battle for Gaul*, VII, 71.
223. "gravestones," "stings": Ibid., 73.
224. Gallic battle figures: Ibid., 76.
224. "Instead of surrendering": Ibid., 77.
224. suffering of the Alesians: Dio, XL, 40.

225. attack on Roman weak point: Caesar, *Battle for Gaul*, VII, 83.
226. Caesar urging on troops: Ibid., 86.
226. Gallic breastplates: Plutarch, *Lives:* Caesar, 27.

XXXV: CICERO

229. "Do not imagine": Cicero, *Letters to Atticus*, V, 2.
229. "Please invite the women": Ibid., 1.
229. "no one could be more good-natured": Ibid.
229. "He says one thing": Cicero, *Letters to His Friends*, VIII, 1.
230. "but our conversation": Ibid., 28.
230. Cilicia: Elizabeth Rawson, *Cicero*, 164–65.
230. "All the people are": Cicero, *Letters to Atticus*, V, 13.
230. "a human being but": Ibid., 16.
231. 12,000 infantry: Plutarch, *Lives:* Cicero, 36.
231. Cicero didn't intend to fight: Cicero, *Letters to Atticus*, V, 7.
231. "Ah, what a long way": Ibid., 19.
231. "I was hailed": Ibid., 20.
231. "With my toil and preparation": Ibid.
231. " 'The Pindenissians!' ": Ibid.
232. "Even when he asks": Ibid., IV, 1.
232. Atticus urges that Cicero cultivate Brutus: Ibid.
232. "Well, I shall be sorry": Ibid.
232. "And much more honorable": Cicero, *Letters to His Friends*, XV, 5.
233. "Forgive me, I cannot": Cicero, *Letters to Atticus*, VII, 2.

XXXVI: CURIO

234. "But suppose that Caesar": Cicero, *Letters to His Friends*, VIII, 8.
234. "Suppose my own son": Ibid.
236. Pompey's homecoming: Plutarch, *Lives:* Pompey, 57.
237. "Wherever I stamp my foot": Ibid.
237. "On the one hand": Cicero, *Letters to His Friends*, VIII, 14.
237. "You are aware": Ibid.
237. "Enjoy your victory": Greenhalgh, II, 123.
238. Marcellus threatens to act: Plutarch, *Lives:* Pompey, 58.
238. "My colleague and I": Ibid., 59.
238. "If there is no better way": Appian, II, 31.
238. December 25 was the date by the Roman calendar without correction. By the
     Julian calendar it was November 5. Marsh, *History*, 229n.
238. "it is late to resist": Cicero, *Letters to Atticus*, VII, 5.
239. "if he should go mad": Ibid., 8.
239. "What will happen": Ibid., 3.
239. Caesar's ultimatum: Appian, II, 32.
239. Antony goes to Caesar: Ibid., 33.
239. Caesar pointed out: Caesar, *Civil Wars*, I, 5.

XXXVII: CAESAR

241. Caesar secretly moves forces: Gelzer, 187.
241. 5,000 armed men: Plutarch, *Lives:* Caesar, 32.
242. "My friends, not to cross": Appian, II, 35.

242. quoting from Menander: Ibid.
242. *"Alea iacta est"*: Suetonius, Julius, 32.
242. Caesar's speech: Caesar, *Civil Wars*, I, 8. Caesar says (*Civil Wars*, I, 5) he was at Ravenna when he addressed the troops. Gelzer, 193*n*, argues persuasively that the speech was given at Ariminum.
243. 4,000 gold pieces: Suetonius, Julius, 33.

XXXVIII: POMPEY

245. "starting to be afraid": Cicero, *Letters to His Friends*, XVI, 2.
245. "Oh, Pompey": Plutarch, *Lives:* Pompey, 60.
246. "I have suddenly": Cicero, *Letters to Atticus*, VII, 10.
246. "wretched madman": Ibid., 11.
246. "Leave the city?": Ibid.
247. patrician senators evacuating Rome: Dio, XLI, 8.
247. consul leaves treasury: Leach, 175.
247. "Is Pompey missed?": Cicero, *Letters to Atticus*, VII, 12.
248. Cicero's women to leave Rome: Ibid., 14.
248. "If he has done nothing else": Ibid., 13.
248. "Pass over other faults": Ibid.
248. "I already knew him": Ibid., 16.
248. recruiters couldn't show face: Ibid., 20.
248. Cicero's response to Caesar: Ibid., 17.

XXXIX: CAESAR

249. Caesar's reception in northern Italy: Caesar, *Civil Wars*, I, 13.
250. march against Corfinium: Ibid., 15.
250. "I do not trouble": Cicero, *Letters to Atticus*, VIII, 11b.
250. "I was glad to read": Ibid., 11c.
250. Domitius prepared to escape: Caesar, *Civil Wars*, I, 19.
251. Roman nobles within the town: Ibid., 23.
251. "You are right to presume": Cicero, *Letters to Atticus*, IX, 16.
251. "Could anything be more cold-blooded": Ibid., 14.
252. Caesar's blockade of harbor: Caesar, *Civil Wars*, I, 25.

XL: CICERO

253. "Be sure that I have": Cicero, *Letters to Atticus*, XI, 6a.
254. "Arpinum, I think": Ibid., 17.
254. "We were mistaken": Ibid., 18.
255. "If I may not use": Ibid.
255. "So we parted": Ibid.
255. Caesar's speech to senators: Caesar, *Civil Wars*, I, 32.
255. "The master of Italy": Appian, II, 40.
255. people's response to Caesar: Dio, XLI, 17.
256. contents of treasury: Gelzer, 210.
256. "will be more gratified": Cicero, *Letters to Atticus*, IX, 19.
256. "would not even give me": Ibid., X, 4.
256. "These are our great men": Ibid.
256. "has turned out the bitterest": Ibid.
256. "Still, I do not fancy": Ibid., 7.

257. "I thought that peace might be made": Ibid., 8.
257. "that queen among women": Ibid., 8a.
257. "Finally, what better role": Ibid., 8b.
257. Cicero prays for victory in Spain: Ibid., 12a.

XLI: CAESAR

258. peace terms for Spain: Caesar, *Civil Wars*, I, 86–87.
258. "If there is any gratitude": Appian, II, 43.
258. left Marseilles (Massilia) unharmed: Gelzer, 219.
259. Caesar punishes mutiny: Caesar, *Civil Wars*, III, 1.
259. Dyrrachium (Durazzo to Italians) became Durres, Albania's chief seaport.
259. "If we can reach": Appian, VIII, 55.
260. Bibulus dies: Caesar, *Civil Wars*, III, 18.
260. "Fight the storm bravely!": Appian, IX, 57.
261. I don't want ships: Ibid., 58.
261. Gabinius ignored order: Ibid., 59.
261. Caesar pardons survivors: Caesar, *Civil Wars*, III, 27.
261. "incredible piece of luck": Ibid.
262. "What wild beasts": Appian, II, 61.
262. "I am wounded": Ibid., 60.
262. overture to Scipio: Gelzer, 232.
263. standard-bearer threatens Caesar: Appian, II, 62.
263. "The enemy would have won": Ibid.

XLII: CICERO

264. "If so, how low": Cicero, *Letters to Atticus*, X, 7.
265. "his cruel and bloody reign": Ibid., 16.
265. "I have lent Pompey": Ibid., XI, 3.
265. Cicero derided: Middleton, 186.
265. "Then why don't you": Plutarch, *Lives: Cicero*, 38.
266. "king of kings": Appian, II, 67.
266. three-vote proposal: Caesar, *Civil Wars*, III, 82.
266. "From then on": Elizabeth Rawson, *Cicero*, 200.
266. Brutus with Pompey: Plutarch, *Lives: Brutus*, 4.
267. Caesar's reception at Gomphi: Caesar, *Civil Wars*, III, 80.
267. 20 legionaries poisoned: Appian, II, 64.

XLIII: POMPEY

268. Why should Pompey retreat: Appian, II, 65.
269. "Do not suppose": Caesar, *Civil Wars*, III, 87.
269. comet debated: Appian, II, 69.
270. Pompey's forces: Ibid., 71.
270. Caesar's deployment: Caesar, *Civil Wars*, III, 89.
271. "This day will decide": Appian, II, 73.
271. "His star has already": Ibid., 74.
271. "let us spare": Ibid.
271. "so that we may have": Ibid.
271. "Today, General, I will": Caesar, *Civil Wars*, III, 91.
271. Caesar's password: Appian, II, 80.

272. "We are contending": Ibid., 72.
273. "Protect the camp": Caesar, *Civil Wars*, III, 94.
273. Pompey slumps in his tent: Appian, II, 81.
273. "What? In our very camp?": Ibid.
273. Crastinus killed: Caesar, *Civil Wars*, III, 99.
273. only Italian losses recorded: Appian, II, 82.
274. Cornelia at Mytilene: Plutarch, *Lives:* Pompey, 74.
275. "ceased to think": Caesar, *Civil Wars*, III, 110.
276. "He that goes once": Plutarch, *Lives:* Pompey, 78.
276. "I'm sure I am not mistaken": Ibid., 79.
277. "Dead men": Ibid., 77.
277. Caesar lands four days later: Grant, *Cleopatra*, 61.

XLIV: CLEOPATRA

278. Alexandria riot: Caesar, *Civil Wars*, III, 106.
278. 17.5 million denarii: Gelzer, 247.
279. Cleopatra enters palace: Plutarch, *Lives:* Caesar, 49.
279. "to seek the source": Von Wertheimer, 86–87.
280. scrolls lost in fire: Gelzer, 249n.
280. Caesar with Cleopatra: Caesar, *Civil Wars*, III, 112.
280. baldness formula: Grant, *Cleopatra*, 67.
281. Cleopatra pregnant: Plutarch, *Lives:* Caesar, 49.
282. restrictions lifted against Jews: Grant, *Cleopatra*, 79.
282. 400 ships: Appian, II, 90.

XLV: CICERO

284. Cicero's lictors: Cicero, *Letters to Atticus*, XI, 6.
284. "I cannot help feeling sad": Ibid.
284. "that I have not entirely:" Ibid., 7.
284. Quintus and son seek Caesar's pardon: Ibid., 8.
285. Caesar greets Cicero: Plutarch, *Lives:* Cicero, 39.
285. powers voted to Caesar: Gelzer, 253.
286. "made my peace": Cicero, *Letters to His Friends*, IX, 1.
286. "I never saw anyone": Elizabeth Rawson, *Cicero*, 224.
286. "She will be a woman": Ibid., 225.
287. "When I come to Rome": Cicero, *Letters to Atticus*, XII, 40.
287. "That cheerfulness": Ibid.

XLVI: CAESAR

288. "Fellow soldiers": Appian, II, 94.
289. "I hold you, Africa!": Dio, XLII, 58.
289. "*That* is where": Plutarch, *Lives:* Caesar, 52.
289. "Couldn't I strangle myself": Appian, II, 98.
289. Cato's suicide: Ibid.; Dio, XLIII, 11.
290. three senators put to death: Suetonius, Julius, 75.
290. Pompey's sons to Spain: Dio, XLIII, 14.
290. Lucius Caesar executed: Dio (ibid., 12) says he was put to death secretly; Suetonius (Julius, 75) claims it was done without Caesar's permission.
291. Caesar ridiculed Republic: Suetonius, Julius, 77.

291. Caesar declined other honors: Dio, XLIII, 14.
291. "Let none of you": Ibid., 15.
292. 1,192,000 enemies killed: Pliny, VII, 92.
293. "Home we bring": Suetonius, Julius, 51.
293. "Gaul was brought to shame": Ibid., 49.
293. "Si bene faxis vapulabis": Dio, XLIII, 20.
293. criticism of triumphs: Ibid., 24.
294. Octavius in triumphs: Huzar, 93.
294. population streamed behind Caesar: Dio, XLIII, 22.
294. quietem Italiae: Gelzer, 217n.
294. limits on consuls: Dio, XLIII, 25.
294. Julian calendar: Ibid., 26, and note.
295. "I hate the queen": Cicero, Letters to Atticus, XV, 15.
296. Gnaeus Pompey: Gelzer, 293.
296. Caesar's headaches and fainting: Suetonius, Julius, 56.
296. letters written in code: Ibid.
297. Antony as Master of the Horse: Plutarch, Lives: Antony, 8.
297. assassin in Caesar's house: Huzar, 68.
297. Antony and Fulvia: Plutarch, Lives: Antony, 20.
298. "I don't know": Ibid., Brutus, 6.
298. "Cassius makes the stronger case": Ibid., 7.
299. "It is not those well-fed": Plutarch, Lives: Antony, 4; ibid., Brutus, 8.

XLVII: BRUTUS

300. Caesar as dictator for life: Suetonius, Julius, 76.
301. "Jupiter alone is king": Ibid., 75.
301. "Long live the king!": Suetonius, Julius, 79.
302. "Brutus was elected": Ibid., 80.
302. Brutus unrelated to Lucius Brutus: Dio, XLIV, 12.
302. Caesar says better to die once: Plutarch, Lives: Caesar, 42.
302. Caesar's proposed journey: Ibid., 48.
303. "Brutus will wait": Ibid., 42.
303. "What shall we do": Appian, III, 434.
304. "Then I will not remain silent": Plutarch, Lives: Brutus, 10.
304. "Do you think it is weavers": Appian, III, 434.
304. "If any man in the world": Cicero, Letters to His Friends, VI, 14. (The letter was written in 46 B.C.)
304. "Let us go quickly": Ibid., VII, 30.
305. "If you were an eyewitness": Ibid.
305. "But why shouldn't we hear": Plutarch, Lives: Cicero, 39.
305. "Oh, Ligarius": Ibid., Brutus, 11.
305. "How well these two bad fairies fit": Catullus, Poem 57, Martin trans.
306. Caesar on extending the mind: Wilkin, 7.
306. "Yet he is not a guest": Cicero, Letters to Atticus, XIII, 52.
306. "Don't think this is": Cicero, Letters to His Friends, IX, 15.
306. "I was given to you in marriage": Plutarch, Lives: Brutus, 13.
307. decision reached in February: Yavetz, Julius Caesar, 190.
307. Romulus' murder: Appian, III, 437.
307. "You concealed the secret": Plutarch, Lives: (Dryden): Brutus, 1193.
308. "What is the best": Appian, III, 439.
309. "Read this, Caesar": Plutarch, Lives: Caesar, 65.
309. "What about your prophecies": Dio, XLIV, 18.
310. Caesar's previous ill omen: Appian, III, 443.

310. "Friends, what are you": Ibid.
310. "Damned Casca!": Plutarch, *Lives: Caesar*, 66.
311. "You, too, my son?": Ibid.; Suetonius, Julius, 82.
311. "Run! Bolt the doors!": Dio, XLIV, 20.
312. Lepidus and troops: Appian, III, 447.
312. praetor is stoned: Yavetz, *Julius Caesar*, 192.
313. conspirators' bribes: Appian, III, 451.
313. Antony collects Caesar's will: Huzar, 82.
313. "Those who are asking": Appian, III, 465.
314. "regard what has happened": Dio, XLIV, 32.
314. "By any chance, do you have": Ibid., 35.
314. only one mortal blow: Suetonius, Julius, 82.
314. Caesar due consular funeral: Huzar, 84.
315. "What, did I save": Suetonius, Julius, 84.
315. Caesar's will: Huzar, 84.
315. "So strong was his natural": Dio, XLIV, 39.
316. "Indeed, if you wished": Ibid., 44.
316. "This better than anything else": Ibid., 46.
316. "Therefore, for the gods": Ibid., 48.
316. Antony's delivery: Appian, III, 497.
316. "And now": Dio, XLIV, 49.
317. wax image: Appian, III, 499.
317. wood gathered for pyre: Plutarch, *Lives: Caesar*, 68.
317. Caesar's robes burned: Suetonius, Julius, 84.
317. Jews especially mourned: Ibid.
317. mourners stayed through night: Appian, III, 501.

XLVIII: OCTAVIAN

318. Octavian in Apollonia: Dio, LXV, 3.
318. Octavian's mother refused permission: Tarn, 9.
319. Antony mocks Octavian: Plutarch, *Lives: Antony*, 16.
319. "He is completely": Cicero, *Letters to Atticus*, XIV, 12.
319. "I have always loved": Ibid., 17a.
320. "For though the tyrant": Ibid., 14.
320. Brutus and Cassius' statement: Ibid., 20; XV, 1.
320. "It was not Caesar I followed": Cicero, *Letters to His Friends*, XII, 13.
320. "Is all our Brutus": Cicero, *Letters to Atticus*, XIV, 10.
321. he scorned the daggers of Catiline: Cicero, *Philippics*, II, 118.
322. Cicero invokes law of Jupiter: Clarke, 52.
322. "but in some respects": Cicero, *Brutus*, I, 17.
322. "Look at your words": Ibid., 16.
323. "to be praised and lifted up": Velleius, 187. The verb *tollere* has the two meanings.
324. proscriptions: Syme, 191n, quotes Appian at 300 senators, Plutarch (*Lives: Brutus*, 27) at 200, but notes that there is "a lack of evidence for the significant category, that of knights."
325. "Who are you?": Plutarch, *Lives: Brutus*, 36.
325. "In that spirit": Ibid., 41.
325. "I seem to be fighting": Clarke, 69.
326. "Yes, indeed": Plutarch, *Lives: Brutus*, 52.
326. Brutus' body overboard: Dio, LXVII, 49.
326. Octavian's punishments: Suetonius, Augustus, 13.
327. Cleopatra's barge: Plutarch, *Lives: Antony*, 26.

327. Antony was susceptible: Grant, *Cleopatra*, 115.
328. "Inimitable Living": Huzar, 154.
331. "Dying Together": Huzar, 224.
333. "Charmion, was this right?": Plutarch, *Lives:* Antony, 224.
334. interest rate drops: Tarn, 136.
335. Cicero's death: Plutarch, *Lives:* Cicero, 48, 49.

ACKNOWLEDGMENTS

337. "intellectually pretentious and thoroughly heartless": Patterson, 232

BIBLIOGRAPHY

Abbott, Frank F. *The Common People of Ancient Rome* (London, 1912).
———. *Roman Political Institutions* (Boston, 1901).
Adcock, F. E. *Marcus Crassus, Millionaire* (Cambridge, 1966).
———. *The Roman Art of War Under the Republic* (Cambridge, Mass., 1940).
Altamira, Rafael. *A History of Spanish Civilization*, trans. P. Volkov (New York, 1968).
Anderson, J. G. C. "Pompey's Campaign Against Mithridates," *Journal of Roman Studies*, 1922, 99ff.
Andrews, Carol. *The Rosetta Stone* (New York, 1985).
Appian. *Roman History*, 4 vols., trans. Horace White (Cambridge, Mass., 1913).
Arnott, Peter D. *An Introduction to the Roman World* (New York, 1970).
Auguet, Roland. *Cruelty and Civilization: The Roman Games* (London, 1972).
Axer, Jerzy. *The Style and the Composition of Cicero's Speech* Pro Q. Roscio Comoedo (Warsaw, 1980).
Badian, E. "M. Porcius Cato and the Annexation of Cyprus," *Journal of Roman Studies*, 1965, 110ff.
———. *Roman Imperialism in the Late Republic* (Oxford, 1968).
Bailey, D. R. Shackleton. *Cicero* (London, 1971).
———. *Onomasticon to Cicero's Speeches* (Norman, Okla., 1988).
Baker, G. P. *Sulla the Fortunate* (New York, 1967).
Balsdon, J. P. V. D. "Consular Provinces Under the Late Republic," *Journal of Roman Studies*, 1939, 57ff.

————. "The History of the Extortion Court at Rome, 123–70 B.C.," in *The Crisis of the Roman Republic*, ed. Robin Seager (Cambridge, 1969).

————. *Julius Caesar* (New York, 1967).

————. *Life and Leisure in Ancient Rome* (New York, 1969).

————. "Long-Term Commands at the End of the Republic," *Classical Review*, 1949, 14ff.

————. Review: "Hans Volkmann's 'Cleopatra,' " *Classical Review*, 1960, 68ff.

————. "Roman History, 58–56 B.C., Three Ciceronian Problems," *Journal of Roman Studies*, 1957, 15ff.

————. "Roman History, 65–50 B.C., Five Problems," *Journal of Roman Studies*, 1962, 134–41.

————. *Roman Women* (London, 1974).

Barnds, William Paul. "Poem of Lament in Catullus," *Classical Journal*, November 1937, 88ff.

Barrow, R. H. *The Romans* (London, 1949).

————. *Slavery in the Roman Empire* (New York, 1968).

Bernal, Martin. *Black Athena* (New Brunswick, N.J., 1989).

Bernstein, Alvin H. *Tiberius Sempronius Gracchus* (Ithaca, N.Y., 1978).

Bevan, Edwyn. *A History of Egypt Under the Ptolemaic Dynasty* (London, 1927).

Boardman, John, Jasper Griffin, and Oswyn Murray. *The Roman World* (Oxford, 1988).

Boissier, Gaston. *Cicero and His Friends*, trans. Adnah David Jones (New York, 1897).

Boren, Henry C. *The Gracchi* (New York, 1968).

Bowder, Diana, ed. *Who Was Who in the Roman World* (Oxford, 1980).

Bradford, Ernle. *Cleopatra* (London, 1971).

————. *Julius Caesar* (New York, 1984).

Braund, David. *Rome and the Friendly King* (London, 1984).

Brogan, Olwen. *Roman Gaul* (London, 1953).

Brown, Virginia. *The Textual Transmissions of Caesar's Civil War* (Leiden, Netherlands, 1972).

Brunt, P. A. *The Fall of the Roman Republic* (Oxford, 1988).

————. *Italian Manpower, 225 B.C.–A.D. 14* (Oxford, 1971).

————. *Social Conflicts in the Roman Republic* (London, 1971).

Buchan, John. *Julius Caesar* (London, 1932).

Caesar, Gaius Julius. *The Battle for Gaul*, trans. Anne and Peter Wiseman (Boston, 1980).

————. *Civil Wars*, trans. A. G. Peskett (London, 1979).

————. *War Commentaries*, trans. John Warrington (London, 1955).

Carcopino, Jerome. *Cicero: The Secrets of His Correspondence*, 2 vols., trans. E. O. Lorimer (London, 1951).

————. *Daily Life in Ancient Rome*, trans. E. O. Lorimer (New Haven, Conn., 1940).

Carney, Thomas F. *A Biography of C. Marius* (Chicago, 1970).

Carpenter, Rhys. "Observations on Familiar Statuary in Rome," *American Academy in Rome (Memoirs)*, XVIII, 1941.

Carter, John M. *The Battle of Actium* (New York, 1970).

Cary, M. "The Municipal Legislation of Julius Caesar," *Journal of Roman Studies*, 1937, 48ff.

Caselli, Giovanni. *The Roman Empire* (New York, 1985).

Castro, Americo. *The Spaniards*, trans. Willard F. King and Selma Margaretten (Berkeley, Calif., 1971).

Catullus, Gaius Valerius. *Poems*, trans. Horace Gregory (New York, 1956).
————. *Poems*, trans. Charles Martin (Baltimore, Md., 1979).
————. *Poems*, trans. Carl Sesar (Middleton, Conn., 1973).
Cicero, Marcus. *Brutus*, trans. G. L. Hendrickson; *Orator*, trans. H. M. Hubbell (London, 1971).
————. *Pro Quinctio, Pro Roscio Amerino, Pro Roscio Comoedo, Contra Rellum*, trans. J. H. Freese (Cambridge, Mass., 1977).
————. *In Catilinam I-IV; Pro Murena; Pro Sulla; Pro Flacco*, trans. C. Macdonald (Cambridge, Mass., 1927).
————. *Letters of Marcus Tullius Cicero*, vol. 1, ed. William Melmoth (London, 1778).
————. *Letters to Atticus*, vols. 1–3, trans E. O. Winstedt (Cambridge, Mass., 1980–87).
————. *Letters to His Brother Quintus*, trans. W. Glynn Williams; *Letters to Brutus*, trans. M. Cary; *Handbook of Electioneering, Letter to Octavian*, trans. Mary Henderson (Cambridge, Mass., 1989).
————. *Letters to His Friends*, vols. 1–4, trans. W. Glynn Williams, M. Carey, M. Henderson (London, 1979).
————. *Murder Trials*, trans. Michael Grant (London, 1988).
————. *The Nature of the Gods*, trans. Horace C. P. McGregor (Middlesex, England, 1972).
————. *On Old Age and Friendship*, trans. Frank O. Copley (Ann Arbor, Mich., 1967).
————. *Philippics*, trans. D. R. Shackleton Bailey (Chapel Hill, N.C., 1986).
————. *Pro T. Annio Milone*, ed. Albert C. Clark (Amsterdam, 1967).
————. *Select Letters*, ed. D. R. Shackleton Bailey (Cambridge, 1980).
————. *Selected Letters of Cicero*, ed. Hubert McNeill Poteat (Boston, 1916).
————. *Selected Political Speeches*, trans. Michael Grant (London, 1987).
————. *Selected Works*, trans. Michael Grant (New York, 1987).
————. *The Verrine Orations*, 2 vols., trans. L. H. G. Greenwood (London, 1978).
Clarke, M. L. *The Noblest Roman* (Ithaca, N.Y., 1981).
Cobban, J. M. *Senate and Province, 78–49 B.C.* (Cambridge, 1935).
Connolly, Peter. "The Early Roman Army," in *Warfare in the Ancient World*, ed. John Hackett (New York, 1988).
Cowell, F. R. *Life in Ancient Rome* (New York, 1980).
Cronin, Vincent. *Italy* (New York, 1972).
Crook, John A. *Law and Life of Rome* (London, 1967).
————. "A Legal Point About Mark Antony's Will," *Journal of Roman Studies*, 1957, 36ff.
Davies, W. V. *Egyptian Hieroglyphs* (Berkeley, Calif., 1987).
Davison, J. A. "Cicero and the Lex Gabinia," *Classical Review*, 1930, 224ff.
Dio, Cassius. *Roman History*, vols. 3, 4, 5, trans. Ernest Cary (Cambridge, Mass., 1984, 1969, 1989).
Dorey, T. A., ed. *Cicero* (London, 1965).
Douglas, A. E. "Platonis Aemulus? Some Reflections on Cicero's Philosophical Writings," *Proceedings of the Classical Association*, 1960, 21ff.
Duberman, Martin Bauml, ed. *Hidden From History*, with Martha Vicinus and George Chauncey, Jr., eds. (New York, 1989).
Duggan, Alfred. *Julius Caesar* (New York, 1955).
Dupuy, Trevor N. *The Military Life of Julius Caesar* (New York, 1969).

Duruy, Victor. *History of Rome*, vol. 2, sec. 2, trans. M. M. Ripley (Boston, 1894).

Feder, Lillian. *The Meridian Handbook of Classical Literature* (New York, 1986).

Ferrero, Guglielmo. *The Life of Caesar*, trans. A. E. Zimmern (New York, 1962).

————. *The Women of the Caesars* (New York, 1911).

Finley, M. I. *The Ancient Economy* (Berkeley, Calif., 1985).

Forsyth, William. *Life of Marcus Tullius Cicero* (New York, 1896).

Fowler, W. Warde. *Julius Caesar* (New York, 1892).

————. *Social Life at Rome in the Age of Cicero* (London, 1908).

Froude, James A. *Caesar* (New York, 1897).

Gabba, Emilio. *Republican Rome, the Army and the Allies*, trans. P. J. Cuff (Oxford, 1976).

Garnsey, Peter, and Richard Saller. *The Roman Empire* (Berkeley, Calif., 1987).

Gelzer, Matthias. *Caesar*, trans. Peter Needham (Cambridge, Mass., 1968).

Goar, R. J. *Cicero and the State Religion* (Amsterdam, 1972).

Goodenough, Simon. *Citizens of Rome* (New York, 1979).

Gotoff, Harold C. *Cicero's Elegant Style: An Analysis of the* Pro Archia (Urbana, Ill., 1979).

Grant, Michael. *The Ancient Historians* (New York, 1970).

————. *The Ancient Mediterranean* (New York, 1988).

————. *The Army of the Caesars* (New York, 1974).

————. *Cleopatra* (London, 1972).

————. *From Alexander to Cleopatra* (New York, 1982).

————. *History of Rome* (New York, 1978).

————. *The Jews in the Roman World* (New York, 1973).

————. *Julius Caesar* (London, 1969).

————. *Nero* (New York, 1970).

————. *The Roman Emperors* (New York, 1985).

————. *The World of Rome* (Cleveland, 1960).

————. ed. *Latin Literature* (New York, 1981).

Graves, Robert. *The White Goddess* (New York, 1948).

Greenhalgh, Peter. *Pompey*, vols. 1 and 2 (London, 1981).

Greenidge, A. H. J., and A. M. Clay. *Sources for Roman History, 133–70* B.C. (Oxford, 1960).

Grimal, Pierre. *Hellenism and the Rise of Rome* (New York, 1968).

Gruen, Erich S. *The Last Generation of the Roman Republic* (Berkeley, Calif., 1974).

Gundolf, Friedrich. *The Mantle of Caesar*, trans. Jacob Wittmer Hartmann (New York, 1928).

Guterman, Norbert, ed. *The Anchor Book of Latin Quotations* (New York, 1990).

Gwatkin, William E., Jr. "The Father of Pompey the Great," *Abstract xxxvii, Transactions and Proceedings of the American Philological Association*, Philadelphia, 1940.

Habicht, Christian. *Cicero the Politician* (Baltimore, Md., 1990).

Hackett, John, ed. *Warfare in the Ancient World* (New York, 1989).

Hamblin, Dora Jane, and Mary Jane Grunsfeld. *The Appian Way* (New York, 1974).

Hamilton, Edith. *The Roman Way* (New York, 1932).

Hardy, E. G. *The Catilinarian Conspiracy in Its Context* (Oxford, 1924).

————. *Some Problems in Roman History* (Oxford, 1924).

Harris, William V. *Ancient Literacy* (Cambridge, Mass., 1989).

————. *War and Imperialism in Republican Rome* (Oxford, 1979).

Haskell, H. J. *This Was Cicero* (New York, 1942).

Havelock, E. A. *The Lyric Genius of Catullus* (Oxford, 1939).

Henderson, M. I. "The Establishment of the Equester Ordo," in *The Crisis of the Roman Republic*, ed. Robin Seager (Cambridge, 1969).

Herm, Gerhard. *The Celts* (New York, 1976).

Heurgon, Jacques. *The Rise of Rome to 164 B.C.*, trans. James Willis (Berkeley, Calif., 1973).

Hirtius, Aulus. *Caesar: Alexandrian, African and Spanish Wars*, trans. A. G. Way (Cambridge, Mass., 1988).

Holliday, Vivian L. *Pompey in Cicero's Correspondence and Lucan's Civil War* (The Hague, 1969).

Holmes, T. Rice. *Ancient Britain* (Oxford, 1907).

————. *Caesar's Conquest of Gaul* (Oxford, 1911).

Hooper, Finley. *Roman Realities* (Detroit, Mich., 1979).

Huzar, Eleanor Goltz. *Mark Antony* (London, 1986).

James, T. G. *Pharaoh's People* (Chicago, 1984).

Johnson, W. R. *Momentary Monsters, Lucan and His Heroes* (Ithaca, N.Y., 1987).

Jones, Francis L. "The First Conspiracy of Catiline," *Classical Journal*, April 1939, 410ff.

Jonkers, E. J. *Social and Economic Commentary on Cicero's* De Imperio Cn. Pompei (Leiden, Netherlands, 1959).

Josephus, Flavius. *Life and Works*, trans. William Whiston (Philadelphia, 1957).

Judson, Harry Pratt. *Caesar's Army* (New York, 1888).

Kaegi, Walter E., and Peter White. *Rome: Late Republic and Principate* (Chicago, 1986).

Kahn, Arthur D. *The Education of Julius Caesar* (New York, 1986).

Kaplan, Arthur. *Catiline* (New York, 1968).

Keaveney, Arthur. *Sulla* (London, 1982).

Keppie, Lawrence. "The Roman Army of the Later Republic," in *Warfare in the Ancient World*, ed. John Hackett (New York, 1989).

Kildahl, P. A. *Caius Marius* (New York, 1968).

King, Anthony. *Roman Gaul and Germany* (Berkeley, Calif., 1990).

Kraemer, Ross Shepard. *Her Share of the Blessings* (New York, 1992).

Leach, John. *Pompey the Great* (London, 1978).

Lefkowitz, Mary R., and Maureen B. Fant. *Women's Life in Greece and Rome* (Baltimore, Md., 1982).

Levi, Mario Attilio. *Political Power in the Ancient World*, trans. Jane Costello (Westport, Conn., 1965).

Lewis, Naphtali. *Life in Egypt Under Roman Rule* (Oxford, 1983).

———— and Meyer Reinhold. *Roman Civilization*, vol. 1 (New York, 1990).

Lintott, A. W. *Violence in Republican Rome* (Oxford, 1968).

Livy (Titus Livius). *The Early History of Rome*, trans. Aubrey de Selincourt (London, 1988).

————. *Rome and Italy*, trans. Betty Radice (London, 1988).

————. *Rome and the Mediterranean*, trans. Henry Bettenson (London, 1987).

Lucan. *The Pharsalia*, trans. H. T. Riley (London, 1853).

Lynn, R. O. A. M. *Selections from Catullus* (Cambridge, 1973).

MacMullen, Ramsay. *Roman Social Relations* (New Haven, Conn., 1974).

McDonald, A. H. *Republican Rome* (New York, 1966).

Marsh, F. B. *A History of the Roman World* (London, 1953).

——. *The Founding of the Roman Empire* (Oxford, 1927).

Marshall, B. A. *Crassus* (Amsterdam, 1976).

Massey, Michael. *Society in Imperial Rome* (Cambridge, 1982).

Masson, Georgina. *The Companion Guide to Rome* (New York, 1965).

——. *A Concise History of Republican Rome* (London, 1973).

May, James M. *Trials of Character: The Eloquence of Ciceronian Ethos* (Chapel Hill, N.C., 1988).

Middleton, Conyers. *The Life and Letters of Marcus Tullius Cicero* (London, 1848).

Millar, Fergus. *The Roman Empire and Its Neighbours* (New York, 1966).

Mitchell, Thomas N. *Cicero: The Ascending Years* (New Haven, Conn., 1979).

Mommsen, Theodor. *The Provinces of the Roman Empire: The European Provinces* (Chicago, 1968).

Murphy, Edwin. *Diodorus on Egypt* (Jefferson, N.C., 1985).

Nicolet, Claude. *The World of the Citizen in Republican Rome* (Berkeley, Calif., 1988).

Nybakken, Oscar. "Progressive Education in the Roman Empire," *Classical Journal*, October 1938, 38ff.

Odahl, Charles Matson. *The Catilinarian Conspiracy* (New Haven, Conn., 1971).

Oman, Charles. *Seven Roman Statesmen of the Later Republic* (London, 1923).

Parker, H. M. D. *The Roman Legions* (Cambridge, 1958).

Paterson, Jeremy. "Politics in the Late Republic," in *Roman Political Life*, ed. T. P. Wiseman (Exeter, England, 1985).

Patterson, Orlando. *Freedom* (New York, 1991).

Perowne, Stewart. *Death of the Roman Republic* (Garden City, N.Y., 1968).

Petersson, Torsten. *Cicero* (New York, 1963).

Pharr, Clyde. "Roman Legal Education," *Classical Journal*, February 1939, 257ff.

Pliny, *Natural History*, 10 vols., trans. H. Rackham, W. H. S. Jones and D. E. Eicholtz (Cambridge, Mass., 1938–63).

Plutarch. *Fall of the Roman Republic*, trans. Rex Warner (London, 1972).

——. *Lives: Cicero, Caesar; Crassus; Pompey*, trans. Bernadotte Perrin (Cambridge, Mass., 1986, 1984, 1968).

——. *Lives of the Noble Grecians and Romans*, trans. John Dryden; revised, Arthur Hugh Clough (New York, 1864).

Poliakoff, Michael B. *Combat Sports in the Ancient World* (New Haven, Conn., 1987).

Pomeroy, Sarah B. *Goddesses, Whores, Wives and Slaves* (New York, 1975).

Posner, Ernst. *Archives in the Ancient World* (Cambridge, Mass., 1972).

Postgate, J. P. "The Site of the Battle of Pharsalia," *Journal of Roman Studies*, 1922, 187ff.

Quennell, Peter. *The Coliseum* (New York, 1971).

Radin, Max. *The Jews Among the Greeks and Romans* (New York, 1916).

Ramage, Edwin S. *Urbanitas, Ancient Sophistication and Refinement* (Norman, Okla., 1973).

Rawson, Beryl. *The Politics of Friendship: Pompey and Cicero* (Sydney, Australia, 1978).

Rawson, Elizabeth. *Cicero, a Portrait* (Ithaca, N.Y., 1983).

——. *Roman Culture and Society* (Oxford, 1991).

Renfrew, Colin. *Before Civilization* (Cambridge, 1979).

Richards, George C. *Cicero* (Westport, Conn., 1935).

Richardson, J. S. "Notice: Grant's Julius Caesar," *Journal of Roman Studies,* 1970, 263–64.

Richardson, Keith. *Daggers in the Forum* (London, 1976).

Rickman, Geoffrey. *The Corn Supply of Ancient Rome* (Oxford, 1980).

Romanelli, Pietro. *The Roman Forum,* trans. Clarice Pennock (Rome, 1950).

Rose, H. J. "Patricians and Plebeians at Rome," *Journal of Roman Studies,* 1922, 106ff.

Sabben-Clare, James. *Caesar and Roman Politics, 60–50 B.C.* (Oxford, 1971).

Sallust's Bellum Catilinae, ed. J. T. Ramsey (Atlanta, Ga., 1984).

Salmon, E. T. *Roman Colonization Under the Republic* (London, 1969).

Seager, Robin. *The Crisis of the Roman Republic* (Cambridge, 1969).

——. *Pompey* (Berkeley, Calif., 1979).

Sellar, W. Y. *The Roman Poets of the Republic* (Edinburgh, 1863).

Sherwin-White, A. N. *The Roman Citizenship* (Oxford, 1939).

——. "Violence in Roman Public," in *The Crisis of the Roman Republic,* ed. Robin Seager (Cambridge, 1969).

Smith, R. E. *Cicero the Statesman* (Cambridge, 1966).

——. *The Failure of the Roman Republic* (New York, 1975).

Snowden, Frank M., Jr. *Blacks in Antiquity* (Cambridge, Mass., 1970).

Spann, Philip O. *Quintus Sertorius and the Legacy of Sulla* (Fayetteville, Ark., 1987).

Stambaugh, John E. *The Ancient Roman City* (Baltimore, Md., 1988).

Stearns, Monroe. *Julius Caesar* (New York, 1971).

Stevenson, G. H. "Some Reflections on the Teaching of Roman History," *Journal of Roman Studies,* 1922, 192ff.

Stockton, David. *The Gracchi* (Oxford, 1979).

Strachan-Davidson, J. L. *Cicero and the Fall of the Roman Republic* (New York, 1894).

Suetonius. *The Twelve Caesars,* trans. Robert Graves (London, 1987).

Sumner, G. V. *The Orators in Cicero's Brutus: Prosopography and Chronology* (Toronto, 1973).

Sutherland, C. H. V. *The Romans in Spain* (London, 1939).

Syme, Ronald. *The Roman Revolution* (Oxford, 1967).

Tannahill, Reay. *Sex in History* (New York, 1980).

Tarn, W. W. "The Battle of Actium," *Journal of Roman Studies,* 1931, 173ff.

—— and M. P. Charlesworth. *Octavian, Antony and Cleopatra* (Cambridge, 1965).

Taylor, Lily Ross. "Caesar and the Roman Nobility," *Transactions of the American Philological Association,* 1942, 1–24.

——. *Party Politics in the Age of Caesar* (Berkeley, Calif., 1949).

——. *Roman Voting Assemblies* (Ann Arbor, Mich., 1990).

Toynbee, Jocelyn M. C. *Death and Burial in the Roman World* (London, 1971).

——. *The Voting Districts of the Roman Republic* (Rome, 1960).

Treggiari, Susan. *Roman Freedmen During the Late Republic* (Oxford, 1969).

Velleius Paterculus. *History of Rome,* trans. F. W. Shipley (Cambridge, Mass., 1929).

Veyne, Paul, ed. *A History of Private Life,* trans. Arthur Goldhammer (Cambridge, Mass., 1987).

Vickers, Michael. *The Roman World* (New York, 1989).

Von Wertheimer, O. *Cleopatra* (Philadelphia, 1931).

Ward, Allen Mason. *Marcus Crassus* (Columbia, Mo., 1977).

Warren, Larissa Bonfante. "Roman Triumphs and Etruscan Kings," *Journal of Roman Studies*, 1970, 49ff.

Watson, G. R. *The Roman Soldier* (London, 1969).

Weigall, Arthur. *The Life and Times of Marc Antony* (New York, 1931).

Weinstock, Stefan. *Divus Julius* (Oxford, 1971).

White, Jon Manchip. *Everyday Life in Ancient Egypt* (New York, 1991).

White, K. D. *Roman Farming* (Ithaca, N.Y., 1970).

Wiedemann, Thomas. *Greek and Roman Slavery* (London, 1988).

Wilkin, Robert N. *Eternal Lawyer* (New York, 1947).

Williams, Gordon. "Some Aspects of Roman Marriage Ceremonies and Ideals," *Journal of Roman Studies*, 1958, 16ff.

Wiseman, T. P., ed. *Roman Political Life* (Exeter, England, 1985).

Wistrand, Magnus. *Cicero Imperator: Studies in Cicero's Correspondence, 51–47 B.C.* (Goteborg, 1979).

Wood, Neal. *Cicero's Social and Political Thought* (Berkeley, Calif., 1988).

Yavetz, Zwi. *Julius Caesar and His Public Image* (London, 1983).

————. "The Living Conditions of the Urban Plebs," in *The Crisis of the Roman Republic*, ed. Robin Seager (Cambridge, 1969).

————. *Plebs and Princeps* (New Brunswick, N.J., 1988).

————. *Slaves and Slavery in Ancient Rome* (New Brunswick, N.J., 1988).

INDEX